T0318161

The German Hanse was the most successful and most far-flung trade association that existed in medieval and early-modern Europe. Inevitably it appears prominently in every general study of trade, sometimes under the label of 'the Hanseatic League'. This, however, is the first study to be devoted to relations between the Hanse and England throughout the entire period of their contact, which lasted for some 500 years.

The relationship between England and the Hanse was based upon commercial exchange, and as a consequence much of this work is devoted to trade. The composition of trade is analysed, and the fluctuations in its volume and value are reconstructed from primary sources, chiefly customs accounts. But trade was often made possible only by intensive political and diplomatic bargaining between the two sides, sometimes at the level of merchant and merchant, at other times between the English government and the Hanse diet, the highest authority within the German organisation. This aspect of the relationship is explored in equal detail. The book also synthesises existing scholarship and makes many original contributions to the study of the Hanse, often by re-examining accepted theories.

ENGLAND AND THE GERMAN HANSE,
1157–1611

ENGLAND AND THE
GERMAN HANSE, 1157–1611

A study of their trade and commercial diplomacy

T. H. LLOYD

Senior Lecturer in History, University College of Swansea

The right of the
University of Cambridge
to print and sell
all manner of books
was granted by
Henry VIII in 1534.
The University has printed
and published continuously
since 1584.

CAMBRIDGE UNIVERSITY PRESS

Cambridge
New York   Port Chester
Melbourne   Sydney

PUBLISHED BY THE PRESS SYNDICATE OF THE UNIVERSITY OF CAMBRIDGE
The Pitt Building, Trumpington Street, Cambridge, United Kingdom

CAMBRIDGE UNIVERSITY PRESS
The Edinburgh Building, Cambridge CB2 2RU, UK
40 West 20th Street, New York NY 10011–4211, USA
477 Williamstown Road, Port Melbourne, VIC 3207, Australia
Ruiz de Alarcón 13, 28014 Madrid, Spain
Dock House, The Waterfront, Cape Town 8001, South Africa

http://www.cambridge.org

First published 1991
First paperback edition 2002

A catalogue record for this book is available from the British Library

Library of Congress Cataloguing in Publication data
Lloyd, T. H. (Terence Henry), 1937–
England and the German Hanse. 1157–1611: a study of
their trade and commercial diplomacy / T. H. Lloyd.
p. cm.
Includes bibliographical references and index.
ISBN 0 521 40442 8 (hardback)
1. Hansa towns – Commerce – England – History. 2. England – Commerce – Hansa towns
– History. 3. Hanseatic League – History. I. Title.
HF455.L56 1992
382′.0942043–dc20 90-27582 CIP

ISBN 0 521 40442 8 hardback
ISBN 0 521 52214 5 paperback

Contents

Tables

Abbreviations

APC	*Acts of the Privy Council*
CChR	*Calendar of Charter Rolls*
CChW	*Calendar of Chancery Warrants*
CCR	*Close Rolls and Calendar of Close Rolls*
CFR	*Calendar of Fine Rolls*
CLR	*Calendar of Liberate Rolls*
CPMR	*Calendar of Plea and Memoranda Rolls*
CPR	*Patent Rolls and Calendar of Patent Rolls*
DI	*Danziger Inventar*
EcHR	*Economic History Review*
EET	*England's Export Trade*
EHR	*English Historical Review*
Foedera	*Foedera, Conventiones, Literae*
Hanseakten	*Hanseakten aus England*
HG	*Hansische Geschichtsblätter*
HR	*Recesse und Andere Akten der Hansetage*
HUB	*Hansisches Urkundenbuch*
KI	*Kölner Inventar*
Letter Book A, etc.	*Letter Books of the City of London*
L & P	*Letters and Papers, Foreign and Domestic, of Henry VIII*
POPC	*Proceedings and Ordinances of the Privy Council*
Rot. Litt. Pat.	*Rotuli Litterarum Patentium*
Rot. Parl.	*Rotuli Parliamentorum*
SPD	*Calendar of State Papers, Domestic*
SPF	*Calendar of State Papers, Foreign*
Stats.	*Statutes of the Realm*

Introduction

The German Hanse is probably more familiar in English historical literature as the Hanseatic League. The latter term has been eschewed for the reasons given by Philippe Dollinger in his general survey of the organisation, but the modern German spelling of Hanse has been used in preference to the Latinised form adopted by him.[1] German Hanse (*Hansa Teutonicorum, dudesche Hense*) was the name used by the members themselves for the greater part of its history. For the sake of convenience the title is generally shortened to Hanse, but the initial capital is retained, not least to prevent confusion with other hanses. Strangely, although the word hanse is Germanic or Scandinavian it seems to have been incorporated in the title of the German Hanse only around the middle of the thirteenth century, a hundred years or so after the birth of the organisation, at the very time it was becoming obsolete elsewhere. Originally, it described a fraternal association formed among travelling merchants, or their monetary contribution to a common fund. In England the nature of a hanse is well illustrated at York where a royal charter of 1154–8 confirmed the city's liberties, which included a gild merchant (*gilda mercatoria*) and 'hanses in England and Normandy'. The institutions themselves were clearly older than this and a charter granted to Beverley *c.* 1130 establishes that a hanse house (*hanshus*) already existed at York. At Leicester, another town with a Scandinavian past, members of the gild merchant still made a payment called hanse when they visited fairs in eastern England at the end of the twelfth century. Some other town charters, such as that of Ipswich (1200), also make a formal distinction between gild merchant and hanse.[2] This suggests that in the past there had been

---

[1] P. Dollinger, *The German Hansa* (London, 1964), p. xx.

[2] E. Miller, 'Medieval York', in P. M. Tillot (ed.), *The City of York* (The Victoria History of the Counties of England, London, 1961), p. 31. A. F. Leach (ed.), *Beverley Town Documents*

I

some degree of separation between the two, if only to the extent that one was an offshoot of the other. By this time the difference was becoming blurred, probably because it was less necessary for a town's merchants to travel together and make collective arrangements for security in their own country. Later forms of association among English merchants trading overseas were organised on a national basis and never incorporated the use of the word hanse. An example of a hanse as a national organisation of merchants in a foreign country is provided by the Hanse of London, a union (either real or planned) of Flemings who came to England to buy wool in the twelfth or thirteenth centuries.[3] Members of the German Hanse may have been slow to adopt the word, or at least to leave evidence of it in their surviving written records, but the element of solidarity between merchants travelling in an alien environment was the essence of their organisation from its beginnings.

An organisation which survived for roughly half a millennium (from the middle of the twelfth century to the mid-seventeenth) was bound to see many changes, but when German historians began to investigate the Hanse in detail they soon began to emphasise one in particular. Traces of this change were detected in the late thirteenth century, but the decisive period was reckoned to be the second half of the fourteenth century. The thesis was that a Hanse of merchants gave way to a Hanse of towns. In the earlier period, membership of the Hanse and the use of its collective privileges appears to have been open to all German merchants who traded overseas. In the later phase, membership was confined to specific towns, indeed it was the towns themselves rather than individual merchants which were now the members of the Hanse. The change was put down to alterations in the economic climate of the later middle ages. On the one hand travelling merchants were superseded, or at least supplemented, by those who remained at home and operated their business by proxy. On the other hand greater collective effort and expense was needed to safeguard the trade and commercial privileges which had been established all over Europe. Only those willing to share the costs might reap the fruits. Later scholars modified the thesis in points of detail, but most accepted the distinction between the Hanse of merchants and the Hanse of towns. Dollinger's agreement is reflected in the structure of his book. The fourth chapter, entitled 'Towards

(Selden Soc., 14, London, 1900), p. 132. M. Bateson (ed.), *Records of the Borough of Leicester*, I (London, 1899), pp. xxviii–ix, 12–35. C. Gross, *The Gild Merchant* (London, 1890), I, p. 7.
[3] T. H. Lloyd, *The English Wool Trade in the Middle Ages* (Cambridge, 1977), pp. 23–4.

the Hansa of Towns (*c.* 1250–*c.* 1350)' begins with the sentence 'As early as the mid-thirteenth century the cities tried to take over from the Gotland Community the protection of German merchants abroad.' The next, 'The Hansa of the Towns: A Great Power in Northern Europe (*c.* 1350–*c.* 1400)', outlines the significant events of this period, including the assembly of 1356, which Dollinger regards as the first full Hanse diet (*Hansetag*). He later refers back to this time with phrases such as 'the formation of the Hansa of towns' and 'from the beginning, that is, from about 1358'.[4] Ahasver von Brandt accepts that a transition was under way by the end of the thirteenth century but emphasises the slowness of change. He writes that even in the second half of the fourteenth century 'Hanse merchant is not someone who is a citizen of a Hanse town, but Hanse town is one whose citizens are engaged in overseas trade and share the privileges without opposition. The German Hanse is not yet personified in the towns.'[5] He regards it as significant that when the towns first identified themselves with the Hanse (in 1358) they did not use the term 'Hanse towns' but 'towns of the German Hanse' (*Stede van der dudeschen hense*). Only around the turn of the century did the older usage give way to 'Hanse towns' (*hense stede*), indicating that the transition was complete.

Most of this book is concerned with relations between England and the Hanse in the era of the Hanse of towns, but that is the consequence of bias in the survival of evidence. The earlier period is just as important, both in its own right and for an understanding of later developments. For details of the general development of the early Hanse, English readers are served most conveniently by Dollinger's book, but here a summary may usefully be provided of von Brandt's views expressed in the article already cited. The latter describes the rise of the Hanse of merchants in four stages, which are partly chronological and partly schematic. This analysis helps to elucidate the enigmatic statement of Fritz Rörig that 'the whole [of the Hanse] was earlier than the parts'.

The beginning of the German Hanse is firmly rooted in the Baltic. For several centuries in the early middle ages this sea was the

---

[4] Dollinger, *German Hansa*, pp. 45–82, 86, 89.

[5] A. von Brandt, 'Die Hanse als mittelalterliche Wirtschaftsorganisation – Entstehen, Daseinsformen, Aufgaben', in A. von Brandt and others, *Die Deutsche Hanse als Mittler zwischen Ost und West* (Wissenschaftliche Abhandlungen der Arbeitgemeinschaft für Forschung des Landes Nordrhein-Westfalen, 27, Cologne and Opladen, 1963), 9–38, especially 25. Dollinger makes a different distinction between 'town of the Hanse' and 'Hanseatic town', *German Hansa*, p. 88.

principal trade route between eastern and western Europe. The west sent cloth, wine and whatever else was acceptable and in return received not only the native products of the north-east Baltic lands but also commodities which came via Russia from Byzantium. Much of the exchange took place in the province of Schleswig, the narrowest part of the Danish peninsula where a land journey of only fifteen kilometres separated the Baltic port of Schleswig from Hollingstedt, which was accessible via the river Eider from the North Sea. From the west came first Frisians and later men from other parts of the Low Countries and the Rhineland. They seldom sailed on the Baltic itself, since goods were brought to them by Scandinavian and Slav merchants. The situation was transformed in 1159, when the city of Lübeck was founded on the Trave estuary in the south-westernmost corner of the Baltic. It was settled chiefly by west-German merchants who immediately took to the sea in cogs, vessels recently developed in the North Sea which proved to be commercially superior to Scandinavian and Slav ships. This was the first of von Brandt's four stages of development. The second embraced the island of Gotland, which had long been a halting place on the route to the east. In 1161 Henry the Lion, Duke of Saxony, made peace between Germans and Gotlanders and, in return for a confirmation of the latter's rights in Saxony, the former were allowed to trade in Gotland. Some Germans settled at Visby on the west coast of Gotland, but more importance is usually attached to the community formed among merchants who merely visited the place ('universi mercatores imperii Romani Gotlandiam frequentes'). Little is known about its origin and early constitution, but it bound together men from more than one home town. In the thirteenth century it was ruled by four aldermen, elected respectively by merchants of Visby, Lübeck, Soest and Dortmund. German historians have long stressed the significance of the Gotland community, but for von Brandt an integral part of stage two is the beginning of German involvement with Skania, in the south-west tip of modern Sweden. Each autumn this region provided the most prolific herring fishery in Europe and disposal of preserved fish formed the basis for more general fairs, which in time came to be dominated by Hanse merchants. Von Brandt's inclusion of Skania is a salutary reminder, for the point is often overlooked that, when English merchants flocked to the Baltic two centuries later, Skania was at first just as much an attraction to them as Prussia.

Stage three of von Brandt's plan, which began *c.* 1200 and lasted until *c.* 1250/70, saw the establishment of the far outposts of the Hanse. It consisted partly of the foundation of new towns such as Riga (1201), Reval (1219) and Dorpat (1224), which accompanied the crusade to subjugate the heathen tribes of the north-east Baltic. The other element was a build-up of trade and the acquisition of commercial privileges in regions where there was no question of conquest and mass settlement, at Novgorod in Russia, Bergen in Norway, in Sweden, Flanders and England. Stage four consisted of the foundation of the towns on the southern shore of the Baltic, from Wismar to Königsberg in the provinces of Mecklenburg, Pomerania and Prussia, Slav lands which became thoroughly Germanised. Chronologically this stage was concurrent with the third, but it is conceptually separate. Unlike the towns of the north-east Baltic these were not founded with overseas trade specifically in mind. In the course of time, however, they built up a thriving trade in the products of their hinterlands, often embellished by their own citizens. Among them were some of the leading members of the Hanse. Only by the terminal date of stages three and four were all the 'parts' of the Hanse in place, yet in Rörig's words the 'whole' had long been in existence.

Before leaving this discussion of the early development of the Hanse, mention must be made of an important contribution by Detlev Ellmers, the purpose of which seems to be to remove any doubts about the leading role of Lübeck at all times in the organisation's history. He states unequivocally 'Lübeck did not at some time or other become the head of the Hanse, but was from the beginning the point of departure and basis of the Hanse.'[6] Ellmers challenges certain long-accepted ideas such as the novelty of the cog to the Baltic in the twelfth century and the view that the Gotland community was the first to embrace German merchants from different towns, but this is peripheral to his main thesis. He accepts that the Gotland community was the core of the Hanse but claims that it was not conceived in Gotland some time after 1161 (von Brandt's stage two), but was part and parcel of the foundation of Lübeck. The community was formed between two groups of settlers – those from Westphalian towns such as Soest and Dort-

---

[6] D. Ellmers, 'Die Entstehung der Hanse', *HG*, 103 (1985), 2–40. Contrast this with Dollinger's statement that Lübeck was not officially recognised as leader of the Hanse until 1418 (*German Hansa*, p. 107).

mund, who had hitherto traded merely on land, and seafarers who
came from Schleswig. Now they combined forces to trade on the
Baltic. Ellmer's argument depends on iconographic interpretation of
the thirteenth century civic seal of Lübeck. This depicts two men in
a ship, one steering (a seafarer) and the other (a merchant) swearing
an oath, that is they are forming a partnership. Details of the ship
were already obsolete when the first seal was cut in 1223, but the
whole design was carefully copied when it was renewed in 1256 and
1281. The archaism is seen as a deliberate piece of propaganda,
intended to demonstrate that Lübeck had been the birth place of the
Hanse and remained its leader. The organisation was and remained
for a century or so a Hanse of Eastlanders. Westphalian merchants
were an integral part of it, but those of Cologne and the Rhineland
towns were not. The former traded overland to Lübeck, but the
latter were seafarers. Sea-borne trade with the north-east continued
on the old route via Hollingstedt and Schleswig, for at first there was
no advantage in shipping to Hamburg and crossing thence to
Lübeck. The sea journey was as long in the second case as the first
and the land crossing much longer. Cologne merchants continued to
have little direct contact with the Baltic until the end of the
thirteenth century and it was probably for this reason that they
played no part in the election of the aldermen of the Gotland
community. After fusion of the latter with Cologne and the western
towns the westerners increased their Baltic trade. Fusion itself took
place in the west – in Norway, Flanders and England, into which
areas the Eastlanders expanded their activities in the thirteenth
century. At first they were opposed by the merchants of Cologne, but
from about the middle of the century it began to be realised that
cooperation would improve the position of all *vis-à-vis* local interests.
For Ellmers, events in England in 1282 marked the final recognition
by Cologne of Lübeck's leadership of the Hanse and the point at
which the Hanse of Eastland became a true German Hanse. These
matters will be discussed fully in the next chapter. The last point
about Ellmer's paper which needs to be noted is that it does not
challenge the traditional thesis of a Hanse of merchants giving way
to a Hanse of towns. Indeed he explicitly endorses the dichotomy.[7]
On the other hand, if his argument about Lübeck finds general
acceptance it may necessitate some reappraisal of the formal role of
towns in the earlier phase of the Hanse's history.

[7] Ellmers, 'Entstehung der Hanse', 8.

The metamorphosis of the Hanse of merchants into the Hanse of towns should not be misconstrued. The organisation remained essentially what it had always been – a community of commercial interest. On the occasion of a major crisis in 1469 the Hanse sought to instruct the English crown about its own true nature. It explained that it was 'a firm *confederatio* of many cities, towns and communities for the purpose of ensuring that business enterprises by land and sea should have a desired and favourable outcome and that there should be effective protection against piracies and highwaymen, so that their ambushes should not rob merchants of their goods and valuables'.[8] It might have been added, though on this occasion it would have been impolitic to do so, that the Hanse also existed to ensure that princes did not burden trade with new taxes or embroil merchants unwillingly in their wars. The greater part of the document in question was taken up by an explanation of what the Hanse was not and what it lacked, and it has frequently been remarked that it is easier to do this than to explain what it was. Though a confederation or 'a kind of alliance', to use another phrase of the 1469 elucidation, the Hanse possessed no common property, no treasury, no seal, no permanent officials (until the mid-sixteenth century) and no navy. Expenditure on a common enterprise had to be financed by loans from individual towns, the common purses of the *Kontore* or private merchants, and attempts made afterwards to recover the costs by the most equitable means. The only common institution was the diet, but full assemblies met comparatively infrequently and often were poorly attended. They were generally convened to discuss specific matters, and towns which did not have a direct interest in the current business resented the expense of representation and either ignored summonses or delegated authority to a neighbouring town which did bother to attend. Regional diets, comprising groups of neighbouring towns, met more frequently. Many ordinances (*Rezesse*) of the diet were of a negative kind, such as a prohibition of trade with a certain party or for a period of time. Ultimately, the matter of obedience lay with individual merchants, but dissidents could be dealt with at *Kontor* level or cited to answer to a future diet. Penalties included fines and the expulsion of individuals, but little could be done about large-scale disobedience condoned by the home town of rebels. Expulsion of a town itself from the Hanse was a sanction of the final resort and rarely used. The

[8] Dollinger, *German Hansa*, document 26, pp. 411–13.

main purpose of such action was to deny the use of any Hanseatic privileges in any place to all merchants of the town in question. The most famous case was the expulsion of Cologne in 1474, because of its refusal to stand by the other towns in their recent struggle with England. The size of the Hanse fluctuated in its later years as new members were admitted and others dropped out, often as a result of sheer inactivity on their part, but sometimes for more sinister reasons. It is impossible now to state how many, or which, towns were members at any particular time. This is because the Hanse itself seldom drew up lists of members and resolutely set its face against supplying details to outsiders, who usually wanted them for a restrictive purpose. Dollinger estimates that there were generally about seventy active members and a hundred or so others, whom he terms passive.[9] Only a very small proportion of these ever engaged in direct trade with England.

The Hanse was not a sovereign body and could never become one, since its members owed allegiance to many different territorial princes, ecclesiastical and lay. Some of the latter had aspirations of their own to sovereign status, which made them particularly jealous of the autonomy which had been acquired by the more important towns. The Margraves of Brandenburg were especially notorious and at some time or other forced almost all of the Hanse towns in Brandenburg and Pomerania to withdraw from the organisation.[10] Straslund alone was able to withstand them, though it too was much weakened in the struggle and by concessions made to the prince. But Hanse towns were not singled out for attack by their overlords either in Brandenburg-Pomerania or elsewhere. Attempts by princes to bring towns to heel were widespread in late medieval Germany. Lacking in sovereignty, the Hanse was also without a place in the constitution of the Empire. Towns such as Lübeck and Dortmund, which enjoyed the status of free imperial cities, occupied seats in the imperial diet, but they were there in their own right not as representatives of the Hanse. For most of its history the Hanse simply ignored the Empire and in return was ignored by the Emperors. Only in the late sixteenth century did the Hanse turn to the Empire for help in its struggle with the English Merchant Adventurers. It claimed that English commercial policy and practice were harmful not merely to the Hanse but to the interests of the Empire as a whole.

---

[9] *Ibid.*, p. 88.　　[10] F. L. Carsten, *The Origins of Prussia* (Oxford, 1954), pp. 136–48.

Although the Hanse won the support of the imperial estates, the Emperor was not won over and for a time he declined to enforce a ban on English trade within the Empire. By then the Hanse was a mere rump of its former self and quite unable to prevent its rivals from first evading the ban and very soon getting it rescinded.

Among many anomalies in the history of the Hanse not the least is the presence of the Grand Master of the Teutonic Order, the only territorial prince admitted to membership. Moreover, he was not just any prince but ruler of the sovereign state of Prussia-Livonia. It is not clear exactly how the Order came to be represented so directly in the Hanse, but its claim might have been justified on either of two grounds. On the one hand it had played a decisive part in the foundation of towns in the eastern Baltic; on the other it possessed vast landed estates, much of whose production was marketed in western Europe through Hanse channels. Because of the key role played by Prussia-Livonia in the unravelling of English interest in the Baltic it is necessary to describe briefly its historical geography.[11] The Teutonic Order of St Mary's Hospital in Jerusalem (known more colloquially as the Teutonic Knights) was founded in the Holy Land in the late twelfth century, but soon transferred its energies to eastern Europe. In the 1220s the Knights were enlisted to help the Christian, Polish, Duke of Masovia against the heathen Prussians and installed at Kulm on the eastern bank of the river Vistula. Instead of merely supporting the Poles, the Knights, with the sanction of papal bulls, conquered the whole of Prussia for themselves, though it took them until 1283 to do so. In 1294 died the last Slav Duke of Pomerelia, the coastal province to the west of the Vistula, which included Danzig at the mouth of the river. After a struggle which lasted until 1308, the Knights won control of the whole country and incorporated it in their state. Poland was now cut off entirely from the sea and its considerable trade with the west was conducted through Prussian ports. These were members of the Hanse in their own right, even though their ruler was also a member. Nevertheless, the Grand Master kept an exceptionally tight control over all the towns, and their freedom of action, both within and without the Hanse, was limited. They chafed under this restraint, none more so than Danzig, which from the mid-fourteenth century rapidly became one of the major ports in the Baltic. More than once

[11] The following paragraphs are based chiefly on E. Christiansen, *The Northern Crusades* (London, 1980).

they flirted with Poland and after a bitter war and civil war lasting from 1454 to 1466, western Prussia, which included most of the towns, was ceded to Poland. The towns remained in the Hanse and, under the suzerainty of the King of Poland, enjoyed greater autonomy than in the past. Only Königsberg and Memel were left to a truncated Prussia, which remained nominally a theocratic state until 1525. Then, Albert of Hohenzollern, the current Grand Master, converted to Lutheranism, secularised the province and made himself an hereditary duke under Polish suzerainty.

Even before Prussia fell to the Teutonic Knights, the Baltic tribes living between the Gulf of Finland and the river Dvina had been partially subjugated, again under the guise of a crusade, for these people too were still heathens. The more northerly area, occupied by Estonians, was made subject to the King of Denmark, though its only substantial town, Reval (now Tallinn), was a German foundation of 1219 and a member of the Hanse. A larger area, then known as Livonia, was centred on the modern state of Latvia and conquest proceeded from Riga, founded in 1201. Pacification was committed to a specially created military order, the Knights of the Sword, but after initial successes it was virtually destroyed in 1236 by the neighbouring Lithuanians. The survivors were then absorbed into the Teutonic Order, which acquired the suzerainty of Livonia, though it was governed as a separate province under a provincial master. In 1343 the native Estonians revolted against their overlords and the Teutonic Order was called in to subdue them. In 1347 the Order bought Estonia from the King of Denmark and it was added to Livonia, which continued to be ruled by the Knights until 1562. The region was then divided up between Russia, Poland, Sweden and Denmark. Livonia was physically separated from Prussia for the greater part of the history of the Teutonic state. A small stretch of coastline between the two was inhabited by the Samogitians, who were subjected to the Knights for only a few years in the early fifteenth century. Inland a much bigger wedge was provided by the Lithuanians, who retained their heathenism and independence, in the form of a grand duchy, until 1385, when the union of Poland-Lithuania was created, a power bloc which ultimately defeated the Teutonic knights.

It was emphasised earlier that the Hanse was from first to last a community of commercial interest. It existed solely to promote and protect the trade of its members, who initially were individual merchants and later citizenships of towns. This meant that as a body it had no concern with political programmes or policies which were not wholly or largely commercial or economic in character. Even in this limited field the Hanse was reluctant to cooperate with outsiders. Naturally, individual towns also had non-commercial interests and therefore occasionally combined with others, within or without the Hanse, to achieve other ends. The circumscribed nature and concerns of the Hanse meant that its relationship with England was limited to commercial matters. England could not look to the Hanse, as it did to the Count of Flanders and the princes of the Rhine (and later the Duke of Burgundy or the Emperor), for a political-military alliance against France. Not until the reign of Henry VIII will we see a purely political engagement between England and Lübeck. Moreover, the latter was then acting independently, not as leader of the Hanse. Later, England tried to get cooperation, though not active military support, from Hamburg in respect of campaigns in Scotland and Ireland. Again this was not something which involved the Hanse as a whole. In stressing that the relationship between England and the Hanse was merely commercial, one does not disregard the fact that this involved much more than the simple exchange of commodities. Trade was supported by constant bargaining of a diplomatic nature and the disruption of trade sometimes gave rise to armed conflict. But only one dispute (1468–74) is generally described as a war. Since the conflicts were commercially motivated they are not in the same category as the power struggles between England and France, which were largely about control of territory. But nor can they be classed with the Anglo-Dutch wars of the seventeenth century. The latter were rooted in commercial rivalry which resulted from conflicting national policies espoused by governments. The former were more pragmatic – the by-product of localised acts of piracy. This is not to deny the very real rivalry which existed between Hanseatics and Englishmen in the middle ages. But one must be careful in trying to equate this, on the English side, with government policy. The Hanse diet was concerned only with commercial matters. But the English government, responsible for a large nation-state, had a much wider range of concerns. Economic matters were low down in its list of priorities, and even when considered often had to be subordinated to other interests. The prime example was the manipulation of the wool trade to support foreign policy from the twelfth century onwards.

Edward Miller, contrasting England with France, believed that in the former 'something like a national economic policy could develop from these dealings with the wool trade and the cloth trade'.[12] This may be so, but not until the reign of Edward IV can one begin to assert with some conviction that a national economic policy was emerging. Nor did this yet include hostility to the Hanse as one of its principal tenets. For that we must wait until 1517, when Cardinal Wolsey began to regard the Hanse as a force which was not conducive to the economic welfare of his country. On the other hand, interaction between the English government and the Hanse long preceded anything which can be termed economic policy. Contact between German merchants and the crown began as soon as the former began to visit England, and the relationship gradually became more complex. Much later, when Englishmen began to venture to regions controlled by the Hanse, it became even more intricate. Englishmen asked for privileges similar to those enjoyed by Hanseatics in their country, and when these were denied they looked to their government to support the demand. The procedure which developed was for the government to negotiate with, rather than on behalf of, the English merchants. It depended upon the merchants for intelligence, but was the senior partner in so far as it alone had the power to impose sanctions on the Hanse. England had no non-economic expectations of the Hanse, so the interests of the merchants did not have to be subordinated to foreign policy, though occasionally they might have to be weighed against those of others among the king's lieges. Some government ministers might be indifferent to matters of trade (and occasionally some might even be susceptible to bribery by the opposition), but on the whole the crown would naturally side with its own subjects, even though this was not yet part of a national economic policy. These engagements began as the Hanse of towns assumed its final form, and from then on we are concerned not simply with merchant against merchant, but with the English government against the Hanse diet.

---

[12] E. Miller, 'The Economic Policies of Governments: France and England', in M. M. Postan, E. E. Rich and E. Miller (eds.), *Economic Organisation and Policies in the Middle Ages* (Cambridge Economic History of Europe, 3, Cambridge, 1963), p. 291.

CHAPTER I

The winning of the Hanse franchises, 1157–1361

A legal compilation commonly termed the Billingsgate tolls shows that subjects of the Emperor (*homines imperatoris*) were trading in London about the year AD 1000.[1] In addition to the regular city tolls they paid the king certain specific dues at Christmas and Easter, in return for which he gave the same protection to their possessions as natives enjoyed. The privilege, no matter how limited, and the discharge of an apparently collective obligation suggests some degree of organisation on the part of these merchants. The only townsmen from within the Empire specifically mentioned in this source are those from the Meuse settlements of Huy, Liège and Nivelles, none of which was ever a member of the later German Hanse. However, the implication is that all imperial subjects shared the privilege and doubtless men from other German towns also came to England at this date. The next evidence survives in a miscellaneous collection put together between 1206 and 1216, which portrays conditions existing in London a century or more earlier. Formerly, historians dated its first compilation to about 1130, but a more recent analysis suggests an eleventh-century date.[2] One manuscript begins with the statement that these were the laws of the men of Lorraine; another shows that they were applicable to all subjects of the Emperor and, possibly, in general terms to all aliens. The laws were intended to define the rights and duties of merchants who arrived by way of the Thames, which must have been the most frequently used route. They could either remain in their ships and sell their goods there or else bring them up into the city. Those who did the former paid no duty except for an impost on wine known as *cornage*, but those who

---

[1] A. J. Robertson (ed.), *The Laws of the Kings of England from Edmund to Henry I* (Cambridge, 1925), pp. 70–3.
[2] M. Bateson, 'A London Municipal Collection of the Reign of John', *EHR*, 17 (1902), 495–502. C. Brooke and G. Keir, *London, 800–1216* (London, 1975), p. 267.

chose the latter had to pay *eschawinge*, a tax on all goods which had been recorded in the Billingsgate tolls. Most merchants were free to lodge wherever they wished within the city walls, but those of Tiel, Bremen and Antwerp had to remain below London bridge unless they were willing to be ruled by the law of the city. Possibly, this meant that they would be required to renounce their right to trial by a form of law merchant, which may otherwise have been used in disputes between aliens and citizens. Those who lodged in the city had to inform the sheriff and await his coming before unpacking their goods, although they might proceed with impunity if he did not arrive within three days. The delay was probably intended to allow time for the king's right of pre-emption. If the right was not exercised then the merchant could sell to others, but in a carefully defined order, with Londoners having first choice, next citizens of Oxford, then those of Winchester and finally any others. Until he had remained one night in the city after unpacking his goods, the merchant of Lorraine could not venture beyond four specified boundary points. This restriction was less than that put upon Norwegians, who were forbidden at all times to go out of the city to trade in markets and fairs. Danes, on the other hand, might go wherever they wished in England. Both Danes and Norwegians were allowed to stay in the city for up to a year, but Lorrainers were required to leave after forty days unless they were delayed by bad weather or unpaid debts.

The main import of the merchants of Lorraine was wine and, besides having a right of pre-emption, the king enjoyed butlerage, which allowed him to purchase a few casks at less than the market price. Except for one cask the rest had to be sold wholesale. The privilege of selling only one cask by retail can hardly have had much economic significance, so possibly its origin lay in the need to offer hospitality or samples to potential customers. Similar restrictions confronted aliens in disposing of the rest of their goods. Cloth might be sold only by the whole piece and other wares could not be sold in less than certain amounts. Other trade goods specifically mentioned in the laws were cups of gold and silver, precious stones, cloths from Constantinople and Regensburg, coats of mail from Mainz, fine linens, fustians, wax, pepper and cummin. The import trade, then, may be summed up as one in which wine was the staple commodity, with a wide variety of luxury goods making up the balance. It is impossible to construct a convincing picture of the exports of these merchants, and statements about restrictions upon their purchases in London merely reiterate, in a garbled form, clauses from the earlier Billingsgate tolls. There is no reason to doubt the continuity implied by these two sources, but nor is there evidence that any specific privilege or form of mercantile organisation survived from this period into post Norman Conquest times.

Given the pre-eminence of wine among German imports in the eleventh and early twelfth centuries, it is not difficult to accept that merchants of Cologne already played a part in the trade. Nevertheless, there is no explicit written evidence of this until the reign of Henry II. A surviving writ of that king orders the sheriffs and bailiffs of London not to molest the men of Cologne, but to let them sell wine on the same terms as Frenchmen. More important is another grant of about 1157, which conferred perpetual protection upon the *homines et cives Colonienses*. As long as they paid established dues they were to be treated as the king's own men and no fresh charges would be levied on them without their consent. By this time they had some form of corporate organisation with a headquarters in London and the king's protection was extended to that place – *domo sua Londonensi*, glossed in a later hand as *gildhalla sua*. In 1194, Richard I, in return for help given to him by the Archbishop of Cologne, conferred upon the merchants of that city the widest measure of privilege which they had yet received in England. The London Gildhall was freed from an annual tribute of 2s and its members were absolved from the payment of all local dues in London and throughout the kingdom; they could attend fairs and buy and sell wherever they wished, not excepting London; finally, they were free to exercise their own customs in England. King John several times granted simple letters of protection to Cologne merchants during the early years of his reign, but he did not confirm Richard's charter until 1210, excepting, however, customs of London. In 1213 he again confirmed the charter as part of the price paid for the support of Cologne for his nephew, Otto, in his struggle with the Hohenstaufen.[3]

It has been assumed that Henry III disregarded the charters of his predecessors and exacted the 2s rent for the Gildhall until 1235. If the payment or non-payment of this trifling sum was merely symbolic then its collection might indeed suggest a reluctance by the

---

[3] *HUB*, 1, nos. 13–14, 40, 84, 89.

king to recognise the privileges which had been enjoyed by the merchants in earlier reigns. However, it is likely that previously historians have misinterpreted the significance of the renewal of the Cologne charter in 1235. It is probable that the merchants sought confirmation that year not because of any hostility shown towards them by Henry III, but rather because of the aggressive behaviour of his subjects. The previous year the king had instructed the authorities of London not to exact murage from any Germans until they had counsel with him, while immediately after the renewal of the charter he ordered the bailiffs of Yarmouth to repay 53s 4d which they had exacted illegally from the merchants of Cologne. This suggests that the confirmation of the charter was intended to publicise the fact that the merchants of Cologne enjoyed a wide measure of immunity from the payment of local tolls. The merchants had indeed temporarily lost seisin of the Gildhall earlier in Henry III's reign, possibly as a result of *quo warranto* proceedings, but had recovered it in 1220 for a payment of 30 marks.[4]

At this date both the English authorities and the merchants of Cologne may have been reluctant to concede common rights to the different groups of Germans trading in England. The Cologners were probably willing to share their privileges with neighbouring Rhineland towns, provided that these recognised the authority of the city, but north Germans were a different matter. Mention has already been made of Bremen merchants in London in the late eleventh or early twelfth century, although then they enjoyed fewer rights than some other aliens. There is no evidence from the late twelfth century about the activities of northerners, except for the grant of a wine-cellar in the parish of St Peter the Less by Richard I to Robert le Herre of Saxony. Nevertheless, it is likely that north Germans came increasingly to England as part of their general expansion in the North Sea region. In 1213 Bremen merchants were given a general safe-conduct during the king's pleasure, while a number of north-German ships received individual letters. Thereafter, English sources are again silent about them until the crisis which followed the death of Philip Augustus of France in July 1223. During this emergency all English and alien ships were placed under arrest in case they should be needed to repel a French invasion. Gradually, writs were issued for the release of ships of friendly powers and for the persons of merchants who had been detained. Orders

---

[4] *CCR*, 1231–4, p. 453; 1234–7, p. 216. *CChR*, 1, p. 214. J. M. Lappenberg (ed.), *Urkundliche Geschichte des Hansischen Stahlhofes zu London* (Hamburg, 1851), 1, p. 9.

given during the course of 1223 and 1224 prove the presence in England of ships from Bremen, Emden, Hamburg, Staveren and Groningen, as well as unnamed subjects of the Emperor and of various German dukes. The only more specific reference to a Baltic merchant in these years is the safe-conduct given in July 1223 to Gilbert of Schleswig, a subject of the Duke of Lüneberg.[5]

In 1237 Henry III issued a charter in favour of all the merchants of Gotland which declared them to be free of customs and tolls throughout England on all their imports and exports. This has always been regarded by historians as an original grant, but it was probably a confirmation of an existing right. Earlier, in 1226, the Gotlanders successfully claimed in the *curia regis* that they should be free of lastage and other customs throughout England, and that they had never paid any before the last war, presumably the disturbance of 1223–4. At that time Henry de Hauvill had begun to exact lastage from them in Boston and Lynn, but they claimed that they still paid no tolls elsewhere, not even in London.[6] But just who were these Gotlanders? One problem about their identity which has exercised some historians is the question of whether by the thirteenth century the original Scandinavian merchants of Gotland had been entirely superseded by the Germans who had settled at Visby.[7] The wardrobe purchases of Henry III indicate that Scandinavians were still prominent among the Gotland merchants, but there seems no reason to doubt that both groups shared whatever rights the islanders possessed in England. Gotland merchants still frequented the east-coast ports in the early fourteenth century, but they handled only a tiny proportion of the northern trade. More important than the ethnic identity of the Gotlanders is their relationship to the Gotland Community of the Baltic which, as we have seen, is widely regarded as having been at the core of the German Hanse. Henry III's charter was granted to 'all the merchants of Gotland' but there is no evidence to link this to the Gotland Community. Moreover, it is quite clear that merchants of Lübeck and other towns of the north-German mainland did not automatically share in Gotland privileges in England.

---

[5] *Rot. Litt. Pat.*, 1201–16, p. 194. *CPR*, 1216–25, p. 376. H. M. Chew and M. Weinbaum (eds.), *The London Eyre of 1244* (London Record Soc., 6, 1970), p. 89. Lloyd, *Wool Trade*, pp. 16–17.

[6] *CCR*, 1234–7, p. 427; 1237–42, p. 38. *CChR*, 1, p. 227. *Curia Regis Rolls*, 12, p. 427.

[7] A. E. Christensen, 'Scandinavia and the Advance of the Hanseatics', *Scandinavian Economic History Review*, 5 (1957), 89–117. G. A. Lönig, 'Deutsche und Gotländer in England im 13 Jahrhundert', *HG*, 67–8 (1942–3), 65–93.

Evidence that Lübeck merchants were coming to England before
1226 is provided in an imperial charter granted to the city that year.
It ruled, *inter alia*, that Cologne must stop exacting illegal tolls from
Lübeck merchants in England. This establishes that there was already
some connection between the two groups, for why else should the
former try to tax the latter in a country which was alien to both? It
could never have tried such a move against Flemings or Italians. No
doubt Lübeck resisted the attempted taxation not merely on
financial grounds, but because payment would have acknowledged
the leadership of Cologners in the German community in England.
For several decades the two groups continued to go their own ways,
but there is little direct evidence that Lübeck formally led a rival,
north-German community. Nevertheless, the growing north-German presence in England forced the government to consider their
claims to parity of treatment with the Cologners. When the city of
London obtained a murage grant in 1234, the mayor and sheriffs
were instructed not to collect it from the merchants of the King of
Germany or the Archbishop of Cologne until the king had a colloquy
with all parties. In 1230 Henry III granted a general protection to
all the men of Otto of Brunswick, who included Lübeck merchants,
though it was conditional upon payment of all established duties. In
1238 certain privileges were granted specifically to Lübeck, but they
were not as wide as those enjoyed by Cologne. In fact they were little
more than the safeguards needed by any merchant venturing abroad
regularly, such as a guarantee against spoilation in the event of
shipwreck. In 1252 the citizens of Hamburg obtained protection for
three years, while in 1257 those of Lübeck were given protection for
seven years, provided that they remained true to Henry III's
brother, Richard, now King of Germany. In this time their goods
were to be spared all royal prises.[8] More significant were
developments in 1266. In November the merchants of Hamburg
received permission to have their own hanse in England, while at
Christmas the men of Lübeck were vested with privileges wider than
any they had yet enjoyed, including the highly coveted immunity
from distraint of goods for any offence or debt other than their own.
The record of the latter grant made no mention of a hanse, although
this may have been an oversight, since a few days later the Lübeckers
obtained a charter which not only reiterated the newly acquired

---

[8] *CPR*, 1225–32, p. 415; 1247–58, pp. 155, 553. *HUB*, 1, nos. 205, 292.

privileges but also added that they could have their own hanse like that of Cologne. It can be no coincidence that these two major cities each obtained a hanse within a few weeks of one another at the end of 1266. Although there is no record of any *quid pro quo*, it is impossible to doubt that they were allowed their hanses in an attempt to soften resistance to the collection of the 'new aid', the English customs duties which had recently been imposed by the crown on both native and alien merchants.[9]

During the second half of the thirteenth century the various groups of German merchants were welded into a single community claiming common privileges. This included the Gotlanders, whose 1237 charter was still in the possession of the London Steelyard in the middle of the fifteenth century. The process of assimilation is not easily reconstructed. Some historians have claimed that the decisive step had been taken by 1260, when Henry III at the request of his brother Richard confirmed the existing privileges of the merchants of the 'gildhalla teutonicorum vulgariter nuncupatur', but without reference to any earlier specific grant.[10] This description of the hall has been taken as proof that merchants from all over Germany were now admitted to the Cologne organisation. There is nothing in the charter to warrant this interpretation beyond doubt, for although an official record it is cursory in the extreme. The common parlance referred to probably had in mind the Cologne Gildhall when it spoke of the Gildhall of the Germans, for then as now the man in the street probably regarded one German-speaker as being much the same as another and would be unable to remark the difference between one from Cologne and another from Hamburg. On the other hand, another document also datable to 1260 refers to the leader of the Gildhall merchants as 'aldermanno mercatorum Alemannie', which perhaps provides support for the theory of a united community at that time.[11] It may be argued that the grant of separate privileges, including hanses, to the merchants of Hamburg and Lübeck in 1266 proves that they were not yet part of a wider community, for if they were why was such independent action necessary? The point is not incontrovertible since both towns acted unilaterally even in the Baltic, where there is less doubt about the existence of a united Hanse. Before 1261 Lübeck obtained privileges for its own citizens in Sweden. In that year they were confirmed and extended to the men

[9] *CRP*, 1266–72, pp. 5, 20, 23. Lloyd, *Wool Trade*, p. 60.   [10] *HUB*, I, no. 552.
[11] Lappenberg, *Urkundliche Geschichte*, 2, no. 28.

of Hamburg, but not to those of other German towns, despite the fact that earlier Swedish rulers had made grants without qualification to merchants of Germany. K. Kumlien interprets this as a significant step in the metamorphosis of the Hanse of merchants into the Hanse of towns.[12] It might be unwise, however, to put the same gloss on the 1266 development in England.

While the 1260 charter does not positively establish the existence of a united commercial community in England at that date, it must be admitted that in later years the Hansards attempted to persuade the English authorities that it did just this, particularly when their liberties were threatened. The 1260 charter was always the earliest put forward by the united German Hanse for confirmation, and its brevity and vagueness became an advantage rather than a disadvantage. After the passage of time it became more and more difficult to prove that the privileges referred to in 1260 should be enjoyed only by the men of Cologne, if that was indeed the case, and not by those who had joined up with them after that date. The first confirmation of the 1260 charter was obtained in November 1281, a few months before the earliest conclusive evidence of a united Hanse. The need probably arose from renewed claims by the de Hauvill family about their rights to lastage in the principal East Anglian ports. Thomas de Hauvill, the king's hereditary falconer, leased the lastage of Boston to two Florentine merchants for two years from 30 November 1281 for 100 marks and there may well have been a dispute about his rights in Lynn. At any rate, it was later claimed that the Germans ceased to pay lastage here on 2 November 1281. There the matter rested until 1291 when, following a *quo warranto* enquiry, de Hauvill again attempted unsuccessfully to establish a right to lastage from the Germans at Lynn. The Cologne men seem to have had no objection to the use of the 1260 charter by the united Hanse, but in 1290 and again in 1321 they took the sensible precaution of renewing and defending their other charters, dating back to the twelfth century.[13] These protected their rights even if the 1260 charter should at any time be declared invalid. There is no evidence that the Hamburg and Lübeck men ever sought separate

---

[12] K. Kumlien, 'Hansischer Handel und Hansekaufleute in Skandinavien', pp. 88–9, in A. von Brandt and others, *Die Deutsche Hanse als Mittler*, pp. 78–101.
[13] *CPR*, 1272–81, p. 465. *Placitorum...Abbreviatio* (London, 1811), pp. 280, 285. H. T. Riley (ed.), *Munimenta Gildhallae Londoniensis* (London, 1859–62), 2, pp. 66–7. *HUB*, 2, no. 381. *Hanseakten*, no. 26.

confirmation of their charters of 1266, presumably because the rights defined therein were narrower than those enjoyed in practice by the end of the thirteenth century.

As already mentioned, the earliest clear reference to a united Hanse is found in 1281, and it is possible that then, or shortly before, the German merchants decided to form a common front against Englishmen, particularly Londoners, who were seeking to curtail their privileges. Early in that year the city authorities tried to make the Germans accept financial responsibility for the repair of the Bishopgate and also to pay murage, a local tax charged on goods entering and leaving the city. The first claim had been made during the hundredal enquiries of 1275, when two juries found that the Germans (*Teutonichi*) were responsible for maintaining Bishopgate, which had fallen into disrepair. Both juries admitted that in return the merchants should enjoy all the liberties of citizens. When the merchants resisted, the city appealed to the king, who summoned both parties to the Exchequer, where judgement was given on 4 July 1282.[14] It was agreed that the Germans should now pay 240 marks to put the gate into good repair, that they should be responsible for future repairs and also that they would bear one third of the cost of keeping a watch at the gate, the city paying the rest. In return it was ruled that the Hanse should be freed from payment of murage in perpetuity. It was also agreed that corn brought into the city by Hanse merchants might be sold from their hospices and granaries within forty days, unless the king or the city authorities needed to order otherwise because of dearth. A third concession was that the merchants should have their own alderman. He was to be elected by them and then presented to the city authorities, before whom he was to swear that he would do right and justice in the Hanse's own court. The office was described as having existed before this, and that was certainly true. Possibly, the present agreement set the seal to a change in status or alternatively afforded formal recognition to what had hitherto existed without the sanction of the crown.

Whether the city or the Hanse gained the greater satisfaction from the agreement of 1282, it is unlikely that at this date the Londoners could have made serious inroads into the liberties of the merchants. Any move in this direction would certainly have been blocked by Edward I, whose policy of protecting aliens culminated in the

---

[14] *Rotuli Hundredorum* (London, 1812–18), 1, pp. 416, 428. *Munimenta Gildhallae Londoniensis*, 1, pp. 485–8.

suspension of London's charter in 1285. Opposition to direct rule and the favouring of aliens is visible from at least 1290, but the king loosened his grasp on the city only in the wake of the constitutional crisis which began in the autumn of 1297. In April 1298 he withdrew the royal warden and restored the mayoralty. The citizens immediately rounded upon aliens who had been bold enough to take advantage of the laxness which had prevailed during the interval of direct royal government. In June 1298 many aliens, including eight Germans, were charged with keeping lodging houses, a practice forbidden by the city although during the suspension of the charter both alien freemen and other aliens of good character had been suffered to do so. Amerciaments and warnings given to those found guilty and to others charged the following year failed to curb the desire of aliens to dwell in their own premises or to lodge with fellow countrymen. In April 1300, ten Germans and eight southerners were again ordered to give up their own hospices and to take up residence with freemen. The attempt by the Londoners to restore old customs was not confined to hosting regulations, for they also tried to enforce other rules, including the forty-day limitation upon residence. In May 1301 a number of citizens were chosen to go with the mayor to Kenilworth to treat with the king about this and other matters. However, the business was repeatedly suspended and it remained unresolved until the grant of the *Carta Mercatoria* in 1303. In the meantime the city was ordered not to molest aliens.[15]

The two groups which stand out most clearly in this struggle between London and the alien community were the merchants of the German Hanse and the Gascon wine importers. The city seems to have mounted a concerted campaign against the pretensions of the Germans in an effort to hamper the growth in their trade. In June 1298 the Hanse was charged with illegally avoiding payment of duties on goods imported into and exported from London. The citizens claimed that the privileges of the merchants provided immunity only for goods which they brought directly from their homeland and that there was no protection for *aver de poys*, drapery and wool, in all of which the Germans had recently begun to meddle. The Hanse was given a day to prove its claim to the wider immunity

---

[15] *Munimenta Gildhallae Londoniensis*, 2, p. 71. R. R. Sharpe (ed.), *Letter Books of the City of London* (London, 1899–1911), C, pp. 16, 65, 95. A. H. Thomas (ed.), *Calendar of Early Mayors' Court Rolls* (Cambridge, 1924), pp. 7–10, 12–13. *CFR*, 1, pp. 439–40. T. H. Lloyd, *Alien Merchants in England in the High Middle Ages* (Brighton, 1983), pp. 21–4.

from duties. A little later two of its members were charged with removing wax from a ship in Greenwich – a breach of the law that imported merchandise should be discharged only within the city. For good measure both were also accused of importing pollards and crockards in breach of the recently enacted statute of Stepney, but in the event the latter charge was disproved. The charges brought by the Londoners receive a certain amount of support from the fact that in May 1298 the king had sent a writ to the sheriffs of the city ordering them to pay particular attention to the activities of the Germans and to stamp out certain offences which he believed them to be committing. He had heard that they were abusing their liberties by avowing other men's goods as their own, and also that they were smuggling false money. It is possible, of course, or even likely that such rumours emanated from the Londoners themselves.[16]

On this occasion the Hanse seems to have made no attempt to argue its case before the city but instead appealed directly to the crown, for a royal writ dated 7 August 1298 was sent to the mayor and sheriffs. It cited the Hanse charter of 1260 and its confirmation by Edward I and alleged that these liberties had been disallowed by the citizens. The latter were now commanded to let the merchants enjoy their rights or else to appear before the king to justify their disobedience. The writ was returned with the observations that the liberties had not been denied and that when the merchants had been summoned before the city they failed to prefer charges against anyone. In the light of the last statement the Hanse thought it advisable to bring a test case, and on 24 August Ralph de Attendorn complained before deputies of the mayor that on two occasions Richer de Refham had unlawfully exacted duty on imported silk. The case probably went against the Hanse and it appealed yet again to the king, oiling the wheels of justice with loans to the wardrobe of 500 marks and 600 marks. Further royal mandates ordering that the merchants be allowed their liberties had no effect and in February 1301 two justices were commissioned to hear their complaints and to enforce their rights. These disputes were soon overtaken by other events, for in 1303 Edward I published the *Carta Mercatoria*, the most important royal pronouncement yet made about alien trade. Extensive privileges valid throughout the kingdom were conceded to all alien merchants, but in return they were required to pay

---

[16] *Munimenta Gildhallae Londoniensis*, 2, p. 196. *Early Mayors' Court Rolls*, pp. 2, 26.

additional customs duties on all their imports and exports. The
Hanse, as one of the leading and most cohesive groups of aliens,
played a major part in the discussions which gave birth to the *Carta
Mercatoria* and it was equally prominent in the struggle to get the
charter accepted in London. For example, when the city made
concessions in 1309 in an important matter relating to the weighing
of goods, the Hanse provided eleven out of twenty-one alien
negotiators.[17]

Since Edward II confirmed the *Carta Mercatoria* shortly after his
accession, and since it appeared to provide safeguards as strong as,
or stronger than, those of their charter of 1260, the Hanse made no
immediate move to obtain confirmation of the older instrument. But
by the summer of 1311 the situation was very different, for the
privileges enjoyed by all aliens were then fiercely under attack and
the *Carta Mercatoria* was soon to be cancelled as part of the famous
ordinances published that autumn. This caused the Hanse to
scrutinise its own charters very carefully and, finding that the 1281
confirmation of the 1260 grant made no reference to the merchants'
heirs, they felt it worth paying £100 for a confirmation by Edward
II which rectified the situation.[18] This was done in June 1311 before
the cancellation of the *Carta Mercatoria*, so that after that the
merchants of the Hanse were legally back where they had been
before 1303.

No sooner had the Hanse obtained confirmation of the 1260
charter than further gaps in its franchises were exposed, although the
events which demonstrated this resulted eventually in the deficiencies
being made good. The cause of the trouble was a series of piratical
attacks upon Englishmen, in which German ships were alleged to
have been involved. The most serious case was the seizure off the
coast of Norfolk of wool and other goods belonging to a group of
Lincolnshire merchants. The culprits were said to have come from
Lübeck, Hamburg, Kampen, Cologne and other towns in Eastland.
In retaliation the Englishmen obtained writs instructing the sheriffs
of Norfolk and Suffolk, Yorkshire, Lincolnshire and Nottingham-
shire to arrest all German-owned property within their bailiwicks.
This provoked the Hanse into making representations to the crown,
and on 10 July 1311 the sheriffs were instructed to release the goods,

---

[17] *Early Mayors' Court Rolls*, p. 43. *CPR*, 1292–1301, pp. 450, 479, 622. *Letter Book* C, p. 41; D,
p. 209. Lloyd, *Alien Merchants*, pp. 27–9.
[18] *CPR*, 1307–14, p. 354. *Rotuli Originalium in Curia Scaccarii Abbreviato* (London, 1805–10),
p. 181.

since the king wished to show special favour towards the merchants of Almain. However, they had to provide surety to answer the charge of piracy in the Chancery on 9 September. As a result of this hearing the sheriffs were ordered to release the mainpernors of the Germans, on the grounds that the original arrest of their goods had been illegal. It is clear that the Lincolnshire merchants lost the first round of their action for damages because they had acted prematurely in seeking the writs of distraint. This was an accepted part of the law merchant, but such distraints should not be made until the aggrieved parties had sought justice from the lords or civic authorities of alleged robbers or debtors. Only if justice was denied should the plaintiffs then have recourse to direct action in their own country in order to speed up the legal process. Since the crime in question had been committed on 24 June 1311, the Lincolnshire men cannot possibly have sought and been denied justice in Germany before the arrests of early July. It was probably on these grounds that the Chancery ruled that the arrests were illegal; the fact that the owners of the arrested goods were not privy to the robbery was not an issue, for provided that due processes had been observed they might legally be called to account for the actions of their compatriots. Although the Lincolnshire men had been faulted on this occasion they were not debarred from continuing their action and in March 1312 they obtained royal letters addressed to the civic authorities of Hamburg, Lübeck and Kampen requesting that the pirates be brought to justice. Hamburg and Lübeck replied in very similar terms, simply denying any involvement of their citizens. Kampen neither admitted nor denied implication in the piracy, but submitted counter-charges of its own merchants. After refusing several times to link the specific charge of the Lincolnshire men to general complaints of Kampen, Edward II finally acceded to a request for a letter of safe-conduct for envoys to come to England to discuss all grievances; two consuls came under the protection of a letter covering the period from 1 May to 1 November 1313. According to the English version of events, these two merely sought to delay settlement of the piracy claim and then broke off all negotiations without justification. After the failure of the talks, writs were issued on 16 November 1313 for the arrest of all goods belonging to Hamburg, Lübeck and Kampen to satisfy the claims of the Lincolnshire merchants.[19]

[19] *CCR*, 1307–13, pp. 111, 364, 378, 541, 543, 578; 1313–18, p. 26, *CPR*, 1307–13, p. 567. PRO, SC1/13/80; 19/71.

Although the seizures noted above were limited to the cities of Lübeck, Hamburg and Kampen, there is no doubt that they were a cause of concern to the Hanse as a whole, for within a few days it had asked the king to command the Chancery to maintain the Hanse in its liberties. In fact, these liberties did not protect the Hanse against reprisals which were soundly based on the law merchant. It is true that the king could and did bestow immunity from arrest upon individuals or groups of merchants where they were not themselves debtors or trespassers, but this was a jealously guarded privilege which had been excluded from the *Carta Mercatoria*. Among the cities of the Hanse only Lübeck had so far obtained this right, although in the present troubles it seems to have been disregarded. The Hanse now made a determined effort to add this plum to its liberties and in April 1314 it was conceded to all the merchants of Almain.[20]

Having obtained the immensely valuable privilege of immunity from general arrest the Hanse had to vindicate it against powerful interests. It was soon an issue in several cases involving English merchants, but the real test became a complaint by William de Widdeslade, citizen of London. Widdeslade had goods valued at £300 taken from a Brabant vessel putting out from Sluys in Flanders, and he laid charges against the men of the Count of Holland and eight named German towns. In January 1316 in the parliament assembled at Lincoln the king's council awarded him the amount of his loss plus £100 damages. The following Michaelmas Widdeslade obtained writs authorising the arrest in Boston and Lynn of goods belonging to men of the Count of Holland and of 'the men whom he shall ascertain'. The Hanse immediately petitioned for the release of the arrested goods, claiming that none of the eight towns were involved in the piracy; indeed, some had actually lost goods in the same incident. Moreover, all were members of the Hanse and therefore enjoyed immunity from general arrest. The plea was accepted and in mid-November 1316 instructions were given for the release at Boston of goods and ships belonging to Lübeck, Münster and Soest. But, in January 1317, Widdeslade obtained a new writ authorising the arrest at London of goods to the value of £300 plus any damages awarded by a city jury. The Hanse appealed yet again and in March the sheriffs were ordered to release Hanse goods valued at £400. By 1317 the immunity of the Hanse

[20] *CChW*, I, p. 394. *CPR*, 1313–17, p. 112.

from arrest was a serious issue and it must have seemed expedient to obtain confirmation at the highest level. On 27 June a royal patent guaranteed immunity until 6 September; on 30 September this was extended until the next parliament, when presumably it was intended to debate the whole matter thoroughly. However, on 7 December 1317 the Hanse confounded its opponents by obtaining a royal confirmation of its charters, for which it paid no less than £1,000. Not only did Edward II confirm the grants of his predecessors and his own award of immunity from arrest but, for the first time, he conceded that neither he nor his heirs would place new impositions on the Hanse without its consent.[21]

The new Hanse charter probably made its enemies even more determined to discuss their grievances in parliament, and the Germans whose goods had been released in London in March 1317 were summoned to the assembly held at York at Michaelmas 1318. It was then urged that, since an award had been made against them before the date of their recent charter, the earlier judgement should be implemented. No agreement could be reached on this matter and a decision was deferred until the next parliament. In fact, it was not until July 1320, after several more reverses, that Widdeslade was finally able to secure the successful execution of a writ of distraint against a group of German merchants. By this time the influence of the Hanse was waning rapidly and in the following year Widdeslade petitioned in parliament for an increase in the amount of damages awarded to him, on the grounds that the Germans had vexatiously delayed a settlement. In consequence of this a London jury increased the figure by £200.[22]

The purchase of the 1317 charter must have convinced the English merchants that they could not secure the abolition of the Hanse liberties and therefore their only course of action was to restrict the number of those entitled to enjoy them. This was no easy matter. Some of the Hanse charters referred merely to the merchants of Almain, while more recent grants to the merchants of Almain of the London Gildhall were hardly more satisfactory, since they seemed to allow the Germans to determine their own membership. In the York parliament of 1318 the Englishmen established that a certain German whose goods had been arrested was no longer a member of the Gildhall, but thereafter they ran into difficulties.

[21] *CCR* 1313–18, pp. 366, 376, 393, 398. *CChW*, 1, p. 447. *CPR*, 1313–17, p. 672. *HUB*, 2, no. 313.   [22] *CCR*, 1318–23, pp. 45–7, 89, 155, 158, 248, 414.

Almost invariably, when German merchandise was arrested, Hanse officials swore that the owners were members of the Gildhall and the goods had to be released. Naturally, the English were not prepared to accept this state of affairs indefinitely and at the end of 1319 they challenged the testimony that certain merchants of Soest and Greifswald were members of the Gildhall. A jury composed of Londoners and non-German aliens then found that the merchants in question had not been members at the time their goods were arrested. In 1320, no doubt in consequence of the conflicting testimony of the Hanse and the London jury, the crown brought a suit in the King's Bench against the former. It was called upon to certify the names of all its members, the towns from which they came and who admitted them. Before this case was concluded it was overtaken by *quo warranto* proceedings arising from the London eyre of 1321. The latter action was the more serious since it was not restricted to the question of membership, and the entire fabric of the Hanse privileges came under attack. The proceedings began in the Chancery but were soon transferred to the King's Bench, where they were repeatedly adjourned. In Hilary term 1324 the merchants failed to appear and the sheriffs were ordered to take their liberties into the king's hands. The next year the merchants paid a fine of £20 to replevy their liberties, but judgement was continually deferred until the matter was closed by the accession of Edward III and a fresh confirmation of the charter of 1317 and all earlier privileges.[23] The precariousness of the collective liberties of the Hanse in the later years of Edward II forced individuals to protect their own interests as best they might. The Cologne merchants did so by submitting their own charter of 1194 to the *quo warranto* proceedings of 1321. Since the privileges which this enshrined were narrower than those enjoyed by the greater Hanse, the charter had been somewhat neglected in recent years and had never been confirmed by Edward II. But should the wider franchises be overthrown and the Hanse disintegrate, the Cologne charter might establish a useful fall-back position for the men of Westphalia. Additionally, from at least as early as the spring of 1323, some German merchants obtained personal letters of protection. At first these tended to be simple letters of safe-conduct, but later documents described the principal liberties claimed by the Hanse and stipulated that they should be enjoyed by the recipient. Some men received progressive benefits; privileges

---

[23] *CCR*, 1318–23, p. 45. H. M. Cam (ed.), *The Eyre of London, 1321*, I (Selden Soc., 85, London, 1968), pp. lxxiv–lxxv, cxvii–cxix; 2 (86, 1969), pp. 180–5.

bestowed at first during royal pleasure, then for life, with a final accolade of denizen status.[24]

Unlike his father, Edward III did not issue a general confirmation of the *Carta Mercatoria* after his accession; instead, individual groups of aliens were left to renew their own copies of the charter. This fact became significant in the early 1330s, when London began to levy murage on alien goods. The city was not simply ordered to desist; instead, Chancery issued separate instructions in favour of any merchants who produced current charters to warrant their liberties.[25] The German Hanse was not among those who thought it advisable to update their copies of the *Carta Mercatoria*, probably because it felt sufficiently protected by its other charters, which were confirmed by the new king as early as March 1327. Its confidence was not without foundation. The liberties granted uniquely to the Hanse by Edward II were in some respects more valuable than those provided by the *Carta Mercatoria*. Moreover, the temporary cancellation of the *Carta Mercatoria* under the terms of the 1311 ordinances had shown that it was vulnerable to political attack. The Germans' own liberties were no more vulnerable; in fact, since they were shared by a smaller group, they might rouse less resentment and therefore be easier to defend. Whether or not the Germans' neglect of the *Carta Mercatoria* was deliberate, they undoubtedly tried to capitalise on the fact in 1330. That year, they petitioned that the duty of 3d in the pound, and by implication all the alien customs duties established in 1303, were being taken from them illegally. But, instead of simply claiming that they did not currently come within the terms of the *Carta Mercatoria* and ought not therefore to bear its charges, they sought to distort the historical record. They alleged that Henry III had granted that no custom should be taken from them without their consent and that Edward I had confirmed this before 1303. Even were it true, this claim would have been irrelevant since the Germans were undoubtedly in the forefront of those who negotiated and gave their consent to the charter of 1303. In fact, while the *Carta Mercatoria* itself contained a vaguely worded promise that aliens would not be subjected to further taxation without their consent, an unambiguous undertaking to this effect unique to the Hanse was given only in 1317. Not surprisingly, the crown rejected the suggestion that Hansards should be exempt from the 1303 duties. In April 1332 Edward III made his first general confirmation of the

---

[24] *CPR*, 1321–4, pp. 280, 434; 1324–7, p. 194. *CCR*, 1323–7, p. 402.
[25] Lloyd, *Alien Merchants*, p. 33.

Carta Mercatoria. Thereafter, there could hardly be any question but that the Hanse was subject to all its provisions.[26]

In 1335 the position of all alien merchants in England was significantly strengthened by a statute made in the parliament assembled at York. Until now their status had depended almost entirely upon the royal prerogative, but many of the privileges which the king had bestowed upon them conflicted with prescriptive and chartered rights of English communities. Conflict was inherent in any attempt to favour aliens, but hitherto in many quarters the claims of natives had been regarded as paramount, by virtue of that bastion of liberties – *Magna Carta.* Chapter 41 of this document attempted to provide a minimum of civilised treatment for visiting merchants, but it ranked well below chapter 13, which said that London and all other towns should continue to enjoy all their ancient liberties and free customs. The statute of 1335 cut through this difficulty by declaring that all chartered franchises and customary usages which interfered with its intent were null and void. Parliament did not, however, explicitly endorse the *Carta Mercatoria* and the short statute did not go into any detail about the points at issue between Englishmen and aliens. It simply stated that aliens might trade in all commodities, although wine could be exported only by royal licence, and that they might deal with whomsoever they wished, whether denizen or fellow alien. Nevertheless, it was clearly the intention of parliament to establish a wide measure of free trade, and when the statute was confirmed in 1351 it was then spelled out that this included the freedom to engage in both retail and wholesale trade.[27]

During wartime all rights to trade, whether established by royal charter or parliamentary statute, were subordinated to other considerations. At the beginning of the Hundred Years War such considerations included Edward III's diplomatic and financial strategies. To assist these a total ban was placed on the export of wool, which was the main English product handled by both denizen and alien merchants. The king sought to reassure aliens and to encourage them to maintain the rest of their trade by letters of safe-conduct. A large number were issued in the early years of the war, some in favour of all aliens, some limited to particular groups. They were generally for a specified period of time, usually from one to three years; however, little if any significance can be attached to the

---

[26] *CPR,* 1330–4, p. 270, *Rot. Parl.,* 2, p. 46. *HUB,* 2, no. 460.
[27] *Stats.,* 1, pp. 270, 315.

time factor. On the one hand, although letters often promised that the *Carta Mercatoria* would be respected during this period there is no suggestion that afterwards recipients would automatically be put outside the charter. On the other hand, one cannot suppose that the king bound himself unconditionally to continue his protection until the end of the given period; should circumstances require, it would undoubtedly be withdrawn. Legally, notice ought to be given if letters of protection were terminated prematurely, so that aliens had time to settle their affairs and depart in peace. Naturally, such a courtesy was not extended to the subjects of any power who behaved unfairly to English merchants abroad. On at least two occasions during the early years of the war the Hanse franchises were put in jeopardy. The first threat arose from the arrest within the territory of the Archbishop of Cologne of one master John Piers, who was released only after payment of a large fine.[28] From 1344 until 1346 his executors sought to recover damages by distraining the property of German merchants in England. Although Piers had been about the king's business, this was a private action; because of this the arrests were limited in scale and ultimately unsuccessful since they were objected to as a breach of Hanse privileges. The second incident was potentially far more serious, since at first the crown chose to treat it as an insult to itself and the entire English nation. It revolved around the execution in Sluys of Richard Curtys of Bristol, on a charge of piracy brought by a German merchant. The English merchants of the staple represented this to their government as judicial murder, procured by perjury and slander. In July 1351 the liberties of the Hanse were suspended and a wholesale arrest made of goods and debts throughout the country. Individual merchants gradually recovered their property by swearing that they had no association with the German Hanse in Flanders, but a shadow lay over them for several years. The franchises were formally restored by June 1354 at the latest, when an elaborate letter of protection shows that they were then being enjoyed by all members of the Hanse in England.[29]

The ban imposed on the export of wool in 1336 was relaxed in favour of the Hanse in March 1338, but the trade remained subject to strict controls and was also burdened with a subsidy additional to the ancient custom of 1275 and the new custom of 1303. At first the rate was 20s per sack for denizens and aliens, while the latter were

---

[28] *HUB*, 3, nos. 39, 42, 65, 77–8.
[29] *Ibid.*, nos. 207–11, 214–15, 222, 233, 235, 238, 258, 298.

also required to pay an equal sum as a loan. Later the amount was increased and aliens were frequently required to pay a higher rate than denizens. Various considerations counselled acceptance of this increase in tax beyond the level agreed to in 1303. Subsidy was paid by natives as well as by aliens; there were precedents from earlier in the reign of Edward III and from that of Edward II; consent was obtained, initially from English merchants and at least a few leading aliens, later from parliament. Most importantly, of course, unless he paid subsidy a merchant simply would not be allowed to export wool.[30]

While there is no evidence that aliens questioned the legality of the wool subsidy, they did not submit so readily to the new taxes on other goods which were introduced in 1347. Most controversial was the levy on English-made woollen and worsted cloths, established by 'common consent' in a great council held in March. Aliens paid 1s 9d for woollen cloths of assise without grain (more for those in grain and half-grain) and 1½d on standard cloths of worsted (more for single and double beds of worsted). The fact that they had to pay this in addition to the cloth duties established in 1303 soon roused protests, probably on the grounds that they had not given consent. As early as October 1347 instructions were given that the new duty was not to be taken at present from members of the German Hanse, although a guarantee was obtained that it would be paid retrospectively should their liability be established. By 20 January 1348 a decision had been made in favour of the merchants and it was ruled that they should pay only the duty of 1303 and be exempt from the new tax. It is far from clear whether this decision was based upon the *Carta Mercatoria* or upon the 1317 privilege of the Hanse. If the German exemption stemmed from the *Carta Mercatoria* one would expect to find parity of treatment between them and other aliens, but this is not the case. There is no record of an order in favour of non-Hanse aliens in 1348, though not until 1351 is it possible to establish whether or not these others were actually paying double duty. From that date there was a lack of uniformity for a number of years. Sometimes non-Hanse aliens paid double duty, sometimes they did not. Whenever they were spared one of the duties it was always that of 1303, not the higher rate of 1347 as in the case of the Hanse. No specific instructions to customs collectors about non-Hanse cloth duties have been found, except for writs sent to Southampton on 25

---

[30] Lloyd, *Wool Trade*, pp. 144–92.

October 1356 and to London on 1 February 1357. In both cases the collectors were told to disregard a previous order exempting merchants of Acquitaine from payment of the 1303 duty, since the king's council had now decided that they must pay both that and the 1347 duty. Although these writs refer only to Gascons it is likely, but not certain, that all non-Hanse aliens paid the same rates in any given port. This attempt by the Exchequer to enforce double payment was not altogether successful and the lack of uniformity continued until 1361. From that date until 1381 non-Hanse aliens paid only the 1347 duty in all ports except London, where they continued to be charged double duty.[31]

The stabilisation of non-Hanse rates in 1361 probably resulted indirectly from the settlement of a new dispute with the Hanse, although this left the Hanse paying only the 1303 duty and confirmed its exemption from that of 1347. It is not clear just how and when the dispute began, but some time before May 1358 the king's council ruled that the Hanse merchants should pay 1s 9d on exported cloths of assise. This was interpreted by the collectors of Boston and Hull as meaning that they should pay 1s 9d in addition to the 1s which they were already paying. On 12 May 1358 they were instructed not to collect the 1s until Michaelmas next, since the Hanse had found mainpernors to pay double duty on all cloths exported between the two dates should their liability be established. On 16 May the collectors at Boston, Lynn, Yarmouth and London were ordered to stop demanding 1s 9d per notional cloth in addition to the 3d in the pound *ad valorem* duty which was already paid on straits and pieces of assise measuring less than half a cloth in length. On 16 October the Boston collectors were informed that the Hansards were to pay only the 1s 9d on cloths of assise, since it would be unjust to make them pay double duty. The London collectors were told the same on 2 December 1358, an earlier writ dated 28 November having confirmed that in the case of worsteds the Hanse was to be charged only with the 3d in the pound of 1303 and not with the 1347 duty. Thus far, then, it had been decided that Hanse woollens of assise were to pay only the 1347 duty and their worsteds and straits only the 1303 duty. In London the Hansards, having paid only 1s 9d on assise cloths in 1358–9, paid 1s and 1s 9d in 1359–60. It is clear that the compromise satisfied neither the Exchequer nor the Hanse, and the situation remained confused until 8 February

---

[31] *CFR*, 6, p. 28; 7, p. 29. *CCR*, 1346–9, pp. 334, 354. *CPR*, 1348–50, p. 201.

1361. It was then decided that henceforth Hansards should pay only the 1303 duty on whole and half woollen cloths of assise and only 3d in the pound on straits, smaller pieces of assise and worsteds. The agreement was honoured for the remainder of Edward III's reign. Only the bare bones of this dispute between the Exchequer and the Hanse about the 1347 duty can be reconstructed and, as already remarked, it is impossible to determine whether the Hanse justified its position primarily by the *Carta Mercatoria* or by the privilege of 1317, though both were cited in the formal verdict of the king's council in 1361. In truth, neither may have been the deciding factor, since the council stated that it favoured the merchants 'in consideration of services by them rendered in the king's war and elsewhere, of aids oft-times granted in time of his need, and of the readiness found in them beyond other alien merchants in the king's business'. Since Hanse loans to the crown had dried up some years previously it must be assumed that some remnant of gratitude remained or else the council had an eye to the future in acknowledging that such services would not be unrewarded.[32]

As well as refusing to pay the permanent new custom on cloth, the Hansards resisted temporary subsidies on other goods, allegedly levied to pay for the protection of maritime trade. The first of these was authorised by the great council of March 1347, the rates being 2s on a tun of wine and a sack of wool and 6d in the pound on general merchandise, to be collected from denizens and aliens from the 18th of that month until Michaelmas. In the event, the tax on merchandise continued until 25 November 1347 and that on wool until the following Easter. In the middle of October the Hanse obtained an order that for the time being its members should not pay this subsidy, just as it gained a respite from the new cloth duty. As we have seen, by January 1348 the dispute over the cloth duty had been resolved in favour of the Hanse, but no record has yet been found of any decision in the other matter. The same problem exists in relation to the second subsidy of tunnage and poundage, which was collected from 28 February 1350 to 28 June and, after a temporary suspension, from 24 September 1350 to 29 September 1351. In April 1350 the subsidy was not charged upon the cargoes of four cogs arriving at Boston, but this may have been an act of special grace. It is clear that during the following winter and spring all Hansards were required to pay the subsidy at the time of export

---

[32] *CCR*, 1354–60, pp. 448, 467, 518; 1360–4, pp. 151–2.

or import unless they found mainpernors to pay later, should it be decided that they were liable.[33] Although no formal record survives of the decision of the king's council in this matter, it appears to have gone against the merchants. Events in the aftermath of the Curtys affair may be indicative. As mentioned earlier, all whose goods were arrested in 1351 gradually recovered seisin, except for Hildebrand Sudermann, alderman of the London Gildhall, whose chattels valued at £207 remained attached and were eventually sold on behalf of the crown. A possible explanation is that Sudermann had pledged members who were unable to put up cash for the subsidy and he remained personally liable until it was paid, so the Exchequer did not need to waste time pursuing recalcitrant debtors.[34] Those whom Sudermann pledged had not necessarily failed his trust, since they may have paid him directly and left him to discharge the debt at the Exchequer. If he did not deliver the money then he was himself responsible for his predicament. When a third grant of tunnage and poundage was collected, between 1 December 1359 and 26 June 1360, there is no record of even temporary respite being allowed to Hansards and, given the current dispute about cloth duties, it is most unlikely that they were spared.

In the light of the fact that the privileges enjoyed by the Hanseatics diminished both the king's own revenues and those of his subjects it is somewhat surprising that the question of eligibility did not figure more prominently than it appears to have done for much of the middle ages. The crown was initially content to grant franchises to the 'merchants of Almain', without seeking to define more closely those who fell within this category. Even when it was made aware of the problem caused by the exercise of these liberties it failed to grasp the nettle by giving a clear ruling as to who should enjoy them. Instead, it adopted a pragmatic policy of asking the officials of the Hanse Gildhall in London to say who was or was not a member as the need arose. These tended to acknowledge almost every German merchant in difficulties as a member of their organisation. Eligibility for membership of the Gildhall stemmed from citizenship of certain German towns; later, birth in such towns was claimed by the English authorities to be a prerequisite. Early fourteenth-century sources establish Cologne, Dortmund, Münster, Soest, Osnabrück, Recklinghausen, Lübeck, Hamburg, Greifswald,

---

[33] *CCR*, 1346–9, p. 334; 1349–54, pp. 167, 259–60, 291, 297.
[34] I.-M. Peters, *Hansekaufleute als Gläubiger der englische Krone, 1294–1350* (Cologne and Vienna, 1978), pp. 287–8.

Gotland and Dinant as places from which merchants categorically and successfully claimed the protection of the franchises when their goods were distrained. Harderwijk merchants advanced a claim in 1305, but their distrained goods were released on other grounds, so on this occasion the question of membership was not put to the test.[35] Merchants from Rostock, Stralsund, Deventer, Staveren and Attendorn can be shown to have been members by other criteria, such as participation in deliberations of the Hanse at Boston in 1303.[36] This list may not include all the towns which supplied members, but it might be a mistake to try to spread the net too wide and claim that membership at this time was open to all German merchants. On the other hand, it is probably more important to stress that it was not limited by any action of the English crown.

Granted that the citizens of an undetermined number of towns were eligible for membership of the Hanse, the question next arises as to whether they automatically became members whenever they came to England or whether they had formally to be admitted into the organisation. If the latter, was membership voluntary or compulsory? Membership was not totally automatic for this would have excluded the possibility of expulsion or resignation, which certainly existed. When a number of north-German ships visited Lynn in 1303 in defiance of a Hanse boycott of the town, the captains and merchants were summoned to appear before senior members of the fellowship at Boston fair and were given the choice either of compounding for their offence or of being expelled from the organisation ('extra judicium ac libertatem Teutonicorum ponerentur').[37] They chose the former. In 1319 a jury found that one Hermann le Skippere had ceased to be a member of the London Hanse, but no further explanation was recorded.[38] Karl Engel favours the idea of both formal and compulsory membership and in support cites a Cologne statute of 1324 which provided that its *Englandfahrer* must belong to a Cologne hanse and that wherever four of them were assembled they were empowered to elect an alderman who had authority over all the city's merchants. There is also evidence for the existence in 1328 at Attendorn of a fraternity of St Nicholas, whose members regularly traded with England.[39] It seems

---

[35] *Early Mayors' Court Rolls*, p. 78.   [36] *HUB*, 2, no. 40.   [37] *Ibid.*, no. 40.
[38] *CCR*, 1318–23, p. 89.
[39] K. Engel, 'Die Organisation der deutsch-hansischen Kaufleute in England im 14 und 15 Jahrhundert bis Utrechter Frieden von 1474', *HG*, 19 (1913), 455–517, especially 458, 469; 20 (1914), 173–225.

likely that disputes about the right to enjoy the franchises would not often have arisen in the case of those who lived permanently in England or regularly visited the main centres of economic activity, but from time to time newcomers must have been challenged. In the late fifteenth century provincial customs officials required a certificate of membership issued by the Steelyard. This they returned to the Exchequer with their accounts as a warrant for allowances. In cases of doubt a similar procedure could have been followed in earlier times, since the London Gildhall was clearly recognised as the chief executive authority of the Hanse before the end of the thirteenth century. When the city of Lübeck complained about the arrest of seven of its ships at Newcastle, Ravenser and Yarmouth in 1295, orders for their release were given after two Englishmen and four Germans resident in London provided sureties that they would not trade with the French and would subsequently account to the Gildhall for their movements.[40] It is not possible to reconstruct the constitutional relationship between the London Gildhall and the Hanse communities which were established at several east-coast ports, but in practice the latter must have enjoyed a considerable degree of autonomy. In large measure they were composed of individuals whose business was confined to these provincial centres and who had little or no interest in the economic life of the capital.

By 1300 the German community permanently settled in London was well over a century old. A few of its members were acknowledged as citizens and denizens and this group probably bore the main burden of administering the collective interests of the Hanse. Its leadership was based not on numbers nor upon current economic strength, but upon the historic role of the community and, more importantly, its proximity to the seat of England's government. Permanent German residents may have been fewer in the provinces, but the number visiting those ports in person or sending goods there in the custody of others was very much greater than in the case of London. Moreover, financial investment in the former places was also greater. During the second half of the thirteenth century the German stake in provincial overseas trade had grown considerably, but involvement in London's trade failed to keep pace with overall growth and in certain sectors there may even have been an absolute decline. The result was that the trade of London-based Germans fell back relative to that of those in the provinces as well as to that of

[40] PRO, E159/68, m. 61.

other aliens operating in the capital. It is difficult to detect when these trends were reversed. London's share of Hanseatic trade in England may not have increased significantly until after the middle of the fourteenth century, though the total Hanse share of alien trade may have received a boost in the early stages of the Hundred Years War. Apart from the obvious fact that certain nationalities were then disadvantaged by being classed as enemies, many German merchants suddenly evinced an unaccustomed willingness to lend money to the king, which may have been accompanied by an increase in trade.

The most sensitive branch of London Hanse trade was also the oldest – the import of Rhine wine. By the end of the thirteenth century this had largely been destroyed by the competition of French wine. In 1315 the Hanse unsuccessfully claimed that their wine imports should not be subject to prise.[41] During the course of the dispute it was alleged that no vessels now came fully loaded with wine, but only a few tuns were brought in as general cargo. As its wine trade dwindled the London Hanse failed to find a niche for itself in important sectors of import growth. Surviving early fourteenth-century customs accounts show that almost half of all imports taxed on an *ad valorem* basis consisted of small miscellaneous goods classed as mercery;[42] Germans had no share in these. Their role in the import of cloth from the Low Countries was negligible; between 29 September 1308 and 31 March 1309 Germans brought in fewer than 100 out of a total of 3,626 cloths, and this is their best performance recorded in the surviving accounts.[43] Even more surprising is the almost total absence of fish and timber products, which made up the bulk of German imports on the east coast. This was despite the fact that Lübeck merchants were among the permanent residents of London and the former city was still the dominant power in the export trade of northern Europe. Since there must have been a market in London for these goods it must be supposed that many were brought there by intermediaries after being landed first on the east coast.[44] Those northern products which do appear in the London customs accounts, viz. wax, furs and copper, were not imported directly, but had been stapled in Flanders. These things, together with battery from the Dinant area and weapons, armour and steel from around Cologne, were virtually all that the

---

[41] *Hanseakten*, nos. 52, 55.   [42] Lloyd, *Alien Merchants*, p. 54.
[43] PRO, E122/69/3.
[44] The London fishmongers claimed a monopoly of fish imports.

Hanse merchants imported. In all of them the Hanse had a near, though not complete, monopoly, but even when added together they made up only a comparatively small part of London's total imports. Furthermore the trade was not immune from disturbance. In July 1309 a number of Germans were prosecuted for conspiring to increase the price of wax.[45] It was alleged that since the previous Christmas they had refrained from importing it and consequently prices had doubled. In defence they claimed that the usual practice was for wax to be shipped from Russia and elsewhere to Flanders about Eastertide, but this year none had arrived so they were unable to replenish their stocks. Customs accounts confirm that there was a sharp drop in wax imports not just in London but throughout the country in 1308–9. London imports averaged 1,075 cwt a year between 1303 and 1308, amounted to 451 cwt (including, exceptionally, 112 cwt belonging to a Genoese and a southern Frenchman) between Michaelmas 1308 and 31 March 1309, but only 106 cwt between the latter date and 28 August 1309. In the first decade of the fourteenth century and for some time afterwards London was the chief port of entry for wax, but from the mid-1320s its imports fell catastrophically. Boston became the centre of the trade, though it did not compensate for London's decline, so total imports of wax were greatly reduced. At the same time the general range of alien imports into London fell by over two thirds, so if the Hanse's share of the remaining trade was no higher than it had been previously then its role in the economic life of the capital must have been much curtailed.[46] Exports were at all times negligible except for wool, but discussion of this activity will be reserved until later.

At the end of the thirteenth century the provincial towns which figured most prominently in Hanse trade were Boston, Lynn, Hull and Ravenser, though other east-coast ports also enjoyed their patronage. The oldest and strongest connections were with the first two places, though in both cases the earliest evidence, dating back to the twelfth century, consists of unspecific references to 'Easterlings' (*Estrenses*). Wool was exported by Germans from Hull at least as early as the 1270s, and in 1294 a general arrest of alien shipping trapped many more Hanse vessels in Yorkshire ports than anywhere else in England. Hull and Ravenser were major competitors to Boston and Lynn for the Hanse trade at the turn of the thirteenth and fourteenth centuries, but by the 1320s the threat had receded

---

[45] *Hanseakten*, no. 40.   [46] Lloyd, *Alien Merchants*, appendix A1.9, p. 219.

and the Ravenser connection was eliminated entirely. In 1303 the Hanse instituted a boycott of the port of Lynn which, although not totally effective, lasted until 1310, when the town authorities agreed to the restoration of the merchants' former privileges. Thereafter it again became a centre of Hanse activity. The overall make-up of Hanseatic trade varied from one to another of the provincial ports, but in all of them the range of both exports and imports was wider than in London. The variety of imports was also much greater at the end of the thirteenth century than it had been some fifty years before, though due allowance must be made for the fact that in the interim Hansards were replacing some other groups in important branches of trade. Initially, German imports from northern Europe had consisted largely of furs, hawks and wax; this trade was retained though overwhelmed in significance by more mundane products. Contrary to London practice, furs and wax destined for provincial markets were not necessarily stapled in the Low Countries; in fact most of the furs came directly from northern Europe. In the case of wax the position varied; at Boston between February and Michaelmas 1303, 184 cwt out of 313 cwt came directly from the north, though at other times the proportions were reversed; at Lynn in the 1320s some undoubtedly came from the north, though the immediate origin of most cannot be determined. Copper coming to the provincial ports in the early fourteenth century, as in the case of London, came chiefly from a Low Countries staple.

Two factors in particular were responsible for the transformation of Hanseatic trade with England in the second half of the thirteenth century; these were the intrusion of Hanse merchants into the economy of Norway and the so-called *Umlandfahrt*, the direct sea voyage from western Europe to the Baltic. The principal products of Norway were fish and train oil. Stockfish was caught in the far north, cured in adjacent villages and exported through a staple at Bergen. Smaller, though significant, quantities of winter herring were caught off the south-west coast of Norway and found a market in England at a time of year when stocks of locally caught herring were becoming exhausted. By the end of the thirteenth century Hanse merchants were handling a large part of this trade, but there is no reason to suppose that they originated it. They were probably displacing both Norwegian and English merchants.[47] Lübeck

[47] *Ibid.*, pp. 153–4.

attempted to monopolise the traffic, and in 1284 the *Englandfahrer* of Stralsund complained of the oppression which they suffered at the hands of merchants from the former city.[48] The early-fourteenth-century customs accounts indicate that Lübeck still dominated the trade, though it did not have a total monopoly, since ships and merchants of Stralsund, Rostock and Hamburg, as well as those of the northern Low Countries can be identified in it. In the first decade the English staples for stock fish were Boston and Ravenser, and at the latter, though not at the former, Norwegians shared the trade with Germans. By the 1320s both Hanse and Norwegian imports to Ravenser had dried up and Boston became the sole staple for stockfish. Herrings were brought chiefly to Hull and Lynn, and in the 1320s particularly to the latter port. Unfortunately, in the 1320s the nationalities of the shippers were not recorded, but it looks as if this trade was less dominated by Germans than the stockfish trade. The fish traders also imported from Norway, although much less in value, timber, goat and deer skins, butter, wool and coarse woollen cloth.

The earliest specific reference to the *Umlandfahrt* occurs in a Kampen source of 1251. The northern Dutch towns of the IJsselmeer and the rivers which debouched into it were pioneers of the voyage and continued to participate in the fourteenth century.[49] By then they had been joined in force by the so-called Wendish towns of the Hanse, i.e. those of Hamburg and the western Baltic. Lübeck shared in the traffic, though not dominating it to the extent that it did Anglo-Norwegian trade. Ships from east of the river Oder appear very infrequently in English sources before the middle of the fourteenth century, though the Lynn and Hull customs accounts record visits by several Gotland ships, and those of Hull one ship from Reval in Estonia in 1304 and one each from Elbing and Kolberg in Prussia in the 1320s. The earliest batch of Hull accounts, but no others, are sufficiently informative to provide some sort of quantitative assessment of the participation of various towns. Table 1 shows Hanse ships (including a few exporting wool only) which can be positively identified in Yorkshire ports between 1304 and 1309, though it is very far from being a complete count of those which came there. Before the inception of the *Umlandfahrt*, goods

---

[48] *HR*, I (i), no. 28.
[49] F. Petri, 'Die Stellung der Südersee- und IJsselstädte im Flandrisch-Hansischen Raum', *HG*, 79 (1961), 34–57.

Table 1. *Hanse ships in Yorkshire ports, 1304–9*

| | Hull | | | Ravenser | | | Scarborough | |
	In and out	In only	Out only	In and out	In only	Out only	In only	Totals
Stralsund	10	10	7	0	4	1	2	32[a]
Hamburg	8	4	2	0	8	1	2	25
Lübeck	1	2	0	1	10	0	0	14
Rostock	0	2	1	0	2	0	0	5
Greifswald	0	1	1	0	1	0	0	3
Wismar	0	1	0	0	1	0	0	2
Visby	0	0	0	0	2	0	0	2
Reval	1	0	0	0	0	0	0	1
Totals	20	20	11	1	28	2	4	84

[a] Two ships entered at one port and left at another.

coming from the Baltic were unloaded at Lübeck and carried across the base of Jutland for reshipment at Hamburg. The new route by reducing transport costs encouraged an expansion in those trades in which this was a significant factor, such as timber. The Baltic timber trade was much more varied than that of Norway, supplying not merely hewn and sawn timber, but many artefacts made of wood, such as bowstaves, spade shafts, barrel staves, gates, troughs, tables and chairs, as well as resins and ashes. Another bulky cargo was corn, although England was not a regular importer and it is a moot point whether any came from the Baltic before the 1320s. The German grain imports at Hull in the first decade of the fourteenth century were all carried in Hamburg and Dutch vessels, which allows the possibility that they had originated in north-west, rather than eastern Germany.

The range of goods leaving provincial ports for the north was much narrower than that of imports, though in contrast to London the Hanse merchants did at least have a stake in the non-wool export trade. The only things which really interested them were salt and woollen cloth. Salt, exported from Hull, Boston and Lynn, was handy cargo for ships which might otherwise have to return home with worthless ballast, and was readily saleable at the Skania herring fishery. This explains the prevalence of Stralsund ships, with the salt customed in the name of the masters. Cloth, again found at all three ports, occupied less space but was considerably more valuable, though falling far short of that taken a century later. This meant that trade between England and Germany was very much out of balance and the Hanse importers had capital to repatriate. Since English bullion laws barred them from exporting cash or specie, the feat had to be accomplished indirectly. The key to the situation may have lain in the provision of finance for England's exports to the Low Countries, particularly Flanders, a substantial proportion of which was handled by Hanse merchants. It must be emphasised that in the early fourteenth century these were not the same merchants who traded between England and the Baltic or Norway, for to all intents and purposes the two groups did not overlap. Only infrequently can 'northerners' be found in Anglo-Flemish trade, even in the case of those like the Thousandpounds at Boston who seem to have had a strong base in England. The interest of the Flanders merchants in direct Anglo-German trade is even less conspicuous. Between 1304 and 1309 none of the regular German wool merchants of Hull traded directly with the north, with the exception of Martin de Raceburgh who exported two small cargoes of salt in 1306. This omission is to be explained by a lack of interest in northern trade rather than a disdain for any commodity but wool. Besides wool, some of the Flanders men exported lead and grain; the latter in particular was not a regular trade, but consisted of occasional, though large, speculations in response to temporary shortages in Flanders, which attracted many other wool merchants besides the Germans. Some of this group regularly imported wax and copper, less frequently furs and infrequently items in which the Hanse had no deep-rooted stake, such as figs, raisins, almonds, rice, onions, in fact anything that might come to hand in the continental marts. Finally it may be mentioned that Hanse merchants owned proportionately more of the woollen cloth imported at the east-coast ports than they did at London, though even here they were not major figures.

Little or no trace survives of business connections between the two groups of merchants distinguished above; such evidence as exists only establishes relationships between individuals or partnerships within one group or the other. Nevertheless, it seems possible that many of those who accumulated surpluses from northern imports lent them to Flanders merchants in return for letters of exchange. If they wished to repatriate money in one transaction rather than several then it may have been advisable to turn to fellow Hansards rather than Italian bankers. The former could have drawn directly upon north-German towns, whereas the financial business of the latter was directed to the Low Countries. Even so, surpluses from the northern trade added to the proceeds of their own imports from the Low Countries would have been insufficient to pay for all the wool bought by Hanse merchants at the pinnacle of their involvement in this trade in the early fourteenth century. This means that they must have imported bullion or, alternatively, borrowed from Italians and repaid in Flanders after selling the wool. A partial, but very infrequent, alternative was to lend money to the English crown on the continent in return for allowances or assignments in England, thereby reducing the sums which had to be raised on this side of the channel.[50] The suggestion of extensive use of credit in English business in this period is supported by evidence from other quarters. A century or so later the Hanse is commonly supposed to have set its face firmly against credit operations, though this traditional picture has recently been queried.[51]

It is impossible now to determine just when Germans began to export English wool. There appears to be no evidence that they did so before 1270, yet in 1271, when wool could be exported only by licence, merchants of towns which were in the process of uniting as the Hanse received licences for over 2,300 sacks.[52] Is it simply that earlier evidence has not survived or were the licensees newcomers to the trade, taking advantage of the current enforced absence of the Flemings who had previously dominated it? Another question which needs to be asked is whether an initial speculation in wool more usually came from a business firmly established in England or one rooted in Flanders. In the former category one must surely put John Brilond, citizen of Lübeck and London, who had been importing wax and furs for two decades before he appears as a wool licensee. John also had connections with York, and in 1267 advanced the royal farm on behalf of its citizens. Brilonds still exported wool in the early 1290s and John, or another of the same name, was cited in the parliament of 1290 for allegedly destroying the poor folk of Norfolk by prosecuting them in the King's Bench on behalf of Lübeck merchants.[53] Another prominent wool licensee was Gerard Merbode, citizen of London and alderman of the Gildhall in 1282; he was the

[50] Peters, *Hansekaufleute*, *passim*.

[51] Dollinger, *German Hansa*, pp. 203–6. S. Jenks, 'War die Hanse kreditfeindlich?', *Vierteljahrschrift für Sozial- und Wirtschaftsgeschichte*, 69 (1982), 305–38. S. Jenks, 'Das Schreiberbuch des John Thorp und der hansische Handel in London, 1457–9', *HG*, 101 (1983), 67–113.　　[52] Lloyd, *Wool Trade*, pp. 48–9.

[53] *CLR*, 1251–60, p. 37; 1260–7, pp. 190, 277; 1267–72, p. 99. *Rot. Parl.*, 1, pp. 46, 52.

son of Merbode of Dortmund, who died in London about 1265. Merbodes also exported wool until the 1290s. On the other hand, many of the Lübeckers who followed the Brilonds in the wool trade may have had a primary economic interest in Flanders. Their absence from the Anglo-northern trade routes suggests that their Anglo-Flemish trade should be seen as an extension of a Lübeck–Flanders trade. Nevertheless, for some of them the wool trade became very big business indeed, which can have been valued no less than that starting and finishing in Lübeck. In the case of the Clipping family the wool trade may even have been responsible for their removal or return from Lübeck to Dortmund. In the 1270s the Clippings of Lübeck were among the leading wool licensees, though even then described as kinsmen of the Merbodes. In the fourteenth century the Clippings, now even more prominent, seem to have regarded Dortmund as their home town. This is not to say that Lübeck interest in the wool trade was in any way diminished. The Revel and Hacthorpe (alias Clericus) families, and probably that of Raceburg, all among the very top rank of wool exporters, hailed from Lübeck, as did many others who were not so important. Lübeck was the only northern town which had anything but the most casual stake in the wool trade and with that exception most Hanse wool merchants came from a small area of West Germany bounded by Cologne and the river Rhine on the south and west, and Münster and the upper reaches of the river Ems on the north and east. At the geographical centre of the latter region lay Dortmund, whose citizens became more and more dominant among Hanse wool exporters, though the neighbouring towns continued to enjoy a share. The fact that Lübeck and Dortmund were so obviously distinct and separate centres of this trade must not be allowed to obscure personal and business connections between the two, which embraced other families besides the Clippings, and extended back to the foundation of Lübeck.

While the Hanse stake in the wool trade must have received a boost from the Anglo-Flemish dispute of the 1270s, it benefited even more from the Anglo-French war of 1294–7 and its aftermath. As well as further diminishing direct Flemish participation in the trade the conflict seriously weakened the big Italian companies who had dominated it in recent years. The surviving customs accounts of the early fourteenth century make it clear that, for a short period at least, the Germans were by far the most important group of alien exporters and this period saw the high-watermark of their involvement in the wool trade. From 1303 all alien exporters were required to pay a duty which was 50 per cent higher than that levied on denizens. It is impossible to determine how far the differential was directly responsible for the marked increase in the denizen share of the trade which followed. However, the trade as a whole was experiencing a massive boom, so that the total alien export, from which a German total cannot be isolated, did not begin to decline for several years. The abolition of the new custom in 1311 might have reversed the decline in the alien share if other factors had not soon intervened. These were political, and they may have caused greater discomfort to Hanse exporters than a higher tax bill. The catalyst was the deterioration in Anglo-Flemish relations after the accession of Edward II. Germans, the Englishmen's major competitors in Flanders, could trade in that country with impunity, while the latter did so only at considerable risk. The Englishmen therefore decided that if they could not venture wool directly to Flanders then no one should be allowed to do so. In 1313 they proclaimed a staple at St Omer in Artois, to which all exported wool had to be taken. This was a neutral town, but easily accessible to Flemish buyers so that Englishmen could trade there without prejudice and in fact might be able to direct affairs to their own advantage. In later years a compulsory staple at Calais was to provide Englishmen with a total monopoly of wool exports, except for those which went to Italy. The first staple did not yield such a result, since many exporters defied the law and continued to trade elsewhere. In 1320 a commission of enquiry singled out German merchants as having been particularly serious offenders. Even so the compulsory overseas staples and the abortive home staples of 1326 and 1333 must have inconvenienced aliens and therefore may have been a factor which discouraged many from continuing in the wool trade.

It is impossible to quantify the Hanse wool trade but a careful study of the surviving customs accounts establishes that it was considerably smaller in the 1320s and 1330s than it had been in the first decade of the century. However, it was by no means finished; nor is there any indication of any significant changes in the way it was organised; some leading families drop out of the picture, but some remain and other prominent figures appear. At the beginning of the Hundred Years War the German wool trade, like that of all private merchants, was brought to a standstill, but was permitted again from the spring of 1338 once it became apparent that the crown could not operate a total monopoly. The trade was closely regulated, but a series of loans to the king's agents in Antwerp and Flanders ensured that those who contributed obtained licences to export throughout the periodic bans on private trade. Repayment of the loans took the form of allowances of duty and grants of wool coming to the king from various levies imposed on his subjects. The Hanse men did not receive all that they were promised from the latter source and the greater part of their stocks continued to come from private purchases. Eventually the sums owing to them became so large that repayments had to be supplemented by a general assignment on the customs and other sources of royal revenue. Although the loans were undoubtedly initiated as a means of obtaining export licences, the later amounts suggest that they had become a commercial proposition in their own right. This is the only period in Anglo-Hanseatic history that the merchants entered into such a relationship with the crown. The series of loans continued until 1350, and a significant change in the method of organisation after the mid-1340s was probably more apparent than real. The earlier loans were put together by a number of separate syndicates, each of which, though not a corporate entity like the Italian societies, was composed of individuals who traded independently but had business connections with one another. The later loans were advanced in the name of Tidemann Limberg, a comparative newcomer from Dortmund, but it is unlikely that he was merely using his own capital. It is safe to assume that he was still drawing upon the collective resources of the Hanse merchants.[54]

Although it is impossible to determine whether the absolute level of Hanse wool exports in the late 1330s and early 1340s was greater than it had been a decade or so previously, there can be little doubt that as a proportion of non-royal trade it was much larger. Thereafter it becomes very difficult to make judgements on such matters. The inventories of Hanse goods arrested in August 1351 contain remarkably little wool, at a time of year when one might expect to find large stocks in hand, but it would be dangerous to read too much into this.[55] From the autumn of 1352 to the summer of 1357 aliens enjoyed a monopoly of wool exports, but the absence of customs particulars makes it impossible to allocate the trade between different nationalities, while other references to German involvement

---

[54] For full details of all loans see Peters, *Hansekaufleute*.
[55] PRO, E101/127/7; 128/8. PRO, E372/192, m. 47; 197, m. 38. *HR*, I (i), nos. 153–7.

are sparse and fortuitous. It may be noted, however, that when home staples were being set up in 1354, four Germans and seven Italians were consulted by the king's council.[56] The compulsory staple at Calais in the 1360s may have jeopardised Hanse participation, though its members were not totally eliminated. John de Hatfield, who figures in the 1351 inventories and appears as a wool exporter in 1358, traded at Calais as late as 1367.[57] Other evidence indicates that Hatfield was thoroughly anglicised. The freedom for aliens to go to places other than Calais in the early 1370s led to an increase in their actual and proportionate exports, but again the Hanse share cannot be isolated. The protest made by the Hanse diet in 1375 against the additional taxes which were charged on wool which by-passed Calais indicates that its members had not yet surrendered all interest in the trade. However, surviving customs particulars from the early part of Richard II's reign indicate that by that time Hanse participation was virtually at an end. To what extent this may have been consequent upon involvement in another branch of England's export trade will be considered later.

To conclude this chapter we may examine the question of whether, or to what extent, Englishmen plied a trade with the Baltic before the middle of the fourteenth century. In the light of repeated claims that English vessels were in the Baltic during the thirteenth century it may seem surprising that the question must be put in such a speculative form. Unfortunately, historians all too often borrow from one another without reconsidering the evidence. Some Londoners who appear to have been trading at Copenhagen in or before 1251 probably did not go there in their own ships. The earliest reference to English ships making the voyage seems to be a document tentatively dated to about 1294.[58] The latter is a request by the town of Zwolle to Lübeck to prevent English ships from entering the Baltic and is generally taken as proof that the latter were in fact making such voyages. However, the letter makes a distinction between Frisians and Flemings, who had visited the Baltic and whom Lübeck had attempted to stop, and English ships whom Zwolle wished to stop. At best this appears to impute a degree of novelty to an accomplished feat, but may indicate nothing more than a fear that Englishmen might try the adventure. Be that as it may, the first half of the fourteenth century provides no further examples of English vessels, or even of English merchants in the Baltic. On the other

---

[56] *CCR*, 1349–54, p. 605. [57] *CCR*, 1354–9, p. 482; 1364–8, p. 363.
[58] *HUB*, I, nos. 405–6, 1154.

hand, since English merchants are known to have freighted goods in Hanse ships from Norway and Denmark it is credible that they also traded with the Baltic by the same means. In 1316 a Ravenser man loaded rye and barley in a Lübeck ship at Ålborg in Denmark, while in 1322 Lynn merchants took goods to Bergen in another Lübeck ship and brought stockfish back in the same.[59] By 1364 English merchants and ships were venturing as far as Prussia, but it is still necessary to make a *caveat*. At this period the export trade was very strictly regulated, but of hundreds of enrolments of licences to Englishmen to export goods or money a mere handful relate to trade with the Baltic.[60] The earliest evidence of Englishmen taking up residence in the Baltic is a licence granted in 1373 to John Swerd, bowyer, of York, to send four yeomen and two grooms of his craft to stay in Prussia for four years to fashion bows and send them home. Three years before, Swerd had been licensed to ship wine to Prussia and import wheat and rye in return.[61] Whether or not Swerd actually went through with his plans, within a few years there undoubtedly were English settlers in Danzig and they introduced a whole new dimension into Anglo-Hanseatic relations.

[59] PRO, SC1/34/62; 36/12.   [60] *CPR*, 1361–4, pp. 497, 511, 517; 1364–7, p. 35.
[61] *CPR*, 1370–4, pp. 60, 264.

CHAPTER 2

The English challenge, 1361–1399

The legal foundation of the privileges enjoyed by the German Hanse in England in the later middle ages was completed in 1317. Negotiations after that were concerned with the interpretation of existing charters in the light of changing political and commercial circumstances. Constant vigilance was needed by the merchants to protect earlier gains. The franchises were the fruit of direct bargaining between the crown and the resident Hanse community, with considerable sums of money changing hands at critical times. The community was autonomous and in these matters may have acted completely independently of the home towns of its members, though there is no sure proof of that. It is more certain that the crown did not negotiate directly with the towns. Occasionally the king wrote to individual towns demanding redress for his subjects alleged to have been injured by their citizens. The formulae used do not differ from those found in letters addressed to Flemish towns about similar matters. They give no indication that the English government was at this time aware of the German towns being part of any association. Until a relatively late date the Hanse merchants in England continued to negotiate without external assistance or interference, possibly because they preferred it that way. As late as the 1360s they were able unaided to vindicate their claim to immunity from the export duty upon English cloth introduced in 1347. A decade later the merchants invoked the assistance of the Hanse diet in another dispute about taxation. Significantly, perhaps, this followed hard upon the heels of the treaty of Stralsund, 1370, which successfully concluded a contest with Denmark, and which has been hailed by some Hanseatic historians as one of the most important events in the transition of the Hanse.[1] After the diet's first

---

[1] D. J. Bjork, 'The Peace of Stralsund, 1370', *Speculum*, 7 (1932), 447–76.

intervention there was no turning back. The London Gildhall was no longer regarded as fully competent to treat with the crown. The English now appreciated that ultimate authority resided in the diet, though it soon became clear that in the case of the Prussian towns parallel or separate diplomacy might be necessary, since in this quarter the Grand Master of the Teutonic Order had the final word.[2]

The first direct contact between the English government and the diet was occasioned by the levy of tunnage and poundage which began in October 1371 and continued with only a short break until Christmas 1375. Notwithstanding the fact that the dispute about cloth duties had been settled in favour of the Hanse, its members were required to pay tunnage and poundage when it was reintroduced. The London *Kontor*[3] complained to the diet which met at Lübeck in May 1373 and again just over a year later. In June 1375, after written representation had been disregarded, the diet resolved that two ambassadors, whom it had sent to Flanders, should go on to England to put its case more forcefully. They arrived in London in November and presented their demands to the king's council, which parried with its own list of grievances voiced by English merchants. The ambassadors asserted that they had no power to deal with counter-complaints and that any Englishmen seeking redress should attend the next session of the diet. This prevented meaningful negotiations, though the meetings ended

---

[2] The first Hanse embassy to England (1375) formally represented the 'High Master of Prussia, the common cities and all the merchants of the Hanse of Germany' ('Monsiour le haut mestre de Pruys, de par les communes citees et touz les marchants del hans d'Alemaigne'; 'De hoghen meester van Prussen, van den ghemeenen citeden ende allen den coopmannen van der anse van Alemaignen'): *HR*, I (iii), no. 317.

[3] The Hanse communities in England are frequently personified by the terms *Kontor* (plural *Kontore*) or Steelyard. These are often used anachronistically, simply for convenience. The former is a general term which can be applied to an organised Hanse community anywhere in Europe. The latter is the name of the London factory or headquarters, which is first found in the late fourteenth century, but does not become common until much later. Use of the word Gildhall tends to disappear, but makes a partial comeback in the late fifteenth century. Much has been written about the derivation of the word Steelyard and its physical relationship to the Gildhall. The factories at Boston and Lynn are sometimes referred to as Steelyards at the end of the fifteenth century. W. Kurzinna, 'Der Name Stahlhof', *HG*, 18 (1912), 429–61. M. Weinbaum, 'Stahlhof und Deutsche Gildhalle zu London', *HG* (1928), 45–65. In their outward letters the London merchants came to follow the common European practice of referring to themselves as 'the alderman and common merchant'. The earliest surviving example (20 June 1374) is in an extended form, 'By deme aldermanne unde deme ghemeynen copmanne van der Dussche hense van Almanien op der tiit to Londen wesende.' In the next surviving letter (10 April 1378) the redundant words 'van Almanien' were omitted. *HR*, I (ii), no. 99; (iii), no. 102.

amicably and the ambassadors were presented with relics of St Thomas of Canterbury, in whose honour there was a chapel near one of the city gates of Lübeck. The king also issued a general letter of protection in favour of Hanse merchants for twelve months.[4]

The council refused to free the Hansards from tunnage and poundage on the grounds that it had legitimately been granted by parliament, that it was a wartime tax levied solely for the protection of commerce and that it was paid by denizens as well as aliens. The logic of the last argument was, of course, flawed by the fact that the Hanse franchises already ensured that they paid a lower rate of cloth duty than denizens. Besides the matter of tunnage and poundage the ambassadors also submitted a number of other complaints about alleged abuses of customs procedure. Briefly, these related to certain imposts on exported wool in addition to custom and subsidy, disregard of accepted practice for valuing merchandise, illegal charges for certain types of cocket letters, the double levying of poundage on a ship at Boston, the levying of an incremental duty on certain cloths of assise (those more than 24 yards long but shorter than 32 yards) and attempts to charge duty on the cargoes of ships driven to take shelter in English harbours but not wishing to unload there. The first four points were summarily dismissed by the council, but the remaining two were referred to a great council or parliament. In the matter of the cloth lengths this yielded the ambiguous reply that customs officers were under orders to honour Hanse franchises. The other decision was that storm-driven ships should pay customs duties on the spot unless they were able to find security to pay in another English port or to take their goods entirely away from England. There is independent evidence that the crown did not in fact sanction attempts to exact payment from ships which had no intention of discharging in England.[5] As well as these charges against the king's ministers, two general charges were laid against his subjects: one alleging disregard of Chancery writs ordering recognition of Hanse franchises, the other that the city of London obstructed retail sales by Rhenish wine merchants. Finally, the ambassadors raised five cases in which Germans were alleged to have been denied justice in England. Three of these were simply wrangles about titles to property, but the others cited attacks upon ships which involved loss of life.[6]

The matters raised by the ambassadors suggest that, while the

---

[4] *HR*, I (ii), nos. 99–103; (iii), no. 68. *HUB*, 4, nos. 469, 520, 526. *CPR*, 1374–7, p. 194.
[5] *CCR*, 1369–74, p. 10.   [6] *HR*, I (iii), no. 317.

Hansards were aggrieved, their dissatisfaction fell short of anything that might have caused them to break off trade. They are, in fact, less significant in the development of relations between the two sides than the English counter-complaints.[7] During the reign of Edward III the main threat to Hanse liberties had been the crown itself. We hear comparatively little about hostility from English merchants and urban communities. However, ill-feeling undoubtedly existed and should the crown decide to mobilise it to counter Hanse resistance to taxation then the latter might find themselves in serious trouble. The conjunction of interests came in 1375, when the ambassadors' charges were met with a catalogue of grievances and demands submitted by English merchants. With the exception of a complaint by John Ward, one-time mayor of London, that in 1365 his apprentice had been forced to pay double duty on battery purchased in Dinant, all the English charges relate to northern trade and resulted from the war fought by the Hanse against Denmark and Norway (1368–70). The most serious allegation was that in 1367–8 the King of Norway expelled the German merchants from their staple at Bergen and allowed the English to take their place; after some four years the Germans returned, attacked the Englishmen and drove them away, causing losses estimated at more than 10,000 marks. The facts are that German merchants began to be harassed by the kings of Norway and Denmark in 1366 and evacuated Bergen hurriedly in the spring of 1368, after being warned that a fleet from the Zuider Zee towns of the Hanse was about to attack Norway. In their haste they left their property behind, which was confiscated by the King of Norway. To make matters worse they had to pay an exorbitant sum to the English and Flemish skippers who carried them to safety. The Germans began to return to Norway in the early 1370s during a series of truces, which were converted into a firm peace in 1376. The peace treaty formally confirmed the Hanse privileges, which gave them a stranglehold on Norway's overseas trade. By this time the English had in their turn been expelled, though this must have been after February 1372, when the Hanse merchants in Bergen reported to Lübeck that there were still many Englishmen in the town.[8] They also complained that the Englishmen had been allowed to charter a great cog at Wismar to take goods to Bergen. As a result, or possibly before then, the Hanse seems to have forbidden its members to carry Englishmen's goods, since this was

---

[7] *Ibid.*, nos. 318–19. [8] *HUB*, 4, nos. 257, 412.

one of the complaints made in 1375. Another grievance was that English merchants had no claim to salvaged goods in Eastland, these still being regarded as a perquisite of the lord of the soil on which they were wrecked. It was only in the Peace of Stralsund (May 1370) that the Hanse managed to get recognition of the right of salvage for its own members. The English were resentful that this had not yet been extended to them, since a more civilised custom had long been allowed to all merchants in their country. A further general claim was that, as German merchants were free to trade throughout England, Englishmen should be allowed to trade in all Hanse towns and their environs. Besides Norway, English enterprise had recently suffered a severe check in Skania, the southern province of Sweden, hotly disputed between the king of that country and the King of Denmark. The autumn fairs of Skania not only supplied vast amounts of herrings, but also provided an important market for west-European cloth, which was redistributed over a wide area of eastern Europe. Their attraction for English merchants is obvious. Until 1368 a fairly liberal regime had prevailed in the fairs, but in that year the Hanse gained control of the province and the King of Sweden conferred upon it extensive privileges, which were later confirmed in the Peace of Stralsund. In February 1370 a Hanse diet ruled that English, Welsh and Scottish merchants should no longer be allowed to purchase fresh herrings and salt them themselves. They were permitted to buy salted herrings, though in the first season of the new regime a number of those who did so complained that consignments paid for were not delivered. This was in the autumn of 1370, and when the English parliament met in February 1371 the king was asked to intercede on behalf of his subjects. It was said that the chief purpose of the Hanse was to prevent the English from selling cloth in Skania. The latter did not usually take cash there, but relied upon the proceeds of their sales to finance purchase of herrings. Edward III duly complained to Rostock, Lübeck and perhaps other towns, but the replies gave little hope of satisfaction.[9]

The programme of the English merchants was ill-defined in 1375, but this was characteristic of all their demands in the late fourteenth century and it did not follow that the Hanse could afford simply to ignore it. For the moment, however, the demand for reciprocity was perhaps less of a threat to the Hanse than anti-alien sentiment in

---

[9] *Ibid.*, nos. 378, 387, 393, 421. *Rot. Parl.*, 2, p. 306.

England. Of course, this was not new and was not directed solely against the Hanse, but it seems to have intensified in the later years of Edward III's reign, during which there was a tremendous growth in alien trade. Although increasingly concentrated at London, alien trade, consisting overwhelmingly of imports, was not necessarily welcomed by the citizens. The total population of England was declining, so that scope for expansion of imports must have been limited and alien growth may have been at the expense of denizen trade. It is significant, perhaps, that in 1354 John Malewayn refused to accept guardianship of a London orphan on conditions which required him to trade with the boy's inheritance, since he claimed that English merchants were not making the same profit as in former times. More was involved than merely the import of goods, for the citizens of enfranchised towns, particularly London, were concerned about how aliens sold them after they had been cleared by the customs officers. Londoners were reluctant to accept that aliens should enjoy freedom of trade, even after their right had been confirmed by parliament. In 1353 and 1356 they pleaded that the city should be absolved from observing the offensive statutes of 1335 and 1351.[10]

The late 1360s saw the beginning of a new campaign against alien participation in internal trade. In May 1368 London petitioned parliament about the loss of its franchises which had debarred non-freemen from retail business. It requested that once more all retailing should be confined to freemen, and that aliens should not sell to other aliens for resale (*pur revendre*). The response was ambiguous. As an act of special grace it was conceded that retail sales of victuals should be limited to freemen, but only in London and only until the next parliament; moreover, this was not to prejudice any aliens who had their own charter or franchises. The concession was evidently accompanied by a writ ordering proclamation of the fact that aliens might sell by retail any non-victuals, but in July 1368 the London sheriffs refused to publish the proclamation.[11] The act was not renewed in the parliament of 1369, so the legal ban on alien victuallers lapsed. In February 1371 the commons requested the restoration of the ancient privileges of towns, on the grounds that this would prevent the decay of trade and the navy. The crown replied that the request was too general, but that

---

[10] *Letter Book* G, pp. 15, 39, 52.   [11] *Rot. Parl.*, 2, p. 296. *Letter Book* G, p. 231.

if they supplied details of their grievances a remedy would be provided. Similar petitions were submitted in the parliaments of 1372 and 1373 and the same evasive answer given.[12] Absence of crown support did not, of course, prevent Englishmen from continuing to harass aliens, and one of the Hanse complaints in 1375 was that its wine merchants were prevented from retailing wine in London.[13] The Good Parliament (April to July 1376) had much to say about financial and commercial malpractices on the part of some supporters of the crown, but there is no evidence that it raised the question of alien trade.[14] Nevertheless, in the following winter the court party, now beginning to re-establish its power, made a concession to anti-alien interests. On 4 December, in response to a petition from the city, the London sheriffs were ordered to proclaim that foreigners should not engage in retail trade nor trade between themselves for resale until the matter had been discussed by the next parliament. Saving clauses were inserted that lords could buy large amounts for their own use and that all the liberties of the German Hanse should be respected.[15] When the last parliament of Edward III assembled in January this letter patent was copied on to the parliament roll, presumably as a record of the fact that the royal proclamation had been confirmed in parliament.[16]

The death of Edward III in June 1377 threw the liberties of the Hanse and all other aliens into the melting pot. It was advisable, to say the least, that all who wished to continue to enjoy established liberties should have them confirmed by the new king as soon as possible. The meeting of parliament (October–November 1377) provided an occasion for interested parties to lobby to have their own franchises confirmed and those of their opponents cancelled. The commons in parliament petitioned for the confirmation of the franchises of all English cities and boroughs, to which the crown sensibly replied that their charters would first have to be examined in the Chancery. A similar request by the city of London produced the answer that the king's council would need to consider what franchises were claimed. More satisfying answers were given to a commons plea that aliens should not be allowed to keep hostels and the renewed London cry that they should not trade between themselves. These were conceded, although in each case a rider was added saving the rights of the king's lieges of Gascony. A further

---

[12] *Rot. Parl.*, 2, pp. 306, 314, 318.   [13] See also *CPMR*, 1, p. 151.
[14] G. Holmes, *The Good Parliament* (Oxford, 1975), *passim*.
[15] *Letter Book* H, p. 53. *CPR*, 1374–7, p. 389.   [16] *Rot. Parl.*, 2, p. 367.

petition, claiming to come from the community of English merchants, called upon the crown not to confirm the Hanse privileges as the latter were now asking. However, on 6 November 1377 these privileges were confirmed in the form of the *Carta Mercatoria* of 1303 and Edward III's 1327 ratification of his father's charter of 1317.[17] Within a short time they had been suspended and, although the exact date cannot be determined, it was certainly before 10 April 1378, when London put into effect sweeping anti-alien measures and the *Kontor* wrote to Lübeck describing these and reporting that the king's council had suspended its charter. The council seems to have acted because of a renewed complaint by English merchants about obstacles to their trade in Norway and Skania. It was claimed that the whole country was damaged by a Hanse monopoly, which raised the prices of imports from those places.[18]

The suspension had a twofold effect upon the *Kontor*. On the one hand, it could not plead immunity from the new anti-alien measures in London, which went beyond those sanctioned by parliament the previous autumn. Each of the principal city mysteries was ordered to appoint searchers to ensure that all strangers should board with freemen, that they should not engage in retail trade nor trade among themselves, and that they must dispose of imports within forty days of arrival. On the other hand, the royal customs collectors, either on their own initiative or upon instructions from the Exchequer, began to demand both the 1303 and the 1347 duties on exported cloth. Lübeck referred the complaint of the London *Kontor* to the Prussian towns and to the diet then about to assemble at Stralsund. In consequence, both the diet and the Grand Master of the Teutonic Order wrote to Richard II and to the city of London threatening a trade boycott unless the franchises were restored and the merchants compensated. The Londoners artlessly replied that the matter lay with king and parliament, while the king's council also answered that nothing could be resolved until parliament met. In fact, the situation had relaxed slightly even before the protest of the diet had been dispatched. On 20 May the Chancery had instructed customs officials that for the present they were not to collect the 1347 cloth duty, but were to take security for it to be paid should the council decide against the merchants.[19]

---

[17] *Rot. Parl.*, pp. 16–17, 27–8. *CPR*, 1377–81, p. 57.
[18] *Letter Book* H, pp. 90–1, 101. *HR*, I (iii), nos. 102–3. *HUB*, 4, no. 600.
[19] *CCR*, 1377–8, p. 61. *HR*, I (ii), nos. 159–64. *Letter Book* H, p. 101.

The parliament which sat at Gloucester in October and November
1378 has generally been regarded by historians as one which looked
favourably upon aliens. The usual explanation is that the country at
large was reacting against sacrifices demanded of it in the interests
of merchants trading overseas and of towns such as London. This
interpretation is hardly borne out by the evidence. A short petition
from the commons asking for free trade for aliens met with a very
long, but guarded, response which was incorporated in a statute.[20]
The king recognised the utility of alien merchants to the realm,
welcomed their activity, extended protection to them during a stay
of unlimited duration and promised immediate redress of injuries.
However, on the matters in dispute they were given only partial
satisfaction. It was agreed that victuals and goods classed as small
wares might be sold by retail as well as in gross, both within and
without enfranchised boroughs. But in boroughs wine and other
great wares might be sold only in gross, and then only to freemen of
the place and not to others. This statutory definition of the rights of
alien merchants left them considerably worse off than they had been
in the reign of Edward III. Little had been gained except a slight
curb upon the excessive zeal which London had used against aliens
during the course of the year. The notion of English disunity in this
parliament is discounted by the response to the Hanse petition
asking for the restoration of their privileges.[21] They were informed
that they would be allowed to trade in England provided that they
obtained permission for English merchants to trade freely in their
country; moreover, they were not to act against English interests in
other places, such as Denmark and Norway. Unless by the following
Michaelmas they produced letters to this effect sealed both by the
Hanse towns and territorial princes, such as the Grand Master of the
Teutonic Order, their own privileges in England would be abolished.
This was the first expression by the crown in parliament of the
principle that henceforth Hanse privileges ought to depend on the
enjoyment of similar rights by English merchants in northern and
eastern Europe.

The English were actually more united in their resolve than the
Hansards at this time, for, while the Prussians favoured a hard line
and demanded the restoration of the privileges without conceding
anything in return, the rest of the Hanse was more conciliatory. The

---

[20] *Rot. Parl.*, 3, pp. 47–8. *Stats.*, 2, pp. 7–8.   [21] *Rot. Parl.*, 3, p. 52.

other towns worked together to restrain the Prussians from taking precipitate action against English interests, and Lübeck attempted to set up a conference to discuss the crisis in the autumn and winter of 1378–9, but the Prussians refused to attend. The Prussian towns persuaded the Grand Master of the Order not to take unilateral action, but during the course of their own diet at Marienburg in April 1379 they received a report of English attacks upon their ships in Flanders. They decided, therefore, that at the next meeting of the Hanse diet they would press for a complete break in relations with England until the latter gave way.[22] When this diet met at Lübeck on 24 June 1379 it rejected the demand for an immediate break, but prepared a plan which was to be put into effect if diplomatic efforts did not bring about a settlement by Shrovetide 1380. This would have brought trade between the two communities almost completely to a halt.[23] Michaelmas 1379 came and went without the English getting the assurances they had demanded as a condition of continuing the privileges of the *Kontor*. However, on 9 October the Chancellor wrote to certain towns saying that England desired amicable relations and urged them to work to this end. As a result of this and a further appeal from the London *Kontor* the Hanse diet authorised two ambassadors visiting Flanders to go on to England. They arrived in London on 21 November 1379 and four days later had the first of a series of discussions with members of the king's council and officials of the city of London. The talks with Londoners were acrimonious, since they attempted to raise matters which lay outside the ambassadors' competence, and thereafter negotiations continued with only the councillors.[24]

It was virtually impossible for the talks to bear fruit since the ambassadors were empowered only to deliver replies to four English demands which had been considered by the diet in June.[25] The first was that English merchants should be free to trade in Reval, Pernow and Livonia and all other regions within the jurisdiction of the Hanse towns or of 'any who were generally of their society'. In all these places Englishmen ought to enjoy whatever rights the Hansards exercised in England. The Hanse answered that it could not give such an undertaking, since its members had no jurisdiction in the greater part of this area, which was subject to different temporal and ecclesiastical rulers. Moreover, it was pointed out, Englishmen had

---

[22] *HR*, I (ii), no. 174; (iii), nos. 113, 116, 118, 122. *HUB*, 4, no. 651.
[23] *HR*, I (ii), no. 190. [24] *Ibid.*, nos. 210–11. [25] *Ibid.*, nos. 212–13.

never before traded in most of these places. The second demand was
that Englishmen should have the right to buy, salt and barrel
herrings in Skania, taking them thence wherever they wished
without discriminatory taxation. This was rejected on the grounds
that the sovereignty of Skania was shared with Denmark. Thirdly,
it was requested that English merchants and their property should
not be arrested in the lands of the Hanse, save for personal debts and
trespasses. This was countered by the claim that Hanse merchants
did not enjoy such immunity in England. In fact, while the
ambassadors cited arrests in London in 1378, the principle at stake was
one of the most valuable immunities won by the Hanse from Edward
II. The final demand was that all places which were members of the
Hanse should be certified to the English authorities. The answer,
that this was simply not possible, might have seemed reasonable to
those who gave it, but clearly would not satisfy the English
government, which was reluctant to allow aliens to enjoy privileges
merely on the strength of their own word that they were merchants
of the Hanse. After this exchange it was suggested to the ambassadors
that the Hanse charter should be restored with a codicil recognising
the rights of Englishmen to trade in Norway, Skania and areas
governed by the Hanse. This offer they rejected, as they did an
invitation to remain in England to await the deliberations of
parliament, which was due to meet in January 1380. By Christmas
they had returned to Bruges and the dispute was still unresolved,
although each side may have gained a better understanding of the
other's position.

When parliament assembled, the *Kontor* submitted two petitions;
one asked for a decision about the restoration of its charters; the
other complained about the reimposition of tunnage and poundage.[26] The latter also instanced five cases of alleged denial of justice
to German merchants, although only one was new, the remainder
having already been complained of by the ambassadors who came to
England in 1375. The English merchants presented a counter-
petition, requesting that the Hanse privileges should not be restored
unless their own demand for freedom of trade was conceded.[27] The
upshot was that the *Kontor* was asked to set its seal to a bill identical
to that which the ambassadors had refused to allow to be attached
to the charters.[28] Answer was given that not only did it lack the

---

[26] *HUB*, 4, nos. 671–2.   [27] *Ibid.*, no. 647.   [28] *Ibid.*, no. 673.

authority, but also that such a step was unnecessary since even without formal guarantees the English already enjoyed greater freedom of trade in Hanse towns than the ostensibly privileged Germans did in England. However, as a good-will gesture the *Kontor* offered to intercede on behalf of its rivals at the next meeting of the diet. In February 1380 the Prussian towns reported that they had persuaded the Grand Master not to take any action against Englishmen until Easter 1381.[29]

When the diet met in June 1380 it decided to give the Englishmen some form of reassurance, with the result that on 23 September 1380 the charter of Hanse liberties was conditionally restored to representatives of the *Kontor* in London. The diet did not concede the four points which had been communicated to it the year before, nor even the watered-down version which was subsequently put forward. All that the English obtained was a statement that they should trade as freely 'in partibus ipsorum mercatorum Alemannorum' as the Germans did in England. No specific privileges were described and all references to Norway, Skania and other places had been deleted. Whether this represented any sort of victory for English merchants is debatable. They appear to have gained nothing that they did not have before, while the guarantee was worded so vaguely that it could not provide authority for settling any dispute which might arise in future about English trade in the north. The return of their charter was hardly a triumph for the Hansards, since it merely restored the *status quo* and left many points still in contention. A few days later the Chancery ordered that the mainpernors for payment of double duty upon cloth exports be released, since the council had ruled in favour of the Hanse. The point seemed to have been even more firmly established in February 1381, when the king formally ratified Edward III's concession of 8 February 1361.[30] However, within a very short time customs officials, despite the merchants' protests, were disregarding this franchise and converting strait cloths and short pieces into notional cloths of assise, upon which they levied 1s instead of the *ad valorem* duty of 3d in the pound. Furthermore, in May 1382 a new parliamentary grant of tunnage and poundage began to be collected and the Hansards again submitted a claim to immunity, but in November the council decided against them and the tax was levied retrospectively.[31] Customs collectors also began to

---

[29] *HR*, I (iii), no. 125.   [30] *HR*, I (ii), nos. 224–5. *CPR*, 1377–81, p. 57.
[31] *CCR*, 1377–81, pp. 401, 407; 1381–5, pp. 174, 192. *HUB*, 4, no. 762.

harass Hanse merchants to pay a second duty on imported goods which, having failed to sell in England, were re-exported; such double collection of tax was forbidden by the *Carta Mercatoria*. About 1384, Christian Kelmar of Dortmund, who had been alderman of the London *Kontor* as recently as 1383, handed over 3s 1½d when he re-exported a pack of ermine skins.[32] His defence, that he had sworn that this submission should not prejudice the rights of his fellows, naturally cut no ice with them and he was expelled from the *Kontor*. In compensation, he was first granted citizenship by the authorities of London and then denizenship by the crown. He continued to be black-balled by the Hanse and lost many of his overseas contacts, so that ten years later he sued them in an English court for £1,000 damages. Continuing hostility from English communities made it dangerous for the Hanse to resist the crown too strenuously. Several towns tried to levy local tolls upon the merchants and in 1384 London revived the claim, first advanced in the reign of Edward I, that their immunity ought to apply only to goods imported from their homeland and not to other commodities, such as Bay salt and Gascon wine.[33] On this occasion the London claim was disallowed, but should the king decide to lend his support then the Hanse would be in trouble.

Local harassment was not confined to one side and in 1384 the Prussians decreed that English merchants must henceforth import their wares only through Elbing. Since Danzig was far more convenient to them, the English saw this as a deliberate attempt to throttle their trade and induced the king to make a formal protest to the Grand Master of the Teutonic Order. Nevertheless, it was neither taxation nor trading rights but allegations of piracy which acted as the catalyst of the next crisis in Anglo-Hanseatic relations. As early as January 1382 both the diet and the Grand Master, while thanking Richard II for the restoration of the franchises, had expressed concern about attacks on shipping.[34] Having due regard to all the circumstances, common piracy does not seem to have been a particularly serious problem at this time. This conclusion is based on several lists which catalogue the losses claimed by Prussian merchants from 1375 to the end of April 1385; these total something over £2,136 sterling for material damage sustained in 22 separate incidents.[35] In addition, there was a demand for an enquiry into the alleged murder of the entire crew of a Danzig ship at Boston in 1384,

---

[32] *Hanseakten*, nos. 226, 277.   [33] *HUB*, 4, no. 806.
[34] *HR*, I (iii), nos. 142–3, 192.   [35] *Ibid.*, nos. 199, 201–2.

for which no figure for damages was calculated since the ship itself had been recovered. Of the 22 incidents, 6 involved piracy, 3 robbery of goods after shipwreck, 2 other robberies on land, 6 relate to embezzlement, extortion and the like, 1 to commercial negligence, while the remaining 4 were claims against the crown itself for seizure of wine and the enforced service of ships. These incidents, resulting from a mixture of lawlessness, dishonesty and reasons of state, amount to a level of provocation which was probably regarded as normal and containable in the middle ages. But on 12 May 1385 an English royal fleet attacked and robbed six Prussian ships anchored in the estuary of the Zwin, for which damages ranging from £2,188 to £2,933 were later claimed.[36] Since England was then at war with Flanders this could be represented as a legitimate action against those trading with its enemies. For the Prussians, of course, it was an intolerable act of piracy. The captains of two ships were abducted and before being ransomed were forced to swear that they would not take legal action to recover damages. Allegedly, they were taunted that they could get redress in Prussia, where there were more than enough English goods to pay for all their losses. While this claim may be true it is just as likely that it was invented by the Prussians to justify their subsequent behaviour since, contrary to accepted practice, they did not give the crown an opportunity to repudiate the actions of its subjects or to offer compensation. On 18 July 1385 a diet of the Prussian towns ordered the arrest of English goods in Danzig and Elbing and banned all trade with England. Only then did it dispatch two envoys to demand compensation for the Zwin incident and all losses over the previous ten years. One of these died in Holland and the other was prevented by illness from continuing the journey, so the mission came to nothing.[37]

News of the arrests had reached England by 3 August at the latest, for on that day Hanse merchants in London were brought before the mayor and told that on no account were they to export any of their property; similar measures were taken at York, Newcastle, Lynn and, no doubt, wherever else German-owned goods were discovered. Later, the king gave instructions for the release of non-Prussian goods.[38] When parliament met in October 1385 the government rejected a request to suspend the privileges of the Hanse and allow English merchants to recover their losses from arrested Prussian goods by a suit of withernam. However, it did make provision for the

---

[36] *Ibid.*, nos. 200, 203.   [37] *HR*, I (ii), no. 309; (iii), no. 204.
[38] *HR*, I (ii), no. 310. *CCR*, 1385–9, pp. 2, 48.

systematic arrest of Prussian property in all ports from London to Boston. Goods which could not be detained indefinitely without deterioration were to be redelivered to their owners under mainprise. By June 1386 sufficient goods had been found to cover English losses in Prussia, and on this account instructions were given to de-arrest a Prussian ship and its cargo.[39] It is clear that responsible Englishmen were anxious not to widen the dispute with Prussia into one with the Hanse as a whole, and to resolve it as soon as possible. Nevertheless, negotiations for a settlement were protracted. As early as October 1385 two Prussian merchants and the ship in which they were travelling were accorded diplomatic status, but they appear to have been merely the bearers of letters between the Grand Master of the Teutonic Order and the king.[40] On Palm Sunday (15 April) 1386 a Prussian embassy, consisting of two representatives of the Teutonic Order and one of the towns, presented its credentials to the king and afterwards spent several weeks in intermittent discussions with his council.[41] The council was unwilling to consider claims relating to incidents antedating that in Zwin and declined to accept responsibility even for this. It proved impossible to reconcile conflicting accounts of what actually happened, but the Prussians were portrayed as having brought misfortune upon themselves by trading with the king's enemies. When the English suggestion of a mutual release of goods currently arrested on each side was rejected they offered to send their own embassy to Prussia to continue the search for a solution.

During the course of the discussions with the ambassadors and in the following months the council frequently summoned before it representatives of the English merchants who had lost goods in Prussia.[42] This was necessary not merely to ensure that the losses were fully catalogued and to provide the council with advice, but also to ensure that the merchants ultimately bore the cost of any actions taken on their behalf. The king made it clear that he would not shoulder any charge beyond the inclusion of one knight in the embassy which was to be sent to Prussia. As an interim measure the mission was funded from the sale of Prussian goods arrested in England. It was originally intended that it should depart in the spring of 1387, but it did not do so then and the stalemate continued

---

[39] *HUB*, 4, nos. 849–50. *CCR*, 1385–9, pp. 54, 146.   [40] *CCR*, 1385–9, p. 21.
[41] *HR*, I (iii) nos. 198, 204–5.
[42] *CCR*, 1385–7, pp. 67, 163, 194, 204, 481, 529. *HUB*, 4, nos. 925–6.

until parliament met in February 1388.[43] The embassy, which finally sailed from Lynn about the middle of June 1388, consisted of Nicholas Stocket, a royal clerk, and two merchants, Thomas Graa of York and Walter Sibille of London. It was accompanied by John Bebys or Bevys of London, who was to act as its 'informer'. They were under instructions to submit a number of requests and proposals which the English regarded as conducive to a lasting settlement between the two sides.[44] Foremost was the demand that the king's subjects be given access to Prussian courts to pursue actions relating to chattels and personal injuries, while all property subject to the general arrest of 1385 be released immediately. In summary, the English council contended that they had already submitted claims exceeding £3,889 6s 10d sterling for the value of merchandise and debts arrested and over £4,000 damages for unjust arrest. It was then proposed that in future the right of Prussian merchants to enter and leave England by any port and to trade wherever they wished within the country should depend upon the enjoyment of a similar freedom by Englishmen in Prussia. In addition, it was requested that the Prussians should recognise a corporate English mercantile organisation headed by a governor. When it came to the Prussian claims, the record of the ambassadors' instructions does not go beyond a lengthy restatement and justification of the English actions in the Zwin.

The ambassadors presented their credentials to the Grand Master at Marienburg on 28 July, and on 21 August came before him again for the sealing of an agreement which had been made with his personal representatives, after the latter had consulted the towns.[45] The settlement provided that all goods and debts arrested by either side during the recent dispute should immediately be released, but no suits would be allowed for damages resulting from the stoppage. Any Prussians who wished to claim for losses in the Zwin incident or in earlier times should attend upon the English ambassadors after their return home, who would help them to lay their claims before English courts. In respect of personal injuries, the ambassadors were themselves empowered to make amends, unless defendants denied

---

[43] F. Schulz, *Die Hanse und England von Eduards III. bis auf Heinrichs VIII. Zeit* (Berlin, 1911), p. 41, states that an embassy was sent in 1387. This is an error which probably results from the misdating (by twelve months) of a letter written by a Thorn merchant to his fellow townsmen, warning that the English were inflating their losses by one third. Dated only 5 April it reports rumours of an impending embassy. This appears to be that which left in June 1388, suggesting that the letter was written in 1388 and not in 1387. *HUB*, 4, no. 888.

[44] *HR*, I (iii), nos. 402–3.　　　　　　　　　[45] *Ibid.*, nos. 405–6.

the charges, in which case the former were to take all steps necessary to ensure that justice was done. Similar arrangements were made for Englishmen who wished to pursue claims in Prussia. As regards general matters, the English had reason to be tolerably pleased. The request for recognition of their corporate organisation was not accepted, but nor was this specifically forbidden; it was simply passed over in silence in the treaty. The right to freedom of trade was rather vaguely worded, probably because of reservations expressed by the Prussian towns, but it did specify that Englishmen might use any port and also trade inland; all the towns had agreed to this, with the exception of Elbing and Braunsberg.[46] A further guarantee, potentially as valuable to Prussia as to England, was that in the event of any future dispute between the two sides merchants should be allowed a full year to wind up their affairs and depart in peace before reprisals would be instituted.

While the English appear to have been satisfied with the treaty of Marienburg, the Prussians soon came to regret it. Their reasons were set out in an angry letter sent by the Grand Master to Richard II on 5 April 1391, though disillusion had set in long before that date.[47] He complained that his subjects were bankrupting themselves in vain attempts to recover their losses in England, while the crown continued to disregard the rights of the Hanse by levying unjust taxes, such as tunnage and poundage. Since England was allegedly breaking the treaty the Grand Master refused to ratify it. These accusations of bad faith, at least with regard to the treatment of Prussian litigants, are probably not justified. It was the complexity of many cases rather than wilful refusal to award justice which was the cause of delay. The king's council was concerned about this and, as recently as January 1391, a commission had been issued to some of the most powerful magnates in the land to sit with a team of lawyers to deal with the cases.[48] The charge of duplicity about taxation stemmed from an unbridgeable difference of opinion between the two sides. On the one hand it is certain that in ratifying the treaty of Marienburg the crown had no intention of renouncing its claim to tunnage and poundage. On the other hand it is easy to understand why the Prussians chose to interpret the treaty as they did. They were simply taking up the English challenge of reciprocity. They accepted the general principle that Hanse rights in England should depend upon the enjoyment of similar privileges by

---

[46] *HUB*, 4, no. 936.   [47] *Ibid.*, no. 1054. *HR*, 1 (iv), no. 6.
[48] *CPR*, 1388–92, pp. 372, 374.

Englishmen, but they stuck to the view that the traditional Hanse rights included immunity from virtually all taxation instituted after 1303. (The only tax established after that date which they never seriously challenged was the wool subsidy.)

The judicial commission of January 1391 was clearly associated with an embassy to the Baltic, preparation for which had begun shortly before Christmas. Both the commission and the embassy were authorised to consider disputes with other sections of the Hanse, but Prussia was the main cause for concern. It was more than a year since the English ratification of the treaty of Marienburg had been sent to Prussia, but the Grand Master had not yet returned his ratification. The ambassadorial credentials were made out in the names of John Pykering, clerk, Walter Sybille and John Bebys, merchants. Bebys also received a royal commission as governor of all the English merchants trading in the Baltic. There is little doubt that he was already in Prussia at the time of these appointments and already acting as governor.[49] The purpose of the royal appointment was probably to add greater weight to the renewed attempt to persuade the Grand Master to afford official recognition to this office. It was not successful. On the other hand it is unlikely that recognition was categorically refused as historians have traditionally argued. The confusion has arisen from the Grand Master's refusal to ratify the treaty of Marienburg.[50] The matter of the governorship was again passed over in silence, as it had been in the treaty. Bebys no doubt continued to act as governor, officially recognised by the English crown but not by the Prussians. Sybille, who arrived in Prussia in March 1391, seems not to have excelled as a diplomat, for he soon antagonised Conrad von Wallenrod, the newly appointed Grand Master, who previously had headed the Prussian team which had negotiated the treaty of Marienburg. Von Wallenrod charged Sybille with slandering his predecessor by falsely accusing him of lying about an alleged English promise relating to the Zwin incident.[51] This seems to have resulted from a misunderstanding arising from a Prussian embassy which had come to England in the summer and autumn of 1389. Its purpose had been to help Prussian merchants prosecute their claims in England and its chief task to ensure that the English judges understood the Prussian evidence and official documents. However, rightly or wrongly, the ambassadors

[49] S. Jenks, 'Die Ordnung für die englische Handelskolonie in Danzig (23 Mai 1405)', pp. 110–11 in B. Jähnig and P. Letkemann, *Danzig in acht Jahrhunderten* (Münster/Westph., 1985), pp. 105–20.   [50] *Ibid.*, p. 111.   [51] *HR*, I (iv), no. 11.

came to believe that the king's council had made an offer of 3,000 nobles in compensation for the attack in the Zwin. It was the denial of any such promise which provoked angry scenes in 1391 and resulted in the failure of Sybille's mission. Nevertheless, although the Grand Master refused to send another embassy to England, the English wished to continue direct negotiations and, in September 1391, the Duke of Gloucester actually set out on a mission to Prussia.[52] After he was forced back by storms the initiative was not resumed. Prussia continued to reproach Richard II for breaking the treaty, though the emphasis came to be more on present wrongs than on old debts.

During the course of its dispute with England, Prussia received little support from fellow members of the Hanse. The Wendish towns continued to export goods of Prussian origin to England, despite attempts by Prussia to prevent them. The crown encouraged this by proclaiming that they were not to be held accountable for English losses, though in practice it was difficult to restrict reprisals to Prussian-owned goods. When parliament met in February 1388 the London *Kontor* complained that its franchises were being flouted by continuing arrests as well as by attempts to make them pay the lay subsidy of tenths and fifteenths.[53] The response was not very satisfactory. It was ordered that perishable goods be released under mainprise and all clearly non-Prussian goods de-arrested, but wherever there appeared to be a possibility of partnership with Prussians then the property must remain attached. Shortly afterwards, Englishmen seized a Stralsund ship laden with goods belonging to some of the leading men of that town, who thereupon secured the arrest of English property in Stralsund. Inevitably, there was retaliation and, on 14 July 1388, orders were issued to arrest everything belonging to men of Stralsund, Lübeck, Wismar, Rostock and Hamburg until they gave assurances not to take anything out of the country without licence. On 26 August, additional powers to treat with the Wendish towns were made out for the English ambassadors then in Prussia. The commission was entrusted to a Hanse merchant about to sail for Skania, who was paid 70s for the estimated additional twelve days voyage to Prussia. However, before the ambassadors can have received the news the immediate crisis had been resolved by direct negotiations between the interested parties in England. On 6 September members of the provincial

[52] T. Walsingham, *Historia Anglicana*, ed. H. T. Riley (London, 1863), 2, p. 202.
[53] *Rot. Parl.*, 3, p. 253. *HUB*, 4, nos. 911–12.

Kontore assembled in London; on 8 September the crown lifted the prohibition (imposed on 3 August) on export by Englishmen to the Baltic; on 20 September trade restrictions upon Hanse merchants were eased after the London *Kontor* had provided sureties for the safety of Englishmen in all Wendish towns except Stralsund. On 18 September the captain of Calais was instructed to deliver the captured Stralsund ship and its cargo, or the value thereof, to the mayor of the English wool staple then located at Middelburg.[54] This order was not carried out, but the English goods in Stralsund were released when the owners undertook to secure compensation for the aggrieved burghers. They failed to do this and there was a new arrest of English goods in Stralsund in 1391. On the latter occasion they were not released, but there was no general retaliation against either the Wendish towns as a whole or citizens of Stralsund. English merchants were obliged to sue individually for damages, but progress was slow, probably because of difficulty in identifying Stralsund-owned goods in England. In 1397 and 1398 John Brandon of Lynn succeeded in making good much of his loss by legally authorised arrests. In turn this action probably prompted the seizure of cloth owned by Coventry merchants in Stralsund in 1398 and 1399.[55]

Although the dispute with Stralsund was contained, the 1390s witnessed a general deterioration in relations between England and the Hanse as a whole, caused chiefly by complaints of the *Kontor* about treatment at the hands of the crown and English towns. The parliament of 1388 had actually attempted to improve the status of alien merchants in general, by reviving the free-trade statute of Edward III and ruling that no franchises or usages should be invoked against it. However, in January 1393, the restrictions imposed on aliens at the beginning of the present reign were re-introduced, and freedom of trade was limited by the proviso that aliens should not deal among themselves and that their retail business should be confined to victuals.[56] The chief complaint of the Hanse against the towns related to attempts to exact local tolls. The leading offender, although by no means the only one, was Southampton, and the fact that it was a growing centre of Hanseatic trade made it imperative to resist. As early as 1381 Southampton was ordered to stop trying to exact any duties beyond those

---

[54] *CCR*, 1385–9, pp. 532, 535. *HUB*, 4, pp. 933–4, 942–3. *Hanseakten*, nos. 248, 250–1.
[55] *Royal and Historical Letters during the Reign of Henry the Fourth*, ed. F. C. Hingeston, 1 (London, 1860), pp. 258–61. *Literae Cantuarienses*, ed. J. B. Sheppard, 3 (London, 1884), pp. 79–81.
[56] *Rot. Parl.*, 3, p. 247. *Stats.*, 2, pp. 82–3.

established by the *Carta Mercatoria* of 1303. In 1387 it was again ordered to stop levying a custom of 2d on each barrel of herrings. When parliament met in November 1390 the *Kontor* complained that Southampton was still taking illegal tolls, whereby its members were likely to abjure the realm and the king would stand to lose 2–3,000 marks a year. In February 1391 the Chancery ordered Southampton and Sandwich not to levy tolls until 16 April and to pay those already taken into the Exchequer for safe-keeping. In the autumn parliament the *Kontor* again complained that not only Southampton but Sandwich, Hull and other ports were taking a toll on all manner of imports. It was ordered that these impositions should cease for two years, within which time the king's council should give a ruling about their lawfulness. No definite pronouncement was made within the time limit, but at the end of it the Chancery repeated the prohibition on the collection of tolls until the following Easter.[57]

Taxation was also the bone of contention between the Hanse and the crown. The merchants were still required to pay tunnage and poundage, which was all the more objectionable since it showed every sign of becoming a permanent part of the king's revenue, rather than a wartime tax for the protection of commerce, which it was alleged to be. More importantly, the Exchequer reneged on the 1361 agreement about the taxation of cloth. Since the early 1380s Hanse merchants had complained about some customs collectors converting straits and pieces into notional cloths of assise and charging 1s duty instead of the *ad valorem* duty of 3d in the pound. At Michaelmas 1388 this became official policy, with straits and pieces rated at 48 yards to the assise and kerseys at 3 cloths to the assise. This step was particularly damaging to the Hanse merchants, who during the first parliament of 1390 claimed that on average they exported 10,000 strait cloths and kerseys each year. On this occasion the commons also objected to the new duty, and it was agreed that collection should be suspended until the next parliament.[58] On 12 November 1390, during the course of the new assembly, collection recommenced, and ever after the cloths in question were taxed like assise cloths. In the autumn parliament of 1391, the Hanse again complained that its franchises were being dishonoured.[59] The merchants could not for long unilaterally boycott the export of kerseys and straits, since this would simply hand the trade over to Englishmen. The London *Kontor* tried, therefore, to get a total ban

[57] *CCR*, 1377–81, p. 447; 1385–9, p. 45; 1392–6, p. 238. *HUB*, 4, nos. 1045, 1073.
[58] *Rot. Parl.*, 3, p. 272. *HUB*, 4, no. 998.   [59] *Ibid.*, no. 1074.

on the import of such cloths into the Baltic region. The Wendish towns would not countenance this move, since they were currently at odds with Scandinavia and Flanders and could not sustain a trade war with England as well. The Prussians proposed that a ban should be enforced as soon as a settlement had been reached with Flanders. They also wanted to retaliate by raising duties on imports by Englishmen into their country, but this measure was overruled by the Grand Master.[60]

On the whole the Hanse favoured diplomacy rather than sanctions, but in 1394 the diet wrote to the king's council and five English towns threatening that unless the Hanse franchises were honoured their own merchants would be burdened with new taxation in Germany. On 3 July 1394 the London *Kontor* reported that it had submitted this letter to the council six weeks previously but had not yet received a reply. It had no idea when one might be forthcoming, but did not expect it to be favourable.[61] The English government ignored the ultimatum, but in November 1394 issued letters of credence to John Huntingdon and John de Wesenham as ambassadors to the Wendish towns.[62] The chief purpose of this mission was to complain about attacks by Mecklenburg pirates known as the *Vitalienbrüder*. These pirates, whose origins were associated with the Scandinavian ambitions of the ducal house of Mecklenburg, had been active for many years but had been particularly dangerous since they had captured Visby in 1391. They were also succoured by the towns of Rostock and Wismar. The English complaint does not seem to have been fully considered by the diet until August 1396, when it decided that attack was the best form of defence. It then wrote to Richard II stating that it had no control over the pirates who, in any case, were doing more harm to Hanse merchants than they were to the English. It requested, therefore, that the king should prevent his subjects from attacking Hanse ships in retaliation for damage done by the *Vitalienbrüder*. The diet further demanded the full implementation of the franchises and threatened that, unless it received satisfaction on all these points, it would not only increase the taxation of English merchants but would also ban the import of English cloth. The diet apparently saw no incompatibility between its own demand for corporate privileges in England and its denial of responsibility for the actions of Rostock and Wismar, important members of the Hanse. This view was not

---

[60] *HR*, I (iv) nos. 26, 28.
[62] *Ibid.*, no. 182.
[61] *Ibid.*, no. 196. *HUB*, 5, nos. 153, 169.

shared by all the towns. As long before as March 1395, Dortmund, fearful for its own trade in England, had written to Lübeck urging that compensation should be paid to the English. The German claim that English merchants made good their losses to the pirates by attacks on other Hanse ships may be true, but there is little evidence to support it. There are few immediately contemporary details of any such attacks, and the charge can be sustained only if a few undated claims made at the Hague conference of 1407 relate to events in the 1390s. There is certainly no evidence of any sustained onslaught on Hanseatic shipping by the English in this decade.[63]

Because of the continuing unrest in northern Europe it was impossible to implement the new threat of discrimination against English merchants and merchandise. In December 1396 even the Prussian towns, the most aggressive wing of the Hanse, admitted this and conceded that for the time being they must be content with further diplomatic representations. By the following spring, however, they were so dissatisfied with the ineffectual protests of the Grand Master that they refused to endorse a letter which he was then proposing to send to Richard II until it was altered to meet their requirements. The letter, finally sent on 31 May 1397, was in fact fairly restrained, but it stated that if England continued to disregard the Hanse franchises then Prussia would consider cancelling the treaty of 1388.[64] At this stage the Teutonic Order, because of its own commercial dealings with Englishmen, was still inclined to treat them favourably. The Grand Master tried to prevent discrimination by ruling that any laws made against the English must be applied equally to other aliens. He was finally obliged to bow to the pressure of the townsmen and, on 2 February 1398, wrote to Richard II and the city of London renouncing the treaty and ordering Englishmen to leave Prussia within a year.[65] The English seem to have taken this news remarkably coolly, for there is no indication that at this stage they threatened retaliation, either against the Hanse in general or the Prussians in particular. In October 1398 the king even ordered London to stop trying to make Hansards contribute to the current tenth and fifteenth.[66] This restraint was amply rewarded, for at the end of a year no attempt was made to expel Englishmen from Prussia and for several more years the campaign of harassment remained at a low key. This was not, however, the result of any change of attitude on the part of the Prussian merchants. The restraining factors were

---

[63] *Ibid.*, nos. 189, 235. *HR*, I (iv) nos. 255, 260–4.   [64] *Ibid.*, nos. 399–401.
[65] *Ibid.*, no. 433.   [66] *HUB*, 5, no. 348. *CCR*, 1396–9, pp. 344–5.

their inability to gain support from the rest of the Hanse and a deterioration in relations between the Teutonic Order and Poland, which threatened war between the two.

The key to relations between Prussians and Englishmen was the ambition of the latter to operate in the internal markets of Prussia and beyond. Even before 1400, exports of English cloth to Prussia by Englishmen were greater than those of native Prussians. Doubtless, this was an annoyance to those Prussian merchants who themselves actively engaged in overseas trade, though any who had an interest in ship-owning gained some compensation from the fact that Englishmen employed a considerable volume of Prussian shipping to bring goods home from the Baltic. Merchants who operated only within Prussia, like their counterparts elsewhere in Europe, were not insurmountably opposed to alien importers, in this instance Englishmen, provided that they were content to deal only with enfranchised citizens on a wholesale basis. What they objected to was any attempt to establish retail businesses, attempts to penetrate inland towns and any dealings, even on a wholesale basis, with unenfranchised merchants visiting the ports from the interior. Englishmen, of course, wanted to do all these things and, moreover, regarded it as their right, since Hanseatic merchants were making precisely the same claims in England. During the 1390s comparatively little was done to squash the pretensions of the Englishmen, who took full advantage of the vague formula of the 1388 treaty, which promised them rights similar to those enjoyed by the Hanse in England. They disregarded hosting laws and rented property, both for living in and for retailing cloth; some formed partnerships with natives, while some established themselves even more firmly by taking up residence and either brought wives from England or married Prussian women. They also ignored local regulations about statutory cloth lengths dating back to before 1388. In 1392, after much debate in the Prussian diet, a new law was made that *halb-laken* (half-cloths), as well as whole cloths, must be sold with lists at each end. Such a regulation had long been in force in Skania, and while its intention is never explained in the sources it would, of course, betray any pieces which had been cut for retail sale. The law was not enforced for several years, and not until 1395 do we encounter a complaint that the authorities of Danzig had confiscated twenty-one dozens from two Lynn merchants on these grounds. Thereafter, some Englishmen breached the law in spirit by cutting cloth along its length, and in 1397 Richard II complained about the confiscation of cloths which, although cut in this fashion, were of full length.[67] The growing tendency of Englishmen to settle in Prussia created a potentially dangerous situation, but became a serious problem only in later years. The sole charge of mass restrictive action against Englishmen in this period is recorded in a list of grievances written after May 1404. It alleged the arrest of thirty-two English ships from Purification to Lammas (2 February–1 August) 1396; no details were given and the action may simply have arisen from the current turmoil in the Baltic and been no more sinister than similar arrests by the English crown, which frequently delayed alien ships or pressed them into royal service. Despite the suspended threat of expulsion Englishmen appeared to be in no immediate danger in Prussia when Richard II was deposed, and the accession of the Prussophile Henry IV might have led them to expect that the situation could only improve. This was not to be, but before seeing how things developed it is appropriate to make a more detailed examination of Anglo-Hanseatic economic relations in the later fourteenth century.

A feature of this period, compared with the early fourteenth century, is an increased tendency for Hanseatic merchants to confine their trade to one port. Then merchants quite frequently figured in the customs accounts of several ports; now it is comparatively rare, though not unknown. If any single factor was responsible for this change it was the withdrawal from the wool trade. The great wool exporters dispatched their sarplers from Hull, Boston, Lynn or London as convenience suited, and also imported at any of these places. Having given up the wool trade, merchants seem generally to have confined their business to one place. A converse of this was that the provincial ports ceased to be patronised by a broad spectrum of Hanse merchants and each became dominated by merchants of one town or region. London was something of an exception since Westphalia, the Rhineland, Prussia, the west Baltic and the North Sea towns were all strongly represented here. When the Steelyard was required to find individual mainpernors for its collective responsibility in 1388, the eighteen names put forward were those of ten men from Cologne, seven from Dortmund and one from Hungary.[68] The list is biased in so far as Wendish merchants were not currently acceptable as sureties and Prussians were still absent

[67] *HUB*, 5, no. 252. *HR*, 1 (iv), nos. 127–8.   [68] *HUB*, 4, nos. 934, 945.

from the city. Nevertheless, the names are those of merchants who appear time and time again in dealings with the English authorities and as the leading importers and exporters recorded in the surviving customs particulars. The total numbers occupying the Steelyard or living elsewhere in London at this time are not known, but in 1381 the collectors of the poll tax counted twenty-eight merchants of Almain who were excused payment because of their franchises.[69]

At the end of the fourteenth century the London *Kontor* overtook that of Boston in economic importance, though until then it may have occupied second place. The degree of uncertainty results from an unknown quantity in Hanse cloth exports from London. These appear to have grown more slowly than those of Boston (see table 2), but trade in non-assise woollen cloths and worsteds casts doubt on the matter. In 1358–9 the Hanse men paid 1s 9d duty on each of 281 cloths of assise and 3d in the pound by value for 1,171 worsteds, while an unknown quantity of strait cloth also paid 3d in the pound.[70] The next year the figures were $263\frac{1}{2}$ assise paying 2s 9d, 2,709 worsteds paying $1\frac{1}{2}$d each and probably also 3d in the pound, and 16,150 yards of strait, deemed to equal 323 cloths of assise, paying 1s 9d and probably also still paying 3d in the pound. In 1360–1, when Hanse rates were altered in mid-term, separate figures do not survive. (The 467 cloths shown as Hanse in *England's Export Trade* is a mistake; these belonged to John de Mary, a Genoese.) From the following year Hanse cloths of assise, now paying 1s, were again recorded separately, but straits and worsteds were included in the total of all alien goods paying 3d in the pound. The only year in which there is a separate record of the latter is 1376–7, when under the description of serges and beds of worsteds their value was given as £1,068 10s 8d. This evidence suggests that in the later years of Edward III non-assise cloths were worth much more in value than cloths of assise. The latter averaged only 135 per annum between 1361 and 1372 and, after a period of customs farming, 183 for the last two Exchequer years of the reign (1375–7). The first enrolled account of the new reign (1377–8) records no Hanse cloth exports before 1 June 1378, but $426\frac{1}{2}$ cloths of assise between then and Michaelmas,

---

[69] *Letter Book H*, p. 164.

[70] In the remainder of this chapter all statements about cloth exports are derived from enrolled customs accounts, PRO, E356/7, 9, 14, unless another source is cited. *England's Export Trade, 1275–1546*, ed. E. M. Carus-Wilson and O. Coleman (Oxford, 1963), omits important information and some figures, while some figures are printed incorrectly.

Table 2. *Hanse cloth customed at assise rates, 1358–72*

Mich.–Mich.	London	Boston and Lynn	Hull	Newcastle
1358–9	281[a]			
1359–60	587[b]			
1360–1	n/a	80[c]	35[d]	0
1361–2	45	145	62	0
1362–3	135	847	107	0
1363–4	92	1,783	169	0
1364–5	178	1,766	350	0
1365–6	77	1,975[e]	303	0
1366–7	70	1,197	70	0
1367–8	46	2,008[f]	151	0
1368–9	153	929[f]	104	3
1369–70	241	1,074[f]	188[g]	0
1370–1	163	1,646[f]	195	0
1371–2	281	1,625	127	28
1372 (to 24 Dec.)	32[h]	76	78	0

[a] After 2 Dec. 1358.
[b] Includes straits.
[c] After 8 Feb. 1381, excused 1s 9d.
[d] Before 8 Feb. 1381, pays 1s 9d.
[e] Includes alien imports.
[f] Includes alien imports and denizen re-exports.
[g] Plus twenty imports or re-exports.
[h] Includes re-exports.

each paying 1s by virtue of a Chancery writ of 20 May. Subsequently the merchants were charged £28 19s 10½d *super compotum*, so that the cloth should answer for the full alien duty; in fact that sum does not fully satisfy the difference between the two rates. It is unlikely that Hanse merchants exported cloth before 1 June, but if they did the duty must be included in the total of £254 6s 1¾d paid for other alien woollens and worsteds for the whole year. (*England's Export Trade* erroneously states that this sum is not recorded.) In 1378–9 Hanse exports are not separately recorded, but included in a total alien payment of £296 15s for woollens and worsteds. In 1379–80 and 1380–1, when the Hanse were again paying only 1s, their cloths of assise still totalled only 389 and 406, but this was followed by a sharp rise. The figures for 1381–2 and 1382–3 were 803 and 793, while the average for 1383–6 was 890; the last figure includes a few alien imports, but probably not enough to reduce the Hanse total significantly; the latest separately recorded figure for alien imports, in 1382–3, was a mere 63. Warfare in Flanders in the 1380s stifled cloth imports into England as certainly as it was the factor responsible for the increase in Hanseatic and Italian exports from

England in this period. The drop in Hanseatic assise exports to an average of 386 in 1386–8 is not readily explicable, though the political events of those years must be borne in mind. Equally, or more likely, is the possibility of a switch in investment to low-taxed kerseys, which were increasingly attracting all groups of exporters. As early as 1384 a tunnage and poundage particular for 1 July–Michaelmas records a minimum Hanseatic export to the continent of 519 kerseys and 128 cloths of assise, while 2 ships obviously bound for Prussia carried 237 Hanseatic-owned kerseys and 13 cloths, together with 254 English-owned kerseys and 24 cloths.[71] Because of the loss of revenue, the Exchequer now ruled that, in addition to poundage, denizens must for the first time pay custom on kerseys and all aliens should pay a specific custom duty in lieu of the *ad valorem* rate of 3d in the pound; the conversion rate for all parties was three standard or two Isle of Wight kerseys to one cloth of assise; any remaining straits, which kerseys had largely replaced in the export market, were also converted to assise cloths. Between Michaelmas 1388 and 2 February 1390, Hanse merchants exported 1,378 cloths of assise and 7,545 kerseys; the latter being valued at £1,796 16s 2d would formerly have paid £22 9s 2½d in tax, but now paid £125 15s 0¾d. Prussian merchants, who returned to England in force after the Marienbad settlement, were treated as aliens until the formalities of the treaty were completed, and between Michaelmas 1388 and 25 May 1389 paid the full alien rate of 2s 9d on another 6,118½ kerseys valued at £1,504 12s. Between 1 March and 30 November 1390, during the temporary suspension of the new policy, twenty-two readily identified Hanse men exported a minimum of 3,354 kerseys valued at £714 7s 4d and 529 cloths of assise valued at £1,120 6s 2d.[72] The valuations of these kerseys were uniformly lower than the averages of 5s 1d and 4s 11d derived from the enrolled accounts of 1388–90. If the current averages of 4s 3d per kersey and 42s 4d per cloth are realistic, then it means that a merchant had the choice of investing £100 in 470 kerseys or 47 cloths of assise; on the former he would currently pay custom of £1 5s and on the latter £2 7s; poundage would be the same in each case. With a price ratio of 10:1 the merchants were obviously affronted at a tax-conversion ratio of 3:1, and when the harsher regime was reintroduced in November 1390 the Steelyard probably ordered a boycott of kerseys. The petty-custom particulars for 1390–1 show

[71] PRO, E122/71/8.   [72] PRO, E122/71/13.

seven merchants exporting 84 cloths of assise and 830 kerseys between 1 and 29 October; 21 kerseys entered on 31 October were first valued at £3 14s 6d and charged *ad valorem*, but were later converted to 7 cloths of assise; in the following eleven months only 145 standard and 3 Isle of Wight kerseys were exported by three merchants, none of them leading members of the Steelyard, compared with something over 1,200 cloths of assise legible in the account.[73] (The figure of 1,581 cloths for the whole year in the enrolled account includes kerseys converted to assise cloths.) Denizens were not put off by the resumption of taxation on kerseys, and from November onwards exported at least 7,347 (including 22 Isle of Wight), compared with somewhat more than 2,623 cloths of assise taken over the course of the whole twelve months. Other aliens exported well over 1,000 kerseys in the autumn, while the matter of taxation was still disputed, but only 190 thereafter; their assise cloths exported over the whole year were in the region of 1,900. Between 6 July and 8 August 1392 Hanse merchants still exported only 280 kerseys compared with 870 cloths of assise, though significantly 200 of the former were owned by Frowyn Stepyng, a leading member of the Steelyard.[74] Hanse exports through London were apparently now building up to an unprecedented boom and, between Michaelmas 1391 and Michaelmas 1395, averaged 4,315 short-cloths (including kerseys), which represented over 60 per cent of all Hanse exports from England. Unfortunately, London customs accounts are lacking from Michaelmas 1395 to 10 December 1397 and by the latter date steam was temporarily running out of the Steelyard machinery, so that between then and Michaelmas 1399 exports averaged only 2,321 short-cloths per annum, about 45 per cent of the current national Hanse figure.

Whatever may have been the precise attraction and characteristic of kersey, if indeed it was yet a homogeneous product, by the 1380s and 1390s it had virtually replaced all other types of English cloth (other than assise cloths) in the export trade of the London Hanseatics. They now handled very few worsteds and even fewer pieces described as strait or serge; pieces of so-called 'Irish cloth' and Welsh cloth are more frequently encountered, though their total value was insignificant. Some textiles were also exported in made-up form, caps, mantles and 'Irish' mantles being the most common. Non-textile exports included gloves, cony skins and lamb skins; tin

[73] PRO, E122/71/16. Some illegible entries make exact calculation impossible.
[74] PRO, E122/71/17.

and pewter constituted a more regular and more valuable trade, both to the Baltic and the near continent, but the Hanseatic share of these products was small compared with that of denizens and Italians.[75]

A full list of Hanse imports would be much longer and more varied than that of their exports. Many items, such as glass, locks, mirrors, pouches, rosaries, geegaws, ciphers, dogstones, querns and more besides, are quite obviously not part of a specialist business. Such things appear among the stock of leading members of the Steelyard, but they are more frequently found against the names of obscure merchants, ships' captains or sailors. In any event the combined values of such things made up an insignificant proportion of total Hanse trade. By far the greatest contribution was provided by the traditional staple goods, which depended upon greater capital and specialised knowledge of the markets. Much of this trade was in the hands of resident merchants, who may seldom have left the city, depending instead upon consignments from agents in the Baltic, Bruges, Antwerp, Cologne or Dinant. The Baltic region was still the ultimate source of most Hanse imports but many of them, perhaps even a majority, were generally brought to London not directly, but via the Low Countries. This practice was not confined to the fur trade, the most valuable sector of imports, though it is most apparent here. In July, August and September 1384, total imports of furs by aliens and denizens amounted to rather more than £3,300 in value, but there were none in eight ships which can safely be claimed as coming direct from the Baltic, except for a mere handful owned by two Englishmen. This short account, which has the most furs recorded in any surviving customs particular, was dominated by Christian Kelmer of Dortmund, alderman of the Steelyard, with fur imports worth £1,045. The trade of eleven other Hanse merchants, among whom were at least five more from Dortmund or Cologne, brought their combined share of fur imports to almost 80 per cent. A complete monopoly eluded them, for besides the two Baltic traders a few prominent Londoners imported valuable consignments from the Low Countries. The sheer volume of furs imported in this period may have been exceptional, and it may even have been a glutted market which caused Kelmer to re-export the ermines which led to his disgrace in the same year.[76] The vast majority of imports, however, consisted of relatively inexpensive squirrel skins, which

---

[75] J. Hatcher, *English Tin Production and Trade before 1550* (Oxford, 1973), pp. 103–5.
[76] See above p. 62.

originated chiefly in Russia.[77] Although there is probably a connection between the tendency to import Baltic furs from the Low Countries and the prominent role of Westphalian merchants, this does not necessarily mean that the latter were uninvolved in the first leg of the trade. Bernard Mechynghous of Cologne, a leading London importer, lost furs in one of three Riga ships attacked on a voyage to Bruges in 1405.[78]

The 1384 account is exceptional in the fact that furs heavily outweigh all other products. The account for the twelve months of 1390–1 is more typical in that the traditional products of the Westphalia-Meuse region are better represented. Copper, steel, iron and laton were imported in the form of ingots, bars and wire and also as battery, basins, plates, dishes, swords, knives and sundry pieces of armour. Together, they made a respectable contribution to the import total, though not on the same scale as those of Baltic origin. The enrolled customs accounts of London and other ports show that the wax trade, which had moved away from the city in the early fourteenth century, returned there after mid-century. Alien trade was decidedly cyclical, reaching a high which averaged 1,142 cwt per annum in 1367–72 and a low of 95 cwt per annum in 1375–80; the late-century peak was 762 cwt per annum in 1391–3, but in 1397–9 the level was down to 115 cwt. It is reasonable to suppose that the bulk of alien wax was owned by Hanse merchants, but they did not monopolise the trade and Englishmen imported significant amounts both from the Low Countries and directly from the Baltic.

Ranked in importance between the traditional staples of furs, metals and wax and the sundry wares mentioned earlier was the Hanse stake, as yet relatively small, in a major growth area of English trade: non-woollen textiles, particularly linens.[79] Hanse imports of linen cloth were dwarfed by those of Englishmen; these had been manufactured in all parts of the Low Countries and Westphalia. A considerable amount of yarn or thread, of various sorts though generally indeterminable, was also imported. The Hanse merchants brought in quite a large quantity of Cologne thread, which was sometimes described as Cologne pack thread and

[77] On the fur trade generally see E. M. Veale, *The English Fur Trade in the Later Middle Ages* (Oxford, 1966). J. Martin, *Treasure of the Land of Darkness* (Cambridge, 1986).

[78] See below p. 113.

[79] V. A. Harding, 'Some Documentary Sources for the Import and Distribution of Foreign Textiles in Later Medieval England', *Textile History*, 18 (1987), 205–18.

possibly intended for stitching up bales rather than for weaving. Even in this commodity Englishmen did a brisk trade, and both communities shared in the import of raw flax. There was a small Hanse trade in fustian and Cologne merchants were already establishing a stake in silk; the latter was generally specified as '*crud*'. (?unthrown), but some consignments described as Cologne silk had a much higher valuation.

Although the London customs particulars of this period provide little information about shipping, it is frequently possible to determine roughly where a ship was laden by studying the mix of its cargoes and the names of the merchants who freighted in it. By this means only eight out of ninety-eight ships entering the port in July–September 1384 may be said to have been involved in direct transport from the Baltic, although two of these, with a small quantity of Cologne thread, Cologne steel and silk, must have touched briefly upon a Low Countries port. The total value of the cargoes was £1,336 (including about £100 for the non-Baltic goods). None of the ships appear to have been skippered by Englishmen, but the bulk of the cargoes was English owned, leaving a maximum of 38 per cent for Hanseatic merchants and sailors. Apart from wax, a little copper and a few furs the cargoes consisted chiefly of traditional, high weight/value goods such as timber, ashes, osmund, pitch, tar, flax and a little stockfish; more novel were Prussian linen cloth and yarn and beer, the new drink promoted aggressively by north-German merchants in the late fourteenth century. The 1384 account is in the wrong season to find imports of Skania herrings, but two years earlier the Hanse merchants had protested when the London collectors of the petty custom began to demand 1s 3d instead of 1s on this product.[80] On that occasion the king's council ruled that the matter should be decided by parliament, and meantime the merchants should give security to pay later, should the decision go against them. Particulars of the 1390s show that the customers did successfully raise the assessed value of herrings from £4 to £5 per last. Hanse merchants imported herrings in 1390–1, none positively said to be from Skania though brought in at the right time of the year. Since the total was comparatively small it may be that the herring trade was largely in the hands of native merchants. On the other hand, during part of this year Hanse merchants may have

[80] *HUB*, 4, no. 759.

imported herrings duty free by royal proclamation. Because of dearth it was ordered that corn and all victuals save stockfish and sturgeon should enter free of custom and subsidy. Some merchants who responded to the opportunity by importing Prussian grain got their fingers burned when the scarcity ended unexpectedly and the city authorities ordered bakers not to buy from merchants until its own magazines had been run down. Consequently, Hanse merchants successfully petitioned to re-export grain duty free to specified places, including Bordeaux, Bayonne and Dordrecht.[81]

Many denizen London merchants routinely imported goods of Baltic or Westphalian origin via Flanders or Brabant, but comparatively few traded directly with the Baltic. All surviving evidence points to the fact that now, as later, Londoners were less active here than English merchants from the east-coast ports. Nevertheless, the London interest should not be judged solely from the record of English goods seized in Prussia in 1385, when eleven Londoners lost property to the value of £353.[82] Six of that group and at least twenty-five other Englishmen had freight in the eight ships coming from the Baltic in July–September 1384, though only three exported there in the same period, sending 254 kerseys, 24 cloths of assise and 16 dozen caps.

In the late fourteenth century Boston was still the chief provincial centre of Hanseatic activity, but the geographic and economic bases on which this *Kontor* rested were narrower than before. Here, as elsewhere, wool exports had been replaced by cloth, directed overwhelmingly to northern Europe; on the import side the Norway trade was even more dominant than before. Between Michaelmas 1390 and Michaelmas 1391 Hanse imports from Bergen amounted to £3,779, 74 per cent of all alien imports, while between the latter date and 8 December they totalled £2,679, 64 per cent of all alien and denizen imports.[83] In the twelve months beginning 28 November 1386, when denizen and alien trade paying poundage was valued at £20,804 – the highest annual figure ever recorded at Boston – Bergen imports accounted for £8,844, 43 per cent of the total and 61 per cent of all imports.[84] Shorter particulars confirm the dominant role of this trade, which consisted almost entirely of stockfish and train oil. Small quantities of other goods, such as timber, pelts and hides, could have come from Norway, but the occasional shipments of beer must have originated in Germany and been re-shipped at

[81] *CCR*, 1389–92, pp. 388, 390.   [82] *HR*, I (iii), no. 404.
[83] PRO, E122/7/22–4, 27.   [84] PRO, E122/7/19.

Bergen. There appears to have been almost no regular import trade direct from the Baltic. Occasional cargoes of Skania herrings brought in by Hanse merchants and goods carried by the masters of ships chartered by English merchants were a small fraction of Englishmen's imports from the Baltic, and insignificant compared with Hanse imports from Bergen. Hanse imports from the Low Countries and the Rhineland were insignificant relative both to Englishmen's imports from this region and total Hanse trade.

Hanse exports consisted almost entirely of cloth, and this *Kontor* was probably the first to venture English cloth on a large scale in the expansionary period which began in the middle of the fourteenth century. Between 1353 and 1372 the cloth exports of Boston are enrolled with those of Lynn, but the bulk of Hanse trade was at the former port. From February to Michaelmas 1361, Hanse merchants handled $79\frac{1}{2}$ cloths, with 145, 847, 1,783 and 1,766 taken in the next four years (1361–5). The Boston accounts of the 1350s pose various problems of interpretation, but even if they conceal Hanse cloth exports in those years it is quite clear that the merchants increased their investment in cloths of assise during the 1360s by a large amount. The average annual export for 1365–72 was rather less than 1,493, since that figure includes a few cloths imported by aliens in five of the seven years and denizen re-exports of imported cloth.[85] Between August 1377 and Michaelmas 1399 Hanse cloth exports from Boston averaged just under 2,000 per annum, an increase of one third on the earlier combined Boston/Lynn figure. A slightly higher average for the 1390s alone reflects the inclusion of previously untaxed straits, but this factor is not as distortive of the true trend as in London. At Boston straits were not a major export and kerseys even less so. On the other hand, some merchants still exported worsteds, which were not counted among the enrolled short-cloth figures. It is difficult to set a value upon exports, but it is quite clear that in the late fourteenth century this *Kontor* had a comfortable surplus of imports over exports.

Almost all Hanse cloth went to northern or eastern Europe. In 1386–7 even James St George and John Noldman, Dinant merchants, seem to have exported substantial quantities to the Baltic.

---

[85] To judge from figures given in A. R. Bridbury, *Medieval English Clothmaking: An Economic Survey* (London, 1982), appendix F, p. 118, Carus-Wilson and Coleman seem to have reduced the figures by 25 per cent to arrive at Hanse exports. This may be too much. Denizen exports at 1s (which can only be re-exports of foreign-made cloth illegally burdened with the 1303 custom) numbered only 15 in 1366–7 and 41 in 1371–2; alien imports in the former year were 118, but the trend was steeply downward.

Comparatively few merchants can be positively linked to specific towns, and the home ports of visiting ships are seldom given. From other sources it is known that Bergen trade was still dominated by Lübeck men and there is no doubt that this group ranked largest among Boston importers. In the long run there may have been a strong correlation between importers and cloth exporters, but within the shorter time-scale of surviving particulars the correlation is very variable. The same is true of the ships employed in these trades, so that no single account provides a picture which is entirely typical. Between 6 December 1383 and Michaelmas 1384 fifteen individuals (none of them ships' masters) imported Bergen goods to the value of £1,620, but only four recur among the twenty-five who in the same period exported cloth to the value of £2,253.[86] A second example shows that between 28 November 1386 and 28 November 1387 Bergen goods were imported to the value of £8,844, of which £894 were owned by ships' captains and sailors and the rest by forty-nine or fifty merchants.[87] Only nine of the latter appear among the seventeen Hanse merchants who exported cloth worth £4,407. Of the fifteen ships employed in the import trade only two obtained a cargo when they left; one entered 4 February and left 20 February with £2,499 of Hanse cloth, the other entered 16 February and left 1 April with £247 of Hanse cloth and £220 of denizen cloth; on 30 April the former of these left again with another ship, between them carrying Hanse cloth worth £1,828, no incoming voyage having been recorded for either of them on this occasion. A final example is provided by the account for Michaelmas 1390 – Michaelmas 1391.[88] Bergen imports worth £3,779 were owned by eighty-two merchants, save for £2 credited to a ship's captain. Cloth exporters numbered seventy-two, virtually all of whom appear also in the list of Bergen importers. Out of five ships which brought Bergen imports on 13 November, three left on 4 January and a fourth on 18 February with a total of 1,004 Hanse cloths and 312 worsteds, and 35 denizen cloths. On 4 April two of these same ships again appeared with Bergen imports and left on 8 and 18 May with 629 Hanse cloths and 135 worsteds, and 133 denizen cloths. Yet another made a return appearance on 1 August, possibly from the Baltic, and left again for the Baltic on 20 August with 270 denizen and 17 Hanse cloths. Despite the large number of merchants' names which may be culled

[86] PRO, E122/7/17.   [87] PRO, E122/7/19.   [88] PRO, E122/7/22–3.

from the Boston particulars it is likely that many of them seldom or never set foot in the town, their business being managed by factors or commission agents. In 1407, when writs of *venire facias* naming fifty-four Hanse merchants were sent to the sheriff of Lincolnshire, only seven came in person to defend themselves in the king's Chancery.[89] The headquarters of most of them, in so far as it was not in their home towns, was the Bergen *Kontor*, and this seems to have induced a reluctance to contribute the costs of the London Steelyard. However, in 1383 representatives of the *Bergenfahrer* and the alderman of the Boston *Kontor* met with Steelyard officials and the aldermen of the Hull and Yarmouth *Kontore* and agreed to pay scot to London.[90]

Relations between established members of the *Kontor* and the townsfolk of Boston were probably amicable and numbers of the former enrolled in local gilds and became benefactors of town churches. Competition between the two groups was limited on the import side, since Bostonians apparently made no attempt to break into the lucrative Norway trade, while they enjoyed a relatively free hand in the Baltic and the Low Countries. In the case of exports, denizens dispatched on average 750 cloths a year through Boston port in 1377–91 and 817 per annum in 1391–1402. All surviving particulars testify to the fact that the vast majority of this cloth was going to the Baltic and very little to the Low Countries or south-west Europe. The 1386–7 account, which exceptionally records the destinations of some outward bound vessels, shows that between August and October seven went to Bordeaux with wheat worth £304, but no cloth; two earlier sailings with £149 of wheat and no cloth may also have gone there. In 1390, however, a ship left with 16 cloths on 1 September and returned on 10 November with Gascon wine. The reliance of Boston-based cloth exporters on the Baltic was a cause of potential rivalry between them and the Hanse merchants, though in practice this may not have been serious. It is likely that most of the Hanse cloth was destined for markets in the western Baltic and, while some denizen cloth was undoubtedly going to this region, Bostonians were also exploring the Prussian market. When English-owned property was arrested in Prussia in 1385 the Boston share was less than that of any other port. One source gives a figure of £300 for Boston and Coventry goods, while another gives

---

[89] *HUB*, 5, no. 779.   [90] Lappenberg, *Urkundliche Geschichte*, 2, no. 41.

£206 11s 4d for twelve Boston men and £98 13s 4d for one from Coventry.[91] Several Coventry merchants can be identified in surviving Boston particulars. Prior to this incident, between 6 December 1383 and Michaelmas 1384 thirteen ships had imported east-Baltic wares to the value of £1,166 (23 per cent of all imports subject to poundage in that period). Only £74 was credited to ships' captains, among whom any denizens are not readily distinguishable from aliens, but most, and probably all, of the twenty-seven merchants who shared the remainder of the cargoes were denizens. Among them, with goods worth £269, were six of the Bostonians involved in the later Prussian seizures. The absence of Skanian herring from this account is not significant; the 1383 imports of herring may have appeared before 6 December; the main shipment of denizen cloth, £1,262 in one vessel in August 1384, was clearly synchronised with the next season's Skania fairs; seven of the Prussian 'arrestees' had cloth on this ship to the value of £273. No goods from the east Baltic were imported either by denizens or aliens between 28 November 1386 and 28 November 1387, during the Anglo-Prussian dispute, but the account covers part of two seasons of the Skania trade. In December 1386 three ships held herrings worth £608, of which £61 belonged to captains and crewmen and the rest to twenty-seven denizen merchants. In October and November 1387 two shipments worth £391 belonged to Hanseatics, but five others worth £651 belonged to twenty-one denizens, except for £57 credited to captains and crews. Two vessels which left on 15 August 1387 with cloth worth £1,044 belonging to eleven denizens and £381 to the Hansard John Noldman returned with herrings on 30 October, but of this group of exporters only Noldman and three of the denizens had returned any herrings by 28 November. Between Michaelmas 1390 and Michaelmas 1391, when Anglo-Prussian relations were back to normal, twenty-six denizens sent 487 cloths to the Baltic in January, February and May, but all went in company with Hansards in three ships employed in the Bergen trade, which may mean that they were going to the western Baltic. The next consignment, of 523 cloths belonging to thirteen from the previous group and fourteen new men, left on 20 August and one of the three ships now employed returned with herrings on 10 November. Any returns made by these cloth exporters later than 8 December 1391

[91] *HR*, 1 (iii), no. 404.

are not known, but twenty-nine denizens (including eight of the August contingent) shared ownership of herrings worth £494 imported on 10 November. In 1397–8 the chronological shipping and shipment pattern of denizen cloth exports was slightly greater than in earlier examples, but out of a total of 800 the most significant shipments were 160 in a Hanse ship in February, another of 87 in April and a total of 462 in five ships on 2 September, suggesting that the gearing of denizen trade to the Skania fairs was still significant.

The northern *Kontor* of the Hanse was at Hull, but as in the early fourteenth century there was some settlement in the hinterland. Henry Wyman, whose trade is recorded in many of Hull's customs particulars between 1378 and 1399, married a daughter of the mayor of York, became a freeman of the city in 1387, was granted denizen status the following year and was himself thrice mayor in the early fifteenth century.[92] Wyman's career was far from typical and must certainly have led to his renouncing membership of the Hanse. The scale of Hanse activity in Yorkshire must be deduced chiefly from totals of cloth exports. The first separately recorded figure in 1360–1 was 35, increasing to 62, 107 and 169 in the next three years, an average of 327 during the next two years, but then falling back to an average of 139 from 1366 to 1372. Between 1379 and 1391 they averaged 319 a year, but despite the inclusion of newly taxed straits declined to an average of 272 over the next eight years. Fragmentary tunnage and poundage accounts show that some straits as well as a few worsteds were regularly exported, but by far the greatest part of the cloth consisted of standard broadcloths of assise, typically valued at less than 30s each. Since the Hanse exported little but cloth, the value of this trade can be clearly defined. Identifying the origins of the merchants and putting a value on imports is hampered by the poor state of most of the surviving particulars. The earliest, 1378–9, shows that trade continued throughout the current crisis in Anglo-Hanseatic relations.[93] Cloth was exported despite the prospect of having to pay full alien rates, while eleven Hanse ships imported alien-owned herrings worth £200, general Baltic wares worth £193 and 16 cwt of wax; at least two other Hanse ships also appear in the heavily damaged export account. Four of these ships belonged to Lübeck, one to Kampen and the remainder were all Prussian, five from Danzig and one each from Elbing, Königsberg and Braunsberg.

[92] J. N. Bartlett, 'Some Aspects of the Economy of York in the Later Middle Ages, 1300–1550' (Ph.D. thesis, London, 1958), p. 456.   [93] PRO, E122/59/1.

The last particular of this period, for tunnage and poundage levied between Michaelmas 1398 and 15 September 1399, is the only one for a complete year which is almost perfect.[94] This was an exceptionally poor year in Hull's trade and details may therefore not be typical. Among the total of eighty-one incoming vessels were twelve Danzig and one Elbing ship, but none from other Hanse ports; only four of these found a cargo for their outward voyage, though one other Danzig ship is also recorded in the export section. Two Oslo-owned ships imported small cargoes, but there is no indication that Hull had any stake in the Bergen staple trade during this period.

Hanse merchants regularly imported goods from the Low Countries, and individual consignments, especially of battery and copper, were sometimes substantial, though they were an insignificant element in total imports from this region and a small part of total Hanse trade. Most Hanse trade was geared to the Baltic and the preponderance of Prussian ships, plus a disproportionately large element of ships' captains' trade, suggests that most of this was in the hands of the eastern bloc. Even so the greater part of the Baltic trade was firmly in the hands of denizens. Despite the attraction of the Prussian market for cloth exporters the possibility of some sale in the western Baltic cannot be ruled out, and the west provided more imports than the east. Yorkshiremen were the largest group among the Englishmen whose goods were seized in Prussia in 1385.[95] The first schedule of claims listed thirty separate items totalling £1,617 on behalf of thirty-three York merchants, and eleven totalling £306 for twelve Beverley men (though two of the latter seem actually to have been inhabitants of Hull). During negotiations the York details were somewhat altered and the agreed total reduced to £1,151 15s 1d, but Beverley submitted an extra claim and its total went up to £324 6s 8d. Additionally, a number of factors sojourning in Prussia on behalf of merchants of both towns submitted claims for alleged physical assaults. While Yorkshire merchants clearly valued trade with Prussia, it is dangerous to conclude that this was the principal market for the very substantial amounts of denizen-owned cloth shipped from Hull in the late fourteenth century. Although it is impossible to determine the proportions of exports going to different regions, much was undoubtedly going to Gascony. Those

---

[94] PRO, E122/159/11.   [95] *HR*, I (iii), no. 404.

who exported regularly through Hull spread their capital very widely and it is unlikely that there were many who were totally dependent upon the Baltic markets. In this respect Hull differs markedly from both Boston and Lynn.

The origin of all imports can be established more precisely than the destination of exports and, while a great deal came from the Low Countries, the parallel importance of the Baltic is beyond dispute. Prussia provided some imports but the greatest part generally consisted of Skania herrings. In 1398–9 the total value of Hull's imports, other than wine, was £3,550, of which £1,715 came from the Baltic. Englishmen imported herrings valued at £1,153 and Hanse merchants another £84. The non-herring trade, totalling £478, cannot be precisely allocated between each group, though Englishmen owned much of it. A clear demarcation exists in the case of shipping employed in the import trade. Seven English ships (Hull three, York two, Beverley one, Newcastle one) were loaded with nothing but herrings, while a second Beverley ship had both herring and a substantial volume of Prussian produce. Three Prussian ships (one freighted exclusively by Englishmen) carried only herrings, while ten others had no herrings and carried all the non-herring Baltic imports, save those in the Beverley ship. The conclusion, that northern English skippers sailed to the Baltic frequently, or usually, with little freight but secure in the knowledge of a return cargo of herrings, is amply borne out by the more fragmentary customs particulars of this period. Each year the number of denizen importers of herrings was numbered in scores or even hundreds, so that while most owned only a small amount the total volume was large and very valuable. This probably means that many importers were passive investors, without an intimate knowledge of the Baltic. The homogeneous character of salted herring bought by a commission agent or skipper in Skania obviously minimised risk. The investment pattern on the export side was not so simple, since the marketing of cloth was less straightforward and probably riskier. The possible business or financial relationships between cloth exporters and the much greater number of herring importers poses an intriguing question, but no light can be shed on the matter here. Most of the herrings were clearly for the home market but re-exports, chiefly to Gascony, provided Hull's main export after wool and cloth.

The third provincial Hanse *Kontor* at Yarmouth was largely monopolised by Hamburg merchants, and the withdrawal of this group in the early fifteenth century, which was recognised as a serious loss to the town, virtually put an end to Hanse trade in the port. The dominant role of Hamburg may be illustrated from the best of the few surviving tunnage and poundage accounts of this period, extending from 20 March to 26 December 1388.[96] On 15 May three Hamburg ships entered with typically northern goods valued at £1,218 and all left on 20 June with £1,344 in cloth and a little cheese; a fourth entered on 16 September with goods worth £276 and left on 18 October with £288 in cloth. Three other Hamburg ships appear as either inward or outward bound with small cargoes owned partly by their captains and partly by natives of Yarmouth. There was no shortage of vessels from other Hanse ports at Yarmouth but, unlike those of Hamburg which were associated with the regular trade of the *Kontor*, the former generally appear to have had a more casual role. Within the period under consideration a Danzig ship brought in £80 of German-owned Baltic goods in September and left with a small cargo of denizen strait cloth and red herrings; another left on Christmas Eve with a little denizen cloth; a Rostock ship came in with German-owned salt and canvas, no doubt from Brittany, and left with denizen salt and wheat; two Lübeck ships also left with small denizen cargoes. The dominant role and regular trade of Hamburg merchants is amply borne out by the town's local customs accounts, though the nature of the sources precludes quantification. Unfortunately, the king's petty custom at Yarmouth was farmed from July 1362 to the end of the fourteenth century. Before that the Hanse do not seem to have exported any cloths of assise, but had a thriving trade in worsteds and straits, manufactured in Norwich and the surrounding region. Because of the method of taxation, figures are not recorded.

While most of the goods imported by Hamburg merchants originated in the Baltic, the natives of Yarmouth may have been in something of a quandary about personal involvement in that region. The principal English return from there was herrings, but importing herrings to Yarmouth was the medieval equivalent of carrying coals to Newcastle. Although its greatest period of prosperity was already past, the town remained the chief centre of the English herring fishing and curing industry. Whether it was the decline of the North Sea fishery which led English merchants to go to Skania, or vice versa, Yarmouth must have regarded the Baltic fish as a detestable rival. On the other hand, the Baltic had proved itself as a market for cloth and the Norfolk industry could not and did not ignore it. Yarmouth itself was not involved in the attempt to reach a settlement with Prussia after 1385 but Norwich, for which Yarmouth was the outport, figures prominently. Fifteen merchants submitted claims totalling £938 for confiscated property, of which ten totalling £731 were accepted.[97]

Lynn was a nodal point in the burgeoning Anglo-Baltic trade, but there was no established Hanse *Kontor* in the port in the late fourteenth century. An explanation may lie in the fact that Lynn men were keen to exploit the trade on their own account and did not welcome Hanseatic merchants. They were also foremost among England's attack on the Hanse monopoly of Bergen trade. The merchants of Bremen, a town expelled from the Hanse organisation in 1275 and re-admitted only in 1358, were excepted from any general hostility. They were the only group which traded regularly, though modestly, at Lynn after establishing a connection in the early 1380s. In 1387 a Bremen ship making for Lynn inadvertently came ashore near Grimsby and, not being known locally, was placed under arrest. It was released after security was given to proceed to Lynn. The Lynn authorities in certifying the Exchequer of its arrival confirmed that the master and merchants had been coming regularly to the town for five years and more and were regarded as 'friends and well wishers of the king'.[98]

The claim for damages submitted by nineteen Lynn merchants in the aftermath of the arrests in Prussia in 1385 totalled £1,913 3s 4d, the largest of any town, though it was whittled away to £1,027 13s 3d.[99] Undeterred, many of these men continued to trade there and figure prominently in the surviving customs particulars of the 1390s, which prove that the town was staking its prosperity on the Baltic and Norway markets. Between 1 April 1390 and Michaelmas 1391 forty-three of Lynn's own ships entered the port with cargoes from foreign parts;[100] eight brought wine from Gascony, five salt (probably from the Bay) and two lampreys; this leaves two from Norway with stockfish (£653), four from Skania with herrings (£1,355) and twenty-two with general Baltic goods (£1,503). But the town's own ships by no means sufficed to carry all the goods

[97] *HR*, I (iii), no. 404. [98] *CCR*, 1385–9, p. 600. [99] *HR*, I (iii), no. 404.
[100] PRO, E122/93/31; 94/12.

imported by its merchants and they had to charter an even larger
number of foreign vessels for their exclusive, or nearly exclusive, use.
In the former category four vessels (Danzig two, Wismar one,
Osterdam one) carried stockfish from Norway (£1,180) and five
(Danzig one, Wismar one, Hamburg two and Brill one) herring from
Skania (£1,742). As in the case of English ships, a greater number
of foreign vessels was needed to carry a smaller (by value) amount
of general Baltic wares, forty-one bringing goods worth £2,313.
Because of damage to the account, this last figure cannot be precisely
divided into English and Hanseatic, but well over 90 per cent was
English owned, with the rest belonging to captains and crewmen.
Most of the ships carrying this general cargo were Prussian (Danzig
twenty-five, Elbing one), with contributions from Bremen (two),
Hamburg (three), Wismar (four), Stralsund (two), Kampen (one)
and Veere (three). In comparison with this English trade exclusively
Hanseatic ventures were few and far between. The only significant
entries were two shiploads (£414) belonging to the Bremen group,
and a Lübeck ship with £136 of cargo owned by a single merchant;
four other vessels (Hamburg two, Wismar one, Stettin one) had
cargo worth a total value of only £25. Finally, mention may be
made of two Hanse ships importing salt from the Bay, one (Wismar)
for English merchants and one (Königsberg) the property of the
captain. A petty custom account for 12 February 1396 to 17
February 1397[101] confirms that the Bremen group was still active at
Lynn, bringing in one ship with a cargo valued at £193. Fourteen
other ships contained alien-owned Baltic goods though only one had
a significantly high value (£93); most or all doubtless carried
English-owned goods; only six ships are identified by their home
port (five Danzig, one Osterdam).[102] A Bergen (Norway) ship with
a small alien cargo was probably also chartered by Lynn merchants.
The picture of Lynn as a town heavily dependent on Baltic trade is
amply confirmed by the surviving export particulars of this period.
Between 30 November 1390 and Michaelmas 1391 only five Lynn
ships left the port with any goods other than cloth, though all carried
cloth as well (cloth £190, other wares £145).[103] Since all carried re-
exported northern goods, these were obviously not bound for the
Baltic; the most likely destinations were Gascony or Calais. In the
same period seventeen Lynn ships sailed with nothing but cloth, to

[101] PRO, E122/94/16.
[102] The identification of Osterdam is uncertain. Its skippers sometimes paid Hanse rates,
which seems to rule out Amsterdam.   [103] PRO, E122/94/13.

a total value of £3,265. While we cannot be certain that all these vessels were bound for the Baltic, there is no doubt that the majority were going there. Out of ten ships which left between 27 January and 7 May six returned with Baltic goods within the period of this account, one on 20 May and five (including one which left as late as 7 May) on 26 June; on their outward leg these six ships had carried cloth valued at £1,432. Of the remaining seven ships, four left on 10 August with cloth worth £1,231; had we a particular for the period after Michaelmas we would doubtless find some or all of these ships returning with herrings. In addition to the cloth which they sent to the Baltic in their own vessels, Lynn merchants dispatched cloth worth £597 and 7 tuns of wine in seven Danzig and three Wismar bottoms, in which they were virtually the sole shippers. Using the same criterion of Lynn ships laden only with cloth as primary suspects for the Baltic trade, in the period 22 February 1392 to 28 January 1393 we find seventeen ships carrying cloth to the value of £1,821, of which eight with more than £80 each accounted for £1,555.[104] In addition Lynn merchants dispatched cloth to the value of £1,670 in thirteen exclusively chartered Hanse ships (Danzig nine, Kampen two, Lübeck one, Elbing one). Lynn's stake in the Gascony/Calais trade in this period was substantially greater than before, though chiefly on account of grain exports, which totalled something like £900; cloth sent there came to just over £300, with small amounts of herrings, haberdashery, rice and a few other goods. This trade occupied eleven of Lynn's own ships together with four chartered from Yarmouth, Danzig, Greifswald and Stralsund. A few Lynn men also sent very small amounts of cloth to the Low Countries in Dutch ships. Finally, we may note the evidence of a petty custom particular, 12 February 1396 to 17 February 1397, in which cloth exports are recorded by number but not by value.[105] This was a disastrous period in Lynn's overseas trade and there can be no doubt that this is to be explained by the mass arrest of English ships in Danzig between February and August 1396.[106] In these twelve months denizens dispatched 153 cloths and 17 worsteds (which cannot have been worth more than £300) in nine Lynn ships and one from Newcastle; these ships may or may not have carried other goods, but are unlikely to have been going to Prussia. On the other hand Lynn merchants did commit 100 cloths and 68 worsteds to four Danzig ships. The only remaining denizen cloth exports in

[104] PRO, E122/94/14.   [105] PRO, E122/94/16.   [106] See above p. 74.

this period were 8 in a Bergen (Norway) ship and 28 in two Dutch ships. The conclusion to be drawn from these particulars is that Lynn merchants sent their cloth overwhelmingly to the Baltic, chiefly to Prussia. They did not much cultivate other markets, so that when there was trouble in Prussia exports were bound to suffer. Because of the practice of customs farming, the Exchequer enrolled accounts have no record of denizen-export totals from Lynn until Michaelmas 1394. Between then and Michaelmas 1399 (but excluding February 1396 to February 1397, with a total of only 289) the average denizen export was 1,602 per annum.

Hanseatic-owned cloth exports from Lynn averaged 200 a year between April 1392 and Michaelmas 1399 and the total is unlikely to have been any higher in the earlier period of customs farming. The modesty of the figure is explicable by the fact that only the Bremen merchants exported regularly, while the balance consisted of a small-scale, casual trade largely in the hands of captains and crewmen. In the period 30 November 1390 to Michaelmas 1391 this Bremen group exported cloth valued at £193 in one ship, in February 1392 to January 1393 £258 in two ships, in February 1396 to February 1397 111 cloths and 23 worsteds in one ship. In the same three periods the total cloth exports of other Hanse merchants was £25, £50 and 99 cloths, spread over six ships which also held denizen-owned cloth and fourteen which did not, while the total of twenty was a minority of all Hanse vessels leaving the port.

Surveying briefly the remaining English ports we find that at Newcastle Hanse cloth exports were few and far between, and in the 1390s still averaged no more than 21 per annum. On the other hand a fair number of surviving particulars prove that cloth figures are not here a reliable guide to overall Hanse trade since, exceptionally, the value of other exports frequently exceeded that of cloth. There was also a regular and not insubstantial import trade. Newcastle-owned ships occasionally ventured to the Baltic, but there is little to show that the town's merchants made much contribution to the English eastward thrust. Ipswich is something of an unknown factor in this period, since its petty custom was farmed with that of Yarmouth until the beginning of the fifteenth century. One of the members of this port was Colchester, an important cloth-making town from which three merchants submitted claims totalling £104 for losses in Prussia in 1385; £43 was proven.[107] A Hadleigh (Suffolk) merchant

---

[107] *HR*, I (iii), no. 404.

who claimed £67 also probably traded through Colchester or Ipswich. No Hanse merchants appear in two short tunnage and poundage accounts of the 1380s, but a cargo of herrings worth £191 imported by seven denizens in a Zierikzee ship on 6 December 1386 is at the right time of year to have come from Skania. A longer account for 1397–8 shows both denizens and Hanse merchants importing a wide variety of Baltic wares, but the scale of the trade was still comparatively modest.[108] At this time Gascony was probably a more important market than the Baltic for the Essex–Suffolk cloth industry and there is as yet no trace of the links with the fairs of the Low Countries, which were to develop a few decades later.[109] The enrolled customs accounts of Sandwich record infrequent and very small quantities of cloth being exported by Hanse merchants, while surviving particulars show that other trade was negligible before the end of the fourteenth century. Only at Southampton among the south-coast ports do the merchants seem to have made an effort to gain a trading foothold. The first recorded cloth exports were in 1382 and from then until 1399 averaged about 20 a year, though there were long periods without any. By chance, a customs particular survives for the year with the largest export (1390–1).[110] Of the total of 114 short-cloths, 12 were taken by one merchant in a Southampton vessel, 89 by six in an Elbing ship and 13 by two in a Lübeck ship. The Hanse may have been less interested in Southampton for cloth than as a potential market for herrings. Kampen ships had brought substantial quantities to the port at least as early as 1371–2[111] and the merchants tried to maintain the trade until well into the fifteenth century, despite the burden of local tolls which they complained were illegally levied against them. The only suggestion of any local interest in the Baltic is provided by the claims of a half-dozen Salisbury merchants for losses totalling £134 in Prussia in 1385 and a Winchester man for £43.[112] These probably exported through Southampton. There was no regular Hanse trade at the ports between Sandwich and Southampton or in any of those in the west country. Very occasionally a Hanse shipmaster ventured a cargo of salt to Bristol, and while such illustrations might be multiplied if all the customs records had survived intact, the total would remain negligible. The Hanse interest in England was overwhelmingly

---

[108] PRO, E122/50/30–2; 193/33.
[109] R. H. Britnell, *Growth and Decline in Colchester, 1300–1525* (Cambridge, 1986), pp. 54–71.
[110] PRO, E122/193/25.   [111] PRO, E122/137/19.
[112] *HR*, I (iii), no. 404.

directed at London and a handful of east-coast ports and the historian does not need to waste much time looking elsewhere.

To conclude this chapter an attempt will be made to set Anglo-Hanseatic trade into the general context of England's overseas trade in the second half of the fourteenth century, and to compare the achievements of Hansards and their English rivals not merely with one another, but also with those of other aliens and of English merchants whose ambitions did not extend to the Baltic and Norway. During this period the historian is able to cast his net more widely than before. Sources are enhanced by records of English-made cloth exports after 1347 and by accounts of tunnage and poundage, levied intermittently from that date and almost continuously from 1386. The importance of these is that for the first time they offer the possibility of studying the trade of Englishmen in commodities other than wool and hides. They do not give up their secrets easily, particularly poundage which in its enrolled form does not distinguish between denizen and alien trade. But by comparing one type of record with another and with the help of judicious estimates it is possible to gain some indication of the size of denizen trade.

The outstanding characteristic of England's overseas trade in the late fourteenth century is the beginning of the long drawn out decline in exports of raw wool. In the 1350s and early 1360s this trade enjoyed an Indian summer, during which exports averaged over 33,000 sacks a year, the best performance since the first decade of the century. Then the trade ebbed and by the 1380s and 1390s exports were running at fewer than 18,000 sacks a year. Despite intense debate it has been impossible for historians to agree on the causes of the decline.[113] Some of the consequences are beyond dispute. What was left of the trade fell largely into the hands of Englishmen, aliens being excluded by the politics of the staple. Only Italian merchants managed to hold on to a share. Hansards, who for a time in the early fourteenth century had been the largest alien group in the trade, were ousted completely. That they were able to weather the economic and financial consequences and retain an important stake in England's trade was no mean achievement. On the other hand one should not make too much of their astuteness in replacing wool exports with cloth; they were not unique in this.

---

[113] Lloyd, *Wood Trade*, pp. 314–16. Bridbury, *English Clothmaking*, pp. 90–7.

The growth of cloth exports is the second main characteristic of England's trade in this period. E. M. Carus-Wilson long ago provided an account of this development which became an orthodoxy.[114] She outlined a resurgence of native industry in the middle years of the fourteenth century, which displaced imported cloth in the home market and began to penetrate overseas markets. Interrupted by set-backs and periods of stagnation, growth in exports was slow until the 1380s, while in the 1390s there was an unprecedented boom. It is not disputed here that there was growth in the 1390s and a possible contributory factor will be discussed later. On the other hand it is suggested that the contrast between the earlier and later periods has been exaggerated by selective use of the sources. This *caveat* applies to exports as a whole and sectional shares. Carus-Wilson, for instance, wrote that cloth exports 'of the Hanse, still only 2,700 in the early 1380s, reached 6,300 in the early 1390s'.[115] This gives a very misleading picture of the true situation. The distortion has arisen from the tendency to measure the growth in exports simply from the receipts of the custom levied on cloths of assise. In the 1390s these were artificially increased by the inclusion of kerseys and straits (converted to notional assise cloths), which previously had not paid custom (though liable to poundage subsidy) when exported by Englishmen, and had paid a different sort of custom when exported by aliens and Hansards. Equally distorting is the fact that for some time after mid-century exports of worsteds (never incorporated in the assise cloth custom) were important, whereas by the 1390s they were very much smaller. These observations are not new, indeed Carus-Wilson herself was aware of them, but in her general assessment of export performance she pushed them into the background, and since then the tendency has been to overlook them completely. What they mean, however, is that cloth exports in the second half of the fourteenth century cannot be measured with great precision and the generally accepted picture to some extent distorts the truth.

Given the uncertainty about cloth exports, alien trade as a whole is best measured by the petty custom of 3d in the pound on the value of merchandise other than wool, hides, wine, wax and cloths of assise. This takes in exports, including all cloths other than those of

---

[114] E. M. Carus-Wilson, 'Trends in the Export of English Woollens in the Fourteenth Century', in *Medieval Merchant Venturers* (2nd edn, London, 1967), pp. 239–64.

[115] *Ibid.*, p. 258.

Table 3. Alien merchandise^a charged at 3d in the pound and wax imports, 1351–99

	All England		London		East coast		South and west coasts	
	Merchandise (£)	Wax (cwt)	Merchandise (£)	Wax (cwt)	Merchandise (£)	Wax (cwt)	Merchandise (£)	Wax (cwt)
Mich.–Mich.								
1351–2	17,955	21	8,244	16	8,206	5	1,505	0
1352–3	30,972	443	18,288	324	10,079	19	2,605	100
1353–4	37,955	490	16,586	288	16,420	202	4,949	0
1354–5	27,539	433	12,992	395	11,861	34	2,686	4
1355–6	37,189	140	19,179	125	13,980	15	4,030	0
1356–7	53,199	566	29,530	444	18,503	116	5,166	6
1357–8	48,283	575	24,137	555	19,160	20	4,986	0
1358–9	48,421	1,212	29,017	1,083	16,687	127	2,717	2
1359–60	48,290	603	28,126	599	17,204	0	2,960	4
1360–1	40,329	670	25,833	629	12,589	41	1,907	0
1361–2	46,972	229	27,012	213	16,878	16	3,082	0
1362–3	44,575	493	24,240	445	18,958	48	1,377	0
1363–4	52,229	425	32,855	398	15,578	27	3,616	0
1364–5	59,749	701	39,274	641	17,885	60	2,590	0
1365–6	67,886	857	39,539	785	24,609	61	3,738	11
1366–7	63,910	511	45,590	446	14,500	65	3,820	0
1367–8	65,305	1,213	45,628	1,082	17,001	131	2,676	0
1368–9	58,887	1,093	46,277	1,015	9,290	78	3,320	0
1369–70	62,750	1,120	42,738	1,035	18,989	85	1,023	0
1370–1	63,890	1,024	44,597	972	17,864	52	1,429	0
1371–2	94,790	1,762	69,160	1,605	20,674	157	4,956	0

1375–6			45,298	170				
1376–7			43,987	119				
1377–8			46,822	0	13,561	35	7,263	0
1378–9	66,888	35	39,919	2	19,706	33	5,601	0
1379–80	70,659	214	45,588	186	19,470	26	4,977	8
1380–1	68,414	578	47,271	516	16,166	54	14,897	0
1381–2	82,625	572	47,868	501	19,860	71	19,142	45
1382–3	74,152	383	39,814	300	15,196	38	14,060	19
1383–4	72,308	999	44,721	929	13,527	51	14,465	314
1384–5	69,350	1,014	36,005	675	18,880	25	10,791	327
1385–6	72,696	680	45,410	314	16,495	39	10,464	210
1386–7	67,962	301	40,118	67	17,380	24	11,302	126
1387–8	62,236	164	43,763	30	7,171	8	12,255	42
1388–9	85,560	570	54,421	439	18,884	89	8,940	48
1389–90	70,130	652	47,953	595	14,369	9	7,808	100
1390–1	64,380	555	44,232	433	12,340	22	8,343	435
1391–2	64,049	1,421	44,307	925	11,399	61	10,896	190
1392–3	66,342	848	42,990	602	12,456	56	5,925	66
1393–4	57,524	269	39,938	171	11,661	32	14,916	43
1394–5	72,448	528	44,097	427	13,435	58	11,763	15
1395–6					13,654	33		
1396–7			32,530^b	229^b	13,600	5	12,608	20
1397–8	51,652	269	34,272	188	9,180	3	8,200	78
1398–9	54,637	262	26,405	127	12,603	37	15,629	98

a Incorporates estimates for some gaps in accounts. Margin of error in totals is not significant. Gaps in this table are caused by customs farming or other gaps in accounts which are too serious to allow estimates.
b 10 Dec. 1396—Mich. 1397.

assise, but the bulk of it consisted of imports. Table 3 shows that from 1351 to the mid-1360s trade increased continuously and rapidly and then more or less stabilised at a level well in excess of £60,000 a year. The increase was most spectacular at London, which by the 1360s handled between two-thirds and three-quarters of all alien trade. Business at east-coast ports, predominantly Hanse, was many times that of the south and west where Hanse trade was insignificant. The petty custom of all England was farmed from Christmas 1372 to 1375, but full returns for most ports are not available for several years after the latter date. By the 1380s the general level of trade had increased again and fluctuated between £70,000 and £80,000 a year. This time the increase was concentrated at Southampton, which accounts for more than 90 per cent of the figures given for the south- and west-coast ports. The explanation is that civil war in Flanders between 1379 and 1385 caused Italian merchants to divert trade to the Hampshire port, and they chose to remain there even when more peaceful times returned to the Low Countries. West of England cloth replaced some of that previously bought in Flanders and there was a ready market for imports, including Genoese alum needed by the expanding English cloth industry.[116] During the 1390s receipts of the 3d custom fell back and the last two or three years of Richard II's reign have the appearance of depression, most noticeably at London. It has to be remembered that the change in the tax structure (1391) which increased the yield of the 1347 custom at the same time decreased that of the 3d custom by absolving some cloth exports from paying the latter duty.[117] Nevertheless, there is a distinct possibility that in the 1390s a decline in alien imports coincided with a real increase in alien cloth exports. How is this to be explained? Serious thought should be given as to whether any part of the change resulted from current English bullion legislation.

Bullion laws were first enacted in the early 1340s and required both alien and denizen merchants to import a specified quantity of coin or plate for each sack of wool exported. The immediate cause was a serious shortage of coin within the country, brought about by recent interruptions of the wool trade and the king's export of money to subsidise foreign allies. In the 1350s there was a great turn-around

---

[116] A. Ruddock, *Italian Merchants and Shipping in Southampton, 1270–1600* (Southampton, 1951), p. 49.

[117] At London the transfer of kerseys from one account to the other would alone have caused a fall of several thousand pounds in the value of goods charged with 3d.

as the boom in wool exports and the successful prosecution of the war brought silver flooding into the country and new money pouring out of the mint (see table 4). Thereafter the tide slowly ebbed again. The trade balance dwindled but overall probably remained positive. What is true of the whole, however, is not necessarily true of all parts. Aliens increased their imports and therefore had more money to repatriate, but at the same time ground lost in the wool trade deprived them of opportunities for doing so. Their cloth exports did not yet suffice to fill the gap. Alien trade may well have been out of balance, with an import surplus being financed by letters of exchange, the export of specie being prohibited. By 1379 parliament was sufficiently disturbed by a deterioration in the balance of trade to enact a new bullion law, though this was limited to the period which should elapse until the meeting of the next parliament, and it was not then renewed.[118] The parliament which sat from November 1381 to February 1382 appointed a commission to advise it on monetary matters. One consequence was a permanent ban on the export of money by exchange. The new law proved to be too severe and in the next parliament it was amended to allow the use of exchange in commerce. A joint petition of the commons and Italian bankers claimed that letters of exchange were essential to the smooth operation of the wool trade. There was no further action on monetary matters until December 1390, when a parliament still uneasy about exchange effected a compromise with aliens. New legislation, generally termed an employment act, permitted the latter to transmit half the proceeds from the sale of imports by exchange, but commanded them to buy English goods for export with the balance. Furthermore, this parliament ordered that the staple be removed from Calais to England and by forbidding denizens to export wool created a monopoly for aliens. One of the intentions of the latter step may have been to provide aliens with the means of legally repatriating proceeds of import sales. For denizen merchants the cure proposed for the country's monetary ills was worse than the disease and in November 1391 they were re-admitted to the wool trade. It might be logical to assume that when their short-lived monopoly of wool exports was removed aliens had to increase other exports, i.e. primarily cloth, or reduce imports (or a combination of

---

[118] Lloyd, *Wood Trade*, pp. 242–4. T. H. Lloyd, 'Overseas Trade and the English Money Supply in the Fourteenth Century', in N. J. Mayhew (ed.), *Edwardian Monetary Affairs* (British Arch. Soc. Reports, 36, Oxford, 1977), pp. 96–127.

Table 4. English mint output, 1303–99

| Period of account[a] | Silver | | | | Gold | | | | | |
| | Weight of coin (pounds) | | Origin of bullion[b] | Composition of coin[c] | London Weight of coin (pounds) | | Calais Weight of coin (pounds) | | Aggregate values in money of account (£ sterling) | |
	Total	Annual average			Total	Annual average	Total	Annual average	Total	Annual average
1303–9	634,381	105,730	99 % F	P99 % F1 % Hnegligible					642,362	107,060
9 Oct. 1311–21	259,705	25,971	99 % F	P98 % F2 % Hnegligible					263,009	26,300
7 Oct. 1322–4	3,826	1,913	E negligible	P91 % F9 % Hnegligible					3,878	1,939
1324–7 May 1335	4,882	461	51 % E	P26 % H1 % F73 %					4,937	466
7 May 1335–41	10,865	2,006	83 % E	H54 % F46 % PNil					11,449	2,114
1341–15 Dec. 1343	22,496	10,187	94 % F	H97 % F3 % PNil					23,620	10,696
20 Jan. 1344–5	57,231	34,339		All P	3,448	2,069			111,185	66,711
1345–24 June 1351	37,521	6,525		P20 % H77 % F3 %	9,810	1,706			180,387	31,372
24 June 1351–8 Apr. 1357	299,445	52,077			29,444	5,121			815,966	141,907
8 Apr. 1357–11 Feb. 1363	48,476	8,310			46,451	7,963			757,360	129,833
11 Feb. 1363–8	10,045	1,786			7,712	1,371	18,803[d]	3,406	410,281	72,939
1368–73	3,926	785			9,786	1,957	9,165[e]	1,767	289,172	57,834
1373–84	13,298	1,209			4,264	388	2,927[f]	266	124,487	11,317
1384–9	2,901	580			4,115	823	2,170[g]	635	97,888	19,578
1389–10 Oct. 1399	7,274	727			11,469	1,147	3,960[h]	410	249,536	24,053

[a] All periods of account start and end at Michaelmas (29 Sept.) except where stated otherwise.
[b] F = foreign coin, E = English.
[c] P = pence, H = halfpence, F = farthings.

[d] To 27 Aug. 1368.
[e] To 17 Jan. 1390.

[g] 27 Aug. 1368–4 Nov. 1373.
[h] 17 Jan. 1390–25 Aug. 1399.

[f] From 4 Nov. 1373.

both) in order to comply with the employment act. Some individuals may have been obliged to react in this manner, but the proposition cannot be substantiated for aliens as a whole. In aggregate they so over-subscribed to the requirement of the employment act that one must conclude either that it was enormously successful or was not necessary in the first place. An estimate of their trade (table 5) between 1391 and 1399 suggests that aliens imported values of around £70,000 and exported values of £66,000, a deficit of only 6 per cent of imports. Given the inevitably wide margins of error involved in the estimate, the deficit may easily have been less.[119] One of the biggest problems in determining the size of alien trade is the difficulty of obtaining reliable figures of non-Hanse alien cloth exports for the whole of Richard II's reign. The estimate given above uses the conventionally accepted figures, but it is possible that they are too low.[120] If that were the case then the value of alien exports would have to be increased and the deficit reduced.

Given the uncertainty about the spread of cloth exports between denizens and aliens in the 1380s and 1390s, it is even more hazardous to compare the overall trade of the two groups than it is to speculate about the alien balance of trade, but the task cannot be avoided. The exercise depends primarily on comparing total values of goods subject to poundage subsidy (everything except wool, hides and wine) with those of alien goods paying the petty custom. The first year, and for a long time the only one, in which this can be done is 1371–2. Table 6 shows the stages which lead to the conclusion that

[119] An increase in the estimated value of wool by £1 per sack would virtually eliminate the deficit.

[120] It is impossible to give an exact picture of non-Hanse alien cloth exports in this period because of accounting methods at London and Southampton, which between them handled almost all such cloth. At the former port denizen cloth can be distinguished from alien in only five years during Richard II's reign (1377–81, 1384–5); at the latter they are not separated in 1391–5. Carus-Wilson claimed 'considerable precision' (*Merchant Venturers*, p. 264) for her estimated division into denizen and alien at times when this is not given in the source. Nevertheless, the result is suspicious. This conclusion is based on a comparison of denizen performance in various ports before and after 1391. Using the *EET* figures, denizen exports for all England averaged 15,519 in 1379–91 and 23,487 in 1391–9 (but excluding 1395–6) – an increase of 51 per cent. There are only three important outlets (Hull, Bristol and Boston) where accounts survive for the whole period and also distinguish between denizen and alien. Their aggregate denizen export averaged 8,892 before 1391 and 9,384 thereafter – an increase of only 6 per cent. This implies that in the remaining ports (but overwhelmingly London) trade increased by 83 per cent. Such a regional disparity in performance is possible, but is it likely? The alternative is that Carus-Wilson overestimated denizen trade in London and underestimated that of aliens. In that event the improvement in other alien cloth exports in the 1390s was greater than implied by the conventionally accepted figures. How much of this was due to the employment act?

Table 5. *An estimate of the alien trade balance, 1391–9*
(annual average)[a]

Imports (£)		Exports (£)	
Merchandise[b]	54,998	Merchandise[b]	6,111
Wax[c]	1,200	Cloths of assise[e]	32,511
Wine[d]	13,845	Wool[f]	27,200
Total	70,043		65,822
		Import surplus £4,221	

[a] Excluding all data 1395–7, because of gap in London petty custom account.
[b] Merchandise charged at 3d in £. Split 90:10, imports:exports.
[c] 600 cwt valued at £2.
[d] 2,769 tuns valued at £5. Alien imports recorded only 1392–5, when they amounted to 15·4% of denizen plus alien total. That proportion applied to denizen plus alien total in other years.
[e] 17,058 valued at 35s Hanse, 40s other alien.
[f] 3,400 sacks valued at £8, including custom and subsidy.

the total value of commodities in denizen trade (other than wool, hides and wine) was around £113,000, compared with an alien value of about £105,000. The removal of cloths of assise gives figures of £100,000 and £98,000 respectively (largely imports, but with some exports). Denizens tended to export more miscellaneous goods than aliens, so it may be predicted that the latter led in the import field. On the other hand it cannot be stressed too strongly that this was a highly exceptional year, in which alien trade was by far and away the largest recorded in the fourteenth century. It was 50 per cent higher than that of the preceding six record-breaking years. Denizen trade cannot be compared with earlier periods, but this was a disastrous year for Englishmen. The renewal of war with France in 1369 had already disrupted trade with Gascony and Spain. This year (1371–2) wine imports were a paltry 5,998 tuns (4,795 denizen, 1,203 alien). Worse still, in August 1371 a simmering dispute with Flanders flared up, with arrests of goods and merchants on each side followed by a prolonged stoppage of trade between the two countries.[121] Dislocation in the wool trade lasted even longer than the breach with Flanders. The English government withdrew its

[121] Lloyd, *Wool Trade*, pp. 217–21. D. Nicholas, 'The English Trade at Bruges in the Last Years of Edward III', *Journal of Medieval History*, 5 (1979), pp. 23–61.

Table 6. *An estimate of denizen and alien trade (excluding wool, hides and wine), 1371–2*

	£	£	£
Total value of goods liable to poundage[a]	217,726		
Value of alien merchandise paying 3d[b]	94,790		
Denizen goods plus alien assise cloth and wax		122,936	
Value of alien assise cloth[c]		6,420	
Value of alien wax[d]		3,524	
Denizen goods			112,992
Value of denizen assise cloth[c]			12,583
Denizen imports and exports, excluding assise cloth			100,409

[a] London, 28 Oct. 1371–28 Oct. 1372. Provinces, 1 Nov. 1371–1 Nov. 1372.
[b] Mich. 1371–Mich. 1372.
[c] Denizen 8,388½, Hanse 2,015¼, alien 2,265½. Valued at 30s. Newcastle, Hull, Boston, Queensborough, Bristol, Exeter (12 Nov. 1371–25 Dec. 1372), Melcombe (28 Mar. 1371–Mich. 1372), London.
[d] Valued at £2 per cwt.

support for the monopoly of the Calais staple and there was a substantial, though temporary, increase in alien wool exports. Unfortunately, in this critical year the accounts of the main ports fail to distinguish between denizen and alien wool so that precise figures cannot be provided. From Christmas 1372 both the petty custom and the tunnage and poundage subsidy began to be farmed, but there is no doubt that trade generally continued to be depressed, with aliens benefiting at the expense of denizens.

Table 7 provides information similar to that in table 6 for the years 1391–9.[122] A definitive peace treaty with France was not made until 1396, but this whole period was peaceful and international conditions conducive to trade. Nevertheless, the average value of goods paying poundage was 11 per cent lower than in the disastrous year 1371–2; denizens had around £98,000 and aliens £95,000. Even more revealingly, when the values of assise cloths are deleted (leaving mainly imports), the figures become denizen £57,000 and

[122] Excluding figures for 1395–7, because of 14½ month gap in London petty custom account.

Table 7. *An estimate of the denizen trade balance, 1391–9*
(annual average)[a]

	£		£		£
Total value of goods liable to poundage	192,952				
Value of all alien goods liable to poundage	94,820				
Denizen goods liable to poundage			98,132		
Value of denizen cloth[b]			40,978		
Value of denizen general imports and exports					57,154

	£			£
Denizen general imports[c]	51,438	General exports[c]		5,715
Denizen wine[d]	75,975	Cloth[b]		40,978
		Wool[e]		120,000
Totals	127,413			166,693

Export surplus £39,280

[a] Excluding all data 1395–7. [b] 23,416 valued at 35s.
[c] Split 90:10, imports:exports. [d] 15,195 tuns valued at £5.
[e] 15,000 sacks valued at £8.

alien £62,000. After due allowance is made for the transfer of some alien cloth from the 3d account to the 1347 account it is clear that alien imports, though substantially lower than those of the 1380s, were not much below those of the late 1360s. On the other hand, no such allowance needs to be made for denizen cloth. We are left with a denizen figure which is little more than half of that of 1371–2 and by implication even worse in relation to denizen trade prior to 1369. Can denizen trade have deteriorated so much?[123] However wide the margin of error it is difficult to escape the conclusion that in the late fourteenth century general imports into England declined substantially, with the bulk of the loss being borne by denizen merchants. In contrast the wine trade in the 1390s was fairly buoyant, imports averaging 17,635 tuns a year and denizens

[123] An alternative scenario is even more untenable. This is that before 1369 denizens imported little merchandise because they were bringing in so much bullion, but in 1371–2 imported less bullion and more goods. This is unacceptable because of the indisputable and massive increase in alien imports in 1371–2. Were it so then total imports in 1371–2 would have been far higher than in the 1360s, which is impossible.

handling around 85 per cent of the total.[124] The decline in wool exports was temporarily halted and denizens finally vindicated their claim to a near monopoly of the trade. Denizen earnings from wool and cloth exports comfortably exceeded their outlay on wine and other imports. Ideally, the balance should have been repatriated in specie, and a bullion law was intended to bring this about. The fact that the output of English mints, though but a fraction of that in the 1350s and 1360s, was rising again during the late 1380s and 1390s suggests that the law may have been partially successful. On the other hand the rigid bullionist policy maintained by Burgundy, England's principal trading partner, made it impractical for Englishmen to bring all their profits home in specie.[125] It was for this reason that aliens importing to England were allowed to export up to half of the proceeds by exchange.[126] This was a necessary corollary to Englishmen's having to repatriate some of their overseas earnings by exchange. Net earnings of Englishmen more than covered the export deficit of aliens and the nation's balance of trade remained positive, though much less than in the heady days of the 1350s and 1360s.

If it were possible to break down alien trade into Hanse and non-Hanse components the former could be compared more directly with the trade of Englishmen, but this can be done only in the case of cloth exports. On the basis of the figures used above, between 1379 and 1391 denizens owned 66 per cent of total cloth, Hansards 13 per cent and other aliens 21 per cent; from 1391 to 1399 the shares were 58 per cent, 16 per cent and 26 per cent. The Hanse share of all trade was obviously less, since they now exported no wool and imported little wine. In the absence of more detailed figures, but drawing upon earlier descriptions, the conclusion must be that at this time Hansards were probably not a major threat to the livelihoods of English merchants and certainly not the main threat. Leaving aside the Mediterranean, the geographical pattern of England's trade may be divided roughly into three. In the south-west (Iberia, Gascony) there seems to have been a tendency to mark time and in

---

[124] Total import figures survive for all years, but the denizen/alien ratio only for 1392–5.

[125] J. H. Munro, *Wool, Cloth and Gold: The Struggle for Bullion in Anglo-Burgundian Trade, 1340–78* (Toronto, 1973), pp. 43–63. Munro's figures for English mint production have to be corrected by figures given in Lloyd, *English Money Supply*, p. 119. But it should be noted that the latter wrongly noted a gap in the Calais mint accounts (the figures themselves are complete).

[126] Unless the English could wrest more of the import trade away from aliens.

any event there is no question of Anglo-Hanse competition here. In trade with the Low Countries Englishmen may have lost ground to aliens, but while the Hansards had some share their role was as yet relatively small. On the other hand, in the Baltic where Hansards were their direct and principal rivals Englishmen put up a better performance than they did anywhere else in this period. Starting from little or nothing in the middle of the fourteenth century they built up a substantial export and import trade. In terms of strictly Anglo-Baltic trade (i.e. disregarding the Hanse imports from Norway) Englishmen appear to have been the more successful of the two groups. Here they established the first English trade organisation after the Fellowship of the Staple – and that in the face of local hostility. One suspects that some of England's most enterprising merchants must have been involved in these ventures. Earlier, credit was given to Hanse merchants for retaining a niche in England after being driven out of the wool trade. Surely the Englishmen deserve greater plaudits for their achievement.

CHAPTER 3

Jockeying for advantage, 1400–1437

In the fifteenth century the defence of the Hanseatic franchises became more important than ever, in the light of increasingly stringent parliamentary legislation directed against alien merchants. Although not continuously enforced, this posed an ever-present threat to individuals and groups who disregarded the letter of the law, and was particularly dangerous during recurring periods of active anti-alien sentiment. The 1303 customs duties were still levied, but the reciprocal privileges conferred by Edward I's *Carta Mercatoria* were virtually forgotten. Only by constantly citing the usage of their own liberties granted before and since that date could the Hanse merchants hope to gain exemption from general legislation. Even then their appeals were not always successful. The threat to aliens was not immediately apparent at the accession of Henry IV, since his first parliament (October 1399) actually confirmed their right to sell victuals by retail as well as in gross. Thereafter, parliaments were almost uniformly hostile. Those of 1401 and 1402 re-enacted the bullion and employment acts and requested the king to enforce them more strictly. The employment act now required aliens to expend the whole of the proceeds from the sale of imports upon English goods, instead of merely half as before. Later parliaments of Henry IV and his heirs enlarged the acts, not merely to ensure obedience but to trammel aliens in other directions. In 1404 alien importers were required to provide surety that they would sell their wares within three months of arrival, they were forbidden to trade with other strangers and had to register with a host who would supervise their activities. In 1406 there was a slight relaxation, when it was enacted that aliens and other non-citizens might trade freely with one another in London and sell there by retail as well as in gross. But in June 1407 the king suspended this statute until parliament should give it more mature consideration, and in the meantime the city's franchise prohibited such trade. When parliament assembled in October it confirmed the king's action and annulled the offending statute. In 1411 the period of grace allowed to sell imports was reduced from three months to forty days. The extremity of these regulations came in 1425 when aliens were ordered to find a host before selling any goods or, at most, within fifteen days; within forty days they had not only to have sold their imports, but also to have bought their quota of English goods, on pain of forfeiture.[1]

Fortunately for the Hanse its franchises were confirmed by Henry IV before the hostility of parliament was manifested and before an outbreak of severe violence between England and a number of Hanse towns. This was done on 24 October 1399, in return for the modest fine of 25 marks, but contingent not only upon the principle of reciprocity for the king's subjects in all parts of Almain, but also upon two more specific conditions. All members of the Hanse were to be authenticated by sealed letters from their home towns and no strangers were to be admitted to the fellowship. Secondly, the Prussian and Wendish towns were to send envoys before midsummer next to answer outstanding claims for damages submitted by English merchants. This was the result of a petition presented to Richard II before his deposition, reminding him that some three years earlier he had informed the Germans that, unless his subjects had been given satisfaction by 8 September 1399, they would be issued with letters of marque, authorising them to take direct action to recover their losses. The conditions attached to the confirmation of the franchises were explained to the English merchant community on 6 December 1399. But, although the Hanse failed to send envoys, Henry took no steps either to cancel its charter or to issue letters of marque, save in one instance, and that as early as Easter 1400. On the contrary, both before and after midsummer many Chancery writs ordered the release of German ships arrested in English ports. These had not been halted in anticipation of the promised action against the Hanse, but simply as part of a general arrest of shipping during a state of emergency.[2]

The violence alluded to above, which soon amounted almost to a state of war, did not flow from earlier events nor from a current increase in commercial rivalry between the two communities.

---

[1] *Stats.*, 2, p. 118. *Rot. Parl.*, 3, pp. 468, 502, 542–3, 598, 612, 661; 4, p. 276. *CCR*, 1405–9, p. 210.
[2] *CPR*, 1399–1401, pp. 57, 140. *CCR*, 1399–1402, pp. 73, 85. *HUB*, 5, nos. 384, 386, 391.

Englishmen started the attacks, which were directed not so much against Hanse ships and merchants trading with England, but against Hanse trade in other areas. To some extent the attacks may be represented as simply part and parcel of an apparently general lawlessness at sea which marred the early years of the fifteenth century. Traditionally, the blame for this was laid at the door of pirates and privateers, whose activities defied their own governments as much as they damaged the international trading community.[3] A revisionist study, based chiefly upon the fortunes and misfortunes of English, French, Flemish and Castilian vessels in the English Channel, has advanced an alternative interpretation, suggesting that the predators were mostly subject to government control and the attacks a matter of policy.[4] This view finds limited support from a survey of Hanseatic losses in this period. Some servants of the English state condoned, encouraged or even participated in the attacks, but, throughout, the judiciary listened to the complaints of the victims, instituted enquiries and ordered the arrest into safe custody, and sometimes the restitution, of the spoils. Taken as a whole the episode cannot safely be written off as a government-sponsored attack on the Hanse.

The catalogue of Hanseatic naval losses in the fifteenth century begins at Easter 1400, when John Brandon of Lynn seized a ship at Boston, but this was legally sanctioned by an English court. More questionable is an incident in the following June, when sailors under the command of the Earl of Northumberland allegedly threw the captain and twelve crewmen overboard and took another ship and its cargo of grain into Hartlepool. It is significant that both these ships belonged to Stralsund, with which there had been a long-running dispute and which had itself confiscated English goods. Then there was a respite until 1402, a fact somewhat remarkable in the light of privateering licences being issued to east-coast merchant-shipowners, authorising them to attack Scottish and Frisian ships and keep the spoils for themselves. At this date all Frisians were treated as pirates, since the *Vitalienbrüder*, recently expelled from the Baltic, had established their base in that lordless country. At the end of May 1400 licences were renewed for John Brandon and other

---

[3] J. H. Wylie, *History of England under Henry the Fourth*, 1 (London, 1884), pp. 379–99. C. L. Kingsford, *Prejudice and Promise in Fifteenth Century England* (Oxford, 1925), pp. 78–105. S. P. Pistono, 'Henry IV and the English Privateers', *EHR*, 99 (1975), 322–30.

[4] C. J. Ford, 'Piracy or Policy: The Crisis in the Channel, 1400–1403', *Trans. Roy. Hist. Soc.*, Series 5, 29 (1979), 63–77.

Lynn merchants to continue marauding with four ships already at sea and to press two more to reinforce the squadron. In June John Tuttebury and William Terry of Hull and John Leget of Whitby obtained licences for four or six ships, while in August William Jonesson of Newcastle was commissioned to press sailors for his own two privateers and lodesmen for the king's great ship, the *Trinity*.[5] The lull between 1400 and 1402 was not devoid of incident, for Lynn men got possession of a ship belonging to the Teutonic Knights, which they claimed had earlier been seized by Scottish sailors. The Englishmen declined to restore the vessel to its rightful owners, since the admiral's court awarded it to them as a legitimate spoil of war. This quickly led to reprisals against Lynn merchants in Prussia. In December 1401 Henry IV gave a warning to the Grand Master of the Teutonic Order, in the form of a request to ban his subjects from trading with the Scots. Not until June did the Grand Master reply, in language nearly identical with that used by the Flemings in answer to a similar request made by Edward II almost a century before.[6] The suggestion was declined, on the grounds that Prussians claimed the right to trade freely with all Christian people. By then the first of a wave of attacks had already been made against Prussian and other Hanseatic ships, for after their warning the English felt free to stop anyone suspected of trading with the Scots. However, the attacks began only after Scots land and naval forces had renewed their own assaults. The first seizure was probably that of two Bremen ships by Jonesson's Newcastle privateers on 15 and 16 April, while on 8 May Tuttebury and Terry's Hull men captured an Elbing ship and about the same time robbed, but did not detain, a Lübeck ship. Most of the damage inflicted on the Hanseatics in 1402 was done by an official fleet under the command of the admiral, Lord Grey of Codnore, mustered in May to intercept a Franco-Scottish fleet assisting the Scottish invasion of the north of England. About midsummer Grey's men attacked two Bremen and a Danzig ship in a Scottish port, burning two and capturing the third. On other occasions they robbed, without detaining, three Prussian and one Stralsund ship. In December a Norfolk master in the king's fleet forced a Hamburg ship to put into Holy Island to be searched for Scottish goods, but the latter was wrecked while entering harbour. The catalogue of losses in the North Sea is completed with the sinking of a Danzig ship by Hartlepool fishermen and the robbery of

[5] *CPR*, 1399–1401, pp. 291, 351–2; 1401–5, p. 55.   [6] *HR*, I (v), nos. 91–2.

a Kampen ship in which Lübeck had an interest. In southern waters Hanseatics were less troubled, but two Prussian ships were robbed by licensed privateers, making a total of four ships captured, four destroyed and eight robbed in 1402.

The next year, Hanseatic ships may have steered clear of Scottish waters for, while northern privateers captured four ships and burned a fifth, two of these were probably near the Dutch coast; a sixth was taken near Norway. The reduction of losses in the north was more than offset by those off the French and Flemish coasts, where the intensity of warfare greatly increased. About Easter ships operating from Calais seized three of the Prussian Bay fleet near Ostend, while John Hauley of Dartmouth took a fourth. During the rest of the year Calais men captured three more ships, a Winchelsea fleet took two ships and Prussian-owned goods freighted in a Flemish ship, a Bayonne master accounted for two or three ships, while two privateers financed by London and Dover interests seized a Prussian vessel making for Southampton. This brings total losses for 1403 to nineteen or twenty ships captured and one destroyed. In 1404 attacks upon Hanseatics continued and total losses recorded in that year were sixteen ships captured and six robbed, while German-owned merchandise was taken from two Dutch ships. One ship was seized near Ostend and taken into Calais, but on the whole the action seems to have moved back to the north. In ten cases where the aggressors were named, Newcastle privateers were responsible for five attacks, East Anglian for four and Hull for one. Failure to identify attackers does not necessarily make accounts less reliable, for they were not certainly identified in the most-documented incident of all. This was an assault against three Riga ships, the worst outrage for loss of both life and property. After sailing from Riga packed with Russian wares they touched upon some of the Wendish towns, before continuing their voyage to Bruges. One, at least, left Wismar about midsummer and was said to have been captured on 13 July and brought to Hull; the exact fate of the others is not recorded. The total of fifty-eight or fifty-nine attacks described above as having taken place between 1402 and 1404 is a minimum and should probably be increased by at least a further five incidents, which are not precisely datable but which certainly fall into this general period.[7]

The Hanse towns and the Bruges *Kontor* protested repeatedly

---

[7] This summary of losses is based on documents submitted to the Hague conference, cited in succeeding notes. It does not include any losses by Rostock and Wismar.

about attacks on their shipping, but at first were reluctant to mount reprisals. In Prussia the Knights reacted quickly to the loss of their own ship by arresting goods belonging to Lynn merchants, claiming that the ship had been seized directly by Englishmen and not taken from the Scots. Restrictions imposed by the Prussian diet upon Englishmen in July 1402 are probably too early to have been made in response to the naval attacks, which were just beginning, and must therefore be regarded as a belated and partial implementation of the threat of expulsion made in 1398. Those married to Englishwomen were to leave the country with their families by the new year. Any married to Prussian women and unmarried men were allowed to remain, though the latter group might no longer lodge with the former and had to find native hosts. All were forbidden to trade beyond the confines of a port of arrival. According to later English complaints, which there is no reason to disbelieve, the restrictions soon went beyond this, at least in Danzig.[8] They were allowed to expose cloth for sale on only three days a week, and might not trade in public places nor in partnership with Prussians. As a final act of indignity and spite, Englishmen were denied entry to the common hall where merchants of all nationalities met; any Prussian who took an Englishman there was fined six barrels of beer. It was alleged that all of these restrictions applied only to Englishmen. This may well have been true, though it was largely the result of the present crisis in Anglo-Prussian relations. The Prussian internal traders were suspicious of all aliens, particularly the Dutch, whom they feared just as much as the English. From the summer of 1402 there was a general deterioration and, by the following spring, arrests were threatened against the property of Dutch and Flemish merchants, as well as that of Englishmen.

The expulsion of the married men deprived the English community of many of its leaders, but a fair number of younger men remained to carry on their business. Their property became increasingly subject to arrest until June 1403, when Henry IV took the initiative and sent an invitation for ambassadors to come to discuss current difficulties. The Prussian diet responded with alacrity by freeing English-owned goods of Prussian origin and allowing them to be exported in English ships or in three alien ships. In return, English merchants still in Prussia gave security for payment

---

[8] *HR*, I (v), nos. 90, 93, 101. *Hanseakten*, no. 322.

of compensation for recent injuries inflicted by their countrymen and also twenty hostages for the personal safety of the ambassadors. Nevertheless, it was prudently decided that Prussians should not send any more goods to England until the envoys returned. The delegation arrived in July, bearing claims totalling 19,119½ nobles (£6,373 sterling). After negotiations with the Chancellor and the Treasurer the terms of a settlement were accepted by the whole of the king's council in the first week of October. It was agreed in principle that ships and merchandise should be restored by each side and compensation paid for any destroyed or consumed; there were to be further talks about the men who had been slain or drowned. Since the current Welsh revolt prevented further progress, a truce was proclaimed until Easter (30 March) 1404. In the interim Englishmen could return to Prussia to settle their affairs and Prussians come to England; all could bring home goods already in their possession, but no new trade was to be initiated.[9]

During the spring and summer of 1404 further negotiations took place in London. Master John Kington, acting on the English side, reported to the king's council on 19 April, but no action was taken because of preoccupation with domestic and French affairs. Because of the lack of progress the Prussians forbade their ships to come to England after the truce expired at Easter; the ban was reaffirmed by the diet at the beginning of June and any captain who disobeyed was to forfeit his burgess rights. Furthermore, no Prussian was to import English cloth acquired since Easter nor export to England pitch, tar, ashes and bowstaves. Once again the English made the first move to restore trade with a letter dated 5 June, suggesting that the truce be renewed until Easter 1405. The next day the king authorised his subjects trading in northern and eastern Europe to elect a governor, apparently the first official act of recognition in the new reign. It is more than likely that John Broun of Lynn, who was entrusted to take the royal letter to Prussia, had already been nominated governor. However, on 16 July the Grand Master wrote to the king refusing his request to renew the truce, and shortly afterwards all Englishmen without burgess rights in Prussia were ordered to leave the country by Michaelmas. In August the English Chancery proclaimed that any merchants who traded with Prussia before the dispute was settled did so at their own risk. The Prussians were encouraged by a hardening of attitude on the part of the rest of the Hanse, which until

---

[9] *HUB*, 5, nos. 590–2. *HR*, I (v), nos. 130–2, 134–5. *Hanseakten*, no. 317. *POPC*, I, p. 218. *Letters of Henry the Fourth*, I, pp. 162–6. *Foedera*, IV (i), p. 57.

now had refused even to accept a ban on the import of English cloth. At the end of May 1404 Stralsund arrested English merchandise in retaliation for the attacks on shipping. The following October a meeting at Marienburg, attended by representatives of the Wendish towns, decided to hold a special diet at Lübeck on 2 February 1405 to coordinate sanctions. It was agreed that in the meantime the Hanse should try to enlist the support of the towns and princes of the Low Countries for a general boycott of trade with England. However, it found little support in this quarter. The Flemings were anxious about the supply of English wool, while Holland was more inclined to side with England than with the Hanse, because of its own dispute with Prussia. Consequently, when the special diet finally assembled at Lübeck on 12 March 1405 the Hanseatic towns of the Low Countries were not represented. The diet banned the import of English cloth and the export of virtually all Baltic wares; the merchants of the Low Countries were ordered to fall into line or suffer the consequences.[10]

The English government was not complacent about the threat of a trade stoppage, since it involved badly needed naval stores. As early as August 1404 Henry IV wrote to the Doge of Venice asking him to supply 80,000 lb of cables and cords and 60,000 lb of hawsers for certain great ships then being fitted out.[11] However, the Hanse's efforts to deny such goods to England were ineffective. In September 1405 the Bruges *Kontor* reported that large supplies of Baltic wares had been brought to Dordrecht and Amsterdam and that there was no shortage, either in Holland or England. Moreover, cloth continued to be smuggled into Hanseatic territories, much of it bought from English merchants in Skania. Already in August 1405, while maintaining the prohibition of exports to England and the import of English cloth, Prussia relaxed its general ban on exports through the Sound, alleging that the diet's decision was disregarded by other members of the Hanse. This unilateral action caused the Bruges *Kontor* to protest that disunity would weaken the Hanse and bring it into contempt. It blamed the Prussians for the recent supply of goods to the west, denying that they had been brought via the Elbe ports or shipped through the Sound by non-Prussians.[12]

The English attempt to improve relations with the Hanse began in the parliament which met at Coventry in October 1404. The

---

[10] *HUB*, 5, nos. 614, 617, 620–1. *HR*, I (v), nos. 198, 202–3, 209, 221, 225–9. *POPC*, I, p. 223. *CPR*, 1401–5, p. 394. *CCR*, 1402–5, p. 382. *Foedera*, IV (i), p. 67.
[11] *Letters of Henry the Fourth*, I, pp. 283–4.   [12] *HR*, I (v), nos. 262, 274–5, 302.

commission was given to Sir William Sturmy, speaker of the commons, William Brampton, a London merchant, and Master John Kington. Sturmy and Kington were experienced diplomats, who had already worked together on several embassies to the continent, while Kington had been responsible for the negotiations with Prussia the year before. Their first task was to coordinate the claims of the English merchants, and they did not leave until the end of May 1405. As well as Sturmy, Kington and William Brampton, the party included James Brampton and John Palleys, a Rhineland knight in English service, chosen because of his fluency in low German. The delegation reached its destination on 8 August but, after preliminary exchanges, discussions were adjourned until Michaelmas so that the Prussians could consult the Livonians and the other Hanse towns. As a result the Grand Master declined to make a separate peace, but on 8 October a provisional treaty was agreed, to take effect after England had come to terms with the rest of the Hanse. This provided for the full restoration of trade, with Englishmen being allowed to deal in Prussia as freely as they had ever done in the past. But they were to obey any lawful regulations made by the Grand Master for his own subjects and aliens, in particular that which provided that fractional cloths should have lists at each end. A conference was arranged for 1 May 1406 at Dordrecht in Holland to try the claims for damages made by the Prussians in 1403 and those which had been submitted since that date. Any claimants who could not attend the conference were allowed until 1 May 1407 to put their cases to the Chancellor in England. From Prussia William Brampton returned direct to England, but the rest of the party went to Dordrecht where it had talks with representatives of Lübeck, Bremen, Hamburg, Stralsund and Greifswald, reaching a conclusion on 15 December. These towns agreed to take part in the conference scheduled for the following May and, pending its outcome, all trade sanctions were suspended until 1 May 1407.[13]

The ambassadors did not return to London until 17 February 1406, a fortnight before parliament met. Sturmy was not a member on this occasion, probably because of the timing of the elections, but at an early stage the Chancellor reported to the lords on the outcome of the mission. Proclamation was made of the truce with the Hanse,

---

[13] *Hanseakten*, no. 308. *HUB*, 5, nos. 687, 697. *HR*, I (v), nos. 261, 290. *Letters of Henry the Fourth*, 2, pp. 80–2. *Calendar of Signet Letters of Henry IV and Henry V*, ed. J. L. Kirby (London, 1978), pp. 78, 84. *Foedera*, IV (i), pp. 80–1.

English merchants and sailors were invited to submit claims for their losses and commissioners were appointed to examine Hanse claims already received. As early as 10 March 1406 the English found it necessary to ask for a postponement of the Dordrecht conference until 1 August. They pleaded the recent late return of the envoys, but they were also hindered by the fact that on his way home William Brampton had been shipwrecked; he escaped with his life but lost some of his papers. Later the Hanseatic negotiators sarcastically remarked that everything favourable to the English case had been salvaged and only documents prejudicial to it lost.[14]

Towards the end of June the English asked for a further delay until 1 March 1407. The German delegates refused, came to Dordrecht at the beginning of August and sent word that they would wait there until the end of the month. Later they extended the deadline until 1 November but, when the English party still failed to arrive, they waited until the end of that month before giving up and going home. These delays allowed time for the intrusion of new factors, which prejudiced a successful outcome to the negotiations. In April 1406, for example, the Bruges *Kontor* complained that England had not reinstated the merchants in their liberties as the ambassadors had promised. In September 1406 an English fleet seized five ships *en route* to Spain, three of them actually belonging to the Teutonic Order; fortunately these were quickly restored after the Prussian delegates waiting at Dordrecht came to England to register a protest. Worst of all was the threat posed by the intervention of the Duke of Burgundy. As early as June 1405 he had offered to ally with the Hanse, provided that it took up arms against England; at the beginning of 1407 he renewed this offer. In February the Grand Master wrote to the Duke saying that the international status of the Order required it to be neutral in disputes between other powers, but the response to a later approach did not give such a definite refusal. This did not mean that the Hanse was seriously considering the offer, for it had nothing to gain and everything to lose from open war with England. However, it was not averse to using the threat of a Burgundian alliance to put pressure on England. The Germans gained from this prevarication, when in May 1407 the Duke of Burgundy ordered his officials in West Flanders and Picardy not to molest their ships and merchants. The repeated postponements of

---

[14] *HR*, 1 (v), nos. 312, 460. *Rot. Parl.*, 3, pp. 568, 574.

the conference by the English simply meant that they were not ready; they had no wish to put it off indefinitely, since this might lead to the renewal of trade sanctions when the truce expired in May 1407. One indication of their desire for a settlement is the small olive branch offered to the Hanse in the matter of poundage subsidy. In June 1406, when parliament decided that aliens should pay an increment of 1s in the pound, the Hanseatics were given exemption. Altruism was supported by logic, since the case for refusing to exempt Germans from the regular tunnage and poundage was based solely on the fact that natives were required to pay. The Venetians were also granted exemption from the increment as a special privilege, while it was abolished prematurely for all aliens. Early in 1407 Sturmy and Kington were ready to negotiate; they wrote to the other participants apologising for their failure to turn up in November and suggested that the conference be convened as soon as possible. About the same time they crossed over to Middelburg in Holland to await the arrival of the Hanse delegates. Now it was the Englishmen who were kept waiting. One cause of delay may have been slowness of communications; for example, the letter sent to Prussia on 14 February did not reach Marienburg until 11 April. Some of the towns were so slow in replying that Sturmy was moved to write to the Bruges *Kontor* asking whether they knew of any reason for this. Further delay was caused by the fact that no member of the Hanse could commit itself to a conference before the meeting of the diet, which was scheduled for Ascension (5 May) at Lübeck. One thing which might have caused a hold-up, but didn't, was the death of Conrad de Ullingen, Grand Master of the Teutonic Order; his deputy undertook that Prussia would not use this as an excuse to denounce the provisional treaty of 1405.[15]

The diet authorised the conference to meet on 1 August 1407 at Dordrecht but, because of disturbances in that town, it actually began at the Hague on 28 August. The terms of reference were simple, being confined to questions of compensation. Claims had either to be settled now or firm arrangements made to deal with any that could not be resolved immediately; agreement also had to be reached about terms of payment for any compensation awarded. Much depended upon a successful conclusion, since the Hanse threatened to renew trade sanctions if a settlement was not made.

---

[15] *Hanseakten*, nos. 309–14. *HUB*, 5, nos. 743, 783. *HR*, I (v), nos. 256, 313, 343, 349, 364, 374, 380–2. *Rot. Parl.*, 3, pp. 578, 598. *Foedera*, IV (i), pp. 104, 108–9, 118–19.

The conference and its aftermath was a diplomatic triumph for the English; despite the recent display of unity by the Hanse, they now succeeded in dividing it. This they did by the simple expedient of dealing with the Prussian and Livonian claims separately from the rest. The former were considered first and a substantial measure of agreement was reached within five weeks. Only then, on 6 October, did they proceed to the claims of the other towns and very little was agreed before the conference broke up, apparently on 15 October. Despite this, and despite the ultimate failure to honour the settlement made with Prussia, trade sanctions were not renewed. The total amount of damages claimed by the Prussians was 25,934½ nobles (£8,645 sterling), made up of the claims submitted in 1403, 1405 and later additions. These did not relate solely to attacks on the high seas, for among them were wrongs allegedly committed in England, including, for example, a case of money forfeited to the crown for an offence against the bullion law. The English envoys accepted as legitimate and outstanding claims involving a total of 8,957 nobles. Of the rest some appear to have been rejected, but many had to be passed over because the facts were still too obscure. In these cases claimants were allowed until Easter 1409 to continue their actions in the English Chancery. A couple of cases, which depended upon the question of whether Prussians had actively assisted the Scots in time of war, were referred to the arbitration of Sigismund, King of the Romans. Total English claims against Prussia amounted to 4,535 nobles (£1,512 sterling), of which 766 nobles were found to be proven and outstanding. Livonian claims for property totalled £8,027 12s 7d, and they also demanded provision for the souls of the men who had been slain. The only matter in dispute in this case was the value set upon the stolen goods; it was decided to refer it to the merchant community of Bruges, who were asked to provide details of prices current there on the date of the attack on the ships.[16]

The English envoys returned home in time to report to the parliament meeting at Gloucester, which dispersed on 2 December 1407. The principal Prussian negotiator, Arnd von Dassel, came to England after that date and learned that those in parliament who had been most opposed to the Hanse were the members for Newcastle. This is no doubt explained by the fact that Newcastle men appear to have been those most involved in the attack on the

---

[16] *Hanseakten*, no. 316. *HR*, I (v), no. 397.

Livonian ships. On 26 December, von Dassel reported to Danzig that he had not yet reached agreement with Kington about the amount of the Livonian compensation, but the king had promised to come to London after Christmas to expedite matters. The work was completed by 26 March 1408 when Henry IV confirmed that within three years of Easter (15 April) he would pay 8,957 nobles to the Prussians and 22,096 nobles to the Livonians in three equal instalments, provided that his own subjects were paid 766 nobles in the first year; he also promised to endow prayers for the souls of the Livonian dead. The obligation seems to have been absolute, since there is no suggestion that it was dependent on the king's recovering the money from those involved in the attacks. The amount and terms of compensation agreed upon so far were not accepted by the Prussian towns until August 1408; shortly after that von Dassel returned to England to follow the progress of outstanding claims, but without plenipotentiary powers. This omission proved to be something of a stumbling block, as he informed his principals in January 1409. He also reported continuing harassment of Prussian merchants. In the past year Hull had forbidden them to sell goods from their ships, insisting that these must first be unloaded and warehoused. Because the king had not intervened, London was now doing the same. More encouraging was von Dassel's intelligence about the shortage of corn in western Europe, which resulted from a combination of a poor harvest and a Prussian ban on grain export of several months' standing. In his first letter he noted that England had had to impose its own ban on export. A few days later he reported that all the corn was lost in the north of England, and he thought that because of this a group of Lynn merchants who had come to London to talk with him would have to accept his claims.[17]

In March 1409 Henry IV wrote to the Grand Master asking him to send envoys fully empowered to settle outstanding disagreements about compensation and also to negotiate a perpetual treaty of friendship; he hoped that, meanwhile, von Dassel might stay in England so that the present talks could continue. In April an assembly of the Prussian towns agreed to send envoys, but these did not leave until high summer. They were instructed to demand the first instalment of the compensation and to settle dates for payment of the rest; they were also to ask for 4,200 nobles for prayers for the

---

[17] *HR*, I (v), nos. 484, 547–8. *HUB*, 5, nos. 830, 847. *William Ashbourne's Book*, ed. D. M. Owen (Norfolk Record Soc., 48, 1981), p. 85.

souls of twenty-eight merchants and ships' captains lost with the Livonian ships; provision for the souls of ordinary seamen was left to the king's conscience. The ambassadors were received by Henry IV on 15 August and afterwards had talks with the council. On 31 August they reported that the king had promised to pay one sixth of the agreed damages at Martinmas (11 November), one sixth at Purification (2 February) 1410 and the rest at Purification 1411 and 1412; they would wait for the first payment and, if instructed to, for the second. They were told to wait until February but no longer, and to take delivery of both the Prussian and Livonian money. On 10 October 1409 Henry IV made formal recognisances to pay at the dates given above, subject to the proviso that payments be made by exchange, not in coin or bullion save for reasonable expenses. The Prussians agreed to begin discussing a treaty of friendship as soon as they received the first instalment. The English negotiators appointed on 14 November to act with John Kington were Richard Merlawe and William Askham, mayor and alderman of London. By 4 December they had finished their work and a provisional treaty had been made. Part of it consisted of an indenture about payment of damages in cases left over from the Hague conference and haggled about for the last two years. It was agreed that nine sums totalling 3,421 nobles should be levied from English merchants and ship-owners and handed over to the Prussians by Purification 1411, together with a further 114 nobles if the claim could be proved by 1 April 1410. Additionally, it was provided that the heir of Henry, Lord Percy, after attaining his majority and being invested with his estates, should pay 838 nobles to the proctor of Marienburg for corn taken by Percy for the garrison at Berwick. In return for this settlement and the sums already promised by the king, the Prussians were debarred from distraining English property for anything done before the date of the treaty. Each side undertook to secure payment of compensation in the event of future crimes, but if nothing was done within six months of a complaint then the aggrieved party might make a distraint.[18]

Turning from the settlement of outstanding damages to the substantive clauses of the treaty, which dealt with the future conduct of trade, there is no doubt that the English got the better bargain, even though the rights of each side were described in identical words.

[18] *HR*, I (v), nos. 578–9, 581, 620, 624. *HUB*, 5, no. 480. *Foedera* IV (i), pp. 159–60, 163–4.

The Prussians were accorded no rights beyond those which were already claimed by the Hanse as a whole by virtue of their ancient charters. Their only gain lay in the fact that henceforth the present treaty, rather than former grants, could be cited as the warrant for enjoyment of trading privileges, and, while the treaty held, the Prussians ought to exercise their rights, even if the other Hanse towns lost theirs by a cancellation of the charters. On the other hand, the English gained rights which they could not legally claim on the basis of the 1388 treaty. In the first place the former treaty recognised only 'liege merchants of England', whereas the present comprehended 'all and each the lieges and subjects of the kingdom of England, and the lands and lordships of that kingdom, of whatsoever status or condition'. The former treaty recognised the rights of Englishmen to trade freely in Prussia 'with all manner of persons', but the present made it clear that they might deal directly with 'Prussians and others, of whatsoever nation or rite', thereby embracing aliens, including Poles and Orthodox Russians. Moreover, the treaty could even be interpreted as giving Englishmen the right to use Prussia as a base from which to trade with those peoples in their own countries. In 1388 they had side-stepped any renewed attempt to restrict them to trading at a single port of the Prussians' own choosing by establishing the right to come to any port and thence proceed to any place within the country, but nothing had been said about entering or leaving Prussia by land routes. Now Englishmen might come and go with merchandise 'by land and by sea', thus giving access to Poland and Russia. Finally, bearing in mind the expulsions of Englishmen from Prussia in 1402 and 1404, the negotiators of the new treaty could not avoid the question of the rights of settlers. A form of words was adopted which was probably intended to convey a general right of settlement, but was so ambiguous that it provided little basis for defining particular rights to be enjoyed by English settlers in Prussia. It was to be the cause of endless disputes in years to come.

The Anglo-Prussian treaty of 1409 was strongly opposed by all the northern towns of the Hanse. Some of the reasons for their opposition are found in correspondence of the Bruges *Kontor*.[19] This group of merchants was not a disinterested party, since it exported Flemish cloth to the eastern Baltic in direct competition with English

---

[19] *HR*, I (v), nos. 659, 674.

merchants. Nevertheless, there is no reason not to accept their account of the negotiations which had taken place in England. In January 1410 they wrote to the Livonian towns reporting that the English were demanding the right to trade in their country; when the Prussian negotiators refused this, on the grounds that Englishmen had never traded in Livonia, they were told that in that case Livonians should not trade in England. The Bruges *Kontor* advised that, rather than submit to blackmail, the Hanse as a whole should renounce its privileges in England and refuse to admit the English to Prussia on any terms. It claimed that they must gain the upper hand since England needed Baltic goods more than the Germans needed English cloth. In February the *Kontor* wrote in similar terms to the Prussian diet, complaining about English designs on Livonia.

Despite the hostility of the rest of the Hanse, indeed despite the hostility of some of his own subjects, the Grand Master ratified the treaty with England. The main reason was the political and military pressure currently exerted against the Teutonic Order by external forces. From the 1340s to the 1380s relations between the Order and the kingdom of Poland had been reasonably stable; thereafter, the *modus vivendi* was threatened by the acceptance of Christianity by the pagan Lithuanians and the union forged between the grand duchy of Lithuania and Poland. At first, the Knights actually made gains from the allies, taking the duchy of Dobrzyń from Poland in 1392 and holding it until 1405, and acquiring Samogitia from the Lithuanians in 1398. A revolt of the Samogitians in 1401 was suppressed by 1405, but in 1409 they revolted again. Although the Lithuanians had accepted Catholic rather than Orthodox Christianity, the Order found it expedient to claim that it was still conducting a crusade against the heathen and sought the aid of western knights. The ship that brought this appeal to England also carried a herald of the King of Poland, bearing his complaints about the Knights. Since Henry IV was himself a Knight of the Teutonic Order, the Poles received little sympathy in this quarter. In January 1410 Dietrich von Logendorf, the Order's representative in England, reported that Henry had promised that if he could make peace with France he would go in person to Prussia, but meanwhile he would not prevent any of his subjects from going there.[20] Von Logendorf suggested that to secure the sympathy of England the Grand Master

[20] *Ibid.*, nos. 639–40.

should allow a few shiploads of corn to be brought to London; because of a second poor harvest and a continued ban on exports from Prussia there was acute dearth in western Europe; in England in 1409–10 prices were double the level of those two years earlier.

Despite a degree of mutual need, ratification of the Anglo-Prussian treaty was a long-drawn-out business, Prussia acceding on 24 December 1410 and England on 24 May 1411. Delay was caused firstly by Henry IV's late delivery of the second instalment of the indemnity and then by Prussian military disaster. When no money was forthcoming in February 1410 the envoys refused to wait any longer, so it was agreed that payment should be made at Bruges on 18 May; it was eventually handed over there several weeks after the new date. Then, on 15 July, the Teutonic Knights were defeated by a Polish-Lithuanian army at Tannenberg. This almost resulted in the annihilation of the Order in Prussia, for the Slavs swept all before them, meeting little resistance until they were held before Marienburg by Henry von Plauen. For this successful defence of the capital, von Plauen was shortly afterwards appointed Grand Master. After Prussia ratified the treaty Henry IV rapidly lost interest in paying any more of the indemnity. He defaulted on the instalment due in February 1411, saying that reports of the death at Tannenberg of Ulrich von Juningen, the Grand Master, and the destruction of the Order, made him afraid that the money might fall into the wrong hands. Two thousand nobles were handed over in 1412, but after that nothing. For several years the Prussians vainly sent envoys to collect the balance; then they stopped wasting time and money on the business, although the claim was not relinquished.[21]

The money actually handed over to the Prussians was a small price to pay for dividing the Hanse, which is what it did. In 1405 Prussia had made a provisional treaty, which it undertook not to ratify until the other members made peace with England. The 1409 treaty was made without reference to them and ratified despite the opposition of the northern towns and regardless of the fact they had not yet made peace. This success was not due entirely to English diplomacy, for the Wendish towns were distracted and divided by social discontent in this period. In particular, popular agitation against the ruling elite in Lübeck between 1403 and 1408 resulted in the exile of a majority of the governing body in the latter year, at a

---

[21] *Ibid.*, nos. 634, 637; (vi), nos. 23, 60, 62, 114–16, 193–5. *HUB*, 5, nos. 981, 1004; 6, no. 74. *CCR*, 1405–9, pp. 357, 366; 1409–13, pp. 265, 283.

crucial stage in the dealings with England. The non-Prussian towns which were represented at the Hague conference came away almost empty-handed. They went claiming 32,016 nobles;[22] English counterclaims totalled 1,662 nobles against Hamburg and Greifs-wald and a large, indeterminable sum against Stralsund, which was said to exceed that town's own claim of 7,416 nobles. Additionally England claimed 32,407 nobles against Rostock and Wismar, chiefly for losses during the 1390s. As already mentioned, consideration of these claims was deferred until those of Prussia had been dealt with, and very little time can have been spent on them before the conference broke up. It is hardly surprising, therefore, that the English accepted claims totalling only 1,372 nobles, in addition to £231 about which terms had been agreed before the conference met. On the other hand, as the ambassadors pointed out with reference to the claims of Stralsund, many cases were very complex and the facts difficult to establish – a few of them dating back as far as the 1380s. As in the case of Prussia, claims not settled at the Hague could be pursued for a limited period in the English Chancery. Some towns sent representatives to England after the conference, but only Hamburg formally accepted the offer made by the Sturmy team, and in October 1409 the king made a recognisance to pay it 417 nobles.[23] In the normal order of things the non-Prussian towns might have called for a renewal of trade sanctions against England when the Hanse diet met at Lübeck in May 1408. Unfortunately, no records have survived from this assembly, which coincided with the climax of the city's internal troubles. This misfortune resulted in a general paralysis of will, for Lübeck was effectively the head of the League and no other town could adequately fill its place. Consequently, while sanctions were not renewed relations with England remained tense for many years. In April 1412 the diet protested about disregard of its franchises, once again singling out Southampton as particularly offending in the matter of local tolls; it was ordered that no member should trade there after the following Christmas. This diet also complained about renewed English attacks on shipping, which can be confirmed from other sources.[24]

---

[22] Details survive of claims by Hamburg, Bremen, Stralsund, Lübeck, Greifswald and Kampen totalling 25,135 nobles. The higher figure of 32,016 probably includes those of Rostock and Wismar, which have not survived. England's claims against Rostock and Wismar (unpublished) are in B. L. Cotton, Nero B IX, fos. 57–62. Details of some English claims against Stralsund are in *Literae Cantuarienses*, ed. J. B. Sheppard (London, 1887–9), 3, pp. 79–85.   [23] *Hanseakten*, no. 362. *Foedera*, IV (i), p. 160.
[24] *HUB*, 5, no. 1047. *HR*, I (vi), no. 66. *Rot. Parl.*, 4, pp. 12, 36.

After the death of Henry IV his son confirmed the Hanseatic charters in November 1413, for a fine of forty marks.[25] However, there was no formal attempt to improve relations between England and the Hanse until the meeting of the council of Constance in 1417. The English delegation was authorised not merely to discuss the business of the church, but also to negotiate with various powers, including the Hanse, on secular matters.[26] The talks took place under the chairmanship of Sigismund, King of the Romans, who entertained grandiose diplomatic ambitions encompassing much of Europe; the previous year he had visited England and concluded a treaty of perpetual friendship. Sigismund's mediation was unsuccessful and relations between England and the Hanse became significantly worse. One action which had unfortunate consequences was the pressing of Hanseatic ships to assist in Henry V's invasion of Normandy. Some ships were arrested at sea and, in order to free them for royal service, their cargoes were forcibly sold in England. Even if the proceeds were handed over immediately to the owner's representatives, such high-handed action might cause great inconvenience; for example, shortly before the Constance meeting ten ships carrying salt from the Bay were seized and treated in this fashion. Furthermore, while payment was promised, at the rate of 3s 4d per ton per month for the ship and 3s 4d per month for a seaman's wage, this was often long delayed. In 1434 the Prussians were still claiming payment of £7,300 for twenty-four ships pressed for the attack on Harfleur, including compensation for five which had been destroyed.[27]

In the aftermath of the Constance negotiations the German community in London was alarmed by the erosion of its privileges. For example, the city sheriffs began to levy tolls on a wide range of goods. When the merchants complained to the mayor in February 1418 it was claimed that these payments ought to be made by all aliens in aid of the city farm. The mayor ruled in favour of the Hanse but the sheriffs continued to demand the tolls, so that the merchants were forced to appeal to parliament and the king's council. The council was reluctant to come to a decision, particularly after the death of Henry V, when the matter was postponed indefinitely. An interim judgement provided that the merchants should not pay the tolls for the time being, but without prejudice to any rights of the

[25] *HUB*, 5, no. 1114. *Foedera*, IV (ii), p. 56.
[26] For the background see L. R. Loomis, *The Council of Constance* (London, 1962).
[27] *HR*, I (vi), no. 451; II (i), no. 385.

sheriffs. Another dispute, which began in 1419 and dragged on for years, was the refusal of the city to re-appoint an English alderman for the Steelyard. The principal function of this official was to assist in the adjudication of mercantile cases between Hansards and Englishmen, but since this involved the withdrawal of cases from the city's own courts the appointment was a matter of great resentment. The increasing vexation of the German merchants in England came at a time when the Wendish towns were beginning to re-establish their unity. While English pressure may itself have contributed to this revival, more important was the restoration of the patriciate in Lübeck in 1416, which was accomplished with remarkably little bloodshed. The formation of a Wendish league did not necessarily mean that it would meet force with force, but in 1417 English merchants returning from Prussia were arrested at Greifswald and imprisoned until they provided sureties that they would return to captivity at Martinmas 1418, unless certain conditions had been satisfied in the meantime. An intervention by the diet which met at Lübeck in June 1418 succeeded only in getting an extension of the time limit until the following Easter.[28]

At the same time as relations with the Wendish towns were deteriorating, English fortunes suffered a set-back in Prussia, which was still isolated from the rest of the Hanse. Hitherto, Henry IV's failure to pay the whole of the indemnity does not seem to have done much harm to his subjects in this region. Admittedly, they did not gain access to Livonia, but in Prussia itself they did well. While Henry von Plauen remained Grand Master the Englishmen probably enjoyed greater freedom than ever before. This may have been a matter of policy, for during the recent war the chief Prussian towns had recognised the suzerainty of the King of Poland and, when the Order re-asserted its authority, von Plauen, after an initial reconciliation, was determined to humble them. In Danzig he removed restrictions which the city had recently imposed on English merchants in defiance of the treaty. There is no independent support for the later English claim that von Plauen gave official recognition to their fellowship, but they had a wide measure of *de facto* freedom. This may have included the right to discipline members with stocks and other means of confinement in their assembly house, though criminal jurisdiction was reserved to the Grand Master. In October 1413, however, Henry von Plauen was deposed by a faction within

---

[28] *HUB*, 6, nos. 144, 332–4, 337, 374, 474–5, 479, 482. *HR*, I (vi), nos. 581–2. *Rot. Parl.*, 4, p. 192. *CCR*, 1422–9, pp. 49, 53, 140, 192.

the Order. The hand of his successor, Michael Küchmeister, weighed less heavily on Danzig and this allowed the authorities to pursue more independent policies. One of their first actions was to outlaw the English fellowship; its factory was closed and the members ordered to live with Prussian hosts. Retribution may not have gone much beyond this, with trade continuing relatively unimpeded until the 1420s. The merchants ignored hosting regulations and rented property, both for living in and for trade. Moreover, despite the closing of the factory, they continued to have, or soon revived, some form of association, since in 1422 one of their number was identified as their alderman. Nevertheless, they registered complaints in England, and in 1419 the king sent Sir Walter Pole and Dr William Clynt to demand that his subjects should enjoy the same privileges as Prussians did in England. The Grand Master disingenuously replied that Prussia had no privileges beyond those shared with all the towns of the Hanse. Though true, this answer overlooked the fact that privileges had been guaranteed to Prussians independently of the Hanse, subject, of course, to the principle of reciprocity. The Grand Master also denied that any wrongs had recently been done to Englishmen, but he promised to safeguard whatever rights they customarily enjoyed.[29]

The Prussians frequently complained to Henry V about interference with their own ships, but there is no record of official reprisals until the *Bartholomew* of Hull was confiscated in July 1420 to pay for losses incurred some two years before. That earlier incident involved the seizure of merchandise from a ship trading with Scotland, which, after the invasion of France by Henry V, had broken its truce with England. The Prussians condemned this as illegal, since no warning had been given about trading with the Scots. In 1422 a second Hull ship, the *George*, was confiscated, but this was overshadowed by general restrictions now imposed on English merchants in Danzig, including those resident there, who at this time are said to have numbered fifty-five. Danzig had for some time been drawing closer to the Wendish league and this probably explains why it acted independently of the other Prussian towns, which had not moved so far in that direction. In March 1422 it was proposed in the Prussian diet that none except burgesses of a Hanseatic town should venture to trade beyond a port of entry, but this was not confirmed, since it was supported only by Danzig.

---

[29] *HR*, I (vii), no. 87. *HUB*, 6, no. 238.

Danzig therefore imposed its own restrictions on Englishmen. Hosting regulations were re-affirmed; they were ordered to trade only on market days; they might purchase certain goods, such as bowstaves and wainscot, only from burgesses. Finally, in July 1422 a poll tax was introduced requiring Englishmen to pay six Prussian marks (16s 8d sterling) immediately, and the same amount at three-monthly intervals if they stayed so long. When they resisted, their alderman and twelve merchants were imprisoned until they submitted.[30]

The death of Henry V in August 1422 came at an inopportune moment for the Hanse, since it meant that confirmation of its charters had to be considered in the middle of the row about English trade in Prussia. The Steelyard sought confirmation when parliament met in November. Its petition has not survived, though there is one asking for a verdict against the sheriffs of London in the matter of the tolls. Nor has the counter-petition of the English merchants survived, although its contents are known from a translation supplied by the Steelyard merchants for the Hanse in January 1423. The latter dwelt largely on events in Prussia (as seen through English eyes) since the deposition of Henry von Plauen, and said nothing about conflicts elsewhere except for the imprisonment of English merchants in Greifswald in 1417. In January 1423 the Steelyard complained about the vigorous campaign which had been mounted both in parliament and in the country against the renewal of its charters. This is borne out by the records of Lynn, where native merchants raised £20 to help finance the cost of the agitation; no doubt other towns acted similarly. Because of the outcry the government deferred confirmation and instead, on 23 April 1423, took all Hanseatic merchants into its protection for one year. Concern about the fate of the franchises was exacerbated by the matter of tunnage and poundage. After the battle of Agincourt, Henry V had been granted this subsidy for life; in November 1422 it was renewed retrospectively to 1 September, but for the first time it was decided that only aliens should pay. Naturally, the Hanse refused to pay, since previous English attempts to justify the charge had revolved around the fact that denizens also paid; only after some of its members had been imprisoned for contumacy did the Steelyard agree to give security for payment while they prosecuted their claim

---

[30] *HUB*, 6, nos. 288, 371. *HR*, 1 (vii), nos. 461, 510, 592; (viii), no. 452.

to immunity. On 3 July 1423 all the king's justices gave an opinion that Hanseatics were liable to the subsidy as aliens, not as denizens, but a few days later the council allowed yet another respite until parliament met in October. When the time came the council ruled against the merchants, who were then required to pay. English merchants again used this occasion to petition about recent mistreatment in Prussia.[31]

The temporary imprisonment of the Hanseatics provided a rallying cry for the Hanse and, when its diet met at Lübeck in July 1423, it proposed that in retaliation English merchants should be imprisoned and their goods arrested in all member towns. However, from correspondence it is clear that with the exception of Stralsund English trade was largely restricted to Prussia. In August the Prussian diet reported that after consultation with the Grand Master it had been unanimously decided that such drastic action was inadvisable. The following April the Steelyard again complained to the diet that steps must be taken to prevent the utter destruction of its liberties in England. When the Prussian diet met in August 1424 Danzig tried to gain support for the restrictions which it had long advocated against Englishmen; they should be confined to ports of entry; they must submit to hosting regulations; resident Englishmen should not act as hosts; they should not observe a fellowship. These proposals were rejected by the diet, but Danzig again tried to impose them unilaterally, ruling also that any burgess who rented property to an Englishman should forfeit his own rights. Such limitations were clearly in breach of the rights guaranteed to Englishmen by the 1409 treaty. In November 1424, following complaints by English merchants, the Grand Master ordered that in time for the next meeting of the diet each town should prepare a written report on its attitude towards English trade. This attempt to redefine Prussian policy was complicated by the revival of demands for payment of the financial indemnity promised in the 1409 treaty, and also by the Grand Master's insistence that any new laws should apply equally to all aliens and should not discriminate solely against Englishmen. It was not only the Prussians who were trying to revise rules about aliens at this time; when the Hanse diet met at Lübeck in June 1426 it, too, discussed the question of English and Dutch merchants residing in Hanseatic towns, but was unable to reach agreement.[32]

---

[31] *HR*, I (vii), nos. 592–4, 611, 671. *HUB*, 6, nos. 504, 528. *Rot. Parl.*, 4, p. 192. *POPC*, 3, pp. 110–11, 117.   [32] *HR*, I (vii), nos. 607, 611, 623, 671, 708, 746; (viii), no. 50.

As late as August 1425 the merchants of the London Steelyard were in despair about their status. Writing to Hanse envoys currently visiting Flanders they referred to the expense they had incurred in vain attempts to get their charters confirmed, and complained that the government turned a deaf ear to all representations made on their behalf by the Grand Master, by territorial princes and by the towns. They requested the envoys to come to England to intercede for them and offered to bear the cost. This invitation was not taken up, but already the heat was going out of the situation, since in that same month of August tunnage and poundage began again to be taken from denizens, which made it unrealistic for the Hanse men to press their claim to immunity from the charge. Moreover, in government circles sentiment was already changing in favour of the Hanse. During the recent session of parliament (June–July 1425) the royal council had ordered the city of London to fill the vacant office of English alderman to the Steelyard. In February 1426 the merchants complained that nothing had been done, and submitted three names to the council, asking it to nominate one of them as alderman; the first, William Crowemere, was chosen. The city refused at first to administer the oath of office and not until February 1427, after a further order from the crown, did it confirm the Steelyard's right to have such an alderman. On the same occasion a compromise was reached about the equally long-disputed matter of the sheriffs' tolls. The sheriffs relinquished all their claim, except for a toll of 4d on each cloth exported; on their part the merchants were to continue their ancient contribution of 40s to the city farm, and as a gesture of goodwill agreed to give the city every February two barrels of herring, one barrel of sturgeon and one hundredweight of wax, the total value reckoned to be £5 6s 8d. Whether these developments represented a change of policy on the part of the city or simply submission to the will of the government is not clear.[33]

Prospects of a further improvement in Anglo-Hanseatic relations in 1427 suffered a set-back because of the outbreak of war between some of the towns and Denmark. This had its origins in an ancient dispute between the Danish crown and the German counts of Holstein about sovereignty of the duchy of Schleswig. In July 1426 hostilities broke out between these two and in September the towns also took up arms, motivated chiefly by the fact that Denmark had

[33] *HR*, I (vii), no. 805. *HUB*, 6, nos. 611–13, 651, 658. *Rot. Parl.*, 4, p. 303. *Foedera*, IV (iv), p. 119.

recently imposed a toll on all ships passing through the Sound. Despite Denmark's provocative action the Hanse was far from united; in fact, the war was supported at first only by Hamburg (a Holstein town), Lübeck, Lüneberg, Wismar, Rostock and Stralsund; later the Saxon towns joined them. When they imposed a blockade on the Sound the Prussian and Zuider Zee towns of the Hanse refused to acknowledge it. In March 1427 the Bruges *Kontor* agreed that its members would not ship goods through the Sound, but reported that Holland-Zeeland and the Zuider Zee towns were preparing to break the blockade. It also passed on reports from London about the possibility of an Anglo-Danish alliance. The war between Denmark and the Hanse was in no way beneficial to England, and this thought was probably not altogether absent from the mind of Cardinal Beaufort when he offered to mediate between the belligerents. However, his letters also express concern that the strife would distract attention away from the international crusade against the Hussites, which he was directing in the summer of 1427. If the English had to choose sides there could be no doubt that they would align with the Danes, since to pursue their trade with Prussia they had to run the Hanseatic blockade of the Sound; obviously, this could be done more easily with Danish assistance. On 30 May 1427 the council decided that English ships might take service with Denmark, provided that they did not attack any vessels friendly to their own king. Another naval group which both Danes and Hanseatics were anxious to recruit was an international force of privateers, latter-day *Vitalienbrüder*; their allegiance was long in the balance, but in the end they chose the Hanse. Before this they had been in English service and spent part of the winter of 1426–7 sheltering in west-country harbours until ordered to leave. In the spring they were reported to have sailed to the Elbe.[34]

Because of the competition of Dutch merchants the Bruges *Kontor* decided that it could no longer afford to obey the order not to send goods through the Sound. Notifying Lübeck of this decision on 5 July 1427 it reported that an eighty-strong fleet carrying Bay salt had already sailed from the Zwin. Unfortunately, six days later a Hanseatic naval force was defeated off Copenhagen. This left the Danes in command of the Sound and enabled them to capture the entire Bay fleet when it arrived there. Some English vessels were already in Danish service and later the Hanse complained that the

---

[34] *HUB*, 6, nos. 661, 694. *HR*, 1 (viii), nos. 266, 336. *POPC*, 3, p. 270.

intervention cost them 200 men killed, 600 captured and goods lost
to the value of 100,000 nobles. About the same time the Prussians
also decided that their economic needs required them to break the
blockade, and on 10 July 1427 Danzig wrote to the Duke of
Burgundy that a fleet should be ready to leave within a week.
Because of possible attacks by both Germans and Danes, all ships,
alien as well as Prussian, were to travel in convoy and be escorted
through the Sound by six heavily armed warships. News of the
capture of the Bay fleet caused a change of plan; on 1 August it was
decided that alien ships could sail at their own risk, but any Prussian
merchants who had goods aboard them, or shares in the vessels
themselves, must sell their interests. Prussian ships of less than sixty
lasts burden were permitted to sail along the coast to Lübeck, but
larger vessels had to stay in port. Shortly afterwards it was decided
to delay all sailings until 15 August, to see if there were any better
news; if there were not, then the arrangements described above were
to stand.[35]

In 1428 Lübeck and its allies were still determined to keep the
Sound closed and to this end were anxious to have advance
intelligence of western plans. This was supplied by the *Kontore* of
Bruges and London, most of the English news coming via Flanders.
This was not done without risk, for the Londoners were in constant
fear that their letters might be intercepted. In February Bruges
reported that eight ships, which had been fitting out in Boston, had
been held back as a result of news from the Baltic. On 17 March,
however, London informed Bruges that fourteen of England's
biggest ships were being equipped to force the Sound. A month later
it was reported that this fleet, now increased in number to seventeen,
would sail on 1 May for Marstrand (an island at the mouth of the
Kattegat). When all ships were assembled there, a balinger was to be
sent to scout in the Sound. In April, after the failure of peace talks,
the Germans invested Copenhagen and on the penultimate day of
that month reported the capture of two English ships attempting to
enter the Baltic.[36]

In 1428 the Prussians again held back their own fleet while they
sent envoys to Lübeck and Denmark to ask for free passage through
the Sound. Western ships were free to depart at their own risk, but
to avoid antagonising the Hanse it was ruled that western merchants
should not freight goods in Prussian ships. When this decision was

[35] *HUB*, 6, no. 679. *HR*, 1 (viii), nos. 218, 237.
[36] *HUB*, 6, nos. 712, 722, 728. *HR*, 1 (viii), nos. 418, 422–4.

communicated to the Duke of Burgundy he asked that the Grand Master should either take the former's subjects into his protection or help them sell their property in Prussia. At one stage it was hoped that the Prussian fleet would depart on 25 July, but it had still not sailed by the middle of September and ships were forbidden to travel even through coastal waters to Lübeck. The Hanse eventually notified Prussia that its ships might trade with other Hanseatic towns, provided that their captains swore an oath not to go to any of the Scandinavian kingdoms and carried a certificate to this effect. No ship would be received without a certificate, but any privateer who attacked a certified ship would be outlawed. Prussian merchants might buy goods in Hanseatic towns, provided that they agreed not to sell them to any enemies. Finally, any Prussian ships which wished to pass through the Sound must come to the Wismar deep or the Trave estuary; only then would the Hanse decide whether they might proceed or, instead, have to discharge their cargoes, which would then have to be sent overland to Hamburg. This last condition was unacceptable to the Prussian diet, which forbade its ships to risk the voyage; it also prevented its merchants from consigning goods to western ships going through the Sound. The Hanse had asked the Prussians to detain the latter, but on 16 October Danzig notified Lübeck that the Dutch and English fleets had already sailed. In December the Prussians finally received a safe-conduct from the King of Denmark, provided that they did not carry goods belonging to any town at war with him; the diet then decided that its ships might risk the voyage through the Sound.[37]

The refusal of the Hanse to open the Sound meant that the Prussians extended a warmer welcome to those English and Dutch merchants who successfully ran the blockade. The Prussians looked eagerly not only for cloth but also for Bay salt, in the absence of which they had to buy the more expensive Lüneberg product. Both English and Dutch also imported herrings, since the Prussians were cut off from Skania. This dependence may have contributed to the improvement of the status of English merchants in Prussia during the course of 1428. As early as March German merchants in London made representations to Prussia on behalf of their rivals, possibly in return for the relaxation of pressure upon them by the city authorities. But since their own countrymen were very much in a minority in the London community the Prussians probably attached

[37] *HR*, I (viii), nos. 453, 455, 507, 508a, 546.

little weight to this appeal. When the Prussian diet met in May the Englishmen sought permission to set up at Dibau an establishment along the lines of the London Steelyard; the proposal was not rejected out of hand, though in the event it was not allowed. The English fellowship still enjoyed a *de facto* existence, since a delegation going from Danzig to Lübeck in June, to work for the opening of the Sound and the release of English personnel and property, was sent by the 'aldermannos societatis mercatorum pronunc in Prussia existenses'. In England on the 20th of that same month the merchants received confirmation from the crown of their right to elect a governor, probably as a prelude to a renewed attempt to gain official recognition in Prussia. This time they were successful and in December 1428 the Grand Master officially confirmed their right to elect an alderman, although at the same time he ruled that Englishmen visiting Danzig should enjoy neither more nor fewer liberties than other non-burgesses.[38]

The following year relations between England and Prussia again began to deteriorate. This was probably due, at least in part, to the fact that having made concessions the Prussians expected to gain something in return, only to find their hopes dashed. Their demands were centred on the financial provisions of the treaty of 1409 and in March 1429 a delegation empowered to negotiate on behalf of the Prussian and Livonian claimants began talks with the king's council, which continued intermittently until May 1430. After consulting parliament the government decided that the king was not legally bound to settle his grandfather's debt, but offered to consider paying *ex gratia* a 'reasonable' sum each year out of the customs duties paid by Prussian merchants in England. This offer was communicated to the Prussians but nothing came of it. About the same time the Treasurer of Marienburg began to clamour for the 838 nobles owed to him by the Earl of Northumberland, whose inheritance had been restored in 1416. In 1429 thirty-six English ships were arrested in Danzig in an attempt to enforce payment of this sum, while the following year Hull merchandise was distrained there for the same reason. In May 1433 the officials of the English society in Prussia were given a quittance for the Percy debt, but they continued to protest about the manner in which payment had been enforced. In the same period distraints were made on behalf of other claimants,

---

[38] *HUB*, 6, no. 723. *HR*, I (viii), nos. 433, 451–3, 546.

including some who had allegedly been awarded damages by the English Chancellor in the aftermath of the Hague conference, but who had so far not been paid.[39]

The English merchants complained bitterly about the renewed harassment in Prussia, but there their treatment was at least cloaked in a semblance of legality. The situation was otherwise in the Sound where force was the order of the day. The same is true of Norway, where the Danish–Hanseatic war prompted one of the periodic returns of English merchants. After their expulsion in the early 1370s there appears to be no evidence of Englishmen visiting Bergen for almost two decades. A royal licence enrolled on 30 June 1389 ordered the port officers of Lynn to release from general arrest two Lynn vessels, belonging to John Waryn and James Hubyn, for a voyage to Norway. They were to give sureties not to go to Scotland and to return immediately for the king's service. A special supplementary account of this voyage, duty of £7 16s 10¼d paid for exports and imports worth £152 16s 6d, is found with the enrolled poundage account for Exchequer year 13 (1389–90).[40] If this was a pioneering voyage it was clearly encouraging, since between 1 April and 30 November 1390 Lynn merchants imported stockfish worth £1,094 in one Lynn and three Hanse ships; between the latter date and Michaelmas 1390 they imported £739 of stockfish in one Lynn and one Danzig ship.[41] These were probably the last voyages made by Englishmen to Bergen for several years, since Lynn merchants later complained that 'circa 14 Richard II' (1391–2) they were set upon in that town by Hanseatics, who destroyed their houses and merchandise to the value of 3,000 marks and written securities for debts owing to them of more than £1,000. The accession of Henry IV, whose daughter was married to the King of Denmark and Norway, emboldened Lynn men to return to Norway in 1400, but at first they were again threatened by the Hanseatics. Their claim of discrimination was denied by the governor of Bergen, who was ordered to investigate, and the fact that the Englishmen later claimed damages only for loss of trade, not for robbery and assault, suggests that the clash was not as serious as the previous one. Nevertheless, the Lynn men complained to Henry IV and in March 1402 a number of Boston *Bergenfahrer* were summoned before the

[39] *HUB*, 6, nos. 779, 860, 934, 942, 959. *HR*, I (viii), nos. 586–90, 666–8, 778; II (i), nos. 168–70. *POPC*, 4, pp. 45–6.   [40] *CCR*, 1389–92, p. 7. PRO, E 356/5, m.28d.
[41] PRO, E122/93/31; 94/12.

king's council and ordered to provide security in the sum of 1,400 marks that Englishmen would not be molested in Bergen.[42] The recognisance was not made, but Lynn men resumed their trade and in October 1402 imported £345 of stockfish in two Hanse ships.[43] The next major incident in this chain of events was in 1406, when a large number of Norfolk fishermen casting their nets off southern Norway were attacked and killed by a superior Hanseatic force, probably from Hamburg. Consequently, in February 1407 the *Bergenfahrer* again appeared before the king himself and gave security of 2,000 marks to appear at a later date; this was remitted in May after they had convinced the council that they and their fellows had had no hand in the crime.[44]

Not content with trading between England and Norway, Lynn merchants upset their rivals even more by attempting to intrude into trade between Norway and Germany. In February 1409 they engaged a ship of Bremen, a town with which they were friendly, to sail firstly from Lynn to Bergen, thence to Wismar and back to Bergen laden with beer. The skipper was prevented from going from Bergen to Wismar and when he returned to Lynn those who had engaged him claimed damages from the *Bergenfahrer* for loss of profits. In 1411 the Lynn men secured the arrest of *Bergenfahrer* in Boston, but suffered a similar fate themselves in Bergen. It is not clear which side made the first move on this occasion, but the Germans, despite a bond of 2,000 marks put up by English associates, were detained from March to September. Two years later *Bergenfahrer* were again arrested at Boston, but this time allegedly at the behest of Boston merchants, who claimed attacks on themselves and their property in Bergen and the slaying there of one of their number and a Lynn merchant.[45] It is probably necessary to be somewhat sceptical about the degree of support given to this action by the authorities and leading merchants of Boston, since it resulted in a three-year boycott of the town by the *Bergenfahrer*, which must have done considerable harm to the economy.[46] The protracted negotiations for a settlement, through the mediation of the King of Denmark, were blamed upon a combination of bad weather and the

---

[42] *Letters of Henry the Fourth*, 1, p. 46. CPR, 1408–13, pp. 383–5.
[43] N. S. B. Gras, *The Early English Customs System* (Cambridge, Mass., 1926), p. 556.
[44] *HUB*, 6, nos. 756, 779.
[45] *CCR*, 1409–13, pp. 152–3, 321; 1413–19, p. 12. CPR, 1408–13, pp. 308, 321, 383–5, 400.
[46] See below, p. 161.

duplicity of the Hanseatics in fixing a timetable which they knew their rivals could not observe.[47] Despite the impasse at Boston, trade between England and Norway, both in the hands of Englishmen and Germans, never came entirely to a halt and by 1417 was more or less back to normal. In April 1417 the King of Denmark summoned English and Hanse representatives and enquired whether they were able yet to settle their differences amicably, or whether they would rather that he imposed a settlement on them. The Englishmen opted for the latter, but since the king did not have time to deal with it at the moment he said that he would give his decision one year hence.[48]

The difficulties in the way of trading with Bergen in the second decade of the fifteenth century caused English merchants and fishermen to direct their attention to Iceland. The first recorded voyage was in 1412 and a rapid build-up followed, a formal prohibition of traffic in 1415, following a protest by the Danish king, having no effect.[49] But when Denmark again attempted to stop the trade in 1426 a majority of the merchant community of Lynn overruled its Iceland section and banned the voyages. This was done in deference to their Bergen trade, the prospects of which seemed bright because of impending war between Denmark and the Wendish towns of the Hanse. Despite the insecurity of the times, Englishmen probably increased their stake in Norway's trade for a half-dozen years or more. Bergen was plundered three times in 1428 and 1429 by privateers sailing under Hanseatic colours, but good luck, or possibly the fact that immediately before that these same robbers had been in English service and perhaps hoped to be so again one day, may have saved the Englishmen from serious damage. At any rate no claims for English losses in these early attacks feature in the comprehensive catalogue submitted to Hanse envoys in 1436. However, claims were submitted for £20,000 for nine English ships seized in Bergen in 1430 and £720 for losses in 1432.[50] On the same occasion the Hanse representatives put in claims amounting to 8,030 nobles for an English attack on Danzig ships in Bergen in 1432 and for 10,000 marks in Lübeck currency for an attack there in 1434. They also asserted that the King of Denmark had instigated the actions against English merchants in

[47] *William Ashbourne's Book*, pp. 88, 90, 93–4.
[48] *CPR*, 1413–16, p. 320, *CCR*, 1413–19, p. 316, *HR*, I (vi), no. 385.
[49] For the Iceland trade see Carus-Wilson, *Medieval Merchant Venturers*, pp. 98–142.
[50] *HR*, II (i), no. 385.

retaliation for depredations allegedly carried out in Iceland by their fellow countrymen. It is undoubtedly true that after Lynn merchants agreed not to visit Iceland in 1426 sailors from other ports such as Hull and Bristol continued to go there. Moreover, the King of Denmark was annoyed because some of the Englishmen who did come to Norway for stockfish were tempted to seek it at source in the northern fishing villages, rather than at the Bergen staple. All these matters were taken up by two English embassies to Denmark in 1431 and 1432. The second resulted in a treaty in which England agreed to forbid its subjects to seek fish in any Danish territory save Bergen.

Despite the generally improved situation of Hanse merchants in England in the late 1420s some Englishmen succeeded in obtaining writs to distrain Hamburg merchants in compensation for their own losses. In March 1430 the government put a stop to this, ordering that all Hanseatics should be treated as the 'king's true friends'. In October it went even further and for the first time in the reign formally confirmed the Hanseatic franchises. This official goodwill was jeopardised in the following March when parliament renewed the tunnage and poundage subsidy. The alien rate of poundage was increased from 1s to 1s 6d and the tunnage on sweet wines was doubled. Denizens did not pay the increment, and to make matters worse their cloth exports were now accorded exemption from the basic poundage. After protests, the king's council on 5 May 1431 respited Hanse payments of the increment for the time being, but required the merchants to find £400 security to pay it if their liability should be established. The Steelyard also protested to the Hanse and the Grand Master and the latter then imprisoned the English alderman and five merchants until they promised to intervene to prevent the increment being levied on Hansards. To ensure their cooperation they were compelled to give personal bonds of £400, the same amount as the security taken so far in England. When parliament next met in May 1432 it was in no mood to agree that the Hanse should be spared the increment and instead suggested that those who had been forced to give bonds in Prussia should be allowed to bring counter-actions in the courts of the city of London. This advice was rejected and the Hanse were eventually excused payment. The crown did, however, at first accept a petition calling for the arrest of goods of Lübeck, Hamburg, Wismar and Rostock to answer for the seizure of a Boston ship in the Sound in March 1431. In August 1432 the writ, issued only the previous month, was cancelled on the grounds that it might jeopardise the embassy which was about to be sent to Denmark and the Hanse.[51]

Part of the purpose of the latest mission was to discuss English losses in the Baltic war. The envoys reached some sort of agreement with Denmark but none was made with the Hanse, and relations continued to be tense throughout 1433 and into 1434. Englishmen complained about increasing restrictions on their trade in Prussia, including the ban on renting property. Because of the accommodation problem they again demanded (unsuccessfully) the right to have a factory similar to the London Steelyard. In January 1434 the Prussian diet reaffirmed the earlier decision of the Grand Master that the English should enjoy no more rights than other aliens. Relations with the Wendish towns were no better and so loud was the clamour in England for reprisals that in December 1433 the crown had to issue a safe-conduct of one year's duration, reminding all officials, both public and private, that Hanse merchants enjoyed immunity from local tolls and from arrest for all debts save personal ones. A letter of the Steelyard reveals that the safe-conduct, though couched in general terms, was designed specifically to protect the goods of Lübeck, Hamburg, Rostock and Wismar from mass arrests. A few months later the Exchequer itself exacerbated the situation in an attempt to increase the yield of import duties. Hitherto duty had been based on the cost of goods in the country of origin; now, officials were instructed to charge duty on current market prices in England, which would have been considerably higher. The Steelyard ordered its members to stop trading and complained to the Hanse diet, which was to meet in June 1434. On 16 June, even before the diet's reaction can have been known in England, the king's council, the Treasurer alone dissenting, reversed the ruling of the Exchequer and restored the former method of assessing merchandise.[52]

The diet of 1434 was particularly well attended, since it was required to consider several matters of great consequence to the Hanse as a whole. Commercial relations with Spain, Flanders and Holland-Zeeland were no less critical than those with England, while a five-year truce with Denmark, made in September 1431 on terms very favourable to the Hanse, had been badly kept and by now had broken down almost entirely. It was decided, therefore, to send

---

[51] *CCR*, 1429–35, pp. 55, 145–6, 155–6. *CPR*, 1429–36, p. 220. *Rot. Parl.*, 4, pp. 369, 403. *POPC*, 4, p. 86. *HUB*, 6, nos. 888, 991–2, 1005, 1037, 1046. *HR*, II (i), no. 147.

[52] *POPC*, 4, pp. 239–42. *HR*, II (i), nos. 169, 241, 319–20. *HUB*, 6, no. 1009.

an embassy to deal directly with each of the powers named above, with the exception of Spain. As a sign of its concern the diet made an ordinance banning the import of English cloth. This decision was probably made easier by the fact that for some time the Duke of Burgundy had been trying to organise a boycott in all his own territories, and wanted the Hansards to suspend their right of transit. The diet also agreed that, if England did not reply favourably to the demands of the envoys, then it would be coerced by a total trade boycott. It was imperative that the Hanse be united at this time; above all, this meant keeping the Prussians in line. To this end, four delegates from the other towns were sent to Danzig to help the Prussians attending the diet explain their plans. From Danzig they were immediately summoned to Marienburg, since the Grand Master had recently repeated his prohibition of any assembly which was not convened by himself. On 4 July they informed him of the demands which were to be made of each of the states to be visited, including an eleven-point programme for England. He promised to back any coercive measures which the towns might introduce, and on 9 July letters were drawn up signifying that the envoys enjoyed the support of the Teutonic Order. Additionally, on 29 July the Grand Master wrote to Henry VI in his own name, complaining about the continued failure to pay the arrears of the 1409 indemnity and the lack of respect for the Hanse franchises in England. He said that at the insistence of his own subjects he had given English merchants six months notice to leave Prussia, unless the Germans were given satisfaction. Copies of his letter were sent to the authorities of London and Lynn, with the suggestion that they should combine with York to put pressure on the government to concede the Hanseatic claims.[53]

Because of military involvement with Poland, the Grand Master did not exercise his right to separate representation in the present negotiations as he had often done in the past. Instead, he agreed that Henry Vorrath and Nicholas Wrecht, respectively burgomaster and secretary of Danzig, who had represented Prussia at the Lübeck diet, should speak for all Prussian interests in the two embassies, one going to western Europe and the other to Denmark. Vorrath arrived in Bruges on 27 September 1434 with Henry Hoyer of Hamburg and John Klingenberg of Lübeck; they were joined a few days later by

---

[53] *HR*, ii (i), nos. 321, 354–7, 359–62.

Everard Hardefust of Cologne. The participation of Cologne in the diet and the ensuing negotiations is a measure of the gravity of the crisis in Hanseatic affairs, but the loyal involvement of this city was short-lived. The delegation remained in Bruges dealing with relations with Flanders until 11 October, when it left for England. The envoys arrived in London on 22 October and on the last day of the month were formally received by a majority of the king's council. During the next few days they submitted a list of complaints, which was referred to a committee of four knights. Their grievances numbered eight: (1) the levy of tunnage and poundage; (2) the collection of a poll tax from travellers entering and leaving English territory at Dover and Calais; (3) prolonged delays in obtaining justice; (4) denial of the right to mixed juries, especially in courts of admiralty; (5) denial of immunity from distraint for debts and trespasses of third parties; (6) delay in payment of goods purveyed for the crown; (7) exaction of local tolls at Southampton and Newcastle; (8) denial of the right to sell wine by retail in London. No protest was registered against wool staple regulations, even though this matter had earlier been discussed with the Grand Master. This undoubtedly reflects the fact that the Hansards now had no direct interest in the export of wool and did not want to be seen as a mouthpiece of Burgundy, which was currently striving hard to overthrow the Calais staple.[54]

At midday on 6 November the envoys were abruptly summoned to the presence of the Chancellor, who informed them that the negotiations must be prorogued, since the council was about to leave London because of an outbreak of plague and would not return till a fortnight after Christmas. Protesting that they could not remain in England that long, they arranged for four merchants of the Steelyard to receive any reply that the council might eventually make. To supplement the general complaints already delivered they now submitted a list of claims for damages. This consisted partly of specific, individual claims, some dating back as far as 1411, and partly of more tendentious demands, such as repayment of more than £100,000 alleged to have been paid in poundage over the previous thirty years and 100,000 nobles for damage caused by English assistance to the Danes in 1427. The envoys were still in London on 17 November, but were back in Bruges by 18 December,

---

[54] *HR*, II (i), nos. 324, 383–4, 392. *HUB*, 7, part 1, no. 39.

after being delayed three weeks at Dover by bad weather. Vorrath immediately sent to Danzig a pessimistic account of the mission. Although the English had given them 'many sweet words', he did not expect much good to result; even while they had been there four Hanseatic ships had been seized. This forecast proved to be correct. When the king's council returned to London in January 1435 it was waited upon by English merchants, who complained about their expulsion from Prussia and demanded that the Hanseatic franchises should not be confirmed without new guarantees for English trade in the Baltic. They also asked that any German financial claims which might be substantiated should be set against the claims of Englishmen. These points were accepted by the council, but since the Steelyard had no authority to consider them the council offered to send a delegation to confer with the envoys, who were still in the Low Countries. Both the Hanse and the Grand Master agreed to this, but the latter warned Vorrath that in no circumstances was he to concede any extension of English privileges; such matters could be discussed only in Prussia. Nor should Vorrath agree that the financial demands of each side be set against one another, since the Prussians had harmed no one. Early in April the German envoys wrote to England that they would wait in Bruges until the end of Easter week (24 April), but advised that they were not fully empowered to negotiate and could only transmit suggestions to the Hanse and Prussia.[55]

The two sides met for the first time in the Carmelite church at Bruges on 5 May. The Hanse team was now reduced to Vorrath and Hoyer, since the other two envoys had recently been withdrawn on grounds of cost. The officially accredited English team consisted of the Lynn merchant, Thomas Borowe, and two lawyers. This was smaller than another commission appointed at the same time to treat with the Flemings; the latter consisted of the same two lawyers and five merchants of the staple. (A number of royal officials at Calais were formally members of both commissions.) Despite advance notification of the limited scope of the talks, the English insisted on submitting their own demands. Because of this the Hanse envoys felt it necessary to make a formal protest that they lacked powers to negotiate, and on 11 May they had this drawn up by a public notary. There the talks would probably have broken down

---

[55] *Rot. Parl.*, 4, p. 493, *HR*, II (i), nos. 385, 407, 421-2, 433, 436.

altogether, had it not been for the mediation of the German alderman of the London Steelyard, who was present in an advisory capacity. As a result of his intervention an indenture was made on 14 May, which provided that the two sides should meet again at Bruges on 13 January 1436. To maintain pressure the Hanseatic envoys wanted all trade to be halted by mutual agreement until the results of the next conference were known. They were already aware that the Grand Master had forbidden his own subjects to trade with England. This suggestion was not welcomed by the English nor by the Steelyard, but as a compromise it was agreed that trade should continue until Whitsun, and that Germans would then be allowed two months to remove themselves and their property from England. In a letter sent to Lübeck and Prussia on 17 May the envoys recommended that the Hanse should break off trade; this proposal was accepted. Officials of the Steelyard subsequently withdrew to Bruges, but some merchants remained in London and elsewhere in England.[56]

When the time drew near for the next meeting it was opposed by English merchants, who urged that it would be a waste of money to send a delegation to Flanders unless parliament first formally revoked the Hanseatic franchises. This advice was rejected by the council, and on 16 December 1435 the same team as before was commissioned to treat with the Hanse envoys. They immediately crossed over to Calais to await the arrival of the Germans. On 18 February they wrote to the Bruges *Kontor* complaining that they had already been kept waiting five weeks beyond the appointed date, but that they would wait two weeks longer. On 12 March the *Kontor* reported to Lübeck that two of the commissioners had returned to England, leaving the third in Calais, where the whole team would reassemble when it was informed that the Germans had arrived. The Hanseatic delegation did not receive its final instructions until after the Englishmen had left Calais. Although the Hanse had fully half a year's notice of the impending conference it was totally unprepared. Lübeck had tried to convene a special diet to discuss the English demands, but was unable to do so. The major obstacles were tension between the Prussian towns and the Teutonic Order and war between the Order and Poland. The Grand Master distrusted Vorrath, whom he already accused of having exceeded his powers.

---

[56] *HR*, II (i), nos. 429–32, 435, 437. *HUB*, 7, part 1, no. 40.

He was unwilling that he should again speak alone for Prussia, but on the other hand he could ill afford to divert any of his best advisers from the eastern to the western theatres of diplomacy. At the end of January the Prussians were still debating whom to send. Eventually, it was decided that Vorrath should be accompanied by John Sobbe, canon of Thorn, and Hildebrand Tannenberg, the Grand Master's secretary. On 14 February the Grand Master wrote to Henry VI apologising for the failure of his envoys to appear in January, but expressing the hope that the conference might now begin at Bruges on Palm Sunday (8 April). If this venue was not possible then the Prussians were empowered to treat elsewhere, for all Europe was aware that, since the failure of the Congress of Arras, war between England and Burgundy was inevitable, and this would close all Burgundian lands to Englishmen.[57]

The Prussian envoys went first to Lübeck, remaining there until at least 20 March, and arrived at Bruges on 3 April together with John Klingenberg and Henry Hoyer. By now it was impossible for the English team to go to Flanders, so Henry VI wrote to the Germans (22 April) inviting them to come either to Calais or to England. Before he received this letter Vorrath had informed Danzig (29 April) that he had given up all hope of getting to Calais. He reported that he was optimistic about renewing the truce with Holland-Zeeland, but advised that no ships should come to Flanders, since conditions were too dangerous and the Duke of Burgundy was pressing Hanseatic vessels into his own service. The Hanse envoys answered Henry on 31 May, regretting that they were unable to reach either Calais or England and that they must go home for consultation; they requested that in the meantime the king extend his protection to German merchants. In writing to Danzig on the previous day Vorrath advised that they should withdraw to Lübeck and then try to cross to England from one of the Elbe ports. This last letter crossed with one dispatched from Danzig on 25 May, urging that the envoys should use every effort to make peace with England, so that if the Hanse was unable to trade with Flanders then the other door would be open again. On 5 June the envoys were in Ghent, where they received news of the massacre of more than eighty German merchants in Sluys. For greater security they immediately moved to Antwerp and shortly afterwards returned to Lübeck. On

[57] *HR*, II (i), nos. 503–6, 508, 523–4, 537. *Rot. Parl.*, 4, p. 493.

24 June 1436 Vorrath informed Danzig that the diet wished to send the delegation to England, and that he awaited instructions on this point. Because of the preoccupation of the Grand Master with Poland these were not drawn up until 30 July, when he and Danzig agreed on the main points to be observed. Vorrath was to be sure to obtain the arrears of the 1409 indemnity and he was not to promise any extension of English privileges; it was again stressed that the latter point could be negotiated only in Prussia. Vorrath's credentials, dated 1 September, made it clear that despite earlier misgivings the Grand Master's powers devolved on him personally, the Order's representatives having been recalled, and he alone was qualified to speak for Prussia. This was very different from the agreement of July 1434, in which the Grand Master had promised to abide by the decisions of the Hanse as a whole. When this became known to the other envoys as they were preparing to sail, Lübeck's representative wrote home pointing out that if Vorrath adhered to his instructions it might not be possible to make peace and asking what they should do in that event. No record of an answer has been discovered, but the prescience of the query has probably influenced historians' interpretation of subsequent events.[58]

The envoys met at Hamburg in mid-September 1436 and sailed from there about a month later, arriving at Orwell on 25 October. Letters of safe-conduct were made out two days later and commissions drafted for English negotiators on 6 November. The latter were the Bishop of Norwich, the Lords Tiptoft and Cromwell, the clerk of the privy seal, two lawyers and Henry Frowicke, alderman of London. Although only the last-named can be regarded as directly representing the trading community, it may be assumed that other merchants were regularly consulted throughout the subsequent negotiations. All the English commissioners save Cromwell were parties to the eventual treaty. Few details survive about the talks themselves, though much is known about efforts made by the envoys to put a stop to trade conducted by German merchants who had remained in England throughout the period of the official boycott and others who were presently visiting the country. The ambassadors were not without a vested interest, since they were themselves expected to engage in private trade to help cover their expenses. They brought so many goods that they overloaded the first

---

[58] *HR*, II (i), nos. 541, 561–2, 566–8, 595–6; (ii), nos. 16–18, 53.

ship they chartered and had to hire a second to carry the excess. But this apart, Henry Vorrath in particular firmly believed that the mission would not achieve its objective if the Hanseatics resumed their business before England set its seal upon a treaty. The Hanse had periodically renewed the trade ban imposed in 1434 and it remained in force even though negotiations had begun. But it was impossible to stop all trade. In April 1436 Danzig wrote to Vorrath that hardly had he left the city than the Grand Master, in return for a promised consideration of 3,000 Rhineguilders, had given permission for six English ships to come to Prussia to trade. In the light of this development the city authorities despaired of being able to maintain the boycott. Writing from Bruges at the end of May, Vorrath reported that the Dutch, although subjects of the Duke of Burgundy, were very friendly towards England, and that English merchants were planning to engage six Zeeland ships to come to Prussia to buy goods. In August, Henry VI notified the Grand Master that he would not molest any German merchants who came to England and asked him to protect the four ships coming with his letter. The leader of this expedition was Nicholas Hassham, alderman of the English merchants, and his licence from the crown refers to a current scarcity of bowstaves and wainscot in England. But it was not merely Englishmen who were anxious that trade should continue. When the Hanseatic delegation finally arrived in England it claimed that many German merchants were actively breaking the sanctions. Among them, allegedly, were Prussians, men from the Zuider Zee towns and the Lübeck *Bergenfahrer*, who not only kept up their trade between England and Norway but also exported cloth to Germany. The most serious sanctions breakers were the men of Cologne, who continued to export cloth and refused to pay fines imposed on them by the Hanse officials at Bruges. On 10 December 1436 the Bruges *Kontor* wrote to England warning the envoys that the Archbishop of Cologne was sending his own embassy to negotiate on behalf of his subjects. The letter did not reach its destination until 10 March 1437, by which time the Cologne delegation, led by John von Coesfeld, had arrived and probably left again, but without accomplishing anything. Wherever the Hanse's own emissaries found merchants importing or exporting they ordered them to attend a diet at Lübeck on 1 May 1437 to answer for their disobedience. Lübeck seems to have regarded the envoys as over zealous in this matter, for on 17 February it advised that it would be time enough to consider how to deal with sanctions breakers after the mission had achieved its purpose.[59]

A progress report sent to Danzig by Vorrath in December, and another sent by the delegation as a whole to Bruges on 9 January 1437, expressed the hope that when parliament assembled (on 21 January) the negotiations would be concluded quickly. Vorrath's letter mentioned that the English had submitted claims for damages amounting to more than £200,000 sterling. It is impossible to doubt that there was a large element of bluff in this, and that much of the figure was simply a counter to set against German financial claims. More than half of the total was made up of taxes allegedly paid in Prussia over a period of many years. Despite subsequent developments it is difficult to believe that at this stage English merchants can realistically have hoped to gain complete immunity from taxation, let alone recover earlier payments. With the exception of a poll tax levied in 1422 there is no record of any earlier resistance to payment of local taxes. As regards the present claims it is certain that one side, or both, lied in the evidence they submitted. It was alleged that £40,000 had been paid to the city of Danzig in the form of a quayage tax known as *Pfahlgeld*. From the German statement that the tax was equal to only 6d sterling on 100 nobles worth of merchandise, it would follow that Englishmen had handled goods worth more than £50,000,000 in the period of less than forty years during which the tax had been levied – a quite impossible figure. On the other hand the notion of any *ad valorem* duty levied at a rate of less than one tenth of one per cent is suspect. Whatever the degree of bluff, the financial claims of each side proved impossible to settle. On 12 March 1437 Vorrath was able to report that agreement had been reached on everything but this matter. The only solution was to set aside most of the claims and they were not even mentioned in the treaty which was drafted within a few more days. Provision was made only for payment of arrears of the indemnity which Henry IV had agreed to pay to Prussia in 1409. An indenture recording the draft treaty was drawn up on 22 March 1437, though it was not confirmed by the application of the privy seal until 7 June. In the meantime none of the concessions made to the Hanse were implemented. Vorrath was in no doubt as to where the blame lay. Writing to Danzig on 18 June, he said that the work would have been completed three months

---

[59] *HR*, II (i), nos. 563, 568, 577; (ii), nos. 20–1, 27, 37, 52, 64, 89. *HUB*, 7, part 1, no. 174. *Foedera*, v (i), p. 35.

since, but for bribes given by English merchants to the Treasurer and Chancellor. Their purpose was not to sink the treaty altogether, but simply to delay it while they prepared their own cloth for export. They now had eight ships nearly ready to sail, while the Germans, to whom the envoys had finally given permission to export, were still hindered by customs officials, who refused to hand over cockets. The Englishmen hoped thereby to get to Prussia first and capture the market for cloth. Vorrath could not prevent this, but he urged Danzig to minimise the damage by delaying their return voyage.[60]

Because of its importance in the history of Anglo-Hanseatic relations in the fifteenth century, the treaty merits careful consideration. The accepted opinion is that it was a great victory for the English, but that the settlement was made possible only because Vorrath exceeded his powers. Professor Postan, for example, wrote that 'Vorrath's position was very difficult, almost tragic. He knew that the negotiations could not succeed as long as he adhered to the Danzig instructions, and the failure of the negotiations might mean the break up of the Hanse... After a great deal of hesitation he was forced to break his undertaking to his own town and negotiate about the position of the English in Danzig.'[61] This echoes the opinion of German historians, some of whom hailed Vorrath as a great Hanseatic statesman, able to set aside his regional loyalty for the greater good. The verdict seems to be based largely upon the speculations of the non-Prussian envoys before they sailed from Hamburg and the recriminations against Vorrath when he returned to Danzig. There appears to be no evidence that he actually experienced the alleged crisis of conscience and, when faced with his accusers, his defence was not that he had made concessions to save the treaty, but rather that he had not exceeded his powers and had not in any way extended the liberties enjoyed by Englishmen in Prussia. These assertions were supported by those who had negotiated with him in England. Letters to this effect were sent by the London Steelyard and Frank Keddeken, a Flemish lawyer who had served as Vorrath's adviser and interpreter, since he himself spoke neither English nor Latin.[62] Rather less positive, but just as suggestive, is a letter sent to Lübeck as early as April 1437.[63] This

---

[60] *HR*, II (ii), nos. 29, 65, 67, 70, 76, 84–5.

[61] M. M. Postan, 'The Economic and Political Relations of England and the German Hanse from 1400 to 1475', pp. 118–19, in E. Power and M. M. Postan, *Studies in English Trade in the Fifteenth Century* (London, 1933), pp. 91–153.   [62] *HR*, II (ii), nos. 224, 226.

[63] *Ibid.*, no. 78.

résumé of the recent treaty said that English merchants had been guaranteed any and all liberties enjoyed within the previous hundred years, but made no reference to immunity from taxation, which was to become the most critical issue in Prussia. It is difficult to see how they could have overlooked such a crucial matter, since any immunity would have applied not merely in Prussia but in all Hanse towns. Nevertheless, the treaty does seem to have guaranteed English merchants immunity from new taxation which might be introduced at some future date and also makes statements, albeit ambiguous and possibly even self-contradictory, about existing taxation. How can these facts be reconciled? Vorrath and his supporters may or may not have been truthful in their claims that they had not wilfully made concessions to the English. They may genuinely have believed that the treaty could not be interpreted in such a way as to support an English claim to greater liberties. Alternatively, they may have felt obliged to assert this, even if it had become as obvious to themselves as it was to others that poor drafting of the treaty on their part opened the way for such an interpretation. This last suggestion implies a charge of carelessness, which is not easy to substantiate, particularly since the negotiators included several lawyers who, unlike the laymen, were not illiterate in Latin, the language of the treaty. There remains the possibility of collusion, which might even account for the ambiguity of some clauses. If the Hanse ambassadors had knowingly exceeded Vorrath's powers they might have instructed their lawyers deliberately to adopt an ambiguous form of words to cloud that fact, and the tenor of which might even be disputed if need arose.

Professor Postan saw the treaty as 'defining and safeguarding the English position in the Hanseatic regions more exactly and fully than any formulas had done in the past'.[64] In fact the statements about rights of trade are rather less explicit than those contained in the treaty of 1409, though the English position was protected by the proviso that they should use and enjoy whatever liberties and free customs they had used and enjoyed at any time in the past. They may have felt some qualms about the qualification of previous usage by the word 'reasonably' (*racionabiliter*) but this was balanced by qualifying the former usage of the Hanseatic franchises in England with the same adverb. Postan also accepted that Englishmen 'were to be free of all taxes imposed in the course of the last hundred years

---

[64] Postan, *England and the Hanse*, p. 119.

and more' (and in the future). The use of the words 'and more' causes some difficulty, since taken literally they could denote infinity, though it can hardly be supposed that the Englishmen believed that they had won immunity from all taxation, no matter how ancient and legitimate. What they were seeking to establish was immunity from novel taxes, though in their eyes 'novel' meant any taxes first imposed within the previous hundred years or so. A word or phrase meaning 'and less' or 'within' would be more appropriate, though it is likely that the English did not wish to be tied to a precise period and may have chosen 'and more' (*et ultra*) for that reason. Comment must also be made about the phraseology used to describe the 'novel taxes' against which Englishmen were apparently to be protected. The actual words were 'prise exacciones nove seu prestaciones', i.e. prises (compulsory purchases, often on terms disadvantageous to the seller), new exactions and prests (forced loans of money). The words themselves are quite inappropriate to describe the taxes actually being levied on Englishmen in Prussia at that time. The intentions of those who framed the treaty could have been made more clear by using Latinised forms of the German names for the taxes in question. The latter course may have been rejected by the Englishmen as too limiting in the safeguards it provided, though conversely the Hanseatics may have regarded such a step as being too explicitly a major concession. Instead, the negotiators in their search for a general formula turned to Edward I's *Carta Mercatoria* of 1303. The last clause of that charter promised that in return for the new customs then granted by alien merchants 'nulla exactio prisa vel prestacio aut aliquod aliud onus' should be imposed on the persons of the merchants or their merchandise and chattels. The choice of the words from Edward I's charter was no accident. It betokened the principle of reciprocity which must have governed the bargaining about taxation during the forging of the present treaty. What the Hanseatics gained in return for their concession will be seen shortly. But first it must be asked whether the treaty incontrovertibly gave Englishmen immunity from novel taxation, meaning any which had been imposed within the previous hundred years or so, as well as in the future. The first clause of the treaty appears to say this, but we are then faced with the problem of the second clause, which appears to say something different. After describing Englishmen's trading rights in Hanseatic regions, it states they must pay 'custumis et deveriis de mercandisis suis debitis et consuetis'. The words 'customs and dues from merchandise', although still not precisely descriptive of the mercantile taxes paid by Englishmen in Prussia, are nearer to the mark than the words used in the previous clause. But the chief problem is caused by the insertion of the words 'due and accustomed'. Common sense would suggest that any tax which had been paid regularly without formal objection would fall into this category and, as already mentioned, there is no record that before this the English had ever objected to the payment of any Hanse tax save the Danzig poll tax of 1422. Only by rejecting the obvious meaning of 'due and accustomed' and limiting it to taxes initiated more than a hundred years before (and no doubt levied continuously in the interim) can the second clause be prevented from contradicting the first. There is, however, one further obstacle to the English claim to immunity from taxes. The final clause of the 1437 treaty stated that nothing contained within it should prejudice any existing treaties between England and Prussia or the Hanse towns. This includes the Anglo-Prussian treaty of 1409, in which both sides had undertaken to pay existing customs. One can only conclude that whatever its true intention the statement of English liability to taxes in the Hanse regions was by no means unambiguous.

If the Hanseatic envoys did indeed knowingly concede immunity from 'new taxes' to Englishmen in 1437 then it can only have been done in return for their own immunity from tunnage and poundage in England, in other words an acknowledgement of reciprocity. The Hanse merchants had unsuccessfully opposed payment of tunnage and poundage since its inception in 1347. At first their resistance to this duty was complicated by the dispute about their liability to the cloth custom of 1347 and by the fact that they paid both custom and subsidy on their exports of wool, apparently without protest. However, once the dispute about cloth had been settled in their favour and they no longer invested in the wool trade then they were effectively paying only the customs of 1303, by now hereditary revenue of the crown, and the subsidy of tunnage and poundage, periodically voted by parliament. This made it easier for them to argue that by the terms of the *Carta Mercatoria* and their own charter of 1317 they ought not to pay any taxes instituted after 1303. Since the promise contained in the *Carta Mercatoria* was totally disregarded in the case of all other aliens it is hardly surprising that the English were unwilling to concede that it was still valid for the Hanse. Now, however, they gave way, conceded immunity from tunnage and poundage, but invoked the principle of reciprocity. If the Hanse were not to pay taxes instituted after 1303 then nor should their own merchants. It would, of course, have been clearer if the date 1303 had been inserted as a *terminus a quo* instead of the vague talk about '100 years and more', but, as we have seen, clarity was not a strong point of this treaty.

There can be no doubt that the Hanse negotiators were promised immunity from tunnage and poundage, but when their merchants resumed exports in the summer of 1437 the customs officials demanded this tax, until the Chancellor gave a ruling that the exemption should be allowed. The cautiousness of the customs officials was not totally unjustified, since the treaty nowhere spelled out the words 'tunnage and poundage' ('tonagium et pondagium'). Instead, the wording of the *Carta Mercatoria* was modified by the substitution of 'or any subsidies' for 'any other charge' ('Nulleque prise prestaciones nove aut aliqua subsidia') at the point where the Hanse immunity from new financial burdens was confirmed (clause 3). Since tunnage and poundage was technically a subsidy, the Hanse liability was implicitly revoked. Yet at the risk of splitting too many hairs it must be pointed out that the addition of a single word in the next clause (4) may have jeopardised the Hanse immunity from tunnage and poundage, just as clause 2 cast doubt on the meaning of clause 1 in the case of the Englishmen. *Mutatis mutandis* clause 4 largely follows clause 2, but whereas the latter refers to Englishmen paying lawful 'custumis et deveriis' the former has the Hanse paying 'custumis et aliis deveriis'. 'Custumis et deveriis' might possibly be construed as a tautology, but the inclusion of the word 'other' may be said to rule out a tautological sense. This means that it might be possible to argue that the Hanse were bound to pay not merely customs as they claimed, but some 'other' due, i.e. tunnage and poundage. Nevertheless, it must be admitted that there is no evidence that the English ever made this claim, even when the Prussians refused to ratify the treaty.

Summarising the remainder of the 1437 treaty we find that, despite acceptance of the fact that Henry VI was not legally bound to pay his grandfather's debt, had agreed to do so *ex gratia*. He promised to pay 500 marks immediately, 500 marks before Easter 1438 and thereafter £500 a year until the debt was extinguished. These terms were probably at least as generous as the English were prepared to concede during negotiations held in 1430, so Vorrath cannot be said to have given anything away on this point. Henry VI paid the first 1,000 marks as promised, and it was not Vorrath's fault that later payments were not forthcoming; nor, for that matter, did the blame lie with the crown, since Prussia failed to ratify the treaty. Contrary to statements by some historians the Hanseatics were not required to renounce claims for recent damage; they were not mentioned at all in the treaty itself. This meant that complainants could exercise their normal rights to sue in English courts, as Englishmen could in German courts. The chances of getting redress may have been slight, but at least they were not debarred by the treaty. In general, chances of obtaining justice in England may have been improved by a clause in the present treaty which provided that henceforth the admiral's court should have no jurisdiction over Hanseatic merchants. This had been a grievance for many years. It was also conceded that cases about breach of contract should be tried outside the county where the contract had been made, and if the Hanse merchants so requested it would be conducted by two royal justices. A further concession provided that any local or royal officials, including those of the customs, arresting or molesting any Hanse merchants or sailors against the terms of their charters would be ordered by the Chancellor to desist from such action immediately on pain of answering for their defiance in Chancery. Finally, in an attempt to prevent future incidents at sea, the English promised to enforce a statute of Edward III, which required ships' captains to find sureties not to molest friendly or neutral vessels; a similar provision was to be made by the Hanse to deter attacks on English ships. Where did the balance of advantage lie in this treaty? It is, surely, very difficult to conclude that England gained more than the Hanse. Henry VI promised to pay arrears of the 1409 indemnity and actually paid some. He relinquished a not insignificant income from tunnage and poundage, while the amount of comparable advantage which was expected to be gained by his own subjects is not known. The Hanseatic privileges in England were confirmed and they made certain legal gains. English rights in Hanseatic territories were confirmed but, except for the dubious matter of taxation, were not increased. For the first time the principle of reciprocity was acknowledged by the Hanse as a whole, but since the English were concerned chiefly about trade in Prussia and the eastern Baltic this was not a significant advance. All in all this was hardly the great victory of English diplomacy and determination which it is generally claimed to have been.

Before examining the consequences of the 1437 treaty it is necessary to retrace our steps to study fluctuations in Anglo-Hanseatic trade from the accession of Henry IV to the later date. It will be seen that for the Hansards there were more downs than ups. The fortunes of Englishmen who invested in this sector are less clear, but there is no evidence of any advance and some indications to the contrary. This state of affairs did not result solely from the vicissitudes of Anglo-Hanse political relations; more general factors also intervened. During the first two or three years of the new reign, cloth exports, which had fallen back during the late 1390s, appear to have made a strong recovery. It would be dangerous to read too much into this, since the alien petty custom receipts do not confirm any general boom in trade and no tunnage and poundage accounts are available until May 1403. What is certain is that from about 1402 all branches of English trade fell into a deep and protracted depression. From 1403 to August 1422 the value of trade subject to poundage subsidy was around 27 per cent lower than in the 1390s, while the receipts of the alien petty custom fell by about 30 per cent.[65] Separate figures for the exports of cloth and wool and the imports of wine confirm the picture of a general slump. The brunt of a decline in imports was borne by aliens and their share may have fallen below that of Englishmen, though the margin one way or the other was not large. There is little question now of aliens having an export deficit, but one should hesitate before going further and claiming that this was the result of the tightening of the employment act. After the death of Henry V (1422) frequent alterations and exemptions in the scope of poundage duty make it more difficult to use this source as an aid to determining the size of denizen trade. Nevertheless, J. L. Bolton has provided decennial figures from 1420 to 1460 dividing overall values of trade into denizen, Hanse and other alien sectors.[66] These suggest that all three groups had an excess of exports over imports in every decade, except for denizens' trade in 1431–42.

---

[65] Derived from the tables in Power and Postan, *English Trade in the Fifteenth Century*, pp. 330–60.

[66] J. L. Bolton, *The Medieval English Economy, 1150–1500* (London, 1980), table 9:2, p. 307. It should be noted that Bolton's division of general imports into denizen, Hanse and alien was based upon each group's share of cloth exports; there is no independent record. Denizen import figures given there are substantially higher than the combined trade of Hanse and aliens, because wine imports are included.

Early in the fifteenth century the enrolment of cloth export duties becomes more complete and provides more details than before. On the other hand, far fewer customs particulars have survived than for the previous period. Cloth made up more than 90 per cent of all Hanse exports, so enrolled cloth figures provide a satisfactory record of this side of their trade. The extent to which they reliably reflect trends in total trade, i.e. including imports, is more debatable. If exports and imports were in balance, or an imbalance one way or the other was constant, there would be little problem. But this was not the case. In the late fourteenth century Hanse merchants enjoyed an import surplus. This was gradually reduced and finally replaced by an export surplus. But whichever side the surplus was on, it was not so large that in this period cloth exports cannot provide a guide to overall trade. Import levels were not yet widely separated from those of exports, as they were to become in the sixteenth century.

Using the totals of cloth exported as indicators, the first three and a half decades of the fifteenth century may be divided into five unequal periods (table 8).[67] An examination of the performance of any one of the three exporting groups, denizens, Hansards and other aliens, might suggest different divisions of time, but obviously their fortunes can only be compared with one another by observing a uniform time-scale. The first three years of Henry IV's reign (1399–1402) saw exports as high as any yet attained, with an average of around 42,300 cloths per annum. Denizens exported 22,800 (54 per cent of the total), Hanseatics 7,400 (17 per cent) and other aliens 12,100 (29 per cent). Prosperity gave way to a twenty-year slump (1402–22), during which total exports fell to an average of 29,200. This was caused not by a failure in supply but by a drop in demand from export merchants, for this was a period of chronic insecurity in overseas trade, brought on by piracy and warfare. The middle years of Henry IV's reign were plagued not only by the Anglo-Hanseatic dispute described earlier, but by quarrels with France and Flanders, which also alienated other trading partners such as Castile. Successive truces made from 1407 onwards were not

---

[67] For the sake of convenience in this and the next two chapters all national annual totals and periodic averages of cloth exports are derived from Bridbury, *Medieval English Clothmaking*, appendix F, pp. 118–22. The figures given there were those calculated by Carus-Wilson and Coleman to draw the graphs in *England's Export Trade*. To produce those figures it was necessary to readjust (on a time basis) many of the actual numbers given in the customs accounts and to make estimates for gaps. Because of the number of gaps in the early fifteenth century I have rounded totals to the nearest 100 from 1399 to 1422. Thereafter gaps are (with a few exceptions) less of a problem. Figures for individual ports are taken directly from, or based on, *England's Export Trade*.

Table 8. England's cloth exports, 1399–1436

	Overall total		Denizen			Hanse			Alien		
	Total	Change	Total	Share	Change	Total	Share	Change	Total	Share	Change
1399–1402	42,300	—	22,800	54%	—	7,400	17%	—	12,100	29%	—
1402–22	29,200	−31%	13,900	48%	−39%	5,900	20%	−20%	9,400	32%	−22%
1422–5	45,803	+57%	24,843	54%	+79%	6,949	15%	+18%	14,011	31%	+49%
1425–8	37,561	−18%	17,480	47%	−30%	5,778	15%	−17%	14,303	38%	+2%
1428–35	41,354	+10%	25,228	61%	+44%	4,214	10%	−24%	11,913	29%	−17%
1435–6	25,298	−39%	10,929	43%	−57%	2,353	9%	−44%	12,016	48%	+1%

scrupulously observed. Moreover, while relations with Flanders were patched up the break seems to have put an end to a promising development which had taken place around the turn of the century. This had been the temporary suspension of the ban against the sale of English cloth in Flanders, which had been in force since 1359. Henry V's renewal of the war with France in 1415 led to further disruption, again estranging the Castilians and also the Genoese, the most important of the Italians currently trading in England. During the slump the denizen group of exporters fared most badly, their average of 13,900 short-cloths being a mere 61 per cent of the former trade and only 48 per cent of the new total. They were, however, spared the wild fluctuations which marked the fortunes of other aliens and reduced the average of this group to 9,400, 78 per cent of its earlier figure. Relatively, Hanseatics did best with trade, holding up to 80 per cent of the former level, 5,900, and also spared too severe annual fluctuations. The prolonged slump gave way to a three-year boom (1422–5) with an annual average total of 45,803 cloths, an increase of 57 per cent on the previous figure. During these years other aliens increased their trade by 49 per cent to 14,011, though their exports had actually increased enormously during the last year of the previous period. The timing indicates that in this sector the settlement of the dispute with the Genoese in 1421 was a more critical factor than the Anglo-Burgundian treaty of 1419 and the more peaceful conditions which ensued from Henry V's victory in northern France. For denizens, whose trade increased by 79 per cent to an average of 24,843, the king's death on 31 August 1422 was a decisive event. After the battle of Agincourt, parliament had voted tunnage and poundage for the term of his life, but for the first three years of the new reign denizens were exempted from the periodic grants made to his successor. This gave them an edge in any markets where they were in direct competition with Hanseatics and other aliens. During these three years Hanseatic merchants increased their cloth exports by 18 per cent to an average of 6,949. This group may have derived relatively less benefit than the others from the return to peace and was more susceptible to denizen competition. Italians, exporting to a market closed to Englishmen, suffered least from the last factor.

Boom gave way to a three-year recession (1425–8), though with an overall average of 37,561 cloths a year (down 18 per cent) the general situation was nowhere near as bad as in the prolonged slump. During this period other aliens actually increased their trade by 2 per cent to 14,303. Denizen exports declined by 30 per cent, though at 17,480 remained well above slump level. Once again the question of taxation has to be taken into account in judging this performance. During the first of these years (August 1425 to November 1426) denizen trade was subject to tunnage and poundage. Thereafter cloth exports were again spared, but imports were charged, except briefly from November 1427 to April 1428. Taxation of returns affected total profitability and may have had some depressing effect on the level of cloth exports, even when the latter were not directly burdened with poundage. During these years Hanseatic exports declined by 17 per cent and at 5,778 were slightly below the level of the long slump. The short recession gave way to a further boom (1428–35) in which exports increased by 10 per cent to 41,354, lower than in 1422–5 but back to within 2 per cent of the 1399–1402 total. Denizens increased their trade by 44 per cent to 25,228 (61 per cent of the overall total), their best performance yet and 11 per cent up on the beginning of the century. It is noticeable that the only two fiscal years (1429–30 and 1434–5) in which exports fell way below the current average coincided with periods when denizen cloth was temporarily subjected to poundage (December 1429 to January 1431 and from November 1434 onwards).[68] The first boycott of English cloth in the Low Countries in this period was simply shrugged off. Other alien trade averaged 11,913 (29 per cent of the total), a decrease of 17 per cent on the previous level, though less than 2 per cent down on that of 1399–1402; moreover, the losses were concentrated in two years in the middle of the period, when alien rates of tunnage and poundage were temporarily increased by 50 per cent. Hanseatic trade was down to 4,214 (10 per cent of the total), a drop of 24 per cent from the previous figure and no less than 43 per cent down on that of the beginning of the century. It should be noted, however, that there was a distinct improvement during the last two years of this period.

The early fifteenth century can hardly have been classed as a prosperous time by Hanseatic merchants trading with England. Their cloth exports declined steadily and their share of the trade was sadly depleted. A dismal picture is relieved only slightly by a temporary rise in market share during the long slump (1402–22); other aliens increased their share by a similar proportion and the

---

[68] The apparent sensitivity of cloth exports to changes in tax rates (which were never very high) suggests that they had a low rate of profit.

effect was due entirely to the very bad performance of denizens. It must be remembered, of course, that the period began with a relationship little short of war between England and much of the Hanse and thereafter the political situation remained very uneasy. The bare totals of cloth exports conceal the fact that significant changes were taking place in the composition of Hanseatic trade with England. In summary, northern merchants were giving way to west Germans, particularly Cologners, while Baltic goods began to be replaced by imports from other parts of Europe, including south Germany. The evidence is provided by a review of the trade of individual ports (table 9). Boston experienced the beginning of the decline of its *Bergenfahrer* trade, long drawn out and subject to periods of recovery, but ultimately doomed. Betwen 1391 and 1402 Hanse cloths exports here had averaged 2,312 per annum, while alien merchandise subject to petty custom, composed overwhelmingly of Bergen imports, averaged £6,054 a year. From 1402 to 1413 the cloth export was down by more than one third to 1,472, though the merchandise figure fell only to £4,955 and is shown by surviving particulars to have been concentrated even more than previously in the hands of Hanse merchants.[69] The next three years (1413–16) saw the absence of the *Bergenfahrer* from Boston, though not from England, because of the quarrel about English trade in Norway. Hanse cloth exports in the port fell to an average of only 152 a year and all alien merchandise to £505. When the *Bergenfahrer* returned to Boston cloth exports climbed to 1,795 (1416–26), though alien merchandise recovered to only £4,081. Despite the absence of particulars from this period the last figures suggest that the comfortable import surplus which can be shown to have existed before 1413 was substantially reduced, though not necessarily eliminated altogether.

At Hull Hanse cloth exports averaged 366 a year between 1391 and 1402 (581 in 1399–1402). Trade remained fairly buoyant throughout the ensuing slump, with exports averaging 408 a year down to 1420 (but excluding 1413–16). The performance of 1413–16 can only be explained by assuming that Hull attracted much of the Hanse trade which had temporarily deserted Boston. In these years Hanse cloth exports averaged 1,221 and all alien merchandise £3,787, compared with averages of 310 and £1,916 in the

---

[69] After 1399 all the figures for alien merchandise paying the petty custom are taken from Power and Postan, *English Trade in the Fifteenth Century*, pp. 330–60. Before 1399 I used my own transcripts of the enrolled accounts.

Table 9. Fluctuations in Hanse trade in selected ports, 1391–1435

Boston			Hull			Yarmouth	
	All alien merchandise (£)	Hanse cloth		Hanse cloth	All alien merchandise (£)		Hanse cloth
1391–1402	6,054	2,312	1391–1402	366	1,672	1399–1403	729
1402–13	4,955	1,472	1402–13	385	1,510	1407–13	752
1413–16	505	152	1413–16	1,221	3,787	1413–14	35
1416–26	4,081	1,795	1416–20	470	1,826	1414–15	642
			1420–35	58	779	1415–35	36

immediately previous three years. In July 1420 the Prussians confiscated a Hull ship and two years later another. Fear of reprisals probably deterred many Prussians from visiting Hull thereafter and explains the abrupt decline in Hanse trade. Hanse cloth exports averaged only 58 a year between 1420 and 1435 and all alien merchandise £779 compared with 470 cloths and £1,826 over the previous four years. Another port which suffered a sudden loss of almost all its Hanse trade was Yarmouth, which until this blow fell was weathering the slump quite well. Here Hanse cloth exports averaged 729 a year from 1399 to November 1403 and 747 from Michaelmas 1407 to Michaelmas 1415, but excluding 1413–14 when the recorded total was only 35. From Michaelmas 1415 to 1435 cloth exports averaged only 36 a year; there was also a marked decline in the petty custom paid on general merchandise, but since this contained a large element of other alien trade the fall is not so spectacular. What happened in Yarmouth was the calculated withdrawal of the Hamburg merchants, hitherto the mainstay of Hanse trade. The loss was so much regretted by the town that as early as April 1416 the present customs officials wrote to Hamburg asking the merchants to return and promising that the cause of their fears had been removed.[70] Wisely, the merchants did not return, for in 1414, if not in other years, they had succumbed to a corrupt customs official and allowed their cloth exports to be underrecorded in return for a bribe. This man had been exposed and an investigation was going on into the extent of his crimes.[71] Even if the Hamburg merchants were the victims of an extortioner rather than willing smugglers they had been guilty of a criminal offence. If they had continued to come to England they would undoubtedly have been punished when the matter was finally dealt with in the king's Exchequer.

At Lynn no figures for Hanse cloth exports are available until 1406. Thereafter, the overall level of trade is little different from that of the late fourteenth century. Until 1428 exports averaged 162 a year, but fell well below that figure in 1408–11, 1415–16, 1421–2 and 1424–5. Three ports had a very minor or irregular trade in cloth between 1399 and 1435. Newcastle saw some in most years, but had an overall average of only 15; Sandwich had nil in twenty-five years

---

[70] Lappenberg, *Urkundliche Geschichte*, 2, no. 62.
[71] Full details are given in S. Jenks, *England, die Hanse und Preussen: Handel und Diplomatie, 1377–1461* (Habilitationsschrift, Free University of Berlin, 1985), pp. 382–4.

Table 10. *Hanse cloth exports at London, relative to all England,*
1399–1436

	All England	London	
1399–1402	7,400	3,430	46 %
1402–22	5,900	3,000	51 %
1422–5	6,949	3,978	57 %
1425–8	5,778	4,189	73 %
1428–35	4,214	3,171	75 %
1435–6	2,353	1,905	81 %

and an average of 8 in the remaining twelve years; Southampton
had nil in nineteen years and an average of 22 over eighteen years.
This leaves only London and Ipswich to be considered. The fifteenth
century saw the continued growth in London's share of Hanse
exports, which had been briefly interrupted in the late 1390s (table
10). Once only was there another serious setback. Between 1414 and
1417 London exports averaged only 1,734 cloths compared with
2,716 over the previous three years. This was against the trend
elsewhere, so that in these years London handled only 38 per cent of
all Hanse exports against 51 per cent over the whole of the 1402–22
period. In reality the trade of the London Steelyard was not quite as
depressed as the above figures suggest, since in these years its
members probably diverted some of their exports to Ipswich. Hanse
cloth exports in the latter port averaged 235 cloths a year between
October 1399 and January 1404 and 250 a year between February
1407 and Michaelmas 1414. They then surged to 737, 1,090 and 677
during the next three years. The port did not revert to being a
backwater after 1417; between then and 1435 Hanse exports
averaged 638 a year. It was clearly establishing itself as an outpost
of the London Steelyard. It was explained in the previous chapter
that, although the nature of the enrolled customs accounts make it
necessary to credit all trade to Ipswich, the real centre of Hanse
activity was the member port of Colchester. By the 1430s, and
possibly earlier, Cologne merchants had acquired property and
settled in the town. In 1431 the London Steelyard made a statute
that its members should only purchase Colchester cloth which
conformed with assise measurements. This may have been no more
than a recognition of a change that had already taken place, since

the town had largely given up the manufacture of non-assise cloths some years previously.[72]

The influence which political and military factors exercised on Hanse trade, though ever present, was probably strongest during the depression of the late 1420s and early 1430s. In the nadir of 1430–2 total cloth exports fell to 3,070 and then 2,387. This resulted from the effects of the Hanseatic-Danish war which began in July 1426, a ban on English-made cloth in the Low Countries and the threat of increased taxation in England, though these were not equally important. The first affected most seriously the *Bergenfahrer* at Boston. From 1419 to 1425 their cloth exports flourished as they had not done since the beginning of the century, with an average of 2,011 cloths per annum. The outbreak of the war may already be slightly reflected in the figure of 1,463 in 1425–6 and certainly is in that of 1,051 in 1426–7. Then came the Hanse military defeats in the autumn of 1427 and trade came to an abrupt halt, with cloth exports at Boston averaging only eighteen a year from 1427 to 1433. The much smaller trade at Lynn was buoyant at first, still averaging 146 in 1425–8, but then fell to an average of 60 in the years 1428–33. For the possible effects of the Low Countries cloth ban one must look at Hanse exports from London, though at the same time it is necessary to point out that the first ban had little effect on denizen exports here, which were at record levels.[73] As early as 1359 Flanders had imposed a permanent ban on the entry of English-made cloth, though later that year it conceded that Hanseatic merchants might carry it through the county, provided that it was not unpacked there. Initially this privilege was useful both to Baltic merchants shipping from Bruges and those going to the Rhineland. Before the end of the fourteenth century the merchants of Cologne and Dortmund were beginning to send cloth to Antwerp in Brabant, where they had colonies. In time the northern route became more important than that through Bruges. The attraction of the former was that it combined transit facilities to west and south Germany with fairs at Antwerp and Bergen op Zoom, which permitted the sale of English cloth. Early in the fifteenth century Hanse merchants were competing with Englishmen in these markets. Gradually, the clothing towns of Holland-Zeeland and Brabant came to resent the competition of English cloth and the idea took hold of excluding it,

---

[72] *HUB*, 6, no. 905. Britnell, *Colchester*, pp. 164–5.
[73] There is no way for apportioning denizen exports between different markets.

as the Flemings did. In July 1428 English cloth, both in transit and brought for sale, was banned from Holland-Zeeland, and a month later a similar measure was taken in Brabant.[74] The Holland-Zeeland ban lapsed early in 1430, but, despite the threats of Cologne merchants to boycott the Antwerp fairs, that in Brabant was not repealed until March 1431. London Hanse exports, which stood at 5,071 cloths in 1427–8, declined to 3,757, 3,650 and 2,138 in the next three years and finally to 2,030 in 1431–2. How much, if any, of this decline was due to the Burgundian ban is problematical; some may have resulted from the Danish war. The abnormally low figures of the last two years may owe something to confusion about Hanse liability to the current surcharge on the alien rate of poundage. A strong recovery in London exports in 1432–3 raised the Hanse national total to 3,671, while a partial recovery at Boston and Lynn and strong trade at Ipswich resulted in totals of 5,310 and 5,872 in the next two years (table 11). The last figure shows that the boycott of English cloth ordered by the Hanseatic diet in June 1434 and the simultaneous reimposition of the ban throughout the Burgundian Low Countries for a long time had no effect on Hanse cloth exports. The following year (1435–6) total Hanse exports fell to 2,353, of which 1,905 passed through London. At the same time the denizen cloth trade was in a parlous way. The reintroduction of poundage duty, Hanseatic and Burgundian boycotts, the ending of the Anglo-Burgundian alliance and the prospect of war between the two powers acted together to reduce denizen cloth exports to 20,559 in 1434–5 and 10,929 in 1435–6. Only the other alien sector of the trade, overwhelmingly Italian, prospered; the alien poundage surcharge had been removed and a relative scarcity of buyers may have brought down the price of cloth. Even so, the exports total of all three interest groups at 25,298 cloths was among the four lowest recorded for any twelve-month period so far in the fifteenth century.

Trends in the export of cloth to Hanseatic parts by Englishmen in the early fifteenth century are not easily established, since total denizen exports can be divided into market sectors only very crudely. The best hope of finding clues is to concentrate on those ports, Lynn and Boston, where denizen cloth exports in the late fourteenth century were directed overwhelmingly to the Baltic. At Lynn denizen cloth exports averaged 1,338 a year from 1394 to 1399

---

[74] Munro, *Wool, Cloth and Gold*, pp. 68–9.

Table 11. A comparison of cloth exports at selected ports, 1425–36

Mich.–Mich.	Hull		Boston		Lynn		London		
	Hanse	Denizen	Hanse	Denizen	Hanse	Denizen	Hanse	Denizen	Alien
1425–6	13	3,005	1,463	606	179	1,908[f]	3,505	4,223	11,602
1426–7	4	2,242	1,051	585	116	538[g]	3,992	3,849	7,260
1427–8	0	2,986	0	831	143	2,012	5,071	3,635	8,353
1428–9	66	6,505[a]	3	1,686[b]	0	1,002	3,757	6,195	7,382
1429–30	122	3,122	17	1,650[c]	95	1,006	3,650	6,973	10,530
1430–1	1	2,935	0	384[d]	59	624	2,138	10,530	5,067
1431–2	13	3,077	41	697	71	430	2,030	13,334	953
1432–3	90	3,535	47	394	79	559	3,141	12,719	498
1433–4	60	2,891	521	507	182	1,775	3,271	9,890	4,520
1434–5	38	1,140	593	651	89	874	4,209	8,699	4,347
1435–6	0	828	3	96[e]	27	569	1,905	2,084	4,555

[a] To 28 Oct. 1429.
[d] To 20 Oct. 1431.
[g] From 20 Oct. 1426.
[b] To 1 Nov. 1429.
[e] To 10 Oct. 1436.
[c] 1 Nov. 1429–1 Nov. 1430.
[f] From 30 July 1425

and, after a gap in the record, 1,497 from 1406 to 1422. This is a buoyant performance when measured against national figures and suggests that Lynn's concentration on the Prussian market was paying dividends. The rise of 29 per cent to 1,933 in the following three years (1422–5) is not as great as the national trend, but this is explicable by the fact that the latter includes a large element of simple recovery from slump conditions. The decline of 29 per cent from the new level to 1,380 in 1425–8 is almost exactly in line with the national trend, but the average disguises massive fluctuations. From the beginning of August 1425 to mid-October 1426 the figure was 1,908, falling after the outbreak of the Hanseatic-Danish war to 538 in the next year, but then recovering to 2,012. The last figure may be regarded as postponed trade and, taking the two war years together, Lynn gained nothing from the discomfiture of the Hanseatics. Finally, when denizen exports at a national level experienced a boom from 1428 to 1435 Lynn's trade languished with an average of only 896. The first two years were poor, the next three and the last disastrous, and only 1433–4 saw what would formerly have been regarded as normal trade, with an export of 1,775 cloths. The poor performance was probably due to the harassment of English merchants in Prussia; it is the good trade of 1433–4 which is difficult to explain.

At Boston, which had averaged 817 denizen cloth exports a year from 1391 to 1402, trade fell to 327 a year in 1402–13. Even if every scrap of this cloth now went to the Baltic, there was a huge fall in the amount going there. During the absence of the *Bergenfahrer* from Boston in 1413–16 denizen exports increased slightly, though hardly significantly, to 360 a year, but then fell to 294 for the remainder of the general slump. A possible explanation for Boston's poor performance relative to that of Lynn may be that the Bostonians, who in the late fourteenth century had still dispatched cloth to the western Baltic, had not cultivated the Prussian market so assiduously as their neighbours. The penalty for this was a loss of markets when relations with the western towns were disturbed, as they were in the early fifteenth century. During the next two periods the denizen cloth trade at Boston was relatively flourishing with averages of 693 in 1422–5 and 674 in 1425–8, though this may have been due to new enterprises in regions other than the Baltic, possibly the Low Countries. In 1428–30 exports soared to 1,686 and 1,650, but while much of this went to the Baltic the credit does not necessarily belong to Boston's own citizens. Correspondence of the Steelyard indicates that Boston was chosen as the port from which to launch English attempts to run the blockade of the Sound and it is likely that many who did not normally ship from this port did so in these years. This concentration was not sustained, but denizen exports remained relatively buoyant, at least by the port's own recent standards, with an average of 526 from 1430 to 1435.

The significance of Baltic markets in the denizen cloth trade of Hull in the early fifteenth century is not easily determined. Exports which averaged 3,004 a year from 1391 to 1402, were already declining in the last four years of that period and slumped to an average of only 1,530 in 1402–22. Hull's exporters were not dependent on the Baltic and there is little reason to suppose that this market sector fared better than any other; indeed it may have suffered more than some others. Hull's ability at this time to challenge Bristol as the second largest importer of wine strongly suggests that there may have been a large export of Yorkshire cloth to south-west Europe. During the boom of 1422–5 Hull's denizen exports, averaging 2,834, slightly bettered the national trend, while in the recession of 1425–8 they held up far better, falling only to 2,744. It would be rash to credit much of this achievement to Baltic exports, since the seizure of Hull ships in Prussia, which was probably responsible for the withdrawal of Hanseatic trade from Hull, must surely have made Yorkshiremen cautious of venturing to that country. However, there is evidence of some trade from the mid-1420s, and the Hanseatic-Danish war may have encouraged bolder spirits to decide that the possibility of enhanced profits was worth a risk. Hull's denizen exports from 1428 to 1435 averaged 3,315 with one exceptionally good year, 6,505 in 1428–9, coinciding with the first of Boston's exceptional years. It may be significant that, while Lynn's exports languished, Yorkshiremen appear to have taken over the leadership of the English merchants in Prussia. Nicholas Hassham of York is named as governor in 1432 and remained in that post at least until the breakdown of trade in 1435.

For other English ports and some inland towns there is evidence of a Baltic trade in the fifteenth century, but no method of quantifying it even roughly. Coventry merchants exported cloth to Prussia in the 1430s, but since they used the port of Boston their contribution has already been taken into account. In 1431 three Bristol merchants complained about the arrest of the *Anna* of Bristol, as she was about to sail from Danzig for her home port with their goods and those of other English merchants. Colchester merchants still frequented Prussia in the 1430s. Southampton merchants were sufficiently well established in the English community at Danzig for one of their number to have been included in the delegation sent with plenipotentiary powers from there to Lübeck in 1428.[75] The most aggravating gap in our knowledge concerns the contribution which London may have made to denizen trade with the Baltic in this period. Londoners appear among named leaders of the Englishmen in Prussia and, although their cloth was probably but a small part of total denizen exports from the capital, it could have made a not insubstantial contribution to overall English exports to the Baltic. On the other hand such exports would have to have risen above the level of the late fourteenth century to compensate for the decline in other quarters. This condition cannot be taken for granted and on balance it seems most unlikely that the total of all denizen exports to the Baltic in the early fifteenth century exceeded, indeed may not have been even as high as, those of the late fourteenth century. At certain times Englishmen temporarily improved the general conditions in which their trade was conducted in Prussia, but this did not necessarily lead to much of an increase in cloth exports to that country. Moreover, any gain in the east could conceivably have been more than offset by contraction of sales in the western Baltic.

While the total of English cloth taken to the Baltic by Hanseatic merchants and denizens either stagnated or declined in the early fifteenth century the position as regards imports from that region may have been even worse. The suggestion must be advanced cautiously, since quantitative proof cannot be supplied and after the death of Henry IV even illustrative material in the form of particular customs accounts is sparse. Earlier, the principal return of denizen merchants was Skania herrings; now the cool reception of Englishmen in the west-Baltic towns may have led to a decline in this traffic. Another contributory factor was the rise of the Dutch herring industry, based on an increase in fishing in the North Sea and an improved curing technology. England could now supply its needs from this quarter, while at certain times both English and Dutch merchants found it profitable to export herrings to Prussia. Hanseatic

---

[75] *HUB*, 6, nos. 875, 942, 1037. *HR*, I (viii), no. 451.

imports from the Baltic may also have been prejudiced by a change in fashion. Previously, squirrel skins, the wearing of which extended to relatively humble social groups, had been one of the most important of all Hanse imports. The squirrel did not disappear overnight but in the fifteenth century it gradually went out of fashion, while the inelastic demand for the more expensive furs worn by the rich resulted in a decline in the fur trade.[76] There is no evidence that any other Baltic goods fell out of demand and it would have been strange had they done so, for they were for the most part everyday necessities. It was for this reason that the anonymous author of the *Libelle of Englyshe Polycye* (written around 1437) looked kindly upon 'Highe Duchmene of Prise and Esterlynges', in contrast to his disdain for Italians, many of whose wares he considered to be superfluous trifles. The German wares listed in the *Libelle* were precisely those found in the fourteenth-century customs particulars. Another reason for preferring Hansards to Italians was that the latter beggared England with their financial practices, while the former enriched it by importing silver.[77]

> Also Pruse men maken here aventure
> Of plate of sylvere, of wegges gode and sure
> In grete plente, whiche they bringe and bye
> Oute of the londes of Béalme and Hungrye;
> Whiche is encrese ful grete unto thys londe.

Denizen merchants trading with the Baltic may have continued to make most or all of their returns in wares rather than silver, but given the stagnation of exports there was little or no scope for any increase in imports. In the late fourteenth century the Baltic had been the principal growth area of English trade, but this was no longer true. After 1409 Englishmen were on the defensive in Prussia. For a long time to come the question of reciprocity in the Baltic continued to dominate Anglo-Hanseatic relations, but with the benefit of hindsight we are aware that the seeds of another dispute were being scattered elsewhere. The future of English trade lay in the provinces of Zeeland and Brabant. Englishmen were beginning to see this region as a growth area for cloth exports and in its fairs they found returns not only in local products but in goods from southern Germany, central Europe and the Mediterranean. But at the same

[76] Veale, *Fur Trade*, pp. 134–6.
[77] G. Warner (ed.), *The Libelle of Englysche Polycye* (Oxford, 1926), pp. 15–17.

time some Hanseatics, particularly those of Cologne, recognised the profits to be made in this trade and began to infiltrate it. The Englishmen were already organising themselves into groups of adventurers, which were eventually to coalesce as the Company of Merchant Adventurers. When this happened latent rivalry became open and in the long run the Merchant Adventurers proved to be a more deadly threat to Hanseatic interests than the English Baltic traders ever were.

CHAPTER 4

Trade, piracy, war, 1437–1474

Henry Vorrath remained in England until the end of July 1437, several weeks after the departure of his fellow ambassadors. On his way home he was imprisoned in the bishopric of Münster as a hostage for the debts of some Prussian merchants. Efforts to secure his release were protracted and not until March 1438 did he reach Danzig, where he received a cool reception. In April, after hearing his own account of his mission, the Prussian diet decided to defer ratification of the treaty, despite its acceptance by the Hanse diet the previous August. In the interim Prussian subjects were allowed to trade with England. At the next diet in mid-May Vorrath appealed to the Grand Master for protection against his fellow citizens, who accused him of having exceeded his powers. They also urged that Prussia should disavow the treaty, being spurred on by demands of newly returned English merchants. For the most part the latter were merely asking for things which they had formerly enjoyed, though not without opposition from Danzig. Nevertheless, in the past the Grand Master and the Prussian diet had often supported English claims. Unfortunately, the merchants also raised the thorny question of taxation. They objected to paying the Danzig *Pfahlgeld*, on the grounds that it had been instituted only thirty-six or thirty-seven years previously. They appear to have been ignorant of the origin of *Pfundzoll*, levied by the Teutonic Order, but nevertheless claimed exemption. Their objection was based on the fact that it was the exact equivalent of the English poundage duty, from which the Hanseatics had just been released, despite having paid it for much of the previous ninety years. Danzig met the English demands by dissecting the Vorrath treaty word by word, complaining about its vagueness, which might cause great difficulties for Prussia, and anticipating that the English would soon invoke it in support of the right to trade in Livonia and Poland. It is clear that Danzig was concerned not merely to prevent any extension of English privileges; it was resolutely opposed to the reintroduction of former practices, such as retail trade in Prussia itself. Only four towns were represented at the May diet and three of these, Thorn, Elbing and Königsberg, were ready to confirm the treaty. However, because of the vociferous opposition of Danzig the Grand Master again deferred a decision.[1]

In December 1439 English merchants complained to the Danzig city council about its refusal to allow their liberties, but they were informed that they should have no more rights than any other aliens.[2] This, of course, led to a clamour in England about the failure to implement the treaty of 1437. The forum was the parliament of 1439–40, which enacted a number of laws directly harmful to alien merchants.[3] The Hanse, because of its franchises, was exempt from the new regulations and taxes, but naturally the English merchants were unhappy that this should continue if they were denied reciprocity. When parliament reassembled at Reading in January 1440, Thomas Ecsame of Newark presented a petition to this effect. Consequently, in February the king wrote to the Hanse and the Grand Master complaining about Prussia's failure to ratify the treaty and setting out a list of grievances.[4] Dissatisfaction was expressed about the Grand Master's taxation of ships and merchandise and about taxation and general harassment by the Danzig city authorities. But outside the confines of Prussia, specific complaints at this stage referred only to injuries allegedly inflicted in the Pomeranian towns of Stettin and Köslin. This letter was probably entrusted to Dr John Norton, who about this time was sent on an embassy to Denmark, Poland and Prussia, but few details survive of his mission.

The general situation in the Baltic was steadily deteriorating as a result of war between a section of the Hanse and Holland-Zeeland. The Dutch began hostilities in April 1438 after the breakdown of talks to renew an earlier truce. Officially, they declared that their enemies were only the duchy of Holstein and the towns of Hamburg, Lübeck, Rostock, Wismar, Stralsund and Lüneberg, but other towns, including Cologne, were soon complaining about interference with their trade. In the north the Dutch not only took a heavy toll of Hanse ships coming out of the Elbe and Weser but also sent fleets to the approaches of the Baltic. At the very start of the war they were reported as having 104 warships there, including 45 equipped with

---

[1] *HR*, II (ii), nos. 187, 189, 193, 214, 220–2.   [2] *Ibid.*, no. 318.
[3] *Rot. Parl.*, 5, pp. 24–5.   [4] *HUB*, VII, no. 527. *Foedera*, v (i), p. 72.

forecastles. In April 1438 the Prussian diet, ignoring Lübeck's warning of Dutch intentions, authorised voyages to the Low Countries, including Holland-Zeeland. It was probably lulled into a sense of security by Dutch offers to respect Prussian neutrality, but these were not honoured and 22 or 23 Prussian vessels returning from the Bay were seized in the early stages of the war. After these losses, but also because of a blockade of the Sound by the other combatants, the Prussian authorities banned sailings to the west by their own subjects, though they did so reluctantly and perhaps at first not very effectively. The Prussians laid the blame for the stoppage of trade as much upon the Wendish towns as upon the Dutch, and the result was disunity within the Hanse. This is apparent in the proceedings of a diet at Lübeck in March 1441, though the Prussian envoys reported home that the Wendish towns were now inclined to make peace. The Prussians then went on to Kampen for talks with the Dutch, where they were able to arrange for a peace conference to be held in Copenhagen later that summer. Writing from Kampen on 14 April they advised their countrymen to send a trading fleet through the Sound, since most of the Dutch ships were about to sail to the Bay and they would therefore have little strength in the North Sea for the next seven or eight weeks. Back in Lübeck on 1 May they reveal their distrust of the Wendish towns in a report telling of fleets fitting out in Lübeck and Wismar, ostensibly to fight the Dutch in the Bay but really to buy salt and wine there to pre-empt the depleted east-Baltic markets. The Prussians acted quickly on the news and by 6 May the Grand Master was writing to the King of Denmark notifying him of a big Prussian fleet ready to leave Danzig and requesting free passage through the Sound. The Prussians' reward for their efforts, besides the resumption of trade, was the promise of a financial indemnity from the Dutch at the Copenhagen peace conference in September 1441.[5]

Despite the prolonged stoppage of native trade with the west the Danzig authorities were far less tolerant of the English than they had been during the Danish war twelve years before. The English later claimed that in this period their assembly hall was closed down, they were dispossessed of their houses and forced to live and trade in cellars, forbidden to retail cloth and salt or to conduct any trade with non-burgesses, while all cloth taken beyond the city was burdened

[5] *HR*, II (ii), nos. 184–5, 202–3, 214, 451–2, 458, 465, 471, 494.

with extra taxes.[6] It was further said that the authorities arrested goods to the value of £5,000 as collective security for debts and alleged acts of piracy. Charges of duplicity were also laid; in 1440 the city council first announced that the English might export anything but certain specified goods, but later prevented them from shipping anything but wheat and rye. Presumably, they allowed grain to leave either because of a glut or because they feared to antagonise the Order, which was a major producer. In addition to harassment in Prussia the English had to run the gauntlet of the Sound. In contrast to the earlier Danish war the Hanse did not countenance direct attacks on English vessels, because it feared for its privileges in England. However, in 1440 ships entering and leaving the Sound were pressed into the service of the Wendish towns and Christopher of Bavaria, allies in a rebellion against Christopher's uncle, King Eric of Denmark, who showed overmuch favour to the Dutch. A number of English grain ships returning from Prussia were not even allowed to discharge their cargoes before being put to use as troop carriers.[7] It was later claimed that, because of an extra twelve weeks at sea and misconduct by the soldiers, the grain was so deteriorated as to be unfit for sale even in Flanders, Bordeaux or Lisbon, which apparently were all less fastidious markets than England.

In November 1441 the English merchants again complained to the king's council and received a sympathetic hearing. It was decided to send an embassy to the Hanse and Prussia, and all English towns known to trade with those parts were instructed to provide details of their losses by the time that parliament assembled in January. The commons then proposed that the Hanse should have until Martinmas to make amends and that meanwhile their franchises should be suspended, except in the case of the merchants of Cologne. The crown agreed to demand redress and the confirmation of the 1437 treaty by Prussia, upon pain of forfeiture of the franchises after Martinmas, but declined to suspend them in the interim.[8] There is no evidence that the proposed embassy was ever dispatched, but the complaints were taken to Prussia and Lübeck that summer by the secretary of the Steelyard, which was seriously concerned about the threat and wanted all the towns to be fully appraised of the situation. This intervention had little effect on the

---

[6] The most detailed of several lists recording English complaints about losses in the Sound and treatment in Prussia at this time is *HR*, II (ii), no. 644.

[7] *Ibid.*, nos. 390–4.   [8] *POPC*, 5, pp. 167, 170–1, 177–8. *Rot. Parl.*, 5, pp. 64–5.

Prussians. Meanwhile, on 11 June 1442 the Danzig city council had summoned Nicholas Hassham of York and six other merchants of Hull, Lynn and London to be examined about the complaints made in parliament. This group, doubtless under pressure, disavowed the agitation in England, saying that they and their fellows had no claims against their host city, the admission being attested by a public notary. In September Danzig disingenuously sent a copy of the disavowal to England, as evidence that there was no case to answer. It laid counter-charges that the English merchants in Prussia were at odds with one another and levied taxes upon themselves without the sanction of the local authorities. Naturally, little credence was given to this and after Martinmas Hanseatic goods in England were briefly arrested and the customs collectors ordered to levy tunnage and poundage as well as customs. By February 1443 the storm had blown over and the king's council, while renewing its demand for compensation for the merchants, restored the Hanse's immunity from tunnage and poundage. Paradoxically, during 1442 whilst Danzig resisted most of the English claims it joined with other Prussian towns in support of their opposition to the Order's levy of *Pfundzoll* or poundage.[9] It did so because its own citizens also had to pay this charge and because of English and Dutch threats of a trade boycott. Soon afterwards the Order bought off the opposition of its own subjects by agreeing to share the proceeds of the tax with the towns.

A period of three years in which there is virtually no record of the dispute between the English merchants and the Hanseatics serves only to highlight the crisis which developed early in 1446. It has also led to the formulation of the theory that this crisis had its origins solely in English domestic politics.[10] It has been suggested that the new attack on the Hanse was a sop thrown by the faction of the Duke of Suffolk, which dominated the king's council, to the mercantile interest in parliament, in order to prevent it from rallying to the support of the Duke of Gloucester. Whatever the truth in this theory, it must not be forgotten that earlier the government had been totally preoccupied by military disasters in France, while the absence of parliament during two of the three years meant that the merchants lacked a convenient forum for their agitation. This was no new crisis, but simply a resumption of that which had been staved off by the action of the king's council in February 1443. When the time was

---

[9] *HR*, II (ii), nos. 638, 642, 644, 655, 658, 682–3; (iii), no. 5; (vii), no. 471.
[10] Postan, 'England and the Hanse', pp. 126–7.

ripe the merchants induced the commons to re-present the bill of 1442 which sought to suspend the Hanse franchises, though on this occasion no exception was proposed in favour of the merchants of Cologne.[11] This move may have been made in the fourth and last of the sessions of the parliament of 1445–6, since the king's response was given on 7 February 1446. He agreed to a renewal of the ultimatum that, unless the demands of the English merchants were satisfied, the Hanseatic franchises would be terminated; ample time was allowed for a settlement, since the dead-line was Michaelmas 1447. The length of the fuse may explain the remarkable coolness with which the London Steelyard faced this threat. Instead of immediately demanding that the present Grand Master should confirm the Vorrath treaty, it observed that he was under no legal obligation to do so, since it had been made in the time of his predecessor. Indeed, concern was expressed lest Englishmen acquire too easily rights in Prussia which equated with those which the Hanse had obtained at great cost in England. What it had in mind particularly was the English failure to maintain payments of the financial indemnity promised in the Vorrath treaty. Finally, the Steelyard suggested that the English ultimatum should be countered by a similar one, though expiring at an earlier date, directed against English merchants in Prussia and the Hanse towns. This advice was taken to Prussia in the summer of 1446 by the secretary of the Steelyard. Given that Cologne merchants were prominent in the Steelyard, the official attitude of this community contrasts sharply with that of the city of Cologne, which in the same period wrote to the Grand Master urging him to come to an accommodation with England.[12] All parties were, however, in favour of the Prussians talking with the English and in April 1447 the former prepared instructions for an embassy to England. The envoys reached London in July, but in August reported that they were unable to find anyone to negotiate with, as the king and the great lords were all away.[13] A letter written the same day by Steelyard merchants refers to plans to evacuate their goods from England, since writs of distraint had already been issued and would be served the moment that the Hanse privileges were suspended at Michaelmas.[14] These reports have given rise to

---

[11] PRO, C49/26/10. Printed in Jenks, *England, die Hanse und Preussen*, pp. 28–30.

[12] *HR*, II (iii), nos. 265–7; (vii), no. 485.   [13] *HR*, II (iii), no. 294; (vii), no. 486.

[14] *HR*, II (iii), nos. 286–7, 295. A writ of distraint against Cologne merchants in Colchester had actually been enforced as early as March 1447 by Henry Spicer of Derby. This was an exceptional case, effected through the favour of the Duke of Buckingham.

the belief that the English had no real wish for a peaceful settlement, and were deliberately delaying talks so that the intended confiscations should be provided with a shred of respectability. Another Steelyard letter, written much later, alleges that English merchants had maliciously told their government that the Prussian envoys had incited the King of Denmark to seize English ships in the Sound.[15] Whatever the true attitude of some Englishmen, the main reason for the failure of the negotiations may be gathered from a letter sent by Henry VI to the Grand Master in December 1447.[16] The Prussian delegation simply was not empowered to confirm the Vorrath treaty, which by now was a *sine qua non* of the preservation of Hanseatic liberties in England. This was not merely the result of the opposition of Danzig, for the envoys' instructions show that the attitude of the Teutonic Order was an equally great stumbling block. The Grand Master was quite unwilling to accept any interpretation of the treaty which would prevent him from imposing taxes on English merchants. Since the envoys could only repeat arguments that had been advanced many times in the past there simply was no basis for negotiations.

When the English ultimatum expired the Hanseatic privileges were suspended, though an undertaking was given that they would be restored as soon as Prussia confirmed the treaty. This meant that all Hanse merchants ought to have paid full alien customs and subsidies. Despite threats which it had made only a few months earlier the Hanse did not impose counter-sanctions. This policy of restraint paid dividends, for since the beginning of 1447 England had been faced with a Burgundian ban on imports of its cloth, which soon encouraged the government to reconsider its position *vis-à-vis* the Hanse and to take the initiative in settling the dispute. In February 1448 proclamation was made of an intended embassy to Denmark (to discuss Iceland trade and the Bergen staple) and to the Hanse and Prussia. All who had suffered at the hands of these powers were invited to send details to the Chancery. Commissions were made out for Sir Robert Shottesbrook, Sir John Bek and Dr Richard Caunton on 24 July, but they did not reach Bremen until late October and arranged to have talks with the Hanse and Prussia at Lübeck on 1 March 1449, after conducting their business in Denmark. In the event the Englishmen appear to have postponed their visit to Copenhagen and waited at Lübeck for the negotiations

---

[15] *HR*, II (iii), no. 464.   [16] *Ibid.*, no. 479.

with the Hanse, which began about the middle of March.[17] The chief obstacle to a successful conclusion of these talks was the very limited powers of the Prussian delegation, which again lacked authority to confirm the Vorrath treaty. Its instructions left no room for misunderstanding as there had been twelve years previously. The English must recognise that, although Prussia would show them 'friendship and accord', these words should not be taken as meaning 'privileges and freedom'. The Prussians were aware that the conference might not reach agreement, and their envoys were instructed that any future talks must be held no further away than Flanders; on no account should they take place in England. In the event it was decided that another conference should be convened in Deventer at midsummer 1451, for which the English demanded the presence of a Prussian delegation equipped with plenary powers bearing the great seal of the Teutonic Order. The Hanse gained the promise that in the interim Hanseatic privileges in England should be reinstated. It also frustrated an English attempt to divide it by excluding Prussia from enjoyment of the franchises, should it continue to withhold ratification of the Vorrath treaty. Lübeck argued that the Hanse's constitution did not allow any of its members to be denied privileges which belonged to the organisation as a whole. It also refused to supply the English envoys with the names of those towns which had declined invitations to attend the present conference.[18] This ploy has been interpreted as part of an English plan either to define membership of the Hanse or alternatively to punish those who hadn't bothered to come, by denying them the use of the franchises.[19]

On 5 April 1449, that is before the end of the Lübeck conference, the English parliament renewed the grant of tunnage and poundage for five years and made it clear that the Hanse merchants were to be charged. In July, a second session of the same parliament imposed a heavy poll tax on alien merchants and again refused to concede Hanseatic immunity.[20] But it was not this which blighted the prospect of better Anglo-Hanseatic relations. Rather, it was the seizure of a great fleet as it passed by the Isle of Wight on 23 May 1449, homeward bound from the Bay. Out of a total haul of 110 to 130 ships, nearly half were Hanseatics, including sixteen belonging to Lübeck and fourteen which were later described as Danzig's

---

[17] *HR*, II (iii), nos. 460, 463, 465–7, 470, 480, 484.   [18] *Ibid.*, nos. 488, 503–5.
[19] W. Stein, 'Die Hanse und England beim Ausgang des hundertjährigen Krieges', *HG*, 26 (1921), 33–5.   [20] *Rot. Parl.*, 5, pp. 142–4.

biggest and best hulks.[21] Burgundian ships, crews and cargoes were immediately released, and soon afterwards those of Kampen, a member of the Hanse. The cargoes of the other ships were sold, and the vessels and the crews were pressed into English service. The seizure of the Bay fleet was one of the two most disastrous and ill-considered episodes in the entire history of Anglo-Hanseatic relations, and it is necessary to give some thought to its cause as well as to its consequences. The coup was carried out by Robert Winnington, better known in German sources as Robert de Cane, who a few weeks previously had made an indenture for keeping the seas against the king's enemies and pirates. Since he appears to have received no financial assistance from the crown he was unlikely to have been too scrupulous in his identification of such people. Professor Postan hinted strongly at prior complicity by certain influential members of the king's council, who had naval interests and were also associated with Winnington. This charge has rightly been discounted by C. F. Richmond, who also more generally rejected Postan's view that throughout the 1440s the naval enterprises of these men had been more criminal than otherwise.[22] There is little doubt that the attack on the Bay fleet was unpremeditated and largely fortuitous. It may even have resulted, as Winnington claimed, from simple anger at the refusal of the foreigners to strike their sails in view of the king's arms. It is true that immediately afterwards Winnington sent news of the feat to Thomas Daniell, one of the councillors in question. But his letter is that of a man surprised at his own success, possibly even overwhelmed by the enormity of what he had done and in need of counsel and assistance at the highest level. Thomas Daniell and his colleagues may be cleared of the charge of having planned the attack on the Bay fleet but there can be no doubt about their complicity in the events which followed. There is no direct evidence about the disposal of the Hanseatic cargoes, but years later the Steelyard alleged that the ships were brought up the Thames and salt warehoused even in the king's palace.[23] There is no reason to disbelieve contemporary stories that much of the proceeds found its way into the pockets of the councillors. This was the obstacle which confronted the Germans in

[21] For a description which quotes from many contemporary sources see Stein, 'Die Hanse und England', 48–53.

[22] Postan, *England and the Hanse*, p. 128. C. F. Richmond, 'Royal Administration and the Keeping of the Seas, 1422–85' (D.Phil. thesis, Oxford, 1963), pp. 192–204.

[23] *HR*, ii (v), no. 263.

their attempts to recover their losses. It is, of course, hardly credible that the men who realised the impossibility of holding on to the captured Burgundian ships believed that they could keep the property of the Hanse without inflicting great damage on the national interest. One may only conclude, therefore, that for the moment national interest was to be sacrificed to the private profit of members of the government and their friends.

The first Englishmen to feel the repercussions of the new policy, or rather the lack of policy, were those who had ventured their property or persons to the Hanse towns. By 18 July 1449 all the Englishmen in Prussia had been arrested; after an initial decision to deport them the authorities decided to hold them as hostages. In August the members of the London Steelyard awaited with trepidation a meeting of the king's council scheduled for 11 September.[24] They felt sure that their own goods would then be seized in retaliation for events in Prussia and Lübeck. Much to their surprise the expected blow did not fall. Professor Postan saw this as evidence that the politicians were surfeited with the spoils of the Bay fleet and had decided to abandon the mercantile interest which they had previously wooed.[25] The truth of the matter is that councillors could not profit from confiscation of goods in the Steelyard, for these would be held in favour of English merchants who had suffered losses abroad. Moreover, the currently desperate situation in English-occupied Normandy meant that it would have been the height of folly to imperil the flow of Baltic naval and military stores. Instead, the council decided to follow the path of diplomacy; on 23 September a commission was issued to Lord Dudley and Thomas Kent, clerk of the council, to treat with Prussia and the Hanse. As a gesture of goodwill the Hanse customs concessions were restored, though on a provisional basis. The new conference was held in Bruges, where Hanseatic envoys were holding talks with the Flemings. On 2 November 1449 the parties signed a provisional agreement that a conference should be held at Utrecht in the following June to settle all outstanding differences. The Hanseatic representatives were unable to accept an English proposal for an immediate release of prisoners, and in any event these seem to have been held only by their side, unless one includes any German sailors still pressed in the English fleet. However, it was thought that if the

---

[24] *Ibid.*, nos. 436, 557, 559.   [25] Postan, *England and the Hanse*, p. 129.

English government, the Hanse and Prussia accepted the provisional agreement then a truce could be instituted and trade resumed under safe conduct until Martinmas 1450. The Hanse delegates in Flanders were under pressure to accept this compromise, particularly from Cologne. The archbishop of that city received an English pension, while its merchants were not prepared to put their trade in jeopardy. It was made clear that if the Hanse could not negotiate a peace with England then Cologne, which as yet had suffered few losses, would seek to make its own settlement. When the English mission returned home in mid-November, the government ratified the agreement and in December formally reinstated the Hanseatic privileges, but excluded the merchants of Lübeck and Prussia. The latter were offered a safe-conduct to trade without privileges, but this would have been very risky. Englishmen were already seizing ships in retaliation for recent losses; in November, for example, two Danzig hulks were captured while returning home from Lisbon. The compromise arrived at in the autumn of 1449 was due largely to Cologne, whose merchants had most to gain by it, but their willingness to countenance the exception of Prussia and Lübeck weakened the unity of the Hanse.[26]

While the English government accepted the proposal for a meeting at Utrecht, it wanted the date advanced to March 1450, and sent this request to the Grand Master on 20 November. The latter at first agreed (27 January 1450), but a few days later (5 February) wrote again saying that the Prussians would not after all be able to negotiate before June. In fact, on 22 December, before either of the Prussian letters had even been dispatched, the English government asked for yet another change of plan. In place of the general conference with the Hanse, or as a preparation, it suggested talks with Lübeck and Prussia. Both agreed and in February Lübeck issued a safe-conduct for English envoys, valid until midsummer 1450.[27] It is not clear whether the original intention was for the talks with Lübeck and Prussia to be held jointly or separately. However, both seem to have been under the impression that there would be joint talks, and when Lübeck discovered that this was not the case it drew back. History had taught the Hanse to be suspicious of negotiations conducted separately by the Prussians and in the present instance Lübeck had everything to lose by allowing them to go ahead on their own. This was the result of the very unequal bargaining strength of the two cities *vis à vis* England. Lübeck had suffered greatly in the Bay seizure, her losses later being estimated at £19,000 sterling.[28] But since the city was off the beaten track of English trade it had been able to arrest very little property in retaliation. In contrast, Prussia in August 1451 claimed to have lost goods worth 53,776 Prussian marks in the Bay fleet (apart from earlier losses), but admitted to having arrested English goods worth 41,527 marks.[29] Given the natural tendency to exaggerate losses and minimise seizures, it is likely that the score was more or less even. This put Prussia in a strong position to bargain. The English government was not deterred by this, since it was anxious to reach an accommodation. This was because of the intrinsic importance of trade with Prussia and also because a settlement here would enable it to take a hard line against Lübeck's claims. So strongly felt was the need for peace with Prussia that allegedly Kent was told that if he failed to accomplish it his head would be forfeit.[30]

Because of its weaker bargaining position it was imperative for Lübeck to maintain the support of the other towns. It proposed to do this by holding a diet at Bremen in midsummer, where a common policy could be worked out before any talks were held with England. The invitation to the Grand Master to send representatives also asked him to delay talks with the English envoys, should they arrive in Prussia before the conclusion of the Bremen diet. The Prussians declined the invitation and condemned a suggestion that the Hanse should join Burgundy in banning the import of English cloth.[31] They had no wish to find their hands tied by the Hanse, which might be persuaded to introduce trade sanctions or even to wage an all-out war against England. The Prussian fears were well founded, since the Bremen diet, while not coming to a final decision, arranged to meet again at Lübeck on 21 September, when one of the motions was to consider a complete ban on trade with England and on English goods. Safe-conducts issued by Prussia in April 1450 covered not merely official English envoys, but also other merchants and the crews and cargoes of two ships. The combination of diplomacy and trade reduced the cost of the expedition, since merchants were

---

[28] Claim advanced in October 1461 (25,600 marks of Lübeck). *HR*, II (v), no. 169. In 1465 the figure was given as 125,000 Rhine florins. *HUB*, 9, no. 196.

[29] *HUB*, 8, no. 84.   [30] *HR*, II (iii), no. 669.

[31] *HR*, II (v), nos. 604, 607–8, 614.

willing to pay generously to send goods to Prussia 'in the diplomatic bag'. As well as Englishmen, merchants of Danzig, Cologne and Herzogenbosch ventured cloth. The principal English negotiators were Dr Thomas Kent, John Stocker, merchant of London, and Henry Birmingham, merchant of Lynn, but Thomas Crouch and John Gosselyn of London and William Cateryk of York also had official roles. Even before the expedition sailed, the safe-conduct issued by Lübeck had expired, which made it doubly unfortunate that the ship carrying some of the envoys was captured in the approaches to the Baltic by Lübeck *Bergenfahrer*; the second ship escaped and arrived safely in Danzig. The captors sent the prisoners to Lübeck, but took the cargo to Bergen, where it was confiscated by officials of the Danish crown. Eventually, some was restored to its owners but most was sent to the western Hanse towns to be sold. The following year the Grand Master warned potential buyers not to bring any of the cloth to Prussia, since he would be obliged to restore it to its true owners.[32]

While the capture of the English envoys was fortuitous, their delivery was too much of a temptation to Lübeck, which declined to release them on the grounds that its safe-conduct had long since expired. This action somewhat ruffled the prevailing desire for peace in England. On 1 September the king sent word to the diet about to assemble at Lübeck that he was as anxious as ever for a settlement, but four days later writs were issued for the arrest of Hanseatic goods. The city of Cologne protested at this action, which it did not expect after so many years of labouring in the king's interest. However, much of the property had been released even before receipt of the next communication from the diet dated 16 October, which reached London on 7 November. By the latter date Hans Winter and other merchants resident in England had recovered their goods and had already sent them off to Zeeland. A week later Winter reported that the Hanse merchants had been confirmed in their exemption from tunnage and poundage, except for those of Lübeck, Rostock, Wismar, Stralsund, Hamburg and Danzig. The government welcomed the diet's offer of another conference and agreed to meet Hanse delegates at Utrecht a fortnight after Easter 1451. Lübeck had to be satisfied with a secret resolution that, if the English refused to attend, or if the meeting proved fruitless, then the Hanse

[32] *HR*, II (iii), nos. 594, 596–7. *HUB*, 8, no. 14. *Foedera*, v (ii), p. 26.

would institute a partial trade boycott after Martinmas 1451. Since the diet had been very well attended Lübeck could reasonably claim that the decision had the authority of the entire Hanse. Even Prussia was represented and, having tried and failed to secure the release of the imprisoned envoys, it had little choice but to participate in general negotiations.[33]

Much now depended on the outcome of the Utrecht meeting, but compared with advance preparations for the Hague conference of 1407 the current English preparations were feeble. Instead of carefully concerting all claims for damages the government seems merely to have proclaimed, as late as March 1451, that complainants must go to Utrecht either in person or in proxy to put their cases before the conference. Lübeck still refused to free the envoys unconditionally, but on 17 March it released John Stocker on parole so that he might attend the Utrecht conference. He was sworn to return if the outcome was unsuccessful. Kent, the more important figure, swore to remain as surety for Stocker, but he afterwards fled the city in obscure circumstances. Both Kent and Stocker were included in the commission sealed on 4 May for the English delegation, which was headed by Robert Botill, Prior of the Order of St John. Henry Birmingham and Dr William Witham were also in the party. On the Hanse side those most dedicated to obtaining a peaceful end to the present crisis were Cologne and Prussia. On 25 February the Steelyard wrote to Cologne urging it to send a delegate to the conference who should be thoroughly committed to peace. It reminded the city that the Hanseatic privileges in England had been won originally by the men of Cologne ('dat unse vorvadere uns met groter swarheit in dessem riike gheworven hebben') and they had no wish to lose them because of the intransigence of the north Germans. Prussia was also for peace, but remained unwilling to yield an inch on the question of English privileges. To this end it tried to probe the strength of their case. On 11 January 1451 the Grand Master wrote to Lübeck saying that he had heard that among the papers of the captured envoys were some which purported to prove the English claim to an ancient grant of privileges in Prussia. While knowing full well that these could not be authentic, he asked that the documents, or copies of them, be sent to him. Lübeck preferred to keep the Prussians in suspense. The Prussian towns briefed their delegates at

---

[33] *CPR*, 1446–54, p. 430. *HR*, II (iii), nos. 642, 651, 659, 666, 669–70, 701. *HUB*, 8, no. 1.

a provincial diet in April. They had full power to negotiate about any damage committed by either side, both before and since the seizure of the Bay fleet. They were forbidden to discuss the matter of privileges and were to state formally that the English should enjoy nothing more than the traditional rights afforded to all aliens visiting Prussia. Should the latter raise old charges, such as their being driven from their houses into cellars, they were simply to say that all these points had been answered in earlier negotiations. Additionally, the envoys were equipped with a set of secret instructions. They were to try to secure the formal release of the English envoys; if the conference could not reach a complete settlement of differences the Prussians were to work for a twenty-year truce on the basis of the *status quo*; if all else failed they could make a separate agreement with England that trade between the two countries should continue under safe-conducts for three or four years, provided that England respected Prussian neutrality in its struggle with France.[34]

The Utrecht conference was dogged by bad luck even before it began. The Prussian delegates were captured and for a while imprisoned in Mecklenburg, while those of Cologne had to wait a week before the arrival of any others and were prevented from leaving only by the entreaties of some English merchants in the town. When the two sides first came together on 28 May the Lübeck delegates refused to attend because of the presence of Thomas Kent, so the city was represented by Frank Keddeken, the Flemish lawyer who had assisted Vorrath in 1437. Only when it became clear that the English delegation was not quorate without Kent did the Lübeckers reluctantly join the discussions. The English then dropped another bombshell by refusing to continue until Kent and Stocker were formally released from imprisonment and their goods and papers restored. This Lübeck refused to do, despite pressure from Cologne, Prussia and elsewhere. An attempt to persuade the English to discuss the question of damages without the participation of Lübeck also failed. The only thing salvaged from the Utrecht talks was a provisional agreement made on 12 June to hold another meeting on 24 April 1452. If this was confirmed then trade might continue during a truce until Michaelmas 1452. Both sides already laid down certain preconditions for a final settlement. The English insisted that

---

[34] *CCR*, 1447–54, p. 267. *HR*, II (iii), nos. 687, 691, 694–5, 697, 702, 708.

there could be no peace treaty without the freeing of all prisoners held by Lübeck and Prussia, whether physically detained there, already released on parole, or freed in return for financial sureties. They also demanded the return of at least half the goods arrested in Prussia. A Lübeck and Prussian precondition was the release of any people and all property detained in England. Before the next conference the good offices of the Steelyard were to be enlisted to weigh the losses and confiscations on either side, and wherever possible to effect an amicable conclusion between individual merchants. The English delegation also asked the Germans to urge Lübeck to temper its harshness to the remaining prisoners, now said to be held in chains, and Prussia to make available part of the confiscated property to sustain destitute merchants still under arrest in that land.[35]

According to Stein, the Utrecht conference of 1451 was deliberately sabotaged by the English, who did not wish to pay compensation or restore the Hanse franchises.[36] From their point of view the postponement of a settlement was a successful outcome. They achieved this with the connivance of Cologne and Prussia, who sold out Lübeck and damaged the unity of the Hanse. Prussia was satisfied that trade should continue without its having to make concessions. Cologne was not unhappy that the northern and eastern wings of the Hanse were unreconciled with England, since this maximised the value of its own trade. For Stein, only Lübeck emerged from the episode with honour, since it was the one party to resist the blackmailing tactics devised to secure the release of Thomas Kent. This analysis is weakened by the fact that it disregards a number of important considerations. There was an apparently widespread and genuine desire for peace in England, much of the Hanse already had *de facto* enjoyment of its franchises, and an attempt to settle the question of damages should start within a few weeks. The tacit abandonment for the time being of the English demand for reciprocity of privileges was itself an important concession. Stein rightly emphasised that the Utrecht agreement marked the beginning of a period of increasing isolation of Lübeck from the rest of the Hanse, but it should be added that this was largely of its own making. The English government informed the Steelyard of its acceptance of the agreement as early as 22 July 1451, while the Prussian diet voted to accept it on 6 August. Lübeck did

[35] *HUB*, 8, nos. 40, 47. *HR*, ɪɪ (iii), nos. 709–12.
[36] Stein, 'Die Hanse und England', 90.

not make known its decision until September, after the deadline agreed at Utrecht. It then announced that it would not participate in another conference unless it received prior satisfaction for its losses in the Bay fleet and unless Kent and Stocker returned to captivity. This was tantamount to an outright rejection of the recent agreement and led to a flurry of correspondence in other sections of the Hanse. On 24 September Cologne wrote to Henry VI regretting Lübeck's reluctance to endorse the Utrecht decision and emphasising its own wish for peace. On 28 October the Grand Master wrote to the king saying that he would honour the agreement so long as the latter maintained his safe-conduct for Prussian merchants. He also wrote to Cologne and Hamburg expressing the hope that, despite the absence of Lübeck, all the other parties would reconvene at Utrecht. Coincidentally, the Steelyard wrote to Cologne on the same day in a similar vein. The foreboding of the Steelyard, Prussia and Cologne that England would use Lübeck's decision as an excuse to renounce the Utrecht agreement was unfounded. No move was made against the ships and merchants of Prussia, Cologne, Hamburg, Bremen and other towns which, expecting ratification, had returned to England in considerable numbers in the autumn. Trade continued throughout the winter and all Hanse towns save Lübeck were allowed the franchises. In November 1451 Danzig advised all Prussian and Livonian ships then in the west to form convoys for mutual protection. However, it was not from England alone, or even primarily, that trouble was expected. The fear was that Lübeck would persuade Denmark to close the Sound to all ships carrying English goods and thus imperil the homeward voyages of Prussian vessels.[37]

Pressure continued to be put on Lübeck to take part in the Utrecht conference. In November a diet of the Zuider Zee towns demanded that she should either agree to attend or else convene a Hanse diet in Nijmegen or Deventer by February 1452 at the latest. In fact a diet was held in February, but at Lübeck where it was very poorly attended, and relations with England were scarcely considered. These stonewalling tactics had the desired effect of sabotaging the Utrecht conference. England had conceded that it should go ahead without Lübeck, provided that Prussia and Cologne could guarantee the presence of enough towns to make it worth while. In mid-April 1452 the Grand Master announced that he

---

[37] *HUB*, 8, no. 100. *HR*, ii (v), nos. 5, 14, 17–18, 20, 34, 42; (vii), no. 526.

would not send a representative, since the condition could not be satisfied. However, he promised to carry on working for a settlement and requested an extension of the truce until Michaelmas 1453. In June, Henry VI agreed to this, provided that he was given a new date for the conference by the coming Michaelmas, and provided also that any Hanse towns which wished to be included in the truce sent their own safe-conducts for English merchants.[38]

Lübeck was able to prevent the conference from taking place in 1452 because a majority of the Hanse was not yet ready to act on the political front without its acknowledged leader. But it could no longer galvanise the membership into supporting trade sanctions or military action against England and, as predicted, turned instead to Denmark. The long-standing dispute between England and Denmark about Iceland trade had been provisionally resolved in 1449, but the Danes had not ratified the treaty and declined to extend the truce when it expired in 1451. Denmark then closed the Sound to English ships, though English merchants continued to export cloth in Prussian vessels. At first the Danes turned a blind eye to this, but in April 1452 they stopped ships in the Sound and confiscated English-owned goods. The King of Denmark informed the Grand Master that the same treatment would be meted out to any vessel which tried to pass through the Belt. This action coincided exactly with the decision of Lübeck to stop the overland passage from Hamburg to the Baltic, by outlawing all English-made cloth from its territory. Lübeck did not stop there, for in May it sent to sea two ships under the command of Bartholomew Voet, the famous privateer of the 1420s. Unfortunately, he was no more discriminating now than then and, under the pretext of searching for cloth, robbed many innocent vessels. When this elicited not merely protests from other Hanse towns and the Dutch but also threats of retaliation, the privateers had quickly to be recalled. The ban on English-made cloth remained, but began to be circumvented by movement from Hamburg to the Baltic port of Neustadt in the duchy of Holstein.[39]

Throughout the summer of 1452 many components of the Hanse laboured in the interests of a settlement. The Steelyard reported that the peace party was still strong in England and the king's council was especially friendly towards Cologne. The Zuider Zee towns informed Lübeck that they had no intention of breaking off trade, and again demanded a general diet. Cologne told the king that every

---

[38] *HR*, II (iv), nos. 41, 55–6, 79, 102.
[39] *HUB*, 8, nos. 122–3, 128, 159, 261. *HR*, II (iv), nos. 24, 69–71, 80–81.

town except Lübeck was eager for the conference, though even she might be won over, and it would go ahead without her if necessary. Early in September, however, the Grand Master regretfully conceded that it would be impossible to fix a firm date in time to meet the Michaelmas deadline. He was optimistic that agreement could be reached by Purification (2 February 1453) and hoped that England would therefore confirm the renewal of the truce until that date. This proposal did not reach the king until 18 October, while his acceptance of the new timetable, sent on 8 November, reached Marienburg on Christmas Day. By this last date Cologne, Hamburg and the Zuider Zee towns had accepted a Prussian invitation to confer with England at Utrecht on 23 April 1453. Unfortunately, three days later Lübeck pulled off a master stroke by convening a general diet at Lübeck on 22 April to discuss the Netherlands staple. Since this matter was equally as important as relations with England, Prussia saw no alternative but to request yet another postponement of the Utrecht conference and an extension of the truce until Michaelmas 1453. In return it promised to send representatives to the diet, who would press the assembled towns to make a resolution about England and also try to persuade Lübeck to lift its own boycott on English cloth. The English government received the set-back with apparent good grace in March, promised to continue its safe-conduct as long as Englishmen were protected in return and endorsed the plan for Prussian participation in the diet. The Steelyard wrote to Danzig advising that all towns represented at the diet be reminded to submit their claims for damages against England. So far only Prussia and Kampen had done so and it was to be feared that, when the conference finally met, the English might refuse to consider any claims which had not been notified in advance.[40]

When the Hanse diet finally met at Lübeck at the end of May there was a strong Prussian presence, made up of a personal representative of the Grand Master and others from Danzig and Elbing to speak for the towns. Nevertheless, the English business hardly figured on the agenda and general attendance was so poor that it was necessary to arrange for a further session to be held at Bremen in October to continue discussions about the Netherlands staple. Danzig wrote to Cologne, Hamburg, Brunswick, Nijmegen and Bremen urging them all to send representatives to the next

---

[40] *HUB*, 8, no. 180. *HR*, II (iv), nos. 87, 122, 133, 135, 150, 154.

session, armed with powers to commit the diet to a conference with England. It pointed out that when the truce expired at Michaelmas Hanseatic trade would once more be in jeopardy. With this in mind the Grand Master wrote to Henry VI asking that he extend the truce for three years in favour of Prussia. The city of Danzig apparently thought such a move impolitic and forbade the Steelyard to deliver the letter to the king, but suggested that it make a similar request on behalf of all members of the Hanse who were not at enmity with England. The consequence was that on 28 August 1453 the truce was extended until Michaelmas 1456, in favour of all towns except Lübeck. When the Steelyard sent a sealed copy of the safe-conduct to Danzig, it pointed out that at the end of the first session of the current parliament (28 March 1453) the commons had made the king a life-time grant of tunnage and poundage, to commence when the present grant expired on 3 April 1454. The terms of the grant included the ending of Hanse immunity. This decision was doubtless influenced by the fact that denizen cloth exports were intended to be made liable to poundage for the first time since 1436, though in the event denizen liability was cancelled before the new grant took effect. The Steelyard officials hoped that the king would use his dispensing power in their favour, but proposed not to ask for this until parliament was dissolved. The dissolution came at Easter 1454, and in the following June, with retrospection to 3 April, the king freed all Hansards, except those of Lübeck, from paying tunnage and poundage for three years and also exempted them from the current alien poll tax.[41]

The Hanse diet which was to have been held in Bremen in October 1453 was postponed until December and transferred to Lübeck; attendance was again sparse and business largely confined to the Netherlands. However, Lübeck finally agreed to confer with England, either in Lübeck itself or in Hamburg, and suggested the following May as the date. Stein saw this as a corollary to growing unrest in Prussia, which promoted self-confidence in Lübeck and encouraged the city once more to assert its leadership of the Hanse.[42] The proposed conference did not take place, because the outbreak of civil war prevented the attendance of the Prussians, without whom there could be no final settlement. At this point the towns of Prussia renounced their allegiance to the Order and accepted the suzerainty of the King of Poland, in the expectation of a greater measure of

[41] *Rot. Parl.*, 5, pp. 228, 230. *HR*, II (iv), nos. 168, 170, 177, 236. *HUB*, 8, nos. 196, 285.
[42] Stein, 'Die Hanse und England', 116.

independence. They then became anxious that England might exclude them from the current truce, since the safe-conduct recently sent to Prussia referred to merchants within the dominion of the Grand Master of the Teutonic Order. Their fears were unfounded; as early as 25 April 1454 the Steelyard obtained a new version of the safe-conduct and sent it to Danzig. In return Englishmen trading with Prussia were issued with safe-conducts for up to twelve years – a clear sign of the desire for peace. Further movement towards a settlement came during a Hanse diet held at Lübeck in July 1454. The city used this occasion to lift its ban on English-made cloth. This brought no immediate benefit to English merchants, but the clothiers gained indirectly from the breathing space provided for Hanse exporters. In the conflict between the Prussian towns and the Teutonic Order the King of Denmark had supported the Knights and this had put voyages through the Sound at risk. Now Prussian merchants could send cloth via Hamburg and Lübeck. More importantly, the diet proposed that an Anglo-Hanseatic peace conference should be held at Lübeck or Hamburg in September. Both the shortness of the notice and the preferred venues suggest that the diet was probing English intentions, rather than seriously expecting the meeting to take place. The reply, delayed until 5 December, pointed out that Lübeck was 'manifeste inimicorum nostrorum sede', while Hamburg was equally unacceptable. Instead, the Hanse was invited to send envoys to England.[43] There was virtually no prospect of this invitation being taken up, not the least of the problems being that of determining who was qualified to speak for Prussia. It appears, therefore, that the door was firmly closed against negotiations – a view supported by the fact that neither side suggested another time and place. This does not mean that England or even any section of the Hanse was seeking to fan the embers of the conflict. There was no guarantee that a definitive peace would emerge from any meeting. It might, like earlier conferences, fail to settle the huge financial claims advanced by each side; in that event trade sanctions or even war might be renewed. Obviously, those with the greatest vested interest in a full-scale conference dedicated to the settlement of financial claims were merchants who had been ruined by the seizure of the Bay fleet or subsequent reprisals. Any who had since mended their fortunes, as well as a new generation of merchants, were more concerned with the preservation of existing

[43] *HUB*, 8, no. 354. *HR*, ii (iv), nos. 235, 263, 304.

trade. For the fact was that with the passing of time trade had begun to recover and with the exception of Lübeck the Hanse was enjoying its franchises on a *de facto* basis. What was needed for a further improvement of trade was not a set-piece conference of doubtful value, but a prolongation of the existing truce. The English government was agreeable to this and, although it did not formally make the first move, it privately made its thoughts known to the other side. The go-between was Henry Grevenstein, clerk of the Steelyard, who in December 1454 carried the invitation for Hanseatic envoys to come to England. When this was turned down, Grevenstein journeyed through the Hanse towns, searching for a peace formula. The first to commit itself, in June 1455, was Danzig, although this was probably because it was the furthest point in Grevenstein's travels. From then on he was returning to England enlisting support as he came. Danzig suggested a truce of eight to ten years during which time the Hanse should enjoy its franchises, while the King of Poland would grant a safe-conduct to English merchants. Hamburg accepted this at the end of July, while a similar proposal from Cologne was dated 9 September. At the end of October England sent word that it was prepared to agree to a long truce, but only after Lübeck formally freed the envoys captured in 1450. When this was done, in January 1456, the last remaining obstacle to a *rapprochement* was removed and in February the government proclaimed an eight-year truce with the whole of the Hanse including Lübeck. During this period all the towns were to be free from tunnage and poundage.[44]

Lübeck's act of statesmanship might, given time, have solved many problems. The longer the truce could be maintained the less likely was either side to take unilateral action to redress old wrongs. In the interim some claims might be settled privately in the law courts and eventually any which were left would cease to be a serious issue, though they would undoubtedly be regarded as a bargaining counter for a very long time. Some gains were reaped from the truce by the Hanse merchants almost immediately, for without it they must surely have suffered the same fate as Italians during the anti-alien riots of 1456–7. There is, however, no record of any attempt to turn the London mob against the Germans at this time. Unfortunately, the period of tranquillity which was needed to restore good

---

[44] *HR*, II (iv), nos. 355, 362, 364–5, 399–400, 450–1. *Foedera*, v (ii), p. 66.

Anglo-Hanseatic relations was soon sabotaged by yet another outrageous action perpetrated by the English side. The blow was struck on 29 July 1458 when the Calais fleet seized eighteen ships of Lübeck, on the grounds that they had refused to salute the English flag. Bearing in mind that Calais had been held by the Earl of Warwick as a Yorkist stronghold since 1456, Lübeck may have expected greater sympathy than it eventually received from the Lancastrian government. The latter's attitude resulted partly from indifference, since Warwick's treatment of aliens was among the least of the government's charges against him, and partly from the sheer impossibility of disciplining him. A commission of enquiry was set up as early as 31 July and in October Warwick came to London to give evidence. On 9 November the earl narrowly escaped with his life from a brawl in Westminster Hall; whereupon he beat a hasty retreat to Calais. In February 1459 the government informed Lübeck that its sailors had only themselves to blame for their misfortune, though it promised to obtain the release of prisoners. Warwick's own letter to the city, sent in April, was in similar vein. Because of this lack of concern, and despite Danzig's plea that nothing should be done to break the truce, in March 1460 Lübeck ships seized a Guernsey vessel. The owners then requested letters of marque against Lübeck, Danzig and Hamburg, alleging that sailors of the latter two towns had participated in the attack.[45]

Despite the seizure of the Lübeck ships and minor injuries allegedly inflicted on other merchants, including some from Danzig and Cologne, the eight years truce held until the deposition of Henry VI.[46] This threw everything into the melting pot. Edward IV took possession of the realm on 3 March 1461 and a few weeks later the Steelyard sent word to Lübeck that steps must be taken to renew the truce and obtain a confirmation of the franchises.[47] This was easier said than done, for vested interests soon began to speak out against the Hanse. Because of his constitutional position there was no question of Edward alienating potential English allies by an early confirmation of the Hanse franchises. Instead, he decided that they should be allowed on a *de facto* basis until 2 February 1462.[48] He also demanded to know the names of all towns which claimed to enjoy

---

[45] *HR*, II (iv), nos. 666, 670. *HUB*, 8, nos. 769, 780, 963, 965. *Foedera*, v (ii), p. 82. P. M. Kendall, *Warwick the Kingmaker* (London, 1957), p. 50.
[46] *HUB*, 8, nos. 946, 972.   [47] *HR*, II (v), no. 117.
[48] This step was probably taken on 9 July 1461. *HR*, II (v), nos. 147, 263. *HUB*, 8, no. 1067.

them, together with the names of their temporal overlords. These towns were to give an undertaking that they would urge their lords to behave amicably towards Edward. The king's own subjects were told that he would deal with the question of the franchises when parliament met in November. This gave both sides several months to organise campaigns for and against confirmation. The English had somehow or other to reconcile several interests which were not totally compatible. In the first place, the Baltic merchants revived their clamour for reciprocity in Prussia and, according to a Hanse source, still demanded access to Poland and Russia. If their own demands were conceded this group would not support any movement for the total abolition of the Hanse franchises. On the other hand the latter was the ambition of most English overseas merchants without a stake in the Baltic. Among these the most important group was the fellowship of Merchant Adventurers, who frequented the Brabant fairs. But the Hanse was represented as a rival to all Englishmen who traded with Holland, Zeeland, Brabant, Flanders, Hainault, the Bay and 'other countries adjoining'. All of these interests were referred to in a petition addressed to 'the right worshipful and descrete commons' in the first parliament of Edward IV, which demanded that the Hanse franchises 'be utterly restreyned and putte in suspence' for the time being.[49] All were also mentioned in a letter sent on 16 July from the Steelyard, advising the Bruges *Kontor* of the gathering clouds in England.[50] This letter described the hostility of the city of London, which had revived its complaint that the exercise of the Hanse franchises was a derogation of its own liberties. The current campaign had begun even before the deposition of Henry VI and, amongst other grievances, the city had resurrected its ancient claim about Bishopgate. It was probably in a vain attempt to buy off opposition in this quarter that in February 1461 the Steelyard gave a freewill offering of £20 to a tax quota of

---

[49] PRO, C49/52/8(2). Printed in Jenks, *England, die Hanse und Preussen*, appendix 1, pp. 1–4. Jenks dates the document as 'late 1440s or early 1450s'. My reasons for disagreeing with this date are as follows. It refers back to the parliament of 1442, but identifies it by *anno Domini* instead of the regnal year. While Henry VI still reigned this form would have bordered on *lèse-majesté*. The first parliament of Edward IV condemned all three Lancastrian kings as usurpers and its records referred to years of their 'pretended reigns'. Such language might have been considered over bold in a petition drawn up by mere merchants (and the political situation was still fluid), but the drafters would no doubt be aware of the Yorkist feelings. Dating by *anno Domini* was neutral and avoided the question of the legitimacy of Henry VI's reign. The date 1461 is therefore suggested.

[50] *HR*, II (v), no. 147.

Dowgate ward. Shortly before parliament assembled the city delegated men to concert the campaign against the Hanse and voted funds for their expenses.[51]

At this critical time the Hanse was again divided about tactics. Danzig and Cologne pressed Lübeck to disregard the latest attack on its trade in order to participate in talks about the franchises. This Lübeck refused to do so long as its losses of 1449 were unsatisfied. Hamburg urged the futility of trying to get a definitive settlement as long as civil war continued in Prussia and argued that until that ended the Hanse should look for nothing more than an extension of the truce and continued *de facto* enjoyment of the franchises. Cologne asked that if the king could not yet confirm the franchises he should guarantee them until at least Michaelmas 1462, since the February deadline afforded insufficient security. In fact, on 22 December, immediately after parliament was prorogued, Edward extended the guarantee until Christmas 1462. The Steelyard claimed credit for this, but said that it had been achieved only with great difficulty and the distribution of bribes amounting to 1,300 nobles. It predicted that in the face of parliamentary opposition no further extension would be granted.[52]

The Steelyard now began to lobby support for a full-scale embassy to be sent to England after a Hanse diet. This plan was endorsed by the Zuider Zee towns meeting at Wesel in March 1462. Hamburg again held out hopes of nothing more ambitious than a three-year extension of the truce. Lübeck, of course, was resolutely opposed. In July the clerk of the Steelyard came to a diet at Lübeck, bringing with him documents setting out current grievances of his members and a history of relations over the past few years. It was hoped that these would form the basis of a case to be put by ambassadors, but the diet could not be persuaded to lend its authority. Time was now running out so the Steelyard had once more to appeal to the Zuider Zee towns, which reluctantly agreed to conduct negotiations by themselves. The envoys provided by Cologne and Nijmegen did not arrive in England until December, and the Steelyard later complained that failure to reach agreement before the franchises expired at Christmas cost its members very dearly. In fact, because of the stiff opposition of English merchants agreement was not reached until March 1463. The government now agreed to a *de facto*

[51] *Letter Book* L, p. 76. *HUB*, 8, nos. 1003–4. *HR*, II (v), nos. 146, 263.
[52] *HR*, II (v), nos. 166–70, 175, 179, 263. *HUB*, 8, no. 1110.

extension of privileges until midsummer 1465 in favour of the citizens of any towns which behaved reasonably towards Englishmen. A further condition was that the Zuider Zee towns should continue to lobby for a full-scale conference to settle all outstanding differences between England and the Hanse and between England and Denmark.[53] While the franchises were continued a campaign was mounted to see that they were limited to *bona fide* Hanseatic merchants. The king's legal officers seem to have scrutinised the ancient charters and revived the idea that only members of the London Gildhall were entitled to enjoy the franchises. Membership was attested by a certificate issued by the 'aldermannus et communes mercatores regni Allemannie habentes domum in civitate London que Guyldehalla Theutoniconum vulgariter nuncupator in eadem civitate nunc existentes'.[54]

The demands of the western Hanse towns for a conference were now supported by Danzig, and in August 1463 Lübeck agreed to take part in talks with England at midsummer in the following year, either at Lübeck or Hamburg. Cologne tried unsuccessfully to get the venue changed to one of the Zuider Zee towns, on the grounds that the English would refuse to come to either of the two places suggested. In fact, Cologne's concern may have been chiefly for the safety of its own delegates. The city was in dispute with the King of Denmark, who in February 1463 rejected a request for safe-conducts for Cologne envoys to attend a northern conference. In the event Edward IV agreed to negotiate at Hamburg and, as early as March 1464, commissions were made out for a strong team, consisting of Richard Caunton, archdeacon of Salisbury, Henry Sharp, doctor of laws and king's protonotary, and seven merchants, none of whom were Londoners. A few weeks later, the two leaders and two of the merchants were also commissioned to treat with the kings of Denmark and Poland. The English party crossed to the continent in good time, but while waiting at Bruges for letters of safe-conduct it was notified that plague had broken out at Hamburg. The sincerity of the desire for a comprehensive peace treaty is suggested by the envoys' offer to go to Hamburg as arranged or to an alternative place. However, this was not to be, for the Hanseatics called off the meeting and suggested that they should try again the following year. Plague was not the only reason for the cancellation, as Cologne later explained. The Prussians could not take part because they were too

---

[53] *HR*, II (v), nos. 212, 218, 220, 254, 263, 282–5. *HUB*, 8, nos. 1234, 1236. *Foedera*, v (ii), p. 113.   [54] See below pp. 378–80.

much involved in peace discussions between the King of Poland and the Teutonic Order, while the King of Denmark was away campaigning in Sweden.[55]

Because of economic problems in other quarters, including a new cloth boycott imposed by Burgundy in October 1464, England remained keen on a settlement with the Hanse and in January 1465 floated the idea of a meeting in the following June, either at Utrecht or in some other place no further from England. If this offer was accepted then the Hanse privileges would be renewed for a further two years in favour of all towns which gave their own safe-conduct to English merchants. In April safe-conducts were issued by the King of Poland, Danzig and Stralsund, despite Danzig's contention that they were not really necessary since a state of friendship existed between the two sides. It was agreed that the venue for the conference should be Hamburg, and this time it did take place, although because of two postponements asked for by the English it was delayed until the middle of September. Amongst other problems the Count of Oldenburg declined to issue safe-conducts for the envoys of England and Cologne to pass through his territory *en route* from Utrecht to Hamburg. The conference got off to a poor start, partly because of language difficulties but more importantly because it soon appeared that the English delegates were not empowered to offer compensation for old injuries. Lübeck and its allies saw little point in continuing and it was only the persistence of Cologne and the representatives of the London Steelyard, with some support from Danzig and Hamburg, which kept things going until a compromise was reached. The memoranda of each side's understanding of the compromise are substantially in agreement, though they contain significant differences of detail. The offer subsequently made by the English government differed yet again. The Hanse version began with the statement that the English ambassadors and the merchants of the Steelyard would endeavour to persuade the king to agree to a resumption of talks at Whitsun 1467 in any Hanse town. Each side was to send envoys armed with plenipotentiary powers to discuss and settle all outstanding claims for damages. The king was to inform the Hanse of his acceptance by Whitsun 1466. If he accepted, then the current truce, which was due to expire at Martinmas (11 November), should be extended for one, two, three or five years. If the king would not agree to the proposed conference then the current truce should

[55] *HUB*, 9, no. 119. *HR*, II (v), nos. 352, 354, 538–41, 564, 566, 570, 583. *Foedera*, v (ii), pp. 122–3.

be extended for one year and a new five-year truce should commence
at midsummer 1466. Throughout this period the Hanse should enjoy
their franchises in England and neither side was to use force to
recoup outstanding damages. The English version began with the
suggestion of a five-year truce from midsummer 1466, during which
time both sides should enjoy their accustomed rights and liberties
and refrain from pursuing old grievances. England was to be notified
of all towns which were members of the Hanse and no others were
to be allowed the franchises. Then came the proposal for a
conference at Whitsun 1467, though this was to be held in any Hanse
town or Utrecht as the king might choose. Even if he was not
prepared to talk, the five-year truce should operate.[56]

The English government took until March 1466 to make a formal
offer of a five-year truce (to midsummer 1471), though this was
qualified by a proviso that the franchises would be suspended at the
end of the first two years if the Hanse had not by then sent envoys
to a peace conference in England. Lübeck refused to participate, on
the grounds that it had been agreed that negotiations should be
conducted in a Hanse town. In March 1467 the Steelyard reported
to Hamburg that the king's council was impatient about the lack of
response to the invitation and recommended that a decision should
be made quickly. The secretary of the Steelyard spent much of that
summer travelling around the northern and eastern towns trying to
win them over, but in November Lübeck and its allies were still
refusing to negotiate in England. As early as May 1467 the city of
Cologne had suggested itself as a venue for the conference, in the
hope that this would be acceptable to Edward IV, but when the
proposal was formally put to him in December he turned it down.
Nevertheless, in March 1468 Edward extended the privileges until
midsummer 1469, provided that the Hanse sent envoys to England
within that time. Once again the secretary of the Steelyard began his
weary circuit of the towns in an attempt to get them to accept the
English conditions. However, his efforts were frustrated by the
beginning of the most serious dispute in the entire history of Anglo-
Hanseatic relations.[57]

The outbreak of war between England and the Hanse is commonly
seen as a consequence of the Anglo-Burgundian commercial treaty of
November 1467. It is argued that England could not afford to be at
odds with two of the leading trading powers of Europe at the same

[56] *HR*, II (v), nos. 645–8, 652, 654, 674, 676, 685, 712–14. *Foedera*, v (ii), pp. 130–1.
[57] *HUB*, 9, nos. 310, 350, 387, 415, 433–4. *HR*, II (v), nos. 469–70; (vi), nos. 49, 55.

time, but that having made peace with Burgundy it could take a stronger line with the Hanse. There may be some truth in this for, though it must not be supposed that the new accord with Burgundy in itself caused England to seek a confrontation with the Hanse, it may well have encouraged her to persist with a course of action in which she was manifestly in the wrong. In October 1465 the English envoys sent to Hamburg had made a peace treaty with Denmark, in which *inter alia* Edward IV undertook to prevent his subjects from going to Iceland. At first, neither he nor the King of Denmark tried to enforce this, since both profited by selling licences of exemption. But, after the murder of the governor of Iceland by Englishmen in 1467, the King of Denmark changed tack and in June 1468 seized seven English ships in the Sound. He may have thought that this action would go unchallenged, since he immediately issued a statement saying that he had arrested some Lynn ships to answer for atrocities committed by men of that town, but that all other English vessels could continue to use the Sound. In fact only two of the ships belonged to Lynn and the English were not disposed to treat the matter lightly, as they soon showed. Little could be done to recover the losses directly, since hardly any Danes ventured goods to England. Therefore, revenge was taken against the Hanse, on the pretext that they were implicated in the incident. It was alleged that Germans sailing from England shortly before their rivals had given notice of their coming, while some Hanse vessels actually took part in the outrage. German historians have tended to discount these claims, on the grounds that the only Hanseatics then in Danish service were ships of Danzig, which were away in Swedish waters. However, it is all but indisputable that some Danzig ships were involved in the attack, while a few English witnesses even swore to the presence of Lübeck and Stralsund ships, though their complicity can probably be ruled out. Of course, aggression by Danzig ships sailing under Danish colours in no way justified the subsequent action taken in England. Reprisals were not altogether unexpected and, long before the news reached England, the Danzig authorities were writing to the Steelyard absolving the city of responsibility. It disclaimed its citizens already in Danish service and cautioned all others to stay out of the conflict.[58]

The ordeal of the Hanse merchants began on 23 July 1468 when officials of the Steelyard were notified that on the following day they

---

[58] *HUB*, 9, 468, 471. *HR*, II (vi), no. 95. *Foedera*, v (ii), pp. 134–5.

must defend themselves before king and council against charges of complicity in the attack in the Sound. The Chancellor brushed aside their privileges and demanded sureties of £20,000 (the alleged total of English losses) as an alternative to the arrest of the merchants and their property. Since no Englishmen were willing to provide sureties the council at first accepted personal recognisances, but soon reversed that decision. On 28 July orders were given that all Hanseatics and their property be arrested and placed in safe custody until 6 October, when the council would consider the matter again. The following day all the residents of the Steelyard were imprisoned in the Ludgate counter. The next day again all those born in Cologne were released, on the grounds that their city was itself in conflict with Denmark. However, they had to promise not to leave the country and at first their property remained under arrest. The other merchants were held in detention for three weeks, until they were blackmailed into lending the king £1,000; so that they could raise the money, goods to the value of 2,000 marks were restored to them. The loan was to be repaid at Michaelmas 1469, either to the merchants themselves, should they be found innocent of complicity, or to their English accusers in part satisfaction of losses. In the event the verdict of the king's council on 21 November 1468 went against the Hanse, which was ordered to pay £20,000 compensation. Only the Cologne merchants were relieved of any contribution to this payment. On 5 December 1468 the Hanseatics were again committed to prison for non-payment of the damages awarded against them, and there they remained until the following April. Punitive measures were also taken against Hanse merchants who arrived in England after the original arrest, or sent merchandise or ships there before news of the disaster had been widely circulated. Two Prussian ships arriving at London, two at Lynn, two at Hull and one at Newcastle were confiscated and the crews detained, in some cases throughout the winter, as was one Lübeck ship at Lynn. By the spring the futility of keeping the Hansards in confinement must have been obvious. Moreover, Edward ran the risk of losing the sympathy of his Burgundian ally if he persisted on the present course. The first appeals on behalf of the merchants had come from the Emperor, German princes and urban authorities, while the King of Denmark had also acknowledged that they had no share in his guilt. In October 1468 the Bruges *Kontor* decided that it was then inopportune to ask the Duke of Burgundy to intercede, but on 2 February 1469 the duke appealed for clemency for the prisoners. A few days later the *vier leden* of Flanders wrote to the king in much stronger terms, protesting that his illegal and unjust behaviour was a threat to the entire world of trade ('reipublice communis mercature'). Such criticism stung the English government into drawing up a 'justification' of its sentence upon the Hanseatics, copies of which were sent to Flanders and other interested parties at the end of March. About the same time the prisoners were released after agreeing that 4,000 nobles should be raised from their goods, which by then had been valued at £3,550.[59] It was proposed to restore the residue and allow them to trade freely until 31 August, provided that the Hanse agreed to negotiate in the interim. In May the Hanseatic privileges, which were due to expire at midsummer, were extended until that date. This was done mainly for the benefit of the Cologners, though the usual *douceurs* and fees to government officials were met out of Steelyard funds.[60]

When it comes to allocating responsibility for the events described above, historians have tended to maintain that the king was unduly influenced by Warwick and his brother, the Earl of Northumberland, who was part owner of one of the ships seized by the Danes. Mercantile and popular hostility to the Hanseatics was also involved. There was some looting of their goods, while an envoy sent by the Emperor to plead for clemency was assaulted in London. On the other hand, William Caxton, governor of the English Merchant Adventurers in the Low Countries, wrote to the government condemning the actions taken against their rivals. A petition, allegedly emanating from Gloucestershire cloth workers, was submitted in their favour and claimed that sales had fallen because of the absence of Hanse buyers. The latter testimonial was not unsolicited and the Steelyard had to dip into its coffers to get support for it. By then, however, the Steelyard community had been virtually destroyed by the actions of the Cologners, who must share much of the responsibility for the fate of their erstwhile colleagues. On previous occasions Cologne merchants had ignored collective decisions and continued to trade in England in times of dispute, but never with such disregard for the consequences as now. As we have already seen, the Cologne merchants were not detained with the

---

[59] Or £5,550 in another source. *HUB*, 9, no. 569; *HR*, II (vi), no. 185.
[60] *HUB*, 9, nos. 467, 478–82, 501–7, 509, 511, 515, 524, 527–8, 530, 549, 554, 569–70, 577, 582. *HR*, II (vi), nos. 111, 165, 185.

others and were allowed access to their chambers in the Steelyard. In October 1468 they received instructions from home that they were not to lend money to merchants of other towns nor to act as sureties for them. Cologne now made a calculated decision that its trade with England was more important than good relations with the rest of the Hanse and must be preserved at all costs. No longer was it to be jeopardised by quarrels which were seen as the concern only of the northern and eastern towns. All the relevant arguments were incorporated in a remarkable memorandum drawn up towards the end of 1468, when Cologne decided not to attend a Hanse diet summoned for the following April. Having decided to distance themselves from their fellows, the Cologners sought to convince the English of their sincerity. From the summer of 1469 their leader, Gerard von Wesel, refused to accept any letters addressed to the alderman and community of German merchants in England, and insisted that natives of the city should trade in their own name and only with their own goods. In December Cologne ordered its merchants to form its own council, to have its own chamber to which no outsiders were to be admitted, and repeated the ban on lending money to, or standing surety for, other Germans. The purpose of all this was to persuade the English government to reissue the Hanseatic franchises in favour of the Cologne merchants and no others. They hoped to achieve that end with the assistance of friends in high places. Among these were Dr William Hattecliffe, the king's secretary, Richard Langport, clerk to the council, the Bishop of Rochester, Keeper of the Privy Seal, and Avery Cornburgh, another member of the council. Despite such friends the king was reluctant to comply with Cologne's repeated requests for a grant of privileges in perpetuity. However, when the last general grant of the franchises expired at the end of August 1469 they were renewed in favour of the Cologners alone until Easter 1470 or 1471. In December 1470 the newly restored Henry VI made a grant for five years, with effect from 10 October past. Edward IV later returned to a policy of annual renewal, the first grant after his recovery of the throne, made in July 1471, being retrospective to the previous Easter. Cologne's determination to go its own way was unshaken by an ultimatum given in a Hanse diet in August 1470 that the city might be expelled from the organisation if it did not adhere to collective decisions by the following February. Although England was the biggest thorn in the relations between the two groups it was by no means the only one. Even before the present crisis Cologne had been in trouble, because of the reluctance of its merchants to pay scot to the *Kontor* of Bruges, on the grounds that most of their business was now conducted in Brabant and Zeeland rather than Flanders.[61]

England's first offer, to discuss the present dispute with envoys of the Hanse, was considered by a diet which met at Lübeck on 23 April 1469. This agreed to talks, but ruled that none of its members should trade with England after midsummer, on pain of forfeiting their Hanse privileges. The meeting was to take place at Bruges and the Hanse case was entrusted to the *Kontor* merchants of that town, the clerk of the London Steelyard and a 'notable doctor', who was to advise them on points of law. The cathedral provost of Lübeck was appointed as the legal expert and his first task, which he completed by 14 May, was to draft a refutation of the 'vindication' of the English council. This answered point by point the arguments of the English, most importantly contradicting their claims about the nature and constitution of the Hanse. It was not a corporate entity like a college or society, but was made up of individual towns each subject to different overlords. The purpose of this was to establish that the Hanse was not collectively responsible for the actions of any of its members. The instructions given to the envoys said that if the Duke of Burgundy, who had offered to mediate, proposed a truce then they might accept, provided that the merchants in England were compensated and released from all financial obligations, or at the very least had all their goods restored. If this was agreed then the envoys could promise a further conference in a safe town. If the English refused then the Hanse would impose a ban not only on English cloth, but also any and all cloth made anywhere using English wool. This would, of course, harm the Burgundians and thus make the duke less disposed to favour England. For the English the negotiations, which began at Bruges in the middle of June 1469, were handled by a strong team which had been sent there to deal with Anglo-Burgundian problems. That the talks, which lasted four weeks, ultimately ran into the sand was due in large measure to the successful rebellion of the Earl of Warwick in July. This development not only inhibited the diplomats, but also cooled the enthusiasm of the Duke of Burgundy to mediate. With his enemy, Warwick, in command in England the Duke was far less concerned to help the country out of its impasse with the Hanse.[62]

---

[61] *HUB*, 9, nos. 482, 525, 537, 540, 549, 603, 779; 10, nos. 40, 93, 195. *HR*, II (vi), nos. 114, 223, 225–6, 356, 511–12. *CPR*, 1467–77, pp. 307, 387. *Foedera*, v (ii), p. 183.
[62] *HUB*, 9, nos. 584–5, 588. *HR*, II (vi), nos. 184–5, 221. *Foedera*, v (ii), pp. 170–1.

The failure of the Bruges talks made English vessels a target for Hanseatic privateers, who commenced operations in the autumn of 1469. Without even waiting for the decision of a diet the Bruges *Kontor* engaged the services of two Danzig vessels to attack English ships. The attitude of the towns varied. Lübeck, despite its past record, was reluctant to go into a privateering war without the sanction of a diet. Danzig was the most belligerent. In December 1469 it announced that it would not attend a diet which was being organised, since money so saved could be better spent in equipping privateers. In January, Hamburg urged Danzig to reconsider, admitting that it too had already licensed privateers, but maintaining that this was not incompatible with participation in a diet. Danzig merely reaffirmed its earlier stand. At first the Duke of Burgundy tolerated the privateers, but in January 1470, after Edward IV had temporarily re-established his personal authority in England, he forbade them to operate from his territory and ordered his subjects not to serve in their ships. When the Hanse diet met in May 1470 some of the assembled delegates discussed the future with confidence. Reval's representative urged that the arming of the Hanse made it sought after by all parties caught up in the current unrest in western Europe, and such statements were not altogether without foundation. In April 1470 and again in May the Duke of Burgundy unsuccessfully tried to bring England and the Hanse back to the conference table, with himself as mediator. On 1 May, Queen Margaret of Anjou, writing from the Duchy of Bar, invited the Hanse to ally with her against the usurper, the Earl of March, as Edward IV was referred to. France, too, was anxious to settle its own differences with the Hanse and offered the use of its ports to the privateers. All these proposals were put to the diet, but because of a very sparse attendance they were deferred for further consideration in August. At the later date the diet again declined to commit itself to either side – a wise decision in the light of the rapidly changing political and diplomatic climate. This diet did, however, rule that after next Martinmas (11 November) no merchandise of English origin was to be imported into any Hanse territory. The King of Poland and the German princes were asked to support the ban and the former signified his consent before the end of the year.[63]

The Hanseatic privateers had letters of marque to attack English

[63] *HUB*, 9, nos. 691–2. *HR*, II (vi), nos. 283, 285, 289, 313, 315, 317, 321–5, 331, 361.

and French shipping, but inevitably neutrals also incurred losses. This brought a protest from the Duke of Burgundy to the diet of August 1470. The delegates promised to prevent any more privateers from being licensed before 2 February 1471, but refused to recall those already at sea. Attacks on neutrals did not cease and caused great disquiet in the Bruges *Kontor*, which was held responsible. In October it demanded that privateers should not be allowed to sell goods in places under Hanse control without producing evidence that they had been taken from an enemy.[64] During the summer of 1470 the privateers, said to number sixteen to eighteen, had a fairly free hand in the North Sea, partly because from June to September many of the ships of England and Burgundy were blockading the fleet of the Earl of Warwick in the Norman ports of La Hogue, Honfleur and Harfleur. Burgundy was involved in this task as a result of piratical activity by Warwick as he fled from England in April after the failure of his rebellion. Denied access to Calais, he fell upon a large Burgundian fleet which was passing through the straits and carried many of them off to France, where he joined forces with Margaret of Anjou and agreed to attempt the restoration of Henry VI. Early in September the Anglo-Burgundian fleet was scattered by storms and Warwick seized his chance to sneak across to England. On 2 October a vanquished Edward IV sailed from Lynn and, to add to his misfortune, was almost captured by Hanseatic privateers, who pursued him all the way to Holland. The Duke of Burgundy was at first lukewarm in his welcome to Edward, but he lost his inhibition when France declared war on him in December 1470, ostensibly on account of his seizure of French-owned merchandise in Antwerp. That action was itself taken in retaliation for the refuge given by France to the Earl of Warwick with the spoils of his attack on the Burgundian ships. The duke now opened his ports to the Hanseatic privateers and invited the Hanse to join him against France and Lancastrian England. No formal alliance was made, but Hanseatic ships, mostly of Danzig, formed part of the fleet which carried Edward IV from Flushing to England on 11 March 1471.[65] Although the Germans were paid cash for this service they were, allegedly, also promised the restoration of Hanseatic privileges in England. If any such promise was given then it was not kept, since

---

[64] *HR*, II (vi), nos. 352, 362, 371.
[65] Continental chronicles variously number the Hanse contribution of ships from seven to eighteen. *HR*, II (vi), p. 399, note 1. *HUB*, 10, p. 2, note.

for the moment Edward preferred still to confine his favours to the Cologne merchants. The Duke of Burgundy once more offered to mediate, but in December his services were politely refused by the Wendish towns, which informed him that there could be no more talks until Edward intimated his willingness to restore the franchises and pay compensation.[66]

In the light of the king's refusal to honour an obligation believed to have been incurred, the Hanse kept up the privateering war, and for the time being the Duke of Burgundy tolerated their use of his ports as bases. In November 1471, however, the duke again closed the ports against them and forbade his subjects either to buy their booty or to sell them supplies. In February 1472 Hanseatic strength was increased when for the first time Lübeck agreed to licence four privateers. In March Cologne was notified that the war was to be intensified and that its merchants would trade with England at their own risk. It answered speciously that its citizens were remaining there only to prevent German trade from falling into other hands during these troubled times.[67] The privateers kept up their attacks throughout 1472, but the tide was beginning to turn against them. The letters of the Danzig captain, Bernt Paws, are most instructive. He left his home port on 19 August 1471, but after arriving in the Low Countries spent only nine weeks at sea, between 20 October and 10 August 1472, when he returned to the Elbe. Paws complained continuously about bad weather, poor port facilities, shortages of supplies and difficult relations with the Bruges *Kontor*. Worst of all was the problem of keeping crews up to strength, because the Duke of Burgundy had forbidden his subjects to serve with the privateers. In June Paws proposed to send to Hamburg for replacements. This shortage of manpower came at a very awkward moment, since France and England were fitting out substantial forces, both to deal with the privateers and to confront one another. On 14 or 15 June elements of the French fleet fought with six Hanse ships near Nieupoort and drove them back into the Wielingen. At the end of that month Paws reported that the French now had command of the sea, but the English soon forced them back into their bases and then themselves turned against the privateers. On 19 July they fell upon the Lübeck ships as they lay at anchor in the Wielingen, with most of their men ashore; some were captured, others were burned. The

[66] *HR*, II (vi), no. 486.   [67] *HR*, II (vi), nos. 444, 506–7, 515, 517.

opposition was further reduced when Bremen ships were wrecked on the Dutch coast.[68]

Tactically it was necessary to clear the seas of the privateers, but strategically it was essential to make peace with the Hanse, so that Edward could concentrate upon war with France, plans for which were being made with Burgundy and Brittany. Moreover, there were those among the English merchants who counselled peace. A team of negotiators commissioned in March 1472 to deal with Anglo-Burgundian matters was also authorised to approach the Hanse, and in May William Rosse, victualler of Calais, and John Berton, merchant of the Staple, had exploratory talks with members of the Bruges *Kontor*. On 21 May they wrote to Lübeck suggesting a peace conference at Utrecht. When this was put to a diet of the Wendish towns in July they refused to negotiate at Utrecht, but offered talks at Hamburg in May 1473. This invitation did not reach England until December 1472 because William Rosse, to whom it had been sent, fell ill at Calais. New commissions were issued and Rosse, William Hattecliffe, the king's secretary, and John Chelley, merchant of the Staple, went to Bruges for more talks with the *Kontor*. The English refused to go to Hamburg, but again offered to confer at Utrecht in July. This time the offer was accepted without preconditions by Lübeck, which had been given executive power to arrange the conference. The suggestion of an immediate truce was not taken up and the war continued, although at a lower pitch. Lübeck had lost interest since its losses of the previous summer; Danzig had withdrawn its ships, except for a great carvel which the city had sold to a syndicate of merchants and was now privately operated; this left mainly Hamburg ships at sea. When the final arrangements for the conference were put into an indenture at Bruges in April 1473 it was agreed that there should be a truce from 25 June to 1 October. A proclamation to this effect was published in England on 21 May.[69]

As already remarked, peace with the Hanse was a necessary condition of a successful war against France. Instructions given to the English team at each stage of the Utrecht negotiations show that the king was willing to make important concessions to gain this end. The matter became even more pressing after the Hanse made its own

[68] *HR*, II (vi), nos. 522–59. W. Stein, *Die Hanse und England. Ein hansisch-englischer Seekrieg in 15. Jahrhundert* (Hansische Pfingstblätter, I, Leipzig, 1905).
[69] *HR*, II (vi), nos. 547–8, 593, 596, 608, 638, 644–5, 651. *Foedera*, VI (i), pp. 14, 25, 30–1.

peace with France in August 1473. However, buying off the Hanse was only part of an overall strategy, which involved making peace with other enemies and concluding alliances with the enemies of France.[70] In the former category were the truces signed in the spring of 1473 with Scotland and Denmark. In the latter was the treaty of Chateaugiron, which in September 1472 temporarily secured Brittany. Burgundy was more difficult to pin down and no formal alliance had been made by May 1473, when the English envoys were ready to begin their journey to Utrecht. Three commissions were issued: one for dealings with the Duke of Burgundy about a political alliance, one for talks with his subjects about commercial disputes and one for the Hanseatic business. Membership of the three groups was not identical, but there was some overlap, the presence of William Hattecliffe, and John Russell, Deputy Keeper of the Privy Seal, being necessary for any quorum. It is clear that they were intended to bear the brunt of the work and in fact few other commissioners attended any of the meetings. Hattecliffe and Russell left Westminster on 28 May and arrived in Bruges on 3 June, but for one reason and another were unable to negotiate about either of the Burgundian matters. They reached Utrecht on 30 June, but had to wait until the middle of July for the arrival of the Hanseatic team, which had been delayed by contrary winds.[71]

The chief concern of the English government, as shown by the instructions supplied to its ambassadors, was that the king's honour should not be impugned by an admission that the 'verdict' of 1468 was in any way illegal or unjust. 'The kinges said ambassiatores shalle for his honour defende and justifie the same processe... and they shalle in noo wise applie to any retrait or revocacion to be made of that jugement.'[72] However, this was merely a matter of saving face, for as long as Edward kept the shadow he was prepared to surrender the substance. The envoys were told that, if necessary, they could promise *ex gratia* compensation to those whose property had been seized in 1468. This was to be paid out of future customs on Hanseatic goods and spread over as long a period as could be negotiated. The envoys were forbidden to entertain any other claims, whether ancient or new. This suggests that English losses in the recent war were not so great as to outweigh their gains in that conflict plus their net advantage in ancient incidents, such as the seizure of the Bay ships. Nevertheless, a claim for losses dating back

---

[70] For a general discussion see C. Ross, *Edward IV* (London, 1974), pp. 205–14.
[71] *HUB*, 10, nos. 236, 241.   [72] *HR*, II (vii), no. 22.

to 1449 was the first matter raised by the Hanse team after the examination of credentials. This led to an acrimonious discussion about which side was responsible for the recent war, until the Hanse suggested that more progress might be made if each side submitted its offers. The English began the bidding by offering to restore the franchises, without at this stage attaching conditions. The Hanse sought to minimise the value of this and returned to the question of financial compensation. After further debate the Englishmen hinted that they might make an offer, but advised the Hanse to bear in mind that the money would have to come out of the king's own pocket, since the 'great ones' who had profited from the attacks on the Germans, that is the Earl of Warwick and the like, were either dead or impoverished. After deliberation the Hanse assessed their losses at £200,000 sterling, but said that they would be satisfied with £25,000 plus the title to the London and Boston Steelyards and a house in Lynn, later named as the 'Checkers'. The following day they made a new condition – that henceforth the Cologne merchants should be denied the franchises.

The English envoys claimed that they were unable to agree a specific sum of money, to the grant of the properties or the denial of the franchises to the Cologners, and also that they would have to communicate with the king. At this point the Hanse reduced its demand to £20,000, while the English revealed for the first time that it would be necessary to have some reassurance about English trade and asked what form this might take. Thus, rather late in the day, they got round to the provision in their instructions that confirmation of the Hanse franchises would depend on acceptance of the principle of reciprocity. On this critical point the English report of the negotiations states,

After a little deliberacion they gave us good aunswer, that they should be entreated as they have been wonte to be in tymes passed. We thoght this a generall aunswer and desired in especiall that they might be tretid according to that was concluded in that behalf in a diete holden at London the yere 1436, whereof we said we wold bring hem a true copie on the morne.[73]

The corresponding passage in a German report reads, 'Se in ere Stede mochten komen, dar ere kopenschup hanteren, gelik aloe se von alders covoren plegen to donde.'[74]

---

[73] *HUB*, 10, no. 241.   [74] *HR*, II (vii), no. 34.

It was decided that, since the king had to be consulted on the few matters discussed so far, he might as well be made aware of the rest of the Hanseatic demands. The Hanse delegates spent the next three days writing these in a book, which made up a lengthy catalogue of minor vexations to which they had been subjected in London and elsewhere in England, as well as a complaint about the quality of English cloth. Afterwards, they allowed the Englishmen to make certain corrections in statements relating to the offers already made to them. The English envoys passed the time copying the clauses of the treaties of 1409 and 1437 touching upon English rights in Prussia. However, they did not stop there. They demanded a clear statement of where, and from whom, aggrieved Englishmen could obtain justice within Hanseatic territories; they asked for a list of all towns belonging to the Hanse; they wanted English merchants to be admitted to the international hall in Danzig; they demanded that the King of Poland should confirm any treaty on behalf of the former subjects of the Teutonic Order; finally and most controversially, they demanded that Englishmen be allowed to trade in Livonia, as they were alleged to have done in former times.[75] These points were put to the Germans and the following day the English 'wer answered of our peticions for our merchauntes to our plesir'.[76] Rightly or wrongly, then, they felt that they had been promised reciprocity.

On 29 July the conference was adjourned until 1 September and Bluemantle herald was dispatched to the king with the German book and advice from his own envoys. Both sides spent the interim in dealing with other matters in the Netherlands and came together again on 3 September. Bluemantle joined the English envoys at Bruges on 24 August, but they sent him off to the Duke of Burgundy and afterwards pretended that he had not returned from England until 4 September. The reply he brought was not to the liking of the Germans, and the conference would have ended there and then, were it not for their fear of going home empty-handed. The king refused to give a positive answer to any of the points on which he had been consulted. This may have been because he wanted to talk personally with his ambassadors, though the reason given was that he needed to debate the matter in parliament, which was to meet in October. After a great deal of discussion the Hanse agreed to prorogue the conference until 15 January 1474 and to extend the

---

[75] *Ibid.*, no. 36.   [76] *HUB*, 10, no. 241, p. 154.

truce until 1 March. The last meeting of the two sides was on 18 September, when they exchanged sealed copies of 'a boke in Latyn of articles', which was in effect a draft of the treaty they were striving for.[77]

The next step in the proceedings as far as England was concerned was an act of parliament, which set aside 'any sentence, jugement, marque or reprisal' given by king and council against Hanse merchants before 19 September 1473, and nullified 'al manner promesses, obligacions, suertees, setting of borowes and all other bondes' made by the merchants by reason of any such sentence. This, in effect, reversed the 'verdict' of 1468, despite the earlier concern about the king's honour. Next, the merchants were given an indemnity for any act of war against Englishmen between 21 November 1468 and 19 September 1473. Parliament then reinstated the Hanse franchises, taking care, however, to tack on the principle of reciprocity:

The kynges subjectes shalle mowe as oft as them like repare and resorte unto the londe of Pruse and other places of the hanze frely and suerly entre the same, there abyde and departe from thense at their plesure to bye and selle withe alle manner persones as frely and largely as any tyme hertofore they have wonte to do, withe enjoiynge alle and everyche their libertees and fre custumes, which they have used and enjoyed any tyme passed; and that no prises exaccions nor prestacions shal be sette uppone their persones or goodes, otherwise thenne have be sette uppone theym any tyme afore this 100 yere now last past or above, whereunto the said marchauntes of the hanze by their oratours have assentid and agreed.[78]

On 20 December the Chancellor was ordered to set the great seal on instructions given by the council to the ambassadors, and signed personally by the king.[79] These took the form of a commentary on the Latin book, that is the draft treaty. Some of the articles were allowed to stand unaltered, but in others they were to strive for amendments. In the last resort they were to back down, so that stubbornness should not destroy the peace:

In all which poyntis the kingis oratours shall by the best discretion they can, enduce thaym of the hanze to hold thaym content with the provisions and answers given above... peraventur the willfulnesse of the Esterlingis at this

---

[77] *HR*, II (vii), no. 44. [78] *Rot. Parl.*, 6, pp. 65–9.
[79] *HR*, II (vii), no. 107.

next diete shal be suche, that they wol have agreed unto thaym thair own provisions in the foresaide poyntis all or parte of thaym or utterly breke, the kingis said oratours rather than so to breke shal finally under as covert terms as they can shewe them condescendable and condescended to that in the said poyntis, withoute whiche the other partie can not or wol not be enduced agre.

This willingness to surrender everything has conditioned historians into accepting that the treaty of Utrecht was a diplomatic disaster for England. This is untrue and does less than justice to the men who negotiated the treaty, for they did not give everything away.

The gravest charge against the diplomats of 1474 is that they abandoned the principle of reciprocity, which had been the main plank of English policy towards the Hanse for a hundred years. They also stand accused of surrendering the fruits of the 1437 treaty. Even if the latter charge were true it would not amount to much, for, as we have seen, the fruits of 1437 were illusory. The English had been totally unable to enforce their treaty rights in Prussia during the intervening period. Yet the diplomats now surrendered only a small part of the English claim and that the most difficult part to defend. To substantiate this statement it is necessary to make a close comparison of certain clauses in the draft treaty, the December instructions to the ambassadors and the final treaty. If possible, the ambassadors were to obtain slight amendments to make the clauses more favourable to the English merchants: 'Touching to the 4 article, the 5, 6 and 7 the kingis said oratours shalle passe in thaym aftir the contente of the same, onlesse they can enduce and bringe the oratours of the hanse to a more ample and more beneficial graunte of agrement for the kingis subgettis.' Now even in their draft form these articles, derived from the 1437 treaty, represented a success for the English diplomats. More accurately, perhaps, they were a demonstration of the shortsightedness of the Hanse team, which was too concerned with its own claims to see the full implication of allowing these articles to be inserted. The implication was not lost on the city of Danzig which, during the adjournment of the conference, protested strongly that they must be deleted. They were not deleted; in fact the English ambassadors actually obtained some of the amendments which the council required. The Hanseatic representatives, according to their own report, only accepted the retention of the articles which were obnoxious to the Prussians in order to save the treaty. Moreover, the Englishmen allegedly promised that, whatever the wording used, the articles should be understood to carry the meaning usually put upon them by Prussia.[80] Since the English report of this part of the conference has not survived, that claim cannot be checked. In any event, whatever the English delegates agreed to verbally was not binding. In years to come English lawyers would argue that the treaty meant what it said, and what it said was that England reserved its claim to reciprocal trading rights.

The articles in question, and their amendments, are as follows:

Article 4. Omnes et singuli mercatores et alii subditi et ligei domini regis Anglie pro tempore existentis, cuiuscumque status fuerint, poterunt et possunt tociens quociens eis libuerit et placuerit salvo et secure terram Prucie et alia loca hanze intrare ibidem morari et conversari, exire et redire, emere et vendere cum quibuscumque personis ita et eo modo ac adeo libere, sicut hactenus ante hec tempore emere et vendere, intrare et exire potuerunt et consueverunt, solutis custumis et deveriis de mercandisis suis debitis et consuetis.

The envoys were urged to secure the replacement of '*hactenus*' by '*unquam*', which they did.

Article 5. Omnes et singuli mercatores et alii subditi et ligei domini regis Anglie hujusmodi in terra Prucie et aliis locis hanze omnibus et singulis illis libertatibus et liberis consuetudinibus uti plene debeant et gaudere, quibus unquam aliquo tempore rationabiliter usi sunt et gavisi, nulleque prise exactiones nove seu prestaciones alique super eorum personas vel bona imponentur aliter vel alio modo quam ante 10 20 30 40 50 ymmo et centum annos et ultra imposite sunt vel fuerunt.

Here the numbers 10–50 were to be deleted, leaving only centum; this was not done. The word 'rationabiliter' was to be removed or, failing this, the same qualification was to be inserted into article 6, which guaranteed the Hanse privileges in England. The latter was done.

One may only speculate whether any significance was attached to the reversal of the order of these two clauses as compared to the 1437 treaty. Possibly it was intended to demonstrate more clearly English acceptance of the fact that they must pay all existing, lawful taxes. However, taking the act of parliament and the treaty of Utrecht

---

[80] *Ibid.*, nos. 66, 131–3, 138, 231.

together it is clear that they persisted in their claim to immunity from any new taxation and also that they ought to enjoy any rights which had ever been exercised by them in the Hanse towns or Prussia.

Turning to the other articles of the draft treaty which the king's council thought might be improved upon, we find first the hope that the cash indemnity might be reduced. In the last hours of the earlier sessions it had been brought down to £15,000; after the adjournment it was reduced to £10,000, although the Hanse insisted upon a further £484, which they claimed should have been contributed by the Cologne merchants to the £1,000 'lent' to the crown in 1468. The Englishmen failed to see the logic of this, since the £10,000 was supposed to cover all losses including that loan, but they agreed to pay it. The properties were conceded with hardly a murmur, although for an undisclosed reason the council successfully demanded that the name 'Checkers' should not be used to describe the house at Lynn. This leaves only the demand for the exclusion of the Cologne men from the franchises. The council was genuinely loath to abandon them, but rather than lose the treaty was prepared to do so, provided that it was done in a way which spared the king's honour. The compromise adopted was the deletion from the main treaty of the reference to the exclusion of the Cologners. In its place was a general provision that any town expelled from the Hanse would be denied use of the privileges until it was readmitted. The Hanse delegates then declared that Cologne had been expelled, and a subsidiary treaty provided, *inter alia*, that its merchants would be excluded from the franchises after 1 August 1474.

The conference was resumed at Utrecht on 1 February 1474, and after hard bargaining the final treaty, the most important points of which have been noted above, was signed on 28 February. The subsidiary treaty, signed the same day, provided that the two sides should exchange ratified copies at Bruges on 1 August 1474. Edward IV ratified the treaty and again confirmed the Hanse franchises on 20 July. The city of Lübeck and representatives of the Hanse assembled there ratified the treaty and separately confirmed the English rights in the towns and in Prussia on 1 May. At least sixteen individual towns ratified the treaty by 1 August and another eight by the end of that month. Danzig did not ratify it until May 1476 and even then insisted that English merchants were to enjoy no special privileges in Prussia. Other towns took much longer to signify their acceptance, yet this did not prevent the exchange of ratifications in September 1475, rather more than twelve months later than originally provided for.[81]

Using cloth exports as indicators of trends in trade, the three decades which separate the Vorrath treaty from the beginning of the war between England and the Hanse may be divided into one of prosperity and two of largely unrelieved stagnation (table 12). Even so, during the latter two, Hanse exports were as high as, or higher than, they had been in the early years of the century and, as a proportion of all England's cloth exports, were greater than they had ever been before. In the late 1430s, slump gave way to boom with extreme rapidity, particularly in the case of the Hanse merchants. The underlying causes were changes in political and fiscal conditions. It will be recalled that the twelve months preceding the arrival of the Vorrath embassy (1435–6) had been disastrous for both denizen and Hanse merchants, with totals of 10,929 and 2,353 cloths respectively. In 1436–7 denizens dispatched 16,437 cloths and Hanseatics 12,120. The latter figure is even more remarkable when it is remembered that the Hanse ambassadors themselves tried to prevent their merchants from exporting until they had concluded the treaty in March 1437, while as late as June Vorrath was complaining that English customs officials were wilfully obstructing the dispatch of Hanse-owned cloth to Prussia. The Hansards must have made a tremendous effort that summer to beat their rivals to whatever markets were open. But, if Englishmen were slow off the mark, they shared fully in the coming decade's record-breaking trade. Fortunately for them their cloth was no longer burdened with poundage, though the rest of their trade was subject to this subsidy after a brief respite from November 1436 to April 1437. All Hanse trade, of course, was spared poundage in consequence of the Vorrath treaty.

For both denizen and Hanse cloth exports consideration has to be given to political relations between England and Burgundy. The duke did not formally lift his latest ban on English cloth until the autumn of 1439 (save for the traditional exclusion from the county of Flanders), but it had long since become an ineffective weapon, as may be seen from the enormous increase in exports in the previous two to three years. Denizen exports to the Low Countries were helped by negotiations with Holland-Zeeland, which began in May

---

[81] *Ibid.*, nos. 142, 144, 146, 152, 307. *Foedera*, VI (i), pp. 36–9.

Table 12. *England's cloth exports, 1435–74*

	Overall Total			Denizen			Hanse			Alien		
		Change	Total	Share	Change	Total	Share	Change	Total	Share	Change
1435–6	25,298		10,929	43%		2,353	9%		12,016	48%	
1436–7	39,973	+58%	16,437	41%	+50%	12,120	30%	+415%	11,416	29%	−5%
1437–47	56,026	+40%	28,683	51%	+75%	11,435	20%	−6%	15,908	20%	+39%
1447–57	37,874	−32%	20,848	55%	−27%	7,920	21%	−31%	9,106	24%	−43%
1457–68	33,647	−11%	17,667	52%	−15%	9,001	24%	+14%	6,979	21%	−23%
1468–74	33,338	+8%	22,000	61%	+25%	2,928	8%	−67%	11,400	31%	+63%

1438, but even before this the Dutch had given little material or moral support to their ruler and continued to trade with England.[82] It is likely that, long before the formal ending of the ban, both Englishmen and Hansards had reverted to former practices and were clandestinely selling cloth in the duke's lands, or in the case of the latter passing through them on the way to Germany. Far from harming the English cloth industry and export trade the dispute with Burgundy probably did a great deal of good, since it meant that the Low Countries were almost totally deprived of English wool for several years.[83] Most clothing towns were not now so dependent upon this as in former times, but some still valued it and the loss resulted in a fall in cloth production, which was compounded by civil unrest in Flanders and a universal dearth of food. A shortfall in any market formerly supplied with Burgundian cloth, not excluding even the duke's own lands, provided a potentially open door for English cloth.

Denizen and Hansards were active in the Low Countries, but each also looked to the Baltic. Here, markets had recently been deprived of Flemish cloth as well as English (as a result of the massacre at Sluys) and were ripe for exploitation by the summer of 1437. Until the outbreak of war between Holland-Zeeland and the Wendish towns in April 1438, the general situation was peaceful. In 1436–7 Hanse exports from Boston, Lynn and Hull were 1,043, 972 and 803 – 2,818 in total and 23 per cent of all Hanse cloth exports from England.[84] Subsequently performances at the three ports diverged. At Boston trade remained fairly stable, averaging 905 cloths per annum in 1437–42 and 1,018 in 1442–7. On the other hand, alien general merchandise averaged only £1,105 and £1,992 in these two periods, which means that imports by the Hanse can barely have sufficed to pay for their exports, the former surplus having been virtually eliminated. At Lynn, cloth exports fell to an average of 260 in 1437–42, but then recovered to 370 in 1442–7. In historic terms this was a respectable performance. At Hull the trend was unrelievedly downward, with averages of 193 and 48 in these quinquenniums. The three ports together handled just over 12 per cent of all Hanse cloth exports in 1437–47, though this does not mean that only a like proportion was taken to the Baltic. London

---

[82] Munro, *Wool, Cloth and Gold*, pp. 114–16.   [83] Lloyd, *Wool Trade*, pp. 262–5.
[84] Figures adjusted to twelve months. The accounts for Boston and Lynn extend to 11 November and the actual figures are 1,176 and 1,089.

and Ipswich, which accounted for virtually all the remaining Hanse cloth, also exported to the Baltic and may have dispatched as much as, or more than, the northern ports. The war between Holland-Zeeland and the Wendish towns provided a temporary stimulus to trade between London and the Baltic; Prussian ships and merchants, defying their diet's prohibition of trade with the west, flocked to England's capital. There was an increase in the import of Baltic goods and many were re-exported by Dutch merchants, since they were now in short supply in the Low Countries. This led to Baltic merchants increasing their exports of cloth.[85] It is impossible to ascertain exactly how much Hanse cloth went from London and Ipswich to the Baltic, but if the amount ever equalled or exceeded that going to the Low Countries or western Germany such a situation was probably short-lived.

Before leaving the topic of Hanse trade in the years 1437–47 a few words may be said about the rise in importance of Sandwich, or more correctly its sub-port of Dover. In the late fourteenth century Hanse trade in the Sandwich complex was negligible, and though a regular import trade was established in the early years of the fifteenth century it was relatively modest, and cloth exports remained insignificant. Cloth exports of other aliens flourished from 1412 to 1431, but then fell to a low level in all but two of the following nine years. But as cloth exports declined there was a sharp rise in all alien imports (including the Hanse component). The number of cloths customed at Sandwich bears no relationship to those actually shipped at the Kent ports, since it was common practice both among other aliens and Hanse merchants to send them down the Thames in barges and then transfer them to larger vessels. To deter smuggling it was obligatory to pay duty before the cloth left London. Conversely, imports had to be declared as soon as they were unloaded at Sandwich or Dover, even though most were intended for the London market. They were then brought to the capital by road or Thames lighters, either to avoid congestion at the city wharfs or to guard against mishaps to large ships in the river. Sandwich and Dover thus functioned as outports for London. The total value of

---

[85] The conclusions of J. L. Bolton, 'Alien Merchants in England in the Reign of Henry VI, *1422–61*' (B.Litt. thesis, Oxford, 1971), appendix, tables 2–3, show that cloth exports from London in 1437–9 by 'Baltic' merchants more or less balanced those by 'Cologners'. But Jenks, *England, die Hanse und Preussen*, tables LI–LII, represents the great majority of exports as still going to the Low Countries.

alien trade (including Hanse) subject to the 3d petty custom in this complex was at record levels from the late 1430s to Michaelmas 1449. An already swollen trade, which averaged £8,554 in 1433–7, reached £12,856, £13,276 and £20,075 in the next three years, and still averaged £12,690 from 1440 to 1449. In 1439–40 Hanse imports totalled £3,579, most of them brought to Dover in ships registered at that port or at Calais.[86] Goods of Baltic origin were in a minority, even when those coming direct from that region are added to the furs brought in from the Low Countries by Cologne merchants. The most important product was fustian from south Germany, which accounted for 46 per cent of imports. Since the amount of Hanse cloth customed at Sandwich (as opposed to that from London trans-shipped there) was exceptionally high (146) in 1439–40, the level of imports may also have been somewhat exceptional. To maintain a perspective it may be mentioned that this year Italian imports were 439 per cent greater than those of the Hansards. Subsequently, Hanse trade in the Kent ports declined, but remained well above the level of the early fifteenth century, since the London community continued to use Dover as an outport.

In the immediate aftermath of the Vorrath treaty denizen exporters to the Baltic momentarily lost ground to those of the Hanse, since some of the former seem to have been slow off the mark. While Hanse merchants exported 803 cloths from Hull in 1436–7, compared with nil in the previous year, denizens managed only 887 to all markets, a scant improvement on the 828 of the year before. Lynn denizens did better with a total of 2,362 from Michaelmas 1436 to 26 October 1437, compared with 569 in the previous twelve months. Subsequently, denizens recovered the lead and unless there was a major shift in market orientation their total exports to the Baltic must have equalled or exceeded those of 1428–35. Lynn's average denizen export in the latter period was 1,745 against 896 in the former, Hull's 3,324 against 3,315, but Boston's was down to 328, compared with 526 between 1430 and 1435. Denizen exports from Ipswich must also be taken into consideration, since Essex and Suffolk cloth was popular in Prussia. These increased from an average of 1,653 (1428–35) to 2,188 (1437–47), but not all were going to the Baltic. London is, as ever, the joker in the pack, for though there is ample evidence about the presence of its merchants

[86] Bolton, 'Alien Merchants', appendix, table 5.

in the Baltic their trade cannot be quantified. When Englishmen were invited to submit claims for injuries done to them in the Baltic between 1438 and 1440, Yorkshiremen were most responsive and more than two dozen York and Hull ship-owners and merchants were mentioned by name. Others named were eight Londoners, four from Ipswich, three from Colchester, three from Southampton and one from Sandwich.[87] However, the detailed information comprehends only a small part of total current claims. In this decade of general prosperity there is little doubt that English merchants increased their exports to the Baltic, but whether their gain was commensurate to the overall rise in denizen exports is another matter.

In the late 1430s England's interest in the Baltic was not simply as a market for cloth. There was also a substantial, albeit temporary, rise in imports. A succession of three bad harvests beginning in 1437 rapidly led to famine conditions in much of western Europe and there was a great demand for eastern grain. Prussia and the Hanse sought to reap political advantage from the shortage by strictly regulating exports, particularly those which might go to the Low Countries. After the massacre of merchants at Sluys in 1436 the Hanse transferred its staple from Bruges to Antwerp and imposed a boycott on all trade with Flanders. The pressing need for grain was the chief reason why Flanders was finally forced in September 1438 to accept the Hanse terms for a return to Bruges – full restoration of their privileges and a financial indemnity. By then Holland-Zeeland was under interdict. On 22 June 1438, for example, Danzig town council required an oath from twenty-one ships' masters who were about to sail that they would take their Prussian and Livonian wares to England or Scotland and not sell them to the Dutch.[88] Doubtless these ships carried grain, since on 21 May the authorities had ruled that, because of favourable prospects for growing crops, wheat and meal, though not yet other grains, might be exported; rye and other grains were freed on 2 June. As early as December 1437 the king and the city of London had written to the Grand Master pleading for ten to twenty shiploads of corn, but the Steelyard covertly suggested that on this occasion they be allowed no more than six to eight shiploads. Following a second harvest failure, Henry VI wrote to the Grand Master on 28 November 1438 telling of a great dearth and again

---

[87] *HR*, II (ii), no. 646.   [88] *Ibid.*, nos. 233, 268–9.

requesting permission for his subjects to export grain. This was conceded and the king wrote on 28 February 1439 sending thanks for the favour, but requesting further facilities since prices were still very high in England. Corn exports from Prussia were again banned for a while in May 1439.[89] After the harvest of 1439 prices fell to a more reasonable level in England, although they remained high compared to those of good years. This meant that Englishmen were probably still interested in buying grain in Prussia, but they may have found themselves obliged to take up more than was prudent when the authorities suddenly put a ban upon the export of everything but grain.[90] This may or may not have been a ploy to get rid of a surplus, but there was still concern about the supply of goods to Holland-Zeeland, and as late as the summer of 1441 a ban was maintained on the export of anything which might assist the Dutch war effort. When English ships were commandeered in the Sound in 1440 no less than 1,100 lasts of grain, claimed to be worth £5,500, were said to have been ruined. The exceptionally large shipments from east to west, coupled with the prohibition against Prussian subjects trading through the Sound, put a premium on shipping space, and between 1438 and 1441 Englishmen bought many ships or shares in ships at Danzig, though in July 1440 they complained about efforts by the Danzig Council to stop this practice.[91]

The decade of prosperity in the cloth trade came to an end in 1447. In 1447–8 total exports were still 50,730 compared with 59,337 in the previous year, but this figure was reached only because of a still buoyant other alien trade (chiefly Italian); denizen trade was already well down, while Hanse trade had collapsed. The total of only 32,071 in 1448–9 was the result of abysmal trade in all three sectors. Other alien trade then recovered for three years, before falling away so badly that for many years it occupied third place behind the still depleted Hanse trade. There is no shortage of factors which contributed to the prolonged slump in cloth exports – political disputes with the Hanse and Burgundy, intensification of the war with France resulting in the loss of Normandy and Gascony, civil war in England. The problem is to evaluate the direct effect of each of these separate blows. First in time was a renewal of the ban upon English cloth in Burgundy, proclaimed in January 1447 and removed between April and June 1452.[92] Towards the end of the

---

[89] *Ibid.*, no. 305. *HUB*, 7, part 1, nos. 320, 404.   [90] *Ibid.*, no. 352.
[91] *Ibid.*, no. 693. *HR*, II (ii), no. 380.   [92] Munro, *Wool, Cloth and Gold*, p. 146.

ban the duke's officials advised him that it was ineffective and served only to deprive him of revenue from tolls. But this is not to say that it had done no damage at all to cloth exports. At London denizen exports fell from 7,827 cloths in ten months (29 September 1446 to 21 July 1447) to 4,413 during the following twelve months and 8,444 over the next twenty months (21 July 1448 to 10 March 1450). Any effect on Hanse exports would have been confined to the London and Colchester communities, whose combined exports fell from a five-year average (1442–7) of 10,842 to an average of around 6,000 between Michaelmas 1447 and May 1452. On the other hand this decline also reflects the loss of Hanse tax concessions[93] (Michaelmas 1447 to December 1449) and any consequences of the seizure of the Bay fleet (May 1449). After the removal of the Burgundian boycott in 1452, Hanse exports from London and Ipswich improved considerably and thereafter remained on a fairly even keel until late in 1464. London averaged 7,250 a year between May 1452 and December 1464, Ipswich 1,485 between Michaelmas 1452 and August 1464. The years 1456–7, 1459–60 and particularly 1462–3 saw well below average trade. But these were also very bad times for denizens, and in the third year there was a complete stoppage of Hanse trade from Michaelmas to March while the question of the franchises was being discussed. In October 1464 the Duke of Burgundy imposed yet another ban on the sale and transit of English cloth.[94] This put a total stop to the trade of the Merchant Adventurers, and London denizen exports were only 775 between 5 December 1464 and Michaelmas 1465. During the next two years, when the Adventurers obtained facilities at Utrecht, outside the authority of the duke, trade improved to 9,342 and 8,133, and finally climbed back to 16,594 in 1467–8 after the removal of the Burgundian ban in November 1467. Hanseatic exports also seem to have suffered and the merchants changed their pattern of trade, possibly because of a shortage of shipping in London. At Ipswich exports of 1,167 cloths from 31 August 1464 to Michaelmas 1465 indicate a normal trade, but London with 2,850 from 5 December 1464 to Michaelmas 1465 was seriously down. In the following year (1465–6) London remained down to 3,816, though this was simply because traffic had been transferred to Ipswich (4,515), or more precisely Colchester. On 6 March 1466 a convoy of five ships took

[93] See above p. 178.   [94] Munro, *Wool, Cloth and Gold*, pp. 164–5.

1,625 cloths from the latter port, followed by another four ships with 1,693 on 1 July.[95] The combined export of London and Ipswich this year was not too much down on a normal year. In the next two years the balance of exports moved back to London with an average of 6,657 compared to 720 at Ipswich.

In the provinces, Anglo-Burgundian relations were less important than the current state of negotiations between England and the Hanse, and the level of taxation. At Hull there were no cloth exports between Michaelmas 1347 and the winter of 1451–2. At Boston only 506 cloths were shipped between 18 July 1447 and 21 November 1448, but then there was a recovery to 1,463 in the twelve months to 21 November 1449. Before the last date trade was paralysed by consequences of the seizure of the Bay fleet. Nor was that the only problem, since a few days before that episode some Hull merchants had secured the arrest at Boston of eighteen great packs of cloth belonging to *Bergenfahrer*.[96] Shortly after 21 November 1449 a few stragglers exported 100 cloths, but then there was nothing for more than four years. At Lynn the withdrawal of the tax concessions seems to have had less effect than the piracy of 1449, with 337 cloths exported between 29 September 1447 and 30 April 1449, but only 156 between the latter date and 10 July 1451. When hopes of a peaceful settlement to the Bay fleet dispute appeared on the horizon in the summer of 1451 some Hanse merchants made a hesitant return to Hull and Lynn, though Boston remained deserted by the Lübeckers. Shortly before Michaelmas 1451 Hanse merchants imported goods worth £109 at Hull and afterwards exported 53 cloths and probably £19 worth of other goods.[97] The following two years (1452–4) saw cloth exports of 396 and 352 at this port; particulars covering the period April to Michaelmas 1453 show four Danzig ships entering on 17 May with goods valued at £469 (80 per cent Prussian owned, 20 per cent English).[98] During the next year (1454–5) there were probably no Prussian ships at Hull, since Denmark closed the Sound to those towns in rebellion against the Teutonic Order; the 28 Hanse cloths exported this year were sent to the Low Countries in a Middelburg ship.[99] From October 1455 to 31 December 1458 cloth exports totalled a modest 606, while between the latter date and 11 April 1461 there were none, save 30 taken to

[95] PRO, E122/52/48–9. Britnell, *Colchester*, p. 174.   [96] *HR*, II (iii), no. 531.
[97] *The Customs Accounts of Hull, 1453–1490*, ed. W. Childs (Yorks. Arch. Soc., 144, 1986), pp. 226, 228.   [98] *Ibid.*, pp. 3–4.   [99] *Ibid.*, p. 15.

the Low Countries in the summer of 1460.[100] From April 1461 Hanse cloth exports were again more regular and ran at an average annual rate of 188 to Michaelmas 1468. A rough calculation of the value of Hanse imports in this last period may be made from the enrolled customs accounts, which each year recorded the total value of Hanse trade potentially liable to poundage, though the duty was not exacted.[101] From Michaelmas 1462 to Michaelmas 1468 the totals amounted to £2,834 8s 6d (of which £1,026 16s 8d belongs to the first year and £1,124 18s 8d to the last). These figures include 1,207 cloths, which seem to have been valued uniformly at £1 each. The deduction of these leaves £1,627 for other exports plus imports, which in 1466–7 were divided in the ratio of 17:83. Applying this to the whole six-year period gives £1,350 for imports and £277 for other exports, indicating a slight excess for all exports over imports. If the surviving particulars are representative then Hanse trade at Hull was largely in the hands of Prussian merchants, who typically chartered two to four Danzig ships each year to bring bulky Baltic goods and took cloth away in the same vessels. Occasionally, one or two merchants exported in one of the few Hull ships still going to Prussia. The trade was based on a quick turn around and did not require a permanent Hanse presence in Hull or York.

At Lynn, Hanse trade from the early 1450s to 1468 may be divided into three periods. As at Hull there was a revival in the winter of 1451–2 and thereafter there seems to have been no complete stoppage, so that cloth exports averaged 195 a year from 10 July 1451 to Michaelmas 1459. Trade then turned down sharply, perhaps in consequence of the second Bay fleet seizure, resulting in an average export of 59 cloths from Michaelmas 1459 to 19 November 1464. After one exceptionally good year (1464–5 with 502 cloths) the trend was again downwards, so that the total was back to a mere 52 in 1467–8, though the average of these last four years was 212. In this final period a more detailed picture of trade can be reconstructed from well-preserved particulars. In 1464–5, eight ships brought in over £600 of northern and eastern wares and took away most of the short-cloths, plus a few Welsh friezes and some coverlets; two Hanse ships which did not enter goods also exported a little cloth.[102] In 1466–7 the corresponding import trade, worth £344, was carried in four ships, though one other merchant brought in £3

---

[100] *Ibid.*, pp. 24–5.   [101] *Ibid.*, table 3, p. 230.   [102] PRO, E122/97/4.

of train oil in a non-Hanse ship. The 145 short-cloths exported (130 in three of the previous ships) were valued at £193 6s 8d; other exports were £20 of frieze and £20 of malt.[103] The next year (1467–8) imports of Baltic goods were worth just under £300, though nine ships claimed a share in their freight; two of these vessels also carried similar goods worth £28 belonging to a denizen merchant. The 52 short-cloths exported (in three ships) were valued at £69 6s 8d; malt (£28) was again exported.[104] Although comparatively small, the Hanse trade at Lynn in the 1460s was clearly well established and engaged the interest of the same ships and merchants year after year, some ships coming two or three times each year. It was essentially an Anglo-Baltic trade, chiefly occupying Danzig and Hamburg ships, and some of it probably followed the Hamburg-Lübeck route. Among the merchants involved can be identified men from Hamburg, Danzig and Cologne, though it is impossible to establish the exact proportions of each.

At Boston there were no Hanse cloth exports from late 1449 until after 10 October 1454, when 138 were dispatched up to 10 October 1455. Lübeckers were not yet covered by the king's safe-conduct, but some merchants connected with that city may have resumed their business after it lifted its ban on English cloth in July 1454. In February 1456 Lübeck was brought within the truce, and in the current year (1455–6) Hanse cloth exports from Boston increased to 535. Over the next two years (1456–8) exports fell to a total of 193, but the alien petty custom figures, which generally provide a fair indication of the scale of *Bergenfahrer* imports, rose considerably and totalled £2,543. There is then a gap of fifteen months in the accounts, which conceals the effects of Warwick's seizure of the Lübeck fleet in July 1458, but by 1460 trade had picked up again. Between 15 December 1459 and 1 September 1460, 948 cloths were exported, though this comparatively high figure may simply be a backlog of trade, since thereafter it again fell back, averaging 491 a year in 1460–2, 365 in 1462–5 and 64 in 1465–8. Hanse trade in Boston never really recovered from the long dispute between England and Lübeck. What was left still depended chiefly on the traditional link with Bergen, but whether any of it remained in the hands of Lübeck merchants is questionable. Between 20 July 1463 and 3 May 1464 the only Hanse ship in Boston belonged to

[103] PRO, E122/97/8.   [104] PRO, E122/97/9.

Table 13. *The distribution of Hanse cloth exports, 1436–68*

	Hull	Boston	Lynn	Ipswich	London	Others	Total	London and Ipswich as % of total
1436–7	803	1,043	972	3,569	5,558	102	12,047	76
1437–42	193	905	260	2,316	6,767	130	10,571	86
1442–7	48	1,018	370	3,098	7,744	67	12,345	88
1447–52	11	414	145	1,023	4,823	13	6,429	91
1452–7	241	151	136	1,576	7,527	61	9,692	94
1457–62	84	408	144	1,658	8,119	87	10,500	93
1462–8	201	154	158	1,446	5,498	196	7,653	91

Stralsund; it brought in Hanse goods, mostly stockfish and oil, worth £538, and took away 102 cloths; it also brought in stockfish worth £15 for four denizen merchants.[105] All of the 450 cloths which left between 25 February and Michaelmas 1465 went in two Bergen ships, save 15 which were entrusted to a Boston ship carrying no other cargo but probably bound for Norway or the Baltic.[106] Out of the total of 193 cloths dispatched between Michaelmas 1465 and 20 December 1468, 128 went in two Danzig ships and 65 in two Boston ships going to the Baltic; Hanse imports from Bergen totalled £970 and engaged only one ship each year (one Kampen, one Danzig and one Boston); in the same period one Danzig ship brought in £50 of Baltic goods.[107] After the initial arrests of the merchants in the summer of 1468 a few Prussian ships unwittingly imported goods to various ports, but until the end of the war Hanse trade was restricted to Cologne merchants, who operated exclusively at London, apart from a few cloths shipped at Ipswich.

During the 'great depression' Hanseatic cloth exports were at their lowest in the late 1440s and early 1450s. Thereafter they made a steady recovery for the better part of a decade, until they were affected by uncertainty about the renewal of the franchises and the reimposition of the Burgundian ban on English cloth. Having said that, it must be stressed that the recovery was due entirely to the performance of the London Steelyard (table 13). Elsewhere trade remained in the doldrums. Lübeck merchants were either unable or unwilling to rebuild their former business at Boston, while trade at

[105] PRO, E122/10/4.　　[106] PRO, E122/10/5.　　[107] PRO, E122/10/7–9.

Table 14. *Denizen cloth exports at four east-coast ports, 1436–67*

	Hull	Boston	Lynn	Ipswich	Total
1436–7	887	352	2,108	2,020	5,367
1437–42	3,399	316	1,668	2,366	7,749
1442–7	3,248	340	1,813	2,011	7,412
1447–52	2,312	340	762	1,246	4,660
1452–7	2,184	171	497	480	3,332
1457–62	1,455	101	353	467	2,376
1462–7	745	200	286	196	1,427

Hull and Lynn, mainly Prussian, simply stagnated. What happened at Ipswich/Colchester is something of a mystery. Throughout the depression Ipswich exports were far in excess of the combined trade of the other provincial ports, but were only half of their former level. The remaining exports probably went to the same market as those leaving London, since Colchester was an adjunct of the Steelyard. This suggests the possibility, to put it no stronger, that the substantial tranche of 'missing' exports represents a trade with the Baltic which had now dried up. It is unlikely that much of the current export from London and Ipswich went to the Baltic, at least not directly. This trade was aimed chiefly at Brabant and Zeeland, where some of it competed with that of the Merchant Adventurers. The Dutch provinces were now the main market for English cloth exporters, so an intensification of rivalry between the two groups was inevitable.

The enfeebled state of Hanseatic trade between England and the Baltic in the 1450s and 1460s did not mean that Englishmen's trade flourished. Indeed, the opposite is true. A rough, though reasonably reliable, proof of this is provided by an examination of denizen cloth exports at the four east-coast ports which have been identified as the main centres of English trade with the Baltic (table 14). By 1462–7 their combined exports averaged only 1,427 a year compared with 7,412 in 1442–7, a drop of 81 per cent. In comparison, the combined exports of the ports from Southampton to Bristol, which suffered from the loss of England's possessions in France, fell by about 55 per cent. London, with its Netherlands trade, saw a fall of only 10 per cent in denizen exports in these two periods, despite the fact that the second coincides with a Burgundian boycott. It might be argued that east-coast merchants suffered because they failed to establish a stake in the Netherlands trade, but that their Baltic trade provided a life-line, taking all their current cloth exports. This is not true, but even if every piece of cloth they exported had gone to the Baltic it would have been far less than in former times. One obvious factor in the declining fortunes of the Englishmen was the erosion of the position which they had established and then held precariously in Prussia during the previous three-quarters of a century. Lynn suffered a sharp drop in trade even before the attack on the Bay fleet in 1449. Cloth exports had totalled 2,129 in 1446–7, but reached only 694 between Michaelmas 1447 and 30 April 1449, and 235 between the latter date and the following Michaelmas, before recovering to 1,188 in 1449–50. Perhaps Lynn's merchants had problems of their own, since trade in the other ports appears to have been normal until 1449. At that point repercussions of the attack upon the Bay fleet inflicted grave damage on trade. The Prussians took immediate action against English merchants and goods already in their country, but having obtained security for satisfaction of their losses were ready to give letters of safe-conduct to any bold enough to mount new ventures. Nor is there any evidence that they imposed more stringent conditions upon trade in these years. They had already squashed English pretensions in this direction and had little need to be more harsh. Consequently, Englishmen faced greater danger in the approaches to the Baltic, where their ships were menaced by privateers of Lübeck and Denmark. The threat from the former was lessened after the city was brought within the Anglo-Hanse truce in 1456, but there was no settlement with Denmark until 1465. At first English merchants sought to overcome the problem by shipping in Prussian vessels. In February 1452 denizen cloth was sent from Lynn by this means, while five merchants (including a woman) imported goods worth £94 10s in four Danzig ships which came to Hull in May 1453.[108] When Denmark began to stop and search Prussian ships for English-owned goods, and again when the King of Denmark sided with the Teutonic Order against its rebellious subjects, English merchants could either trade via Hamburg-Lübeck or risk sending their own ships to the Baltic. The latter course was probably adopted only when it was possible to obtain very specific guarantees of safety. In May 1457, for instance, the Danzig authorities issued a safe-conduct valid until Michaelmas

---

[108] *HUB*, 8, nos. 122–3. Childs, *Accounts of Hull*, pp. 3–7.

1458 in favour of two Hull ships and one of Lynn, and ten merchants.[109] In April 1465 they answered a request for safe-conduct with the observation that this was not really necessary, since a state of peace prevailed between England and Poland. Nevertheless the city sent its own safe-conduct and promised to get one from the King of Poland.[110]

A glimpse of English trade at this time may be gained from the reconstruction of a voyage of three Hull ships which probably went to the Baltic in 1464.[111] The first departed on 2 October with a cargo of lead worth £56 13s 4d, 366 denizen cloths and 62½ Prussian-owned cloths. The other two left on 16 November with 286 denizen cloths and £66 13s 4d worth of lead. Despite the absence of any Hanse exports there is little doubt that these were bound for the same destination as the first ship. Forty English merchants shared in the venture, the largest consignment of cloth being 73 pieces, though this was exceeded in value by one of 64 cloths and £37 worth of lead. The first ship to leave returned to Hull on 3 March and the others on 23 February and 2 April. None of them came direct from the Baltic, for as well as goods which originated there all carried other things which could only have been bought in the Low Countries, including Rhenish wine, sweet wine, soap, eastern fruits and spices and much more besides. In fact, although the values of the two sorts of goods cannot be precisely disentangled, it is clear that in every ship the total value of the Baltic goods was much less than that of the other sort. In view of the long absences the implication is that the ships made a triangular voyage, first going northwards and eastwards and then to the Low Countries, where they may have disposed of some of the goods acquired in the north and obtained new cargoes. The same merchant capital financed each leg of the voyage. This is borne out by the fact that of the forty original exporters twenty-eight were among those with goods in the ships when they returned; two brought goods home from the Low Countries in other ships, while the other ten brought nothing from there within the period of account (Michaelmas 1464 to Michaelmas 1465). The last fact is not significant, since there were many merchants importing in the three home-coming ships whose names were not in the outward manifests, and some of these bore the same surnames as some of the 'missing' exporters. Even without the

[109] *HUB*, 8, no. 574.   [110] *HR*, II (v), nos. 647–8.
[111] PRO, E122/62/5, 7. Childs, *Accounts of Hull*, pp. 65–96.

coincidence of surnames there is a strong possibility of business connections between at least some of those exporting only and those importing only in these ships. Of the forty exporters only one, and one other denizen, imported goods in three Danzig ships which came to Hull in May and September 1465, and these were worth only £4. This suggests that Yorkshiremen, and no doubt other Englishmen also, had abandoned the practice of permanently maintaining representatives in Prussia. Caution prescribed a rapid turnover of capital, which meant exporting cloth, disposing of it quickly and repatriating the proceeds in the same ship or ships. Factors travelling with the ships took the place of the former residents. This parallels the practice of the Danzig merchants trading with Hull in this period and the two communities probably regarded each other very warily.

In the 1450s and 1460s the hostility of Denmark was a major obstacle to English trade with the Baltic, but the peace treaty signed in October 1465 offered hopes for the future. Cloth export figures show that at first the merchants were cautious. A staged return is also visible in the customs particulars of Boston, where hitherto denizen trade with the Baltic had been more modest than at any of the other English ports best placed to exploit it. Boston's new interest was probably roused by the desertion of the town by Lübeck merchants and, more positively, by contacts with Danzig merchants who began to take their place. As already mentioned, in December 1463 four denizens imported stockfish from Norway in a Stralsund ship, while the next surviving particular shows a Boston ship going either to Norway or the Baltic in July 1465.[112] On 27 March 1466 Henry Wiske, William Sibsey, Richard Curson and Henry Bukholt shipped 26 cloths, 100 lambskins and 2 tables of alabaster in a Danzig ship in a company with four Hanse cloth exporters.[113] No Boston ship went to the Baltic in the next twelve months, but on 27 April 1467 Wiske and Curson dispatched 41 cloths in William Wakeleyn's Boston ship, which also carried cloth belonging to a Danzig merchant, whose company they had enjoyed the previous year. There can be little doubt that this was an exploratory voyage to Danzig. The same source shows Thomas Hayward bringing his ship the *Gabriel* in from Norway with Hanse-owned staple goods in January 1468.[114] At Lynn no denizens imported or exported in any of the numerous Hanse ships which visited the port between 19

---

[112] PRO, E122/10/4, 5.   [113] PRO, E122/10/7.   [114] PRO, E122/10/8.

November 1464 and 19 November 1465.[115] But moving on to the period 2 November 1466 to 2 November 1467, one may safely conclude that, when Richard Outlawe sailed on 4 October 1467 with 80 cloths and £19 of worsteds, coverlets and candles belonging to three denizens, this was another exploratory voyage to Prussia.[116]

The success of the ventures in 1467 probably encouraged English merchants to revive their fellowship, which seems to have lapsed in recent years, and make a concerted effort to recover their lost market. It is difficult otherwise to account for the enterprises mounted simultaneously in the following year in Boston, Lynn, Hull and London, and possibly in other ports. Fourteen days before the attack by the Danes on English ships in 1468, two other vessels were allowed to pass peacefully through the Sound. These were probably the two Newcastle ships which, with one of Bristol, were already in Danzig at the time of the attack.[117] It was probably arranged that the main fleet of seven ships should rendezvous before entering the Baltic, but as they arrived at the Sound between 5 and 8 June they were seized by the Danes. Other details of the expedition may be pieced together from depositions[118] submitted to the enquiry held after the disaster and from customs particulars of Lynn and Boston.[119] At Lynn twenty-one merchants ventured a total of 911 cloths, 17 tuns of wine and a few worsteds, coverlets and Suffolk cheeses. This was all the denizen cloth exported from Lynn between 2 November 1467 and 2 November 1468 and half as much again as the total dispatched during the previous $3\frac{1}{2}$ years. Most of the cloth and the wine was put aboard the *James*, skippered and one-quarter owned by Richard Outlawe. Outlawe also had a half share in the *Mary*, which was a balinger, a small type of vessel which had room for only 49 cloths. This left 130 cloths, which after paying custom at Lynn had to be taken over to Boston to be put aboard one of the ships loading there. The Lynn ships sailed on 2 May, followed on 6 May by three ships contributed by Boston. These were the *Gabriel*, now commanded by William Wakeleyn, the *George* under Thomas Hayward and the *Christopher* under Robert Watson. None of these skippers had a share in the ownership of the ships. At Boston eighteen adventurers put together 345 cloths (apart from those brought from Lynn) and a little lead, wine and worsteds.

---

[115] PRO, E122/97/4.
[117] *HUB*, 9, nos. 519, 524.
[119] PRO, E122/10/9; 97/9.

[116] PRO, E122/97/8.
[118] *HUB*, 9, nos. 478, 519–20.

Additionally, the Boston ships carried 56 cloths belonging to five Hanse merchants. Depositions submitted to the later enquiry record that five Hanse merchants (one of them a Lübecker) travelled in the *Gabriel*, three of whom can be identified as owners of cloth and two having different names. The Lynn customs particular makes no mention of Hanse cloth in either of its ships, but much later Hans Barenbroek of the Steelyard claimed to have shipped cloth with Richard Outlawe from Lynn as well as in the *George*, a London-owned ship which sailed from the capital. Barenbroek demanded that the English should compensate him for his cloth, even though it had been seized by the King of Denmark. The London venture was financed by eleven merchants whose leader, George Heryott, and possibly some of the others, went in person to Prussia. The last of the ships was the *Valentine* of Newcastle, partly owned by the Earl of Northumberland. The thirty York merchants who chartered her claimed that their losses amounted to over £5,000. While this may have been an exaggeration it cannot be doubted that they had ventured a great deal, probably the greater part of Hull's denizen cloth exports in 1467–8, which at 1,449 pieces were more than three times the total of the previous two years. Given the preparations which must have gone into the expedition and the hopes pinned on it, it is small wonder that the English merchants suspected that the Danes had been urged into the attack by Hanseatic merchants wishing to eliminate competition in Prussia. Whether there were any real grounds for suspicion is a different matter. The magnitude of the disaster meant that the plan to revive trade in Prussia received a severe set-back. In addition many English merchants faced the prospect of ruin or great hardship. Sheer frustration at their inability to hit back at the Danes must have caused them to institute legal proceedings against the Hanseatics. The escalation into all-out war was the fault of politicians and they, rather than English merchants, must bear the blame for this episode in Anglo-Hanse relations.

CHAPTER 5

Rivalry at Antwerp, 1474–1551

Following the settlement at Utrecht relations between England and the Hanse remained remarkably tranquil until almost the end of Edward IV's reign. During the 1470s the waters around the British Isles were largely free from assaults on shipping. The only piratical incidents recorded are the seizure of a Stralsund ship in 1474 and a Lübeck ship in 1475, while a Danzig ship and its cargo were pressed into the king's service by the admiral, Lord Howard, in 1478. This unaccustomed state of affairs was not, however, unique to Anglo-Hanseatic relations. Overall, there was a dramatic fall in the number of piracies, as a result of the reassertion of the king's authority and the general peace which existed, apart from the brief expedition to France in 1475. A number of Hanseatic ships were pillaged after being wrecked on English coasts, but looters recognised neither friend nor foe, so this activity does not indicate any special animosity against Germans. In any case, the crown ordered the investigation of all reported incidents, and satisfaction was probably given, since few of them reappear in any of the detailed lists of damages submitted to the conferences held to consider such matters during the reign of Henry VII. Hanse merchants were just beginning to sail to Iceland, where the English had half a century's start on them, and a number of clashes occurred between the two groups in these waters, now one side and now the other being cited as the aggressor. From 1481 conditions gradually deteriorated. At first the Hansards suffered a number of losses as a direct or indirect consequence of English naval expeditions against Scotland. In 1481 the Prussians lost a ship to Newcastle sailors; the next year two more vessels were taken from them by the men from the same port and a third was seized by the Duke of Albany, renegade brother of the Scots king.[1]

---

[1] *CPR*, 1467–77, pp. 493, 605; 1476–85, pp. 23, 49, 145, 344. *CCR*, 1476–85, p. 336. *HUB*, 10, nos. 470, 489, 1201. *HR*, III (ii), no. 509.

The accession of Richard III saw the area of insecurity extended to the southern North Sea and the Channel, as France and Brittany were drawn into the conflict. In February 1484 the Steelyard merchants sent word to Danzig that England, France and Brittany all had warships at sea and that there was little hope of getting compensation for any prizes taken by them.[2] The record of Prussian vessels allegedly seized or robbed by the English was one in 1483, six in 1484 and eight in 1485, while other ships were arrested for long periods. Cologne's losses in these years were limited to relatively insignificant seizures of wine and other goods in 1484 and 1485. Lübeck alleged five separate attacks on her ships between June 1481 and July 1483.[3] Detailed claims for damages sustained by other towns have not survived, but there is evidence of a Hamburg crayer seized by pirates near Dover in January 1484 and of another Hamburg ship taken by a royal squadron; the crown also compulsorily purchased a Lübeck ship at Dartmouth in January 1485.[4]

Richard III confirmed the treaty of Utrecht and the Hanse franchises on 18 July 1484, and on 5 December he agreed that the Steelyard should continue to retain the petty customs until the financial indemnity was fully paid.[5] Nevertheless, the franchises were already being undermined by legislation of parliament and various actions taken by royal and urban officials. How soon and how deeply parliamentary legislation began to bite is uncertain, since the first recorded complaints date from after the accession of Henry VII and relate chiefly to events of that reign. But the first of the Tudors merely strengthened legislation which had been initiated by the Yorkists. This is seen most clearly in the context of the cloth trade. In 1468 Edward IV prohibited the export of unfinished woollen cloth, but at first little or nothing was done to enforce the ban. This was partly because the wording of the act of parliament was deficient and partly because the prohibition sought to be too all-embracing. Henry VII provided clearer definition of what was intended and limited the scope of the ban to a more practicable level. Certain named types of cloth and any generally priced at £2 each or less were exempted from the requirement. This measure was incorporated in a parliamentary statute in the autumn of 1487, but it was

---

[2] *HUB*, 10, no. 1125.
[3] Full details of Danzig, Cologne and Lübeck losses between 1474 and 1490 were submitted to the Antwerp conference in 1491. *HR*, III (ii), nos. 509–10. *HUB*, 11, nos. 445–6.
[4] *CPR*, 1476–85, p. 425.   [5] *HUB*, 10, nos. 1149, 1172.

put into effect by royal proclamation as early as December 1486.⁶ Moreover, steps were now taken to see that the law was obeyed, at least in so far as the Hanseatic merchants were concerned. The Steelyard complained to a Hanse diet held in May–June 1487, citing the testimony of Joris Tack of Duisburg that he had been obliged to have 500 cloths sheared unnecessarily. In April 1489 the London cloth workers, allegedly with the connivance of the customs officers, secured the arrest of cloths which had already been put on board ship. These were released only after the merchants had provided sureties not to export any more unfinished cloth. This incident became a major *cause célèbre*, with the Hansards claiming that the legislation was being used simply to harass them. The Cologne merchants complained bitterly, alleging that not only had they to pay for finishing cloths in England, but also that the work was done so badly that they commanded a lower price on the continent. In 1491 they claimed that since 1485 (*sic*) they had needlessly finished 13,650½ cloths at a cost of 2s each and lost a further two florins (8s 8d) on the sale of each of them.⁷

In 1483, at the request of London silk-women, a ban was imposed on the import of certain articles made of silk. This was aimed chiefly at Italian merchants, and Jews and Saracens were named as the principal manufacturers of the articles in question, but Cologne silks were specifically included in the ban. It was first intended to last until Easter 1487, but after only one year it was extended to 1497 and in 1485 was further extended to 1507.⁸ The first recorded confiscation of silk from a Cologne merchant is dated September 1486,⁹ but there may have been earlier cases. Legislation designed to increase the import of bowstaves was more of a nuisance than a threat to trade, and in any event there is no evidence that it was enforced at this time, since it does not feature among the grievances voiced by the Steelyard.¹⁰ In London the Hansards fell foul of officialdom when they claimed that their privileges provided immunity against the price-fixing policy which the city introduced for a wide range of goods during the 1480s. The earliest case for which precise details are supplied was in 1484, when a Cologne merchant refused to part with 4,840 bushels of salt for less than 1s 4d per bushel, although the mayor had fixed the price at 1s. Later, he

---

⁶ *Rot. Parl.*, 5, p. 621. *Stats.*, 2, pp. 422, 920. *HR*, III (ii), no. 109.
⁷ *HR*, II (ii), nos. 118, 298–301, 508.
⁸ *Rot. Parl.*, 6, pp. 222–3. *Stats.*, 2, pp. 472, 493, 506.   ⁹ *HR*, III (ii), no. 508.
¹⁰ *Rot. Parl.*, 6, pp. 156, 222, 494. *Stats.*, 2, pp. 432, 472, 521.

had to sell at 6d a bushel, when the general price fell and his own stock deteriorated because of poor storage. In February 1486 the mayor closed down four German wine cellars, because the owners refused to accept his assise price of 10d per gallon for Rhine wine. He tried to have the wine condemned as bad and, although this move was defeated by an appeal to the royal butler, a big import of Bordeaux wine brought down the general price level and again the Hanse merchants had to sell at a loss. In the provinces Hanseatics met with most opposition in York and Hull. As early as the first parliament of Henry VII the town's members called for the enforcement of the fourteenth-century employment acts, which required aliens to buy English goods equal in value to their imports. In fact Yorkshiremen tried to enforce a strictly regional interpretation of the acts, demanding that when imports were sold in the 'north parts' the corresponding exports should be bought there and not in other areas of England. The Hanse men resisted this on the grounds that they could not find good quality cloth in Yorkshire. The locals reinforced their campaign by claiming that, since Englishmen going to Danzig were not allowed to go outside that town to trade, Hanse merchants should not go beyond Hull or York. In several ports customs officials began to demand full alien rates of duty on all imports not originating in Hanse towns and upon all exports not shipped to such places.[11] Apart from increasing revenue, this was designed to discourage Hansards from sharing in the trade between England on the one hand and Burgundy, France and such places on the other.

While the growing tension of the early 1480s is clearly reflected in Hanseatic complaints, there is at first little record of English losses, apart from the robbery of two Bristol vessels by one of Hamburg near Ireland in September 1483 and attacks on three English ships off Iceland by another Hamburg ship early in 1485.[12] A long list of English losses submitted to the Hanse in 1491 contains a few undated incidents, which possibly occurred before the accession of Henry VII in August 1485, but the majority belong to the later period.[13] By the time of Henry's first parliament in November 1485 English merchants were complaining bitterly about attacks, chiefly in Norwegian and Icelandic waters. The situation was complicated by the fact that the chief culprits were notorious Hamburg privateers,

---

[11] *HR*, III (ii), nos. 26, 508. M. Sellers (ed.), *The York Mercers and Merchant Adventurers, 1356–1917* (Surtees Soc., 129, 1917), pp. 107–8.
[12] *CCR*, 1476–85, p. 360. *HUB*, 10, no. 1201.   [13] See below p. 244.

Pinning and Pothorst, who sailed under the Danish flag. The Hanse disclaimed responsibility for their actions, on the grounds that they had long abjured their native city. In his study of English trade in the early Tudor period George Schanz advanced the idea that Henry VII was hostile to the Hanse privileges from the very start of his reign.[14] This view has to contend with various marks of favour shown by the king to the merchants during his first nine months. When parliament met in November 1485 and voted a subsidy of tunnage and poundage a schedule was attached to the grant, to the effect that nothing therein, nor in any other act, statute or ordinance made in the present parliament, should be prejudicial to the Hanse privileges.[15] On 9 March 1486, a few days after parliament was dissolved, the king confirmed the franchises; on 29 June he confirmed the treaty of Utrecht, so that the Steelyard could continue to receive the petty customs levied on Hanse trade.[16] To explain these facts Schanz was obliged to assume that Henry VII acted out of fear – the insecurity of his hold on the throne making him reluctant to antagonise a strong foreign power. Logically, one is then obliged to suggest the same feeling of insecurity as the cause of other actions – the reversal of the anti-Italian trade legislation of Richard III and the confirmation of customs concessions granted to Spanish merchants in 1466. However, any attempt to construct a general thesis that Henry VII's early economic policy was dictated by the fear of antagonising foreigners runs up against other measures taken by his first parliament – the confirmation of the silk act and the imposition of a ban on the import of Gascon wine in alien bottoms. Some historians still accept that Henry VII's concessions to the Hanse were motivated by the initial weakness of his constitutional position,[17] but it is equally or more plausible to argue that any sense of insecurity ought to have caused him to side with his own subjects against them, or at least to play for time as Edward IV did for so long at the beginning of his reign. As we have seen, English merchants brought their protests to Henry's first parliament, so he would have had a good excuse to temporise.

The complaints of the Englishmen and the Steelyard's counter-complaints were discussed in a diet of the Wendish towns on 9 March 1486. On 14 March, ten days after the dissolution of

---

[14] G. Schanz, *Englische Handelspolitik gegen Ende des Mittelalters* (Leipzig, 1881), 1, p. 183.
[15] *Rot. Parl.*, 6, pp. 268–70.   [16] *HR*, ii (ii), nos. 30, 33.
[17] R. B. Wernham, *Before the Armada* (Oxford, 1966), p. 71. S. B. Chrimes, *Henry VII* (London, 1972), p. 235.

parliament, a more up-to-date version of this intelligence was sent to Danzig, together with the news that the king had confirmed the franchises. For the time being, at least, he was prepared to accept the argument that the Hanse had no control over Pinning and Pothorst. But as the reign progressed English shipping losses increased and the victims grew more vociferous in their demands that the Hanse should pay. On several occasions in October and November 1486 representatives of the Steelyard were summoned before the king and council and challenged that they or the Bruges *Kontor*, or the two in concert, were financing Zeeland privateers and buying their spoils.[18] Specifically, they were accused of lending the privateers 3,000 marks and offering to put up another 1,000 marks. Nothing seems to have come of this charge, but the general reference to the role of Zeeland is supported by details of English losses submitted to the Antwerp conference of 1491. These show that during this period Pinning made a speciality of seizing English ships, taking them into the port of Veere and holding them to ransom. It is likely that German merchants acted as intermediaries for ransoms, so that suspicion was bound to fall upon them even if they were not directly involved in the crimes.

In 1487 the Steelyard merchants fell foul of the government as a result of the invasion of England by Lambert Simnel, supported by 2,000 German mercenaries led by Martin Schwarz and financed by Margaret of Burgundy. They were forbidden to import any goods and all their cloth was put under arrest. Fortunately, a general Hanse diet, the only one held between 1476 and 1494, was just assembling at Lübeck, so the merchants had a forum for their complaints. The arrest of cloth topped a long list of grievances, but the letter was sent too early to report the confiscation of goods imported after proclamation of the ban simply because there had been insufficient time to countermand sailing orders. Other complaints related to attempts by the king's council to limit the Hanse customs concession to goods originating in, or destined for, their own towns; attempts by customs officials to change the procedure for valuing merchandise; the ban upon the export of unfinished cloth; poor-quality cloth and the absence of machinery for securing redress; the ban on silk imports; the mayor of London's interference with the sale of wine, herrings and wainscot, and discrimination against Hansards in their disputes with city mer-

---

[18] *HR*, III (ii), nos. 26, 31–2, 103–6.

chants; the attempted ban on inland trading at Hull; finally, attempts still being made to hold the Steelyard responsible for the actions of privateers sailing under the Danish flag. Discussion of the affairs of the Steelyard occupied the diet for ten days in June, though not all this time was taken up by discussion of the grievances. More effort went into dealing with the Steelyard's account of its stewardship of the retained petty customs and apportioning the balance among those who had suffered losses in England in 1468–9. Eighty four per cent of the 1474 indemnity had been recovered by 22 August 1485, when Henry VII succeeded to the throne. Repayments were slowed down by the trade stoppage of 1487, but by then very little of the debt was outstanding. The diet also set up a committee to draft a protest to the king about the present situation in England. At the beginning of October Henry formally rejected the complaints, saying that the new legislation about unfinished cloth applied to all merchants not merely to Hansards, while the ban on general trade had been purely temporary and had now been lifted. He welcomed the idea of a conference between the two powers and proposed that it should be held in England at Whit 1488. In fact the diet had specifically rejected a suggestion of a conference, on grounds of insecurity of the English throne. The Steelyard merchants, ignoring that decision, had themselves raised the matter with the king, and on 4 November wrote again to the towns urging them to accept his invitation. They predicted that parliament, which was due to assemble in a few days' time, would again be the scene of an attack on the Hansards. This proved correct. The Hull members raised the question of English trade in Prussia and more immediately demanded letters of marque against the Hanse for the loss of two of their own ships. The council turned this down, on the grounds that the Hull claims must wait until a conference was convened. The Hull men were far from satisfied and threatened action against the first Hanse ship to visit their port. Certain members of the king's council privately advised the Germans to avoid Hull, and in February 1489 a diet of the Wendish towns put the port under a temporary interdict, but again refused to take part in a conference.[19]

Early in 1488 the Hansards again fell victim to the dispute between England and Burgundy, being forbidden to send any cloth to or through Burgundian territory. This was particularly hard on

[19] *Ibid.*, nos. 160–1, 188–9, 193, 217–18.

Cologne merchants, for whom trade via north-German ports was time-consuming and expensive. Permission to trade through the Hanse town of Kampen provided some relief, but their request to trade through normal channels went unanswered, despite a promise to pass their wares unopened through Burgundy. This state of affairs lasted throughout 1488 or beyond, since England and Burgundy did not settle their differences until February 1489. By then Hanse merchants were again being harassed for alleged breaches of the law forbidding the export of unfinished cloth. At the end of the 1480s, therefore, it was clearly necessary that there should be a full-scale conference between England and the Hanse. It was not simply a question of trying to reconcile recent English legislation with the Hanse privileges; more serious was the need to prevent privateering from developing into all-out war. In the last two years of the decade the number of incidents increased enormously, and the English merchants continued to hold the Hanse responsible for their losses. They retaliated at first with unauthorised attacks on Hanse ships, but in 1489 they finally persuaded the authorities to issue letters of marque. In March 1490 Henry VII renewed his suggestion of a conference to discuss all outstanding differences, to be held at London, Calais or Antwerp. The Steelyard supported this move on the grounds that it was the only way to disprove the false claims submitted by English merchants to the king's council. By now the leading towns realised that they had no choice but to negotiate, and offered to meet at Utrecht or Antwerp on 1 May 1491. The English finally settled on Antwerp, on the grounds that it was unsafe for their people to go to Utrecht. In October the Wendish diet ordered merchants to submit details of their losses and advised that all towns should limit their trade with England until the conference was concluded, so that there would be a minimal amount of goods held there as hostage to the outcome of the negotiations. Such was the lack of trust among the Hanse members that Danzig would have nothing to do with the advice unless it was made binding on all.[20]

The towns represented directly at the Antwerp conference were Lübeck, Hamburg, Danzig, Cologne, Münster and Deventer, together with the Steelyard and the Bruges *Kontor*. Some other towns had delegated full powers to one or other of those attending, for example Osnabrück to Münster, Königsberg to Danzig, Kampen to

[20] *Ibid.*, nos. 339–40, 360, 375, 405, 407.

Deventer. Others, such as Bremen, Stralsund and Lüneberg, intimated that they wanted nothing to do with the conference. All the Hanse delegates were at Antwerp by the end of the first week of May, but had to wait until the end of the month for the arrival of the English. News that they had got as far as Bruges reached the Hansards only just in time to prevent them from making a formal protest and leaving for home. Many rumours had circulated to account for the lateness of the English, including one that they were deliberately held back until the king knew the outcome of negotiations between England and Denmark. In fact, those talks had been completed and a treaty made by 20 January 1491. The official explanation for the delay was the illness of the leader of the delegation. The conference began badly and ended in total failure four weeks later. Broadly speaking, there were two items on the agenda: first, the question of Hanse privileges in England and the reciprocal rights claimed by the English merchants; secondly, the matter of compensation to be paid for the losses suffered by each side in recent years. Under the former heading the Hanse claims were largely the same as those put forward by the diet in 1487, but there were a number of important additions. One concerned Henry VII's navigation act. His first parliament had designated that Gascon wine should be imported only in ships belonging to the king's own subjects, but it was valid only until the following parliament, when it was not renewed. In any event, the Hanse was provided with exemption by the schedule attached to the grant of tunnage and poundage. The parliament of 1490 renewed the legislation and added Toulouse woad. By August of that year cases were reported of confiscation of German-owned French wine which had not been freighted in English ships. Another complaint was that port officials were levying a great custom (poundage) on Hanse exports of lead and tin, on the grounds that these were staple goods and not covered by the general immunity. Finally, the same officials were demanding payment of duty upon all items recorded in a ship's manifest, regardless of the fact that sometimes goods were not there, because they had been delivered too late to be loaded.[21]

As regards compensation claims, the only surviving lists on the Hanse side are those of Cologne, Danzig and Lübeck. The first, totalling between £15,000 and £16,000 sterling, were absurdly

---

[21] *Ibid.*, nos. 515, 520.

unrealistic.[22] A few claims dated back to 1427, though the majority fell into the period between 1464 and the present. Almost half of the total was made up of losses allegedly sustained because of the ban on the export of unfinished cloth. Another £1,100 resulted from a robbery committed by forces of the Earl of Warwick during his rebellion in 1471. Danzig, whose case was much more carefully put together, claimed a total of £5,289 for attacks on its ships between 1478 and 1490, plus a few hundred pounds for attacks which had been reported since the main brief was prepared.[23] English claims totalled £14,670, of which well over half were submitted by Yorkshire merchants and fishermen.[24] The total number of incidents was forty-one, though some involved attacks on more than one vessel; ten incidents were undated and thirty-one placed between 1486 and 1490. With the exception of one Sandwich ship, all the attacks were made against vessels belonging to Calais, Lynn, Yorkshire and Northumberland. This imbalance is not explicable by attacks being confined to northern waters, since many were made near the Low Countries and against ships returning from Poitou. There appears to have been a degree of selectivity in Hanse attacks, either because they felt that they were acting legitimately against the ships in question, or because they feared retaliation if they molested ships belonging to ports such as London, where their own merchants still had a large trade.

Given the near impossibility of verifying the financial claims advanced by each side, it is hardly surprising that the conference ended in stalemate – although a later Hanse diet sought to lay the blame on the Steelyard for going inadequately prepared. On 28 June it was formally agreed that the conference should reconvene on 1 May 1492; meanwhile the *status quo* was to continue. Naturally, the English insisted that their rights in Hanse regions should be reserved, using the form of words contained in the Vorrath treaty and the treaty of Utrecht. The Prussians, however, had profited from their experience at Utrecht and their delegates had gone to Antwerp briefed to stand firm against their fellow negotiators on this point. In the event, a compromise was agreed. On 22 June the Danzig delegation made a sworn declaration before a public notary that they dissented from certain articles in the treaty of Utrecht. The same day the other Hanse representatives also made a formal, public

---

[22] *Ibid.*, nos. 507–8. Confusion and repetition in the two lists precludes an exact total.
[23] *Ibid.*, nos. 509–10. Lübeck's claims are difficult to add up and convert to sterling. *HUB*, 11, no. 445.   [24] *HR*, III (ii), nos. 554–63.

acknowledgement that the relevant clauses should never bear any interpretation other than that given to them by the Prussians. The Danzig declaration stated that the English fellowship had never formally been recognised in their land and that they had never been free to trade with Poles, Letts, Russians and other aliens. On the other hand, it was agreed that they should exercise any rights which they had enjoyed within the previous sixty years. Among these were admission to the *Curiam Artes* or *Artushof*, where international merchants congregated, equality with non-Prussian members of the Hanse and freedom to trade with anyone in Danzig at the time of the annual Dominic mart.[25] German historians have been divided in their opinion as to whether this degree of admission represented any advance on the previous Prussian attitude. Schanz believed that it did; Schulz demurred, arguing that the English were already allowing entry to the *Artushof* and may also have traded freely during the Dominic mart, since the temporary suspension of local monopolies was a common feature of medieval fairs.[26]

The Anglo-Hanseatic conference, instead of reconvening in 1492, was repeatedly postponed, first by one side and then the other, until June 1497. One problem was that for much of that time it was impossible to meet in Antwerp, and neither side was willing to go to a place within the other's domain. In some respects the Hanse's stubbornness was self-defeating, for as Danzig pointed out in March 1495 the current Anglo-Burgundian dispute was a factor which might have served Hanseatic diplomacy. The intervening years were far from trouble free. There were incidents at sea, though fewer than in the 1480s, and there was still official interference with Hanse trade. Most serious were the repercussions of the breach between England and Burgundy. In September 1493 Henry VII imposed trade sanctions on the latter, in retaliation for aid given to the latest impostor, Perkin Warbeck. These applied to aliens as well as to his own subjects, and the Steelyard was required to give a surety of £20,000 that they would respect them. They were forbidden to import from, or export to or through, any part of Burgundy or the neighbouring provinces of Utrecht, Friesland, Kampen or Guelders. The restrictions continued until February 1496. The hardship was greatest for those wishing to take cloth to Cologne or Frankfurt, since they had to make a detour through north Germany. Cologne repeatedly, but unsuccessfully, petitioned the king to open the

---

[25] *Ibid.*, nos. 497–8, 502, 504–5.
[26] Schanz, *Englische Handelspolitik*, p. 189. Schulz, *Die Hanse und England*, p. 143.

Zeeland ports, or at the very least to allow them to trade via the Hanse ports of Kampen and Groningen. A Hanse diet at Bremen in May 1494 tried to impose counter sanctions by forbidding both the Steelyard merchants and those of the Bruges *Kontor* to resort to the cloth staple which the English established at Calais, but by the end of 1494 some were reported to be going there. Danzig suggested a ban on the export of Hanse goods to England to hurry along the proposed conference, but though the idea was cautiously supported by Lübeck and Hamburg nothing came of it.[27]

In June 1497 there was a brief encounter between England and Hanse representatives at Antwerp. This was never intended to be a full-scale conference and was little more than a side-show at the formal signing of the Anglo-Burgundian commercial treaty, nick-named the *Intercursus Magnus*. The talks ran into trouble when the English raised objections to the credentials of the Hanse men. The latter immediately sent to Lübeck for fuller powers, but by the time the messenger returned the conference had broken up, with nothing more to show than a recommendation to meet again in a year's time.[28] Contact was fitfully maintained and on 13 June 1499 the long-overdue conference gathered at Bruges. The English envoys were William Warham, Master of the Rolls, Sir Robert Sampson, Keeper of Calais, and Dr Robert Middleton. After little more than a week's fruitless discussion, the Hansards were ready to abandon the conference, but reluctantly agreed to an adjournment while the English sent home a report of all that had been said so far, together with a request for fresh instructions. Both the report and the response of the king's council have survived.[29] During the first session the English proposed that although their own financial claims exceeded those made against them there should be a mutual cancellation of all claims, because of the difficulty of establishing proofs. This was not acceptable to the Hanse, which resubmitted those brought to the 1491 conference, together with claims for losses incurred since that date.[30] Curiously, most of the resistance came from Cologne, whose own claims would be the most difficult to substantiate, some because they related to incidents so long ago that there could hardly be any living witnesses, but most because they involved nothing so tangible as robbery, but only incidental losses caused by English trade legis-lation. When the Hanse refused to abandon their claims the English

[27] *HR*, II (iii), nos. 259, 273, 290, 333, 353, 358, 379, 383–4, 386, 394, 401. *HUB*, II, nos. 710–12.   [28] *HR*, II (iv), no. 8.   [29] *Ibid.*, nos. 145, 180–1.
[30] *Ibid.*, nos. 13–15.

next suggested that individuals should sue for recovery in the courts
of the power responsible for their injuries, but to save them expense
witnesses should be examined by impartial persons in their own
country and sworn depositions accepted as evidence. The Hanse
rejected this, because of the possibility that witnesses might be
suborned. They wanted the Bishop of Cambrai to act as a neutral
judge, with all claimants and witnesses appearing in person at his
court. When this proposal was referred to the English council they
turned it down. They repeated their preference for mutual
cancellation, but said that the furthest they would go in trying to
settle individual claims would be to appoint a judge to sit at Calais,
if the Hanse would name one to hold a court at Bruges or Antwerp.

When it came to trading rights the English made it abundantly
clear that the principle of reciprocity was far from dead, at least in
so far as it could be employed as a negotiating pawn. They produced
some rather poor testimony of Hull and London merchants who had
allegedly been in Prussia where they were forbidden to buy or sell
except with burgesses. The Prussians claimed that, while they were
willing to allow any rights enjoyed within the past sixty years, the
English had never had the freedom to trade with whomever they
wished and in that respect were on equal footing with non-Prussian
members of the Hanse. The English conceded that it was reasonable
to draw a parallel with other members of the Hanse, but urged that
it was therefore equally valid to argue that Hanseatics should not be
more privileged in England than natives. The Hanse reply was that
their franchises had been granted by earlier kings, whose charters
could be produced to authenticate them. They defied their
opponents to produce evidence in support of the claim that they had
once possessed in Prussia a house and corporate organisation like the
Steelyard and that Vorrath had promised to restore this to them.
The English envoys, referring obliquely to the documents allegedly
taken from Thomas Kent, responded that it was unreasonable to rob
a man of his evidence and then demand that he produce it in defence
of his case. These English arguments were endorsed by the council
during the adjournment and the envoys were instructed to persist
with the demand for equal rights in Prussia and the restoration of the
house allegedly taken from their ancestors.

Statements made by English envoys alleging mistreatment of their
compatriots in Prussia are obviously partisan, and cannot be
accepted as evidence of the normal conditions under which English
merchants were allowed to trade in Prussia at the end of the fifteenth

century. Counter-statements made to rebut these allegations are hardly more reliable. On the other hand, discussions between the Hanseatics themselves must be treated with more credibility. These suggest that Danzig was not hostile to Englishmen prepared to abide by its own rules and, more reluctantly, accepted their right to trade in a limited number of other places. The towns of Elbing and Thorn were anxious to establish their own credentials, and in May 1498 their representatives at a general Hanse diet questioned whether the Antwerp treaty of 1491 confined Englishmen to Danzig.[31] They were assured that this was not the case and invited to send representatives to the next Anglo-Hanseatic conference. In preparation for this the towns enlisted the support of the King of Poland, who in April 1499 published a declaration addressed to the King of England and the Hanse stating that Englishmen were free to trade throughout his Prussian territories on the same terms as non-Prussian Hanse towns.[32] Elbing and Thorn then deputed the secretary of Thorn to represent them at the Bruges conference, but, though he was kept informed of what went on, he was not allowed to participate directly in the negotiations. This decision was probably the result of Danzig's fear that he would concede too much to the English. A declaration of English rights submitted by the Thorn secretary certainly has the appearance of naivety when compared with an amended version prepared by Danzig's secretary.[33] The former stated that Englishmen were free to trade in Danzig, Thorn, Elbing and other places with all inhabitants of Prussia and other members of the Hanse, upon terms as free as had ever existed in past times. The latter stated that they might trade in Danzig, Thorn and Elbing with the citizens of those places, upon the same terms as non-Prussian Hanseatics, and as they had done within the previous sixty years and within human memory. This last condition was clearly intended to overrule claims about the greater freedom alleged to have existed in the early fifteenth century.

At the time of the Bruges conference the English were probably encouraged to press their claims about Prussia by the fact that they seemed about to realise their long-cherished ambition of winning the right to trade in Livonia. This province was still subject to the Teutonic Order and, since its towns had never acceded to the treaty of Utrecht, their merchants were not now allowed to share the Hanse privileges in England. In November 1498 Riga sent an ambassador

---

[31] Ibid., no. 79.   [32] Schanz, Englische Handelspolitik, 2, pp. 414–15, nos. 89–90.
[33] HR, III (iv), no. 168.

to London and within no time at all he had negotiated a draft treaty, which, it was hoped, would be ratified within five months.[34] It was proposed that English merchants be allowed to export to Riga and its dependent territories all manner of goods produced in England itself, taking them either in their own ships or by other means. They could abide and trade freely in the province and bring away whatever they wished. All this trade was to be free of Livonian customs duties. Subjects of Riga could trade in the produce of both countries subject to Hanseatic rates of duty, but if they traded between England and a third party then they had to pay alien rates. England would pay the arrears of the financial indemnity promised to Riga in 1409, provided that within four months the city delivered the original English letter of obligation to the governor of the Merchant Adventurers at Bruges or Antwerp. The Steelyard merchants were thoroughly alarmed by this treaty, not because of the prospect of Englishmen trading in Livonia, but because of an undertaking to pay alien rates of duty on third-party trade. If the English were able to enforce it in this instance it would greatly strengthen their hand in trying to make all Hanseatic merchants liable to alien rates upon a large part of their business. Nevertheless, the city of Riga at first proposed to go ahead with ratifying the treaty, and in April 1499 wrote to the Bruges *Kontor* enquiring of the whereabouts of Henry IV's letter, which when last heard of had been at Kampen. The Bruges merchants were unlikely to lend assistance in such a cause and the delay provided time for the Hanse to put pressure on Riga not to go ahead with the scheme. Lübeck claimed that Riga would be entitled to enjoy the Hanse privileges simply by acceding to the treaty of Utrecht and promised to assist her in this. This apparently satisfied Riga and the 1499 treaty remained unratified.[35]

During the discussions at Bruges about inroads recently made into the Hanse franchises in England, neither side was anxious to debate the king's right to annul the franchises. The English did indeed contend that it was fully within his power to do so, and even asserted that the franchises were now founded on nothing more than Edward IV's grant of 1474, since all earlier rights had been forfeited during the troubles. However, they gave assurances that Henry VII had no wish to annul Edward's charter. Their main concern was to establish that recent parliamentary legislation was applicable to Hansards and not in violation of the franchises. The prohibition of Hanse imports of silk and French wines was justified because these were not products of their own lands, while the ban on the export of unfinished cloth was defended on the grounds that no new tax had been introduced. The adjournment of the conference, during which the English delegates consulted their government, failed to produce a softening of attitudes. Talks were resumed on 16 July but broken off only three days later, nothing having been agreed except the recommendation of a two-year truce and a further meeting in July 1501. This conference did not take place, being repeatedly postponed first by one side and then the other.

When parliament met in 1504, for the first time since 1497, it provided that no act, statute or ordinance, either already in existence or made in the future, should detract from the Hanse franchises.[36] The force of this was slightly diminished by a separate schedule attached to the original act of parliament, stating that nothing contained in this act was to prejudice the liberties of the city of London. This left the way open for the city to continue its age-old opposition to the exercise of the franchises. Notwithstanding this reservation in favour of London, the act has puzzled historians, some of whom see it as a complete capitulation on the part of the king. The explanation generally offered is that he was forced into it by the need to cut off possible Hanse support for the White Rose, Edward, Earl of Suffolk, Yorkist pretender to the throne.[37] The parallel drawn with Edward IV and the Hanse in 1471 is questionable. Suffolk was not a king in exile and, anyway, Henry VII probably knew how little the restoration of Edward really owed to the support of the Hanse. The apparent concession was probably little more than a cynical move to put an end to the interminable talk about the need for a major conference to settle Anglo-Hanseatic differences. It enabled Henry to write to Lübeck in May 1504 stating that the Hanse merchants no longer had any cause for complaint and therefore the conference could be adjourned *sine die*. Jubilation expressed in the Steelyard was short-lived, for the act had no practical effect and before the end of the year the English were again riding rough-shod over the franchises.[38]

The main grievance throughout 1505 and into 1506 was another ban on the export of all cloth to or through Burgundy, because of the

---

[36] *Stats.*, 2, p. 665.
[37] Wernham, *Before the Armada*, p. 73. Chrimes, *Henry VII*, p. 230.
[38] *HR*, III (v), nos. 20–1.

renewal of England's commercial dispute with that country. Financial sureties were again taken from the merchants to enforce their compliance. Unfortunately, the Hanse towns were not now in a strong position to lend much support to the Steelyard, because of their strained relations with a number of European powers. In particular, from 1503 there was increasing hostility between Denmark and Lübeck, which was to result in war breaking out in 1509 between Denmark and the Wendish towns. This could do nothing but harm to English trade, and as early as January 1507 Henry VII backed Scotland's attempts at mediation, but to no avail. In December 1509, and again the following autumn, Denmark tried to enlist the active support of Henry VIII, but this was refused. If aid had been provided, Danish promises of safe-conduct through the Sound would, of course, have been nullified by the attacks of the Hanse. However, even neutrality could not save the English from all injury, and in November 1511 the Steelyard reported that attempts were being made to make it accountable for attacks alleged to have been committed by ships of Lübeck and Stralsund.[39]

Henry VIII succeeded his father on 22 April 1509 but did not confirm the treaty of Utrecht and the Hanse franchises until 20 February 1510, towards the end of his first parliament. In response to a Steelyard petition a *proviso* was also made that no act made in the present parliament should prejudice their franchises. This was necessary because Henry VII's grant of 1504 had run up against the maxim that no king or parliament could bind his or its successor. This was demonstrated firmly by the commons, whose grant of tunnage and poundage contained a declaration that it was applicable to the Hansards. Thereafter Hanse petitions for a renewal of the proviso became a routine precaution whenever parliament was summoned. When parliament next met in February 1512, John Belle, member for Hull, took up the cause of English merchants who had recently suffered losses in the Baltic. A bill condemning the Hanse passed the commons and was read twice in the lords, but then seems to have been stopped. However, the lords may have refused to support the renewal of the proviso, since the Chancellor ruled that the attachment of the great seal was sufficient to warrant it. The proviso was particularly important on this occasion, since the act banning the export of unfinished cloth was renewed, amidst complaints that of late it had been little enforced. As a concession to

[39] *Ibid.*, nos. 29, 217, 518, 533; (vi), nos. 137, 270.

exporters the price of exempt cloths was raised from £2 to 4 marks. Nevertheless, in June 1513 the Cologne merchants were again complaining that they were being forced to comply with the ban.[40]

Despite the attitude of the lower house of parliament and some harassment by officialdom, there is no evidence of general government hostility towards the Hansards until June 1515, when the council accused them of colouring the goods of strangers. Only a few weeks prior to this the house of lords had renewed the proviso, to take account of enactments in Henry's third parliament, though it was not sent down to the commons. ('Domini decreverunt consuetam quamdam provisam pro mercatoribus de Hansa esse sufficientem licet non sit missa in Domum Commune.')[41] From then on the pressure on the Steelyard grew steadily stronger and it was again confronted with the demand that its members confine their trade to the products of their own regions and English goods intended to be sold there. This meant that they should not meddle in trade between England and Burgundy. The merchants were reminded that the king held their bond for £20,000 that they would not export cloth to Burgundy or import anything from there. This had been intended only to secure their compliance with the trade boycott of 1493–6. At Bruges in 1499 the Hanse representatives unsuccessfully asked for the return of the bond. Now the government unscrupulously and illegally threatened to make it forfeit unless the Germans withdrew from the trade between England and the Low Countries even in time of peace.

Contemporary correspondence laid the blame for the attack on the Hansards directly at the door of Cardinal Wolsey. This has been accepted by historians, though no explanation has been provided for the abrupt change in government policy. Moreover, the notion that Wolsey deliberately sought a quarrel with the Hanse may seem difficult to reconcile with the modern opinion that the key to his statecraft was a concern to preserve international peace. Yet the pacific foreign policy pursued by Wolsey once he was firmly entrenched as the king's chief minister may explain the timing of the attack on the Hanse, if not the reason for it. From April 1512 to August 1514 England was at war with France. Throughout this time, and before then as preparations were made, the king was buying munitions from Hanse merchants. The principal items were an amalgam of medieval and modern warfare – bowstaves, copper

---

[40] *L & P*, 1, nos. 381(68). *Journals of the House of Lords*, 1, pp. 7, 13–14, 15–17. *Stats.*, 3, p. 29. *HR*, III (vi), no. 484.   [41] *HR*, III (vi), no. 687. *Lords Journals*, 1, p. 41.

for artillery and saltpetre for gunpowder. Henry also bought a huge warship from Lübeck. When peace was made, the king was no longer so dependent on the Hansards and he actually refused to take delivery of munitions which had been contracted for.[42] The fact that the king broke his contracts still does not provide a motive for Wolsey's wishing to destroy the privileges of the Hanse. Could he have been impelled by simple economic nationalism? The cardinal does not seem to have been credited with a coherent policy along these lines, but he has been said to have been directly associated with the limited overseas exploration by Englishmen in this period.[43]

In June 1517 the secretary of the Steelyard went to a Hanse diet to complain about the towns' failure to support the merchants. As well as reporting widespread encroachments on the franchises he said that their goods were under threat because of the robberies of 1511. Stralsund now accepted responsibility for the outstanding claims, which related to one ship of Lynn, and agreed to send an envoy to try to settle the affair. This envoy, George Sibutus, came to England at some point during the next twelve months and was referred by the king to Wolsey. The cardinal refused to treat with him and publicly humiliated him for coming armed with letters issued by an 'unknown and inferior prince'. The details of this incident are obscure, but when the Steelyard secretary came again to a diet in June 1518, rather than blaming Wolsey, he chided Stralsund for sending a 'mere *medicus*' as its messenger, instead of a doctor of laws. Following Sibutus' mission, or perhaps before that, Wolsey forced two members of the Steelyard to give a bond of £500 that no merchants of Lübeck, Rostock, Stralsund or Wismar would leave England or export their goods until the case was settled. The matter was finally concluded in the summer of 1519, when the Star Chamber awarded the Lynn merchants damages of £500. About the same time Hull men were awarded £250 on account of a piracy allegedly committed near Wismar as recently as April 1519.[44] The fact that in this case the pirates were Danes seems to have been disregarded.

In 1519 the position of the Steelyard merchants must have seemed critical, for in addition to the Stralsund affair Wolsey decided to press ahead with prosecutions against merchants charged with exporting unfinished cloth. One was fined £126 and fourteen others

[42] *L & P*, 1, nos. 1395, 1513–14; 2, no. 2832.
[43] J. J. Scarisbrook, *Henry VIII* (London, 1968), pp. 168–71.
[44] *HR*, III (vii), nos. 39, 108, 204–7. *L & P*, 3, no. 1082.

compelled to find sureties totalling £18,880 to answer similar charges. Wolsey also made it known that he intended to levy alien rates of duty on all goods which were regarded as lying outside the legitimate area of Hanse trade. If the merchants resisted then the bond of £20,000 levied in the 1490s would be declared forfeit. Worst of all, the Cardinal seemed to have set his face against negotiations. In July 1518 the diet invited the king to send envoys to Antwerp in the following October or in May 1519. In March 1519, no reply having been received, a diet of the Cologne third asked Lübeck to write again, saying that if the king continued to ignore them it would be advisable for the merchants to leave England. In August Lübeck wrote to Cologne and Danzig advising evacuation. Danzig was against immediate action and urged a further approach to the king; Cologne could not reply at once, since its *Englandfahrer* were then away at Frankfurt fair. By the time they returned at the end of September word had been received unofficially that the merchants could enjoy the franchises until midsummer 1521, provided that the Hanse agreed to confer before then on all matters currently in dispute. However, not until November did the Steelyard manage to get Wolsey to send a formal invitation.[45]

Anglo-Hanseatic talks were scheduled to begin at Bruges on 15 June 1520, but the English envoys, Dr William Knight, Thomas More, Sir William Hussey and John Hewster, governor of the Merchant Adventurers, did not arrive until 19 July. Compared with the other affairs of state which engaged the king and Wolsey that summer, this was a mere side-show. In May Henry entertained Emperor Charles V at Sandwich, in June he met Francis I at the Field of the Cloth of Gold, in July he conferred again with Charles at Gravelines and Calais. Only when Henry returned to England did his envoys come to the waiting Hansards, representing Lübeck, Cologne, Stralsund and the London Steelyard. Despite their protestations of friendliness there can be no doubt that the English came to Bruges not to negotiate, but to force the Hansards to surrender a large part of their traditional privileges. There is no evidence that they had any constructive suggestions and they did not even get around to tabling any financial claims before the conference collapsed. The general grievances of the Hanse are, for the most part, already familiar to the reader, since they were the same as those raised at earlier conferences. There were, however, a couple of

---

[45] *HR*, III (vii), nos. 188, 203, 229–31, 239, 254, 257.

complaints which were new. One was that English buyers of their imports often promised payment in gold, but then paid the sum in silver which had a lower intrinsic value, pleading an act of parliament which forbade the delivery of gold to Germans. The other concerned a dispute between Hanse ship-masters and the aldermen of the pilots' gild (the Brethren of Trinity House, incorporated in 1514) about the question of legal liability for ships coming to harbour. These complaints about the franchises, together with claims for damages submitted by private individuals, were handed over to the English on 23 July for them to consider privately. Three days later Dr Knight replied briefly to all the points which had been made. His answers were bound to be unsatisfactory, for in almost every instance he and his colleagues pleaded ignorance of the facts. However, the English attitude is adequately portrayed by the remark which Knight made about the franchises; his team could make no comment on them, since they were not familiar with the privileges themselves. Was ever an embassy so badly briefed? Their bluff was called when the Hanse men presented them with copies of the franchises. After studying or feigning to study these, the envoys demanded that every single Hanse complaint should be justified by reference to a specific clause in the franchises. The Germans were now thoroughly suspicious, but nevertheless agreed to appoint a small committee to sit with the Englishmen to do this. In the next full session, on 4 August, the English orator was Thomas More, but his argument was much the same as that put earlier by Dr Knight. He contended that Henry VIII was sovereign in his kingdom, so that neither Roman civil law nor canon law could be used to judge matters affecting his people, only English law and the natural law of justice and reason. The legislation of parliament did not conflict with natural justice, since it was made for the utility of the whole realm. The Germans attempted to counter this line of argument with the claim that the ban on the export of unfinished cloth served only the interests of the London cloth finishers, but the result was stalemate.[46]

It was now obvious that no more progress could be made and the English proposed that the conference be adjourned. The Hanse had no choice but to accept this, but then came the problem of drawing up a final treaty or communiqué. Each side was determined that there should be a form of words which did not prejudice its own case, and because of this a mutually satisfactory draft was not finally put

---

[46] *Ibid.*, nos. 332, 337–8, 340–40a.

together until 12 August. One of the main concerns of the Hanse was that all the current legal actions against its members in the Exchequer should be suspended and no more begun. The English said that they could not bind the king to this, but promised to try to persuade him to do so of his free will. When the Hanse kept returning to this point Thomas More produced a trump card. He said that while the conference was under way a copy of the Hanse credentials had been sent to England and had been found to be inadequate. Consequently, the English envoys had been instructed not to commit themselves to anything. Faced with this the Hanse delegation was divided. Some wanted to abandon the conference entirely, on the grounds that the English were deliberately seeking to wear them down with expensive and tedious negotiations. Other counsel prevailed and in the end they accepted a treaty which confirmed the *status quo* until the conference should reconvene on 1 May 1521.[47] The failure of the conference left the Hanse delegates in a pessimistic mood. Before departing from Bruges they warned the Steelyard officials to be ready to evacuate their goods, but not to do so yet and to do nothing to offend the English. To some of Wolsey's advisers the failure offered a good opportunity to break with the Hanse. Spinelli, writing from Antwerp in August after hearing the news, was one of these. He first incited the cardinal by reporting that the Germans were openly retailing English cloth in the city and flaunting the arms of England to advertise the fact. He then suggested that in alliance with the Emperor and the King of Denmark the Hanse might be humbled without open war. Indeed, he had already taken soundings about such an alliance.[48]

At the request of the Hanse the reconvening of the conference was postponed until September 1521, and in the meantime a Hanse diet considered the possibility of evacuating the Steelyard if negotiations failed again.[49] The proceedings opened at Bruges on 12 September with a bromide speech from Dr Knight, in which he referred to the favours showered on the Hanse by all English kings down to Edward IV.[50] Unfortunately, since that time the merchants had abused their privileges and resisted all the appeals of Henry VII and Henry VIII to mend their ways. The English then showed their teeth, demanding to know the names of all towns which belonged to the Hanse, since it was intolerable that they should allow privileges to an undefined

[47] *Ibid.*, no. 336.
[48] *State Papers during the Reign of King Henry VIII* (London, 1830–52), 6, pp. 65–6.
[49] *HR*, III (vi), no. 413.   [50] *Ibid.*, nos. 448, 450.

group. The German delegates, as always, were reluctant to supply such information and attempted to instruct their adversaries about the constitution of the Hanse. The English were unimpressed, and in the face of their persistence the Hansards eventually handed over a list of thirty-eight towns,[51] while insisting that this should not prejudice the rights of any which had been left out. Once this information had been supplied the two sides exchanged details of their complaints against one another. The Hanse grievances were virtually identical with those submitted the previous year,[52] but this was the first time that the English had formally presented theirs. The latter may be divided broadly into three groups; first, private claims for damages; second, general complaints by merchants about treatment meted out abroad; third, complaints by the crown about abuse of the Hanse franchises.[53] In the first group were eight cases of alleged robbery and miscarriage of justice since 1500, and a further two cases dredged up from the dim and distant past, but there appears to have been no reference to the heavy losses of the 1480s and 1490s. Next, the merchants complained that they were denied access to the Cologne mart and Frankfurt fair, that they were denied their rights in Prussia and that within the past ten years Danzig had imposed a new tax on wine imported by Englishmen. The crown's case was very intemperate. It was alleged that the Hanse exported cloth to the Low Countries, despite having given sureties not to do so; that their imports from that region had cost £100,000 in lost revenue; that Dinant's false claim to privileges had cost £40,000; that a further £94,000 had been lost because Cologne enjoyed the franchises while expelled from the Hanse. A general charge that Steelyard merchants coloured the goods of non-members was supported by the allegation that one Gover Slotkin handled imports worth £6,000 for Italians resident in Antwerp and exported cloth worth £4,000 for the same firm; named individuals were said to have been born outside Hanse towns and so to be ineligible for membership of the Steelyard; finally, we find a revival of the ancient demand that aliens should not remain in England for long periods, and the unsupported claim that Hanse merchants were defaulting on payment for goods sold to them on credit.

The two sides deliberated privately for six days and then intermittently spent a week together making replies and counter-replies to specific complaints. As one might guess, no progress was

---

[51] *Ibid.*, no. 453. Another report (no. 450) states that forty-five towns were named, but these are not printed.   [52] *Ibid.*, no. 454.   [53] *Ibid.*, nos. 455–6.

made, since all the charges were either denied or justified, or the envoys simply pleaded ignorance of the facts. On 5 October the real English attitude was made abundantly clear by Thomas More. The king could drive the Hansards from his country any day that he chose, but he had no wish to do so – provided that they listened to reason. The choice was entirely theirs – either they must leave England or surrender their ancient privileges and negotiate a new treaty of commerce. Four days later Knight and More were summoned to Wolsey, who was then at Calais, from whence Knight alone returned on 19 November. In the meantime the talks were at a virtual standstill, for the Englishmen who remained could do nothing without further instructions and despite the impatience of the Hanse envoys they refused to write to Wolsey, on the grounds that he was too busy with other matters. However, Knight did not come back to resume the present talks. He brought a letter from Wolsey saying that he understood that the Hansards were ready to negotiate a new treaty, but that since the question of privileges now depended entirely on the king's grace this could be negotiated only in England, whither they were invited to come in May 1522. This astonished the Hansards, who vigorously denied what had been imputed to them and refused to go to England.[54] The delegates lingered in Bruges for a few days more, but when the English refused to reopen the talks they departed, without even the formality of a treaty, which was the usual method of bringing the conferences to an end.

In the spring of 1522 the Steelyard merchants were apprehensive about the future of their franchises and took the precaution of sending Henry VII's charter of confirmation to Lübeck for safe-keeping. But May, the month appointed by Wolsey for the negotiation of a new treaty, came and went and no blow fell upon them. Their reprieve was due entirely to the vicissitudes of English foreign policy. Wolsey had been forced by the king to abandon his policy of studied neutrality, in favour of an alliance with Emperor Charles V against Francis I. He had pledged that England would declare war on France in May 1522 if Charles had not by then made his own peace with Francis. That month Charles came to England to ensure that the promise was kept. There is no record of any representations which Charles may have made on behalf of the

[54] *Ibid.*, nos. 462–4.

Hanse, but it would clearly have been impolitic to take repressive measures against his subjects while he was in England or immediately afterwards. Another factor which Wolsey had to take into account was the revival of the threat to the dynasty posed by the White Rose, Richard de la Pole, Earl of Suffolk. Francis I proposed to finance an invasion of England by Pole, launched from the duchy of Holstein and hopefully supported by the Hanse. It was mooted that the Hanse could be won over if Pole promised to pay them the 200,000 angels which they claimed from England, provided of course that his coup was successful. The plan also posited the cessation of hostilities between Denmark and Lübeck and its allies, so that the former might be enlisted against England. The prospects of success appear to have been so slight that it is unlikely that Wolsey felt the need to buy off the Hansards out of fear. However, it would obviously have been an unnecessary complication to curtail their privileges at this particular time. Finally, mention may be made of a £1,000 loan which the Steelyard tactfully made to the king in aid of his war preparations.[55]

In 1525 English diplomacy made another about-turn, when Charles V reneged on his promise to marry Henry VIII's daughter, Mary, in favour of a Portuguese princess. England then made peace with France and the Emperor became the main adversary. This meant that it was no longer necessary to maintain the Hanse franchises merely for the sake of the Habsburg alliance, if indeed this had ever been the case. However, Wolsey was by then losing interest in his plan to destroy the base of the Hanse's economic position in England. In the later years of his life he was far more concerned about the contaminating effect of the Steelyard upon his country's religion. Merchants were uniquely equipped to import heretical writings and from 1526 they were frequently questioned about their reading habits and personal beliefs. After Wolsey's death this harassment ceased, for in the 1530s the king's divorce was the main objective of the government and it was anxious to gain the intellectual support of the Lutherans in this matter.[56]

During the late 1520s there was a revival of economic opposition to the Hanse. A diet meeting at Lübeck in 1530 complained about breaches of the franchises, and in particular about the ban on the

---

[55] *L & P*, 3, part 2, nos. 2184, 2340, 2483 (p. 1049), 2622.
[56] *L & P*, 4, nos. 1962, 2168–70, 2179. R. Pauli, 'Die Stahlhofskaufleute und Luthers Schriften', *HG* (1871), 153–62.

export of unfinished cloth. This protest had no effect and informations continued to be made against Hanse exporters. However, the main field of conflict was Iceland. English fishermen still had a strong attachment to these waters and they now went there with the permission of the Danish crown and the full support of their own government, even to the extent that the latter sometimes provided escorting warships in times of danger. But the Hanse also visited Iceland and, as we have seen, there were clashes between the two groups in the late fifteenth and early sixteenth centuries, which now began again. Frederick I, elected King of Denmark in 1523 after the deposition of Christian II, was also Duke of Holstein, and therefore nominally lord of Hamburg and Bremen. This being the case, it is hardly surprising that he took the side of these towns following a major clash between their seamen and Englishmen in Iceland in 1531, in which forty to fifty Englishmen were killed. In reply to protests, Frederick alleged that the Englishmen had behaved atrociously, so that the Icelandic authorities had legitimately invoked the aid of the Germans as fellow subjects of the King of Denmark. The English did not wish to involve the Danes in the dispute, but they continued to demand satisfaction from Hamburg in 1532.[57]

How far the English government might have gone to enforce payment of compensation, and whether reprisals would have been instituted against the Hanse as a whole, is an open question, since the interests of the English fishermen and merchants were sacrificed to those of diplomacy. Ironically, this new episode, involving at one stage the candidature of Henry VIII for the elective crown of Denmark, was one of the most ill-judged diplomatic ventures of the period. It seems to have resulted chiefly from Henry's exaggerated notion of the power and importance of Lübeck, at that time under the virtual dictatorship of Jürgen Wullenwever. The Hanse as a whole was not involved, only Lübeck and to a lesser extent Hamburg. The episode began with the death of King Frederick I in April 1533. During his reign the Reformation had made considerable headway in Denmark, but the Catholic party sought to check its further progress by preventing the succession of Frederick's elder son, Christian, Duke of Holstein, who had Lutheran sympathies. By delaying the election they hoped to secure the crown for the younger

[57] *L & P*, 4, no. 4740; 5, nos. 768, 1417, 1587, 1633.

son, John, on whom they might exert greater influence. Christian then made an alliance with Mary of Hungary, regent of Burgundy, which promised commercial privileges in Denmark for Dutch merchants. This caused Lübeck to declare against Christian and to prepare a fleet to fight his Dutch allies. On the other hand, Lübeck's support was given not to John, but to the former King Christian II, deposed in 1523 and for some years past a prisoner in Denmark. Charles V, a brother-in-law of Christian II, was not prepared to support him, but maintained the claim of his daughter, the Emperor's niece. She was married in September 1535 to Frederick, Count of the Palatinate and Bavaria, who then became the imperial candidate for the Danish throne. This complicated affair continued to bedevil European politics for many years after the Duke of Holstein secured the election in 1534 as Christian III.

England may have been drawn into the struggle almost fortuitously. In the summer of 1533 a large Lübeck fleet entered the English Downs to await the arrival of a Dutch fleet. It was allowed to revictual, but ordered to respect the neutrality of English territorial waters. Far from doing so, it seized two Spanish vessels and robbed a number of small English ships of goods worth just over £500. The Lübeckers then had the audacity to try to land artillery at Rye, the better to assault some Dutch hulks which had arrived there. The Rye authorities seized and detained the Lübeckers' leader, Marcus Meyer, after which his fleet left without him. The alleged capture of Meyer is suspect, for no attempt was made to rescue him and he was soon being treated not as a prisoner, but as an honoured guest. Henry VIII knighted him, gave him a pension and sent him home in January 1534. These marks of favour cannot have been necessary merely to get Meyer to intercede with his masters for the release of the English and Spanish goods. To achieve that end the threat to distrain property in the Steelyard would have been more effective. It must be presumed, therefore, that during Meyer's sojourn in England the basis was formed for an understanding with Lübeck. Initially, the object of English diplomacy was simply to prevent Lübeck from making peace with the Dutch and reconciling itself with the Emperor. The more Charles V was distracted the better pleased was Henry VIII. Imperial envoys attending a diet convened at Hamburg in March 1534 to negotiate peace were no doubt correct in their claim that it failed to achieve its objective largely because of the support given to Lübeck by

England. They were mistaken, however, in their statement that 30,000–40,000 angels had already been promised to Lübeck to sustain a war against the Emperor. To be sure, Henry VIII seems actively to have encouraged such rumours and even exaggerated the size of the proposed subsidy. He tried to get Francis I to contribute 50,000 crowns towards the cost of electing a pliant King of Denmark, claiming that he had given that much himself.[58]

In June 1534 envoys of Lübeck and Hamburg came to England and after lengthy talks the informal understanding with Lübeck was strengthened into an alliance. The main political objective was the election of Henry VIII or his nominee as King of Denmark. In aid of this project Lübeck was to be lent 20,000 guilders (about £3,333 6s 8d), but the king was reluctant to part with the money without receiving sureties for repayment from the Steelyard merchants, and final details had not been settled by late August. Each side also had other aims. The good doctors from Hamburg and Lübeck were hopeful of converting the king to the Lutheran faith, while he wanted facilities for recruiting German mercenaries to serve in Ireland. The envoys left England in September, evidently with some sort of draft treaty, but in May 1535 the king was complaining that this had not yet been ratified by Lübeck. In July, Edmund Bonner, Bishop of London, and Richard Cavendish were sent to north Germany, ostensibly to try to make peace between Lübeck and the newly elected Christian III, but really to watch over the king's interests. Attempts were made to draw England more deeply into the morass of Danish politics, and Henry prepared to send three warships to the Baltic. Then came news that Christian had arrested twelve or thirteen English vessels and pressed three of them into his service, so the king's ships were held back. Henry's cause, such as it was, was lost when Wullenwever was overthrown in October 1535, but it took some time longer to disengage totally. Lübeck's concern ended in February 1536, when it recognised Christian III as King of Denmark and he confirmed the city's commercial privileges in his lands.[59]

The factors which guided English policy towards Denmark and

[58] *L & P*, 5, no. 377; 6, nos. 428, 972, 1012–13, 1018, 1029, 1062, 1510; 7, nos. 394, 397, 697, 958.
[59] *L & P*, 7, nos. 737, 873, 957, 1060; 8, nos. 121, 759, 848, 1065; 9, nos. 287, 290, 434, 831. G. M. V. Alexander, 'The Life and Career of Edmund Bonner, Bishop of London, until his Deprivation in 1549' (Ph.D. thesis, London University, 1960), pp. 114–68.

the north-German towns in the mid-1530s were largely political, but economic matters were not forgotten. According to Chapuys, the resident imperial ambassador in England, Hamburg was less willing than Lübeck to send envoys to England in 1535 and did so only because commerce was also on the agenda.[60] Even so, Henry insisted that talks about trade concerned only England, Lübeck and Hamburg, not the Hanse as a whole. As Chapuys makes, clear, uppermost in English minds was the fear that Charles V was about to put a stop to trade between England and the Low Countries. This would have meant finding an alternative to Antwerp as a staple for English cloth. Now, as three decades later, the Merchant Adventurers were prepared to consider transferring their business to a north-German port, provided that they were assured of freedom of trade. Any hopes there may have been about secrecy were frustrated, since Chapuys reported that the Hamburg envoys intended to go home via Antwerp, where they proposed to have talks with the regent.

It is unlikely that the Steelyard community derived any tangible gain from the short-lived alliance between England and Lübeck, and within a little while it was again under pressure. Allegations of harassment for exporting unfinished cloth headed a long list of grievances submitted to Henry VIII by a Hanse diet which met in June 1540. Another was that the king's purveyors waited for ships coming from Danzig and Hamburg and took timber at unfair prices – clearly an echo of the great ship-building programme in which the crown was currently engaged. English merchants registered their own complaint at this diet about their treatment in Danzig. It dwelt on the age-old ban on trading with non-burgesses, and there is no evidence of any new restrictions having been recently introduced. The most likely explanation is that increasing numbers of Englishmen coming to Danzig simply strengthened their ambition to recover the long-lost liberties believed to have been enjoyed by their predecessors. Dissatisfaction continued to smoulder until January 1542, when a delegation came before the king's council with a 'book of complaints' against Danzig. Representatives of the Steelyard, who were summoned to answer the charges, denied their validity, but since none of those present were Danzigers they were ordered to write to the city and get a satisfactory rebuttal by Whitsun. A few

---

[60] *L & P*, 7, no. 871.

days later adventurers of the fishmongers' company complained to the council about Hamburg and Bremen, probably on account of clashes in Iceland. Because of the threat which these complaints posed to the franchises, an envoy of Lübeck, who arrived in June 1542 to discuss terms for repayment of the king's loan to the city, was empowered to suggest a full-scale Anglo-Hanseatic conference to settle all outstanding differences. This was accepted, Antwerp named as the venue and 1 November as the date. In September the Hansards begged to be excused from the engagement, on the grounds that disturbances which had broken out in Antwerp and lower Germany made the region unsafe. England was probably just as willing to cancel the conference, since the country was actively preparing for war with France and Scotland.[61]

In February 1543 Henry VIII concluded an alliance with the Emperor Charles V, though it was kept secret until May. In June, once Scotland seemed to be on the point of submission, he began hostilities against France. In September 1544 Henry was deserted by the Emperor, but England, now herself in grave danger of a French invasion, did not manage to disengage until June 1546. The threat was greatest in the spring and summer of 1545, so that Henry sought the assistance of the Protestant princes of Germany. In April of that year Christopher Mont and John Bucler were sent to try to forge an alliance with the princes and the King of Denmark, though the latter, because he was still at odds with the Emperor, was currently allied to France. The attitude of the German Protestants towards England was determined by the Emperor's intentions against them. As imperial pressure increased throughout the summer they leaned more towards England, so that by August they were almost ready to make a defensive alliance. A precondition was that Henry should deposit 200,000 crowns at Hamburg, to be used when or if the Emperor attacked the Protestants. In return the princes agreed that the king might recruit mercenaries in their territories, though since the Emperor controlled the land routes to Calais these would have to be shipped at Hamburg or Bremen. In July John Dymmock, one of Henry's agents in the Low Countries, went north to try to arrange transport, but it was a fruitless mission. The Landgrave of Hesse had predicted that the Hanse towns would consider nothing more than a defensive alliance, but Dymmock did not find them even that accommodating. A French ambassador had preceded him and they

[61] *L & P*, 15, no. 855; 16, no. 392; 17, nos. 736, 1146. *POPC*, 7, pp. 301, 307, 317. *APC*, 1, p. 11. *DI*, nos. 1317, 1362, 1378–9, 1404.

now declared their neutrality. Pleading an imperial ban on the recruitment of mercenaries they refused either to provide ships or to allow embarkation at their ports. On the other hand they claimed that they had stopped trading with the Scots and would not start again. Dymmock also managed to get permission for five shiploads of victuals and fish to sail from Hamburg to England and four shiploads of corn from Bremen. The latter was originally intended for Lisbon, but was held back after reports that the French were seizing similar south-bound shipments on the excuse that they might fall into English hands.[62] Apart from these provisions the only help that Henry got from the German Protestants as a result of his overtures in 1545 was an unsuccessful attempt to mediate between him and Francis I. Their concern was to put an end to the strife between the only two powers likely to help them when the Emperor finally made up his mind to crush them.

The peace made between England, France and Scotland in June 1546 was so fragile that Henry VIII continued to flirt with the German Protestants, though his true intentions towards them are obscure.[63] Increasingly, the princes became the suitors as the Emperor gained the upper hand over them. After Henry's death in January 1547 the new government was doctrinally sympathetic, but had to tread even more warily so as not to upset the Emperor. The latter was urged by the Pope to support the claim of his cousin, Mary Tudor, to the English throne. Charles was not disposed to do anything so rash, but it would be dangerous for England to help the Protestants too openly. This was foremost in the minds of the council in March 1547 when it received an embassy from the Duke of Saxony and his allies requesting financial aid. A promise was made that if the Protestant league, which included Lübeck, Hamburg and Bremen, lasted through the summer then, in three or four months' time, it would receive a loan of 50,000 crowns. Because of the need for secrecy the loan would be made through the merchants of the Steelyard, and could be represented as an advance payment for naval stores. For the English this had the added advantage that Hanseatic trade would provide security for repayment. The stratagem was never put to the test, for on 21 April 1547 Charles V smashed the Schmalkaldic League at the battle of Mühlberg. Despite this reverse the political stance of the Hanse towns continued to be significant, particularly after Protector Somerset invaded

---

[62] *L & P*, 20, nos. 46, 69.   [63] Scarisbrook, *Henry VIII*, pp. 601–3.

Scotland in September 1547. The towns had to be dissuaded from assisting the Scots, either by way of trade or more directly. Fortunately, the new government had behaved circumspectly towards the Hanse. In June, Henry VIII's charter of 1510 was confirmed and this was repeated in December. Moreover, when in November the Merchant Adventurers persuaded the government to suspend the ban on the export of unfinished cloth, the Steelyard merchants were given the same privilege until Christmas. It may have been with some confidence, therefore, that in December 1547 William Watson, the late king's chief agent for purveying Baltic goods, was commissioned to seek the cooperation of Hamburg, Bremen and Lübeck. The following month he reported that he had received assurances from the towns and was satisfied that they were not acting against English interests. However, in March 1548 Dr Nicholas Wotton reported a rumour that the King of France had sent money to Hamburg, Lübeck and other Hanse towns to victual his troops aiding the Scots. Throughout 1548 and into 1549 the Hansards continued to protest they were not involved with the French or Scots, but at the same time refused actively to help England. They again declined the use of their ships and ports for the embarkation of mercenaries, pleading that if they did so their own vessels would be attacked by the French and Danes. Eventually, in May 1549 the Hamburg senate agreed to allow the secret embarkation of mercenaries at Friburg, a small port some seven leagues from their city.[64]

Despite the lack of Hanse cooperation some German mercenaries saw service in the English army in Scotland, and in any event the Hanse could hardly be blamed for the ignominious peace terms accepted in 1550. No doubt resentment was harboured in England, but this cannot be related directly to the blow struck against the Steelyard at the beginning of 1552, particularly since by then Somerset had himself fallen from grace. The new moves were based on commercial and fiscal considerations. An English government had finally steeled itself to execute the plan considered by Wolsey thirty years previously. This was the beginning of the end of the Hanseatic privileges, though in the event it took longer than anticipated to remove them entirely. That is the theme of the last chapter of this book.

[64] *APC*, 2, pp. 60–1, 142–3, 189. *SPF*, 1547–53, pp. 14, 28, 30–1, 33.

Any attempt to describe in a few pages the whole of England's overseas trade between 1474 and the middle of the sixteenth century would be presumptuous. Fortunately, the convention of using cloth exports as an indicator of trade is particularly useful now. In the long run, exports of raw wool continued their remorseless decline, while those of cloth finally realised their earlier promise and came to dominate the export trade completely. Most historians of the late Yorkist and Tudor age have agreed that cloth exports provide the key to an understanding of England's overseas trade. This is particularly true with regard to the Hanseatic share. Far more than in the case of either Englishmen or other aliens, they depended on cloth exports; imports played a declining role in their trade.

The late 1460s and most of the 1470s were a period in which England's cloth exports as a whole marked time (table 15). Hanseatic exports, sustained only by Cologne merchants during wartime, fell to a very low ebb and recovered only slowly after the treaty of Utrecht. Denizen trade, which showed great promise after the ending of the Burgundian boycott in 1467, was blighted by political unrest during the years of Warwick's rebellion and the restoration of Henry VI, and again made a slow recovery. Only the alien sector was buoyant, performing better than it had done since the early 1450s and as well as it was to do until the sixteenth century. A turning-point occurred about 1477, when total exports moved up quickly to the level of the prosperous decade following the Vorrath treaty of forty years earlier. This established what may be regarded as a normal level of trade for the rest of the fifteenth century. It is customary to describe the reign of Henry VII as the beginning of England's domination of international woollen markets, but there was no real leap forward until the end of the century. Earlier than that, but not until Henry had been on the throne for three years, trade simply recovered from a six-year trough into which it had fallen towards the end of Edward IV's reign. That recession was due entirely to the very poor performance of denizen merchants. Even after 1488 the latter did not perform well and until the end of the century their exports, both in absolute figures and as a market share, were significantly down on the years 1477–82. The real achievers were the Hanse merchants, who held their trade in the 1480s and, despite harassment in the matter of unfinished cloth, increased it substantially in the 1490s.

Taken as a whole, the last quarter of the fifteenth century may be

Table 15. England's cloth exports, 1468–1546ᵃ

	Overall total		Denizen			Hanse			Alien		
	Total	Change (%)	Total	Share (%)	Change (%)	Total	Share (%)	Change (%)	Total	Share (%)	Change (%)
1468–74	36,338		22,000	61		2,938	8		11,400	31	
1474–7	41,411	+14	23,384	56	+6	7,713	19	+163	10,314	25	−10
1477–82	59,967	+45	36,848	62	+58	12,288	20	+59	10,831	18	+5
1482–8	46,265	−23	23,200	50	−37	12,445	27	+1	10,620	23	−2
1488–99ᵇ	57,386	+24	30,679	54	+32	15,611	27	+25	11,096	19	+4
1499–1507	77,953	+36	45,268	58	+48	17,613	23	+13	15,072	19	+36
1507–20	88,153	+13	49,625	56	+10	19,973	23	+13	18,555	21	+23
1520–3	75,943	−14	44,583	59	−10	16,721	22	−16	14,639	19	−21
1523–30	93,456	+23	56,763	61	+27	20,591	22	+23	16,102	17	+10
1530–2	84,293	−10	46,157	55	−19	21,086	25	+2	17,050	20	+6
1532–8	102,816	+30	61,879	60	+34	29,079	28	+38	11,858	12	−21
1538–46	119,081	+17	56,308	47	−9	28,334	23	−3	34,439	30	+190

ᵃ Using Bridbury's figures until 1544. When he declines to give an annual total (because of gaps in Bristol accounts) figures have been calculated from *England's Export Trade*, and 2,000 p.a. estimated for Bristol. For 1544–6 figures are taken from J. D. Gould, *The Great Debasement* (Oxford, 1970), appendix C, p. 173.
ᵇ Excluding years 1494–6, because of gap in London accounts.

said to have had an export ceiling of 60,000 cloths a year, no higher than that of the 1440s. The ceiling was raised when the average rose to 78,000 a year in 1499–1507. All three sectors moved ahead, but it may be noted that, while denizens gained most in absolute numbers, their trade was still only 23 per cent up on 1477–82, compared with an alien increase of 39 per cent and a Hanse increase of 43 per cent. In 1507–8 total exports for the first time exceeded 90,000 and did so again in six of the next twelve years, giving an average of 88,000. All three sectors contributed to the surge, but the palm for achievement should probably be awarded to aliens, who were, of course, still handicapped by fiscal discrimination. The early 1520s saw a two- to three-year recession, felt by all groups of exporters and probably a consequence of the war with France. After 1523 trade recovered and exports averaged over 93,000 a year down to 1530. Now the best performers were denizens, increasing their market share at the expense of aliens, whose exports were below those of 1507–20. The 1530s began with a two-year recession, restricted to the denizen sector, but this was followed immediately by the breaching of a 100,000 ceiling. Between 1532 and 1538 exports averaged almost 103,000 a year. Two years into this period alien exports slumped badly, falling back to fifteenth-century levels. The chief beneficiaries were Hanse merchants, whose exports were up 41 per cent on the level of the 1520s, compared with a rise of 9 per cent in the denizen sector.

The slump in other alien cloth exports was dramatically reversed by a change in customs rates made by royal proclamation on 26 February 1538 with effect from 6 April.[65] It was decided that for an experimental period of seven years aliens would be required to pay only denizen rates on all imports and exports. The motive for this is uncertain, though in September 1540 Chapuys, the imperial ambassador in London, claimed that the step had been taken 'for fear of war and stoppage of trade'.[66] It is just possible that the exercise was undertaken to see whether the reduction in alien rates would generate enough extra trade to increase total revenue. On the other hand it is doubtful whether statistical techniques at that time were sufficiently advanced to analyse the result accurately. The government was obviously concerned to monitor the effect on revenue, and it was calculated that in the first year and a half the

---

[65] P. L. Hughes and J. F. Larkin (eds.), *Tudor Royal Proclamations* (Newhaven and London, 1964), I, pp. 281–3.   [66] *L & P*, 16, no. 5.

total amount of custom remitted to aliens was £15,450 9s 3d.[67] There is no evidence of any attempt to estimate how much of this loss was offset by the increase in the amount of basic tax paid. Early in 1540 parliament sought to mitigate some of the consequences of the grant by ruling that the concession should only be allowed to aliens who imported or exported in English ships, Hanse merchants excepted. Because retaliation was anticipated, enforcement of the ordinance was delayed until September 1540. Inevitably, reprisals led to counter-reprisals. In December the Emperor prohibited all merchants trading within his dominions from lading in English ships. England countered by forbidding Dutch merchants to trade in their own ships even if no English vessels were available, and then imposed further restrictions on trade with the Low Countries, including a ban on the export of wool. The Emperor's response was a ban on the export of munitions of war desperately needed by England at this time. By June 1542 the futility of the action was obvious and England agreed that merchants of Spain and the imperial Low Countries should be exempt from the provisions of the recent navigation act.[68]

The experiment in customs equalisation was allowed to run the full seven years but was not renewed, so that the former rates of duty were then restored. In the interim both Hanse merchants and other aliens were relieved of the petty custom of 3d in the pound on general merchandise imported and exported, while the latter also gained from the ending of discriminatory poundage on tin, pewter and hides and custom of wine. However, the biggest gain was experienced by other alien exporters of cloth, where the specific custom of 2s 9d per short-cloth was cut back to 1s 2d and the poundage of 5 per cent *ad valorem* was completely abolished. This had an immediate and lasting effect on alien exports, chiefly at the expense of denizens. In 1538–9 denizens exported 49,588 cloths compared with 65,229 the previous year, while aliens exported 33,145 compared with 7,717. From 1538–46 denizen exports averaged 56,308 compared with 61,879 over the previous six years, those of aliens 34,439 compared with 11,858. Hanse exports suffered only a slight decline, averaging 28,334 compared with 29,079. Although the general political and military situation in the 1540s was worse than in the 1530s the combined exports of all three groups increased from an average of

<hr />

[67] *L & P*, 16, no. 90.   [68] *L & P*, 16, nos. 374, 484, 511, 524, 838; 17, no. 440.

102,816 in 1532–8 to 119,081 in 1538–46. This strongly suggests that the reduction in alien rates of duty did not simply transfer trade from denizens to aliens, but was directly responsible for a real increase in exports.[69] On the other hand when alien exports collapsed after the end of the experiment in equal customs rates, total exports did not fall back to earlier levels. Exact figures cannot be established because of gaps in the customs records,[70] but alien exports are unlikely to have been much more than 16,000 in 1546–7, even if they reached that figure, while their annual average between 1547 and 1552 cannot have exceeded 3,500. Total denizen exports are not known for 1546–7 and 1548–9, since the London figures do not survive in these years. But for the other years between 1547 and 1552 denizen exports averaged around 85,500, surpassing all previous totals. Hanse exports were also at an all-time record, averaging 41,795 from 1546 to 1551. Then in December 1551 the Merchant Adventurers and the government mounted a fierce attack on the Hanse franchises which brought their trade to a standstill, so that the export figure for 1551–2 was a mere 13,824. The continued buoyancy of total cloth exports after the removal of the incentive to alien trade in 1545 suggests that one or more new factors had been introduced. That which has received most attention is the possibility that currency depreciation cheapened the price of English cloth in overseas markets and so stimulated sales. Fisher contended that depreciation of the pound sterling against the Flemish pound had for many years been the chief factor stimulating cloth exports. This view was rejected by Stone and Gould.[71] Gould made a very detailed examination of the possible effects of exchange depreciation upon exports during the currency debasements of the 1540s. He concluded that even now it was not a significant factor, except perhaps for a short period towards the end of that decade.

The arrangement made for the liquidation of the indemnity agreed in the treaty of Utrecht, namely the assignment to Steelyard officials of the petty custom paid by Hanse merchants, provides for a few years a more complete picture of Hanse trade than in any

---

[69] J. D. Gould, *The Great Debasement* (Oxford, 1970), p. 147, is firmly of the opposite opinion. But he overlooks the fact that aliens received an abatement of poundage as well as the reduction in custom.

[70] For cloth export figures in the late 1540s and 1550s see *ibid.*, pp. 173–81.

[71] F. J. Fisher, 'Commercial Trends and Policy in Sixteenth Century England, *EcHR*, 10 (1940), 95–117. L. Stone, 'State Control in Sixteenth Century England', *EcHR*, 17 (1947), 103–20. Gould, *Great Debasement*, pp. 114–60.

Table 16. *Hanse trade, 1474–86**

	Excluding Cologne*ᵃ*, 1474–8			Including Cologne, 1478–86		
	Merchandise (£)	Cloths	Wax (cwt)	Merchandise (£)	Cloths	Wax (cwt)
London*ᵇ*	8,478	4,816	1,111	19,705	11,607	1,880
Provinces	2,641	1,128	47	5,006	955	34
Total	11,129	5,944	1,158	24,711	12,562	1,914

* Twelve-monthly averages.
ᵃ Cologne cloths 2,528, London.
ᵇ 5 June 1475–4 July 1478.

earlier period. The general starting date for the retention of the custom was 5 June 1475, but many ports outside London effectively distinguish between Hanse and other alien payments from the previous autumn. Until 19 November 1478 the crown kept the custom of Cologne merchants for itself, but thereafter allowed it to go towards the indemnity. This increased the rate of repayment, but has the side effect of obscuring the distinction between Cologne and non-Cologne trade. Once the indemnity was fully paid, which happened very early in Henry VII's reign, no purpose was served by continuing to record Hanse customs payments separately from those of other aliens, and the practice was gradually abandoned port by port. It was not revived until 1538. Full details of Hanse trade are given in appendix 2, but a summarised version is given in table 16.[72] The latter does not go beyond the autumn of 1486, since at that point the normal pattern of trade was distorted by the Anglo-Burgundian dispute.

The effects of the isolation of the Cologners may be gauged from their cloth exports, which were fewer than they had been during the Anglo-Hanseatic dispute and less than half the present exports on non-Cologne merchants. Little can be said about their imports, since at London their customs payments on general merchandise were usually combined with those of other aliens. The only Cologne trade at provincial ports was 33 cloths at Ipswich in 1477–8 and a small amount of merchandise at Sandwich, which in 1476–8 totalled

[72] Derived from enrolled customs accounts, PRO, E356/22–3.

£118. The non-Cologne merchants maintained a regular trade at
Hull, Boston, Lynn, Ipswich and Sandwich, but well over 80 per
cent of their business was carried on at London. It is likely that these
merchants had a slight surplus of exports over imports, though the
exact size cannot be determined. The main problem is that of
estimating the value of Hanse cloth exports. The figure of £1 per
cloth generally used by Hull customs officials in this period is far too
low for an overall average, but the £4,005 valuation set upon 1,138
cloths exported from London between 21 August and 17 September
1485 gives almost £3 10s each, which is too high. Putting the overall
average at £2 (possibly on the low side) gives an annual value of
around £12,000, to which may be added £1,100 for other exports
(estimated at 10 per cent of all merchandise paying the *ad valorem*
duty). Import values consist of £10,000 for the remaining
merchandise and £2,300 for wax (estimated at £2 per cwt). Wine
imports are ignored, since no figures are available, but they were not
substantial. The annual shortfall of imports was therefore in the
region of £800. A similar exercise covering the years 1478–86 (but
now including Cologners) gives cloth exports of around £25,000,
other exports of £2,500, merchandise imports of £23,100 and wax of
£3,800, the shortfall being still around £800. Allowing for margins
of error one way or the other it may be concluded that in the early
1480s Hanseatic trade was either roughly in balance or carried a
slight export surplus.

The next opportunity to value Hanse trade comes as a result of the
customs equalisation of 1538. Throughout the seven years' experiment the Exchequer kept a record of customs remitted, and for
most of that time those of Hansards were kept separate from those of
other aliens.[73] In London imports and exports were recorded
separately, but not in other ports; the latter have been allocated in
the same ratio as the former (table 17). At this date cloths cannot be
valued at less than £3 each, which gives an annual bill of around
£80,500. Exports of other goods averaged around £1,700. To
support this trade Hanse merchants imported around £17,600 of
general merchandise and 890 cwt of wax, which has been valued at
50s per cwt, giving a total value for all imports of around £20,000.
This is less than the comparable figure for the 1480s. Wax imports
were currently only one third of those in 1532–8, when the average

---

[73] See tables in Schanz, *Englische Handelspolitik*, 2.

Table 17. Hanse trade, 1538–44

	Exports				Imports			
	Cloths		Merchandise (£)		Merchandise (£)		Wax (cwt)	
	London	Provinces	London	Provinces	London	Provinces	London	Provinces
1538–9	31,143	7	2,903	346	11,052	1,304	683	38
1539–40	27,261	54	1,473	132	21,909	2,061	679	159
1540–1	27,619	34	1,520	86	18,276	989	850	6
1541–2	23,412	58	751	88	12,538	1,373	542	0
1542–3	24,226	43	1,836	11	12,068	73	1,054	0
1543–4	27,052	21	1,046	27	23,340	655	1,330	0
Averages	26,786	36	1,588	115	16,531	1,075	856	34

was still 2,458 cwt, although even then the trade was much down on earlier years. The most likely explanation is that the influence of the Reformation had already led to a reduction in the demand for church wax, and then came the dissolution of the monasteries which removed many of the chief customers. The massive Hanse trade deficit, in the region of £60,000 or three times the value of the import trade, may have been at an all-time high in the 1540s, but had probably been growing steadily as imports failed to keep pace with the increase in cloth exports.

For the greater part of Henry VII's reign the total value of alien merchandise paying the 3d petty custom (including Hanse and mostly imports) grew comparatively slowly.[74] After 1500 the rate of increase speeded up until 1520, when a decline set in. From 1509 the London record (which accounts for around 80 per cent of the total) distinguishes between imports and exports. This enables us to calculate a rough, overall balance for alien trade (table 18). At first there was a slight deficit of exports which persisted even in the 1520s, when imports began to decline. Thereafter, the continued decline in imports and the growth of cloth exports produced a substantial export surplus, which became massive after 1538. In the last period the Hanse import deficit still exceeded that of other aliens, despite the great increase in cloth exports by the latter. This does not necessarily mean that Hansards had been responsible for all of the earlier decline in imports, but it supports the view that they were the weaker of the two groups on this front.

One of the reasons for the large adverse balance of Hanse trade in the sixteenth century was the failure of the London Steelyard to increase its imports sufficiently to compensate for the decline of the provincial *Kontore*. By the 1480s and throughout the first half of the sixteenth century substantial quantities of stockfish were brought to London, where its import had been insignificant when Boston had been the staple for this trade. Now Hamburg merchants were the dominant force and the fish came from Iceland rather than Bergen, but it did not equal the amount brought to Boston in its heyday. Later, the Londoners failed to take over the great import trade which was established at Hull in the early sixteenth century by Danzig merchants. When this was lost to the Hansards it probably fell into the hands of Englishmen. Of course, it would be unrealistic

Table 18. *Hanse and alien balance of trade, 1509–44*

	Imports					
	Merchandise (£)		Wax		Wine	
	London	Provinces[a]	Cwt	Value (£)[b]	Tuns	Value (£)[c]
1509–20	84,392	20,597	3,338	8,345	2,245	11,384
1520–3	70,182	14,317	2,102	5,255	1,941	10,664
1523–30	72,544	18,474	5,787	14,468	1,889	10,310
1530–2	61,567	17,936	1,992	4,980	3,118	15,345
1532–8	53,634	12,819	2,448	6,120	1,845	9,216
1538–44	51,338	13,757	856	2,140	2,096	12,535

	Exports						
	Cloth			Wool		Merchandise (£)	
	H	A	Valued (£)[d]	Sacks	Valued (£)[e]	London	Provinces[a]
1509–20	20,138	17,478	94,040	509	8,144	9,980	2,546
1520–3	16,721	14,639	78,400	710	11,360	6,396	1,245
1523–30	20,591	16,102	91,733	322	5,152	12,221	3,007
1530–2	21,086	17,050	95,340	544	8,704	9,142	2,680
1532–8	29,079	11,858	102,343	533	8,528	8,342	1,916
1538–44	26,821	29,250	168,213	438	7,008	12,486	3,439

	Balance		
	Total imports (£)	Total exports (£)	Surplus or deficit of imports (£)
1509–20	124,718	114,710	+ 10,008
1520–3	100,418	97,395	+ 3,023
1523–30	115,796	112,113	+ 3,683
1530–2	99,828	115,866	− 16,038
1532–8	81,789	121,129	− 39,340
1538–44	79,770	191,146	− 111,376

[a] Exports and imports separated in same proportion as those at London.
[b] Valued at 50s per cwt.
[c] Using values suggested by Schanz, namely non-sweet £4 per tun, sweet £6, malmsey, £10.
[d] Valued at 50s until 1538, £3 thereafter.
[e] Valued at £16 per sack, but possibly too low, since Italians now handled only the very finest wool.

to blame the Steelyard for this latter development. There would have been no point in trying to meet Yorkshire's demand for Baltic goods by importing them through London.

It is easy enough to describe the decline of the provincial *Kontore*, but it is more difficult to decide whether they failed from lack of support or because of circumstances beyond the control of the Hanse merchants. Even in the 1450s the role of London in Hanse trade far outweighed that of all the provincial ports, yet the delegates sent to Utrecht in 1473 were briefed on measures to safeguard the latter interests. As well as strengthening their title to the London Steelyard they gained similar rights to substantial properties in Boston and Lynn.[75] At Boston there had been an organised *Kontor* for two or three centuries and the Hanse may already have been in possession of the building in question, though there is no proof of this. At Lynn there does not seem to have been a recognised *Kontor* since the early fourteenth century and there is no evidence that the merchants held property in the town in 1468, though the possibility cannot be dismissed. Any hopes of re-establishing the former glory of the Boston *Kontor* were soon disappointed. From 1474 to 1485 there was a regular but modest trade, averaging 118 cloths a year and £365 in merchandise imported and exported. After a break of two years there was an irregular trade for a further dozen years or so, but after that the Hanseatics were finished with Boston. The return to Lynn was somewhat more long-lasting. From 1474 to 1508 cloth exports averaged 154 a year and were supplemented by other goods, which regularly included lead. Interest in the latter possibly means that the trade in general merchandise, averaging £551 between 1474 and 1490, contained more than the 10 per cent conventionally allotted to exports. Surviving particulars suggest that at first it was mainly Hamburg shippers and merchants who frequented Lynn, but from 1489 they were almost exclusively Danzigers.[76] After 1508 the level of cloth exports was much reduced, averaging only 29 a year down to 1529, when they virtually ceased. At Colchester there was still a Hanse settlement for some years after the treaty of Utrecht, but it failed to generate anything like the previous level of cloth exports from the town's own quay or at Ipswich. The average between 1474 and 1492 was 293, though that of the last six years of the period was

[75] A survey of the properties made in April 1476 is in *HUB*, 10, no. 477. See also V. Parker, *The Making of Kings Lynn* (London, 1971), pp. 114–17.
[76] PRO, E122/97/17; 98/2, 10, 16; 99/2, 6, 9.

as high as 473. The trade then came to an abrupt halt and it is likely that direct connections with this region were severed. Essex-Suffolk cloth was still popular in the Baltic region, but it was now exported from London and probably bought there as well.

The most thriving provincial centre of Hanse trade in the last decades of the middle ages was Hull. Here the merchants not only withstood the hostility of the townsmen in the early years of Henry VII's reign, but afterwards expanded their business, so that until 1530 it was greater than at any time since the beginning of the fourteenth century, when the port was used for Hanse wool exports. The trouble between the town and its visitors caused a big drop in cloth exports for half-a-dozen years, but cloth figures do not adequately tell the story of Hanse trade here. In fact, it is likely that the main impetus to trade did not come from exports, even when a considerable weight of lead was added to cloth, but from imports. Danzig merchants found a ready market for a wide range of east-Baltic products, and the trade imbalance about which Yorkshiremen complained in the first parliament of Henry VII persisted and worsened in the reign of his son, despite an overall increase in activity. From 1474 to Michaelmas 1486 Hanse cloth exports averaged 461 a year, while general merchandise, consisting predominantly of imports though already containing an element of lead exports, averaged £1,790 worth. In the next twelve months only 68 cloths were exported, while the average for the six years down to 1492 was 80. The record of general merchandise in this period, though incomplete, suggests that the import trade was more patchy than that in cloth, but overall not so depressed. In 1486–7 the merchandise total was still as high as £2,509 and in 1491–2 probably not far short of £2,000. Between times it was £319 in 1487–8, probably some £500–£600 in 1488–9 and £1,184 in 1489–90. The merchants disregarded the instruction of the diet to boycott Hull, and only in 1490–1 was there a complete absence of trade, with no cloth exports and almost certainly no other exports or imports.

Despite the failure of the Anglo-Hanse talks at Antwerp in 1491 the merchants returned in force to Hull the following year and may even have gained a temporary victory over the customs officers of the port. The Hanse delegates had complained about the levy of a great custom on lead and tin, by which they probably meant the imposition of poundage on top of the petty custom. In 1492–3 the merchants exported 146½ tons of lead from Hull, and the enrolled account duly notes that they paid £7 6s 3d in petty custom, but made no reference to poundage. This was the only year in which lead was mentioned in the enrolled accounts separately from other *ad valorem* merchandise, and if poundage had been levied one might expect to find a note to this effect. The customers were obviously unsure of their case, but the silence about poundage probably means that it was not paid this year. The Hanse merchants were still discriminated against in so far as their lead was valued at £4 a ton, whereas that of denizens was always rated at £3 6s 8d. In any event the apparent victory was short-lived, for by the beginning of Henry VIII's reign Hanse merchants were again being charged petty custom and poundage, a total of 5s per ton. This was a subject for renewed complaint at the Bruges conference of 1520.[77]

Between 1492 and 1509 Hanse cloth exports averaged 620 per annum and 697 from 1510 to 1521. The fall to 77 in 1509–10 was either a side-effect of the current clash between Denmark and Lübeck or of Henry VIII's apparent hesitation in confirming the Hanse franchises, or a combination of both factors. In the same year exports from London plummeted and than as abruptly recovered. In 1510–11 cloth exports from Hull totalled 1,150, while around 250 tons of lead, valued at £1,000, was exported.[78] Export values, however, fell far short of general imports worth £7,139 and 171 cwt of wax, the latter pushing the total to over £7,600. This year's cloth exports were the highest ever recorded at Hull in a twelve-month period, but imports were probably higher in 1514–15 and as high in 1516–17. The total value of merchandise paying the petty custom, overwhelmingly Hanseatic and predominantly imports, was £9,190 in 1510–11, £10,768 in 1514–15 and £9,226 in 1516–17; Hanse wax imports in the latter two years were 231 cwt and 94 cwt. The averages for the entire period 1510–21 were £7,186 (Hanse and other alien) and 239 cwt of Hanse wax. These figures establish beyond any doubt that there was a large surplus from the massive imports brought to Hull every summer in a fleet of up to a dozen Danzig ships.

On 2 October 1521 a Danzig ship left Hull with 19 cloths,[79] but in the next two summers the usual fleets failed to arrive and Hanse trade was at a complete stop until after Michaelmas 1523 or even

---

[77] *HR*, III (ii), no. 506; (v), no. 337.
[78] PRO, E122/60/3. The precise figure for lead is not recoverable, because of damage to the ledger. [79] PRO, E122/64/6.

until the following summer. This was presumably a result of the failure of the Bruges conference and Wolsey's threat to cancel the franchises. But once their fear on this count was removed the Danzigers returned, cloth exports averaging 530 between 1523 and 1530, general merchandise £5,146 (including other alien) and Hanse wax 283 cwt. After Michaelmas 1530 cloth exports fell abruptly, a year or so after the abandoning of Lynn. In 1533–4 they recovered temporarily to 622, but the overall average from 1530 to 1546 was only 99. There is no obvious reason for this change in commercial practice and, although the Hanse diet of 1530 complained about harassment over the export of unfinished cloth, it is unlikely that Yorkshire cloth was sufficiently valuable to fall within the scope of the law. The Danzigers tried, with limited success, to maintain their imports and these did not fall so much as cloth exports. The average for all alien merchandise from 1530 to 1538 was £3,543 while from 1538 to 1546 the Hanse average was £1,278 and that for other aliens £533. Danzigers retained a favourable balance of trade, but their reluctance to export cloth, and quite possibly lead, must have made it more difficult to dispose of imports, many of which may have depended on semi-barter arrangements. On 2 October 1531 a Danzig ship departed with a piece of worsted and coney skins worth £18 and 56 cloths, the entire cloth export for 1531–2.[80] No Danzig ships came the following summer, but a Hamburg vessel brought in £64 of Baltic wares in July and then seems to have been sold to a Danzig man, before leaving in August with $4\frac{1}{4}$ tons of lead and 24 chaldrons of sea coal. Two Danzig ships finally came in November 1532 with 54 cwt of wax and other goods worth £1,353.[81] They left in January with lead worth £15 7s, coverlets valued at 16s 8d, two cloths and £3 of denizen-owned lead. Four more Danzig ships came in April with 86 cwt of wax and merchandise valued at £1,719, while in May two Königsberg ships brought 8 cwt of wax and £733 of other wares. All of these ships left before the end of May, having acquired only 17 cloths and £103 of lead. More importantly, they re-exported ashes and tar worth £53 and $45\frac{1}{2}$ cwt of wax and were illegally made to pay duty on them. The ashes and tar were charged 3d in the pound, but the collectors seem to have baulked at levying the specific duty of 1s per cwt on the wax and valued it at £2 per cwt, so the

---

[80] PRO, E122/64/10.　　　　　[81] PRO, E122/202/6.

merchants escaped with 6d per cwt. Notwithstanding this surfeit of imports three more Danzig ships came in June and two in July, bringing another £3,558 in wares and 239 cwt of wax. None of these ships left before Michaelmas, and it is impossible to check whether they took away any of the imports. Part of their profits were invested in some, or all, of the 622 cloths which, as already mentioned, were the last major consignment of Hanse cloth from Hull. It is also significant that never again did Hanse imports in a single year approach anywhere near the amount brought between November 1532 and July 1533. The Prussian merchants must have realised that on this occasion they had overreached themselves and were not inclined to repeat the mistake. By the early 1540s denizen merchants were bringing as much Baltic produce to Hull as Prussians were (though their combined effort did not equal that previously brought by the Hansards alone) and Danzig shippers were happy to help them carry it.[82]

In the aftermath of the treaty of Utrecht there was a redistribution of trade among the Hanse towns represented in England, but not all the changes proved to be permanent. For the merchants of Cologne the treaty was a bitter blow. Should it be ratified they faced the prospects of being denied use of the Hanseatic privileges and of having to surrender the London Gildhall, which had been theirs for some 300 years. Before and after the February 1474 meeting at Utrecht they pestered their English friends to intercede with the king and persuaded the imperial authorities to do the same. Edward's initial misgiving at his abandonment of Cologne turned to impatience when the city persisted in showering him with recriminations. He blamed it for failing to make its own peace with the Hanse in the interval which had elapsed since the exclusion of the city was first mooted. Nevertheless, he continued to provide a breathing space. When the current grant of privileges to Cologne expired at Easter 1474 it was first continued until 31 July, and then further extended until such time as the king should recall it. In fact, the grant was not revoked. Meanwhile the city was desperately seeking to be reconciled with the Hanse, playing upon the sympathy of its Westphalian neighbours and again invoking the mediation of the imperial authorities. Reconciliation was the more imperative because in the summer of 1474 all the Burgundian lands were closed

---

[82] See below p. 288.

to Cologne merchants, in consequence of a quarrel between the duke and the Emperor. This meant that Cologne's overseas trade, including that with England, had to be conducted through Hanseatic ports and was dependent on letters of safe-conduct, which were requested from Hamburg, Bremen, Stade, Groningen and Kampen.[83]

At the beginning of October 1474 Herman Wanmate and Arnold Brekerfield, appointees of the Hanse delegates at Utrecht, came to London to take possession of the Steelyard. This was still held by the Cologne men, for, although the king had originally ordered them to vacate the premises by 31 July, they obtained an extension and did not finally leave until December. Thereafter, they continued to wrangle with the new occupants about things they had left behind, such as glass in the windows of the chambers. For Gerard von Wesel, leader of the Cologners, loss of face weighed more heavily than financial loss, since his windows depicted his family coat of arms and now he feared that his enemies gloated at them. Wanmate and his associates did not actually take possession until April 1475, the delay being caused by the transfer of legal titles, settlement of quit rents and so forth. It will be remembered that by the terms of the treaty the merchants obtained the freehold of the entire Steelyard, which had grown considerably in area since the Gildhall was originally established. Another significant step forward was taken on 12 May, when the common council of London set its seal to a confirmation of all the privileges which the Hanse merchants had enjoyed in the city in former times. In October 1475 the merchants reported that England had now fulfilled all its treaty obligations, save for depriving Cologne of its use of the franchises and paying the £484 indemnity, which had been promised as an addition to the £10,000 being recovered from retention of their customs liability.[84]

The king's determination to keep faith with the Cologne merchants is perhaps slightly surprising, since he was thereby depriving himself of the revenue which would otherwise have accrued from their liability to tunnage and poundage. Meanwhile the city was still seeking reconciliation with the Hanse. After the failure of the overture of 1474 it appealed to a diet which met at Lübeck in May–June 1476. On this occasion the request was denied, but many delegates were anxious that Cologne should be readmitted and it was decided to reconsider the matter at a diet due to be held

[83] *HR*, II (vii), nos. 209, 211, 215–16, 229–30, 279–80. *HUB*, 10, nos. 282, 318, 320, 371.
[84] *HR*, II (vii), nos. 257–9, 287–9, 311. *HUB*, 10, nos. 320, 386–9, 414–15.

at Bremen a few weeks later. Here in September, despite continued opposition from the *Kontore* of London and Bruges, the town representatives relented and Cologne was accepted back into the Hanse as a full member. The London merchants were ordered to admit Cologners into the Steelyard as soon as they returned its archives, which they had removed to Cologne in May 1474. They were also fined £250 sterling, which was to be settled by payment of double scot on their trade. But although Cologne was re-admitted to the Hanse in 1476 it took much longer to reconcile the rival factions in England. The northerners continued to exclude Cologners from the Steelyard, on the grounds that certain documents were missing from the archives. The bulk of these were restored in February 1477, but some items had been mislaid. Even after the discovery and return of one of the most prized items, Henry III's charter to the Gotland merchants, the resistance continued. As late as August 1478 the Cologners were still complaining that they had not yet been readmitted and there was again talk of applying to the king for a separate grant of privileges for their own organisation. However, in November 1478 the reconciliation was finally made, when the Cologne merchants agreed to pay £400 in place of the original £250 fine and also promised to do their best to find an important register that was still missing. The northerners last act of revenge was to exclude from the amnesty Gerard von Wesel and his sons. Not until October 1479 did the Wesels succeed in gaining a ruling from Lübeck and the Wendish towns that they should be readmitted to the Steelyard.[85]

It may be presumed that, in the absence of the Cologners, authority in the Steelyard would be shared out among the merchants of the leading towns, with some regard to their relative numbers and trade. In October 1475 the administrative council of twelve consisted of four merchants of Danzig, four of Hamburg, two of Soest, one of Münster and one of Nijmegen.[86] Diplomatically, the position of alderman was conceded to one of the Soest men, while Hamburg and Danzig supplied two deputies. This arrangement gave equal recognition to each of the thirds into which the late medieval Hanse was divided, but still poses certain questions. The absence of any representative of Dinant, whose citizens had been very active in London in the 1460s, is not particularly surprising, since its status as a Hanse town had always been ambivalent and remained so. In the

[85] *HR*, II (vii), nos. 347, 390, 406; III (i), nos. 31, 35–6, 169, 195. *HUB*, 10, no. 528.
[86] *HR*, II (vii), no. 311.

Anglo-Hanseatic conferences of the 1520s the English went so far as to claim that since the treaty of Utrecht Dinant had enjoyed customs concessions under false pretences. The omission of Lübeck is less easily explained, but if it betokens the absence of its merchants from London at this date the situation did not last long. They soon returned and remained active until the reign of Queen Elizabeth I. After their readmission to the Steelyard, Cologne merchants also returned in force and, as we have seen, were vociferous in their complaints about restrictions in cloth exports in the 1480s and 1490s. They remained a major element in the trade of the Steelyard, but had passed their relative peak before the mid-sixteenth-century crisis in Hanse affairs. The surviving London customs particulars are comparatively few in number, but each is vast in size and the precise identification of Hanse merchants depends on intimate local knowledge, which has not yet been applied to this task. Only Hamburg's share of the trade has been studied in detail, and that only for the reign of Henry VIII and later.[87] This shows that in 1513–14 Hamburg merchants handled 12 per cent of Hanse cloth exports from London, but 23 per cent, 21 per cent and 22 per cent in 1534–5, 1545–6 and 1553–4. Their proportion of the import trade cannot be given with such precision, but it was much greater than the former figures. The dominant role played by Hamburg in the reign of Elizabeth was therefore not an entirely new phenomenon; it had been becoming ever more prominent since the 1460s.

There is no evidence that in the late fifteenth century Hanse imports from the Baltic region were burgeoning. This being the case it might seem that there was plenty of scope for enterprising English merchants. Yet accepted historical opinion holds that the treaty of Utrecht effectively closed the door to Prussia against Englishmen, and in so doing was one of the factors which prompted them to target their cloth exports at the fairs of the Low Countries. Against this it must be emphasised that by the 1460s denizen cloth exports to the Baltic were at such a low ebb that the total deflection of an equivalent amount to the Low Countries in the late 1470s would have had marginal significance for the latter region. It must also be repeated that the treaty of Utrecht made no real difference to the legal status of English merchants in Prussia or elsewhere in the Baltic. Had they wished they could have resumed their trade under the same constraints as had existed for many years before the war.

[87] K. Friedland, 'Hamburger Englandfahrer, 1512–57', *Zeitschrift des Vereins für Hamburgische Geschichte*, 46 (1960), 1–42.

If denizen trade continued to stagnate in the late fifteenth century, as it probably did, then explanations must be sought either in factors outside the Baltic region, or in conditions there which do not involve the legal status of Englishmen in Prussia. In the latter category the most obvious choice is the state of relations between England and Denmark. Whenever the King of Denmark closed the Sound to Englishmen or licensed privateers to attack their ships then denizen trade with the Baltic was bound to suffer. In 1473 the hostilities which had begun in 1468 were terminated by a series of short truces, the last of which expired on 30 September 1482. The truce was not then renewed and, even before it expired, Denmark had closed the Sound. On the other hand, the fact that English merchants had less to fear from the Danes in the 1470s did not necessarily mean that they flocked to the Baltic. The bitter memory of 1468 must have remained with them. Danzig harbour accounts for 1474–7 record two ships coming from England in the first year, seven in the second and twelve in the third, but none of them seem to have been English.[88] They freighted very little English cloth, though substantially more was brought to Danzig from Lübeck, probably having arrived there by way of Hamburg. English ships did return to the Baltic, however; in November 1481 two Lynn ships returned home with cargoes belonging to both denizen and Danzig merchants.[89] Englishmen also shipped in Hanse vessels until the King of Denmark put a stop to this in September 1482. Correspondence between him and Danzig in 1483 referred to English merchants stranded in the city, because they could not obtain safe-conduct to repatriate their goods.[90]

Peace talks between England and Denmark began in August 1489 and a treaty was sealed in January 1491, but in the intervening years the Baltic was not entirely empty of English ships. Most of the credit for keeping the flag flying should probably go to the men of Lynn. In November 1483 a Lynn ship returned home with wax belonging to a Danzig merchant, probably having broken the Danish blockade.[91] Evidence of Lynn ships in the Baltic after that date comes from the Antwerp conference of 1491.[92] Lynn merchants then submitted claims against the Hanse for losses totalling £2,308 in thirteen incidents since 1485. In a majority of cases there are positive

---

[88] W. Lauffer, 'Danzigs Schiff und Wahrenverkehr am Ende des XV Jahrhunderts', *Zeitschrift des Westpreussischen Geschichtsverein*, 33 (1894), 8.   [89] PRO, 122/97/17.
[90] *HUB*, 10, nos. 1003, 1028, 1036–7.   [91] PRO, E122/98/2.
[92] *HR*, III (ii), no. 511.

statements, or prima-facie evidence, indicating Baltic trade. The
Anne and her cargo (£546) were seized and some men killed while
returning from Danzig; William Dreve was robbed while sailing
from Prussia in 1489; William Dalle was robbed and imprisoned on
the way home in 1490. Richard Paskelle bought a ship in Prussia in
1490 and was robbed while coming home, though apparently
keeping the ship. Two denizen merchants freighted in a Danzig ship
coming to Lynn in May 1490.[93] All this does not prove a large trade;
moreover, denizen cloth exports from Lynn to all destinations
averaged only 90 a year between 1482 and 1492. Hull's cloth trade
was not so badly decayed as that of Lynn, but Yorkshiremen had
abandoned Prussia even more completely. Their claims submitted in
1491 totalled £8,381, but there is no evidence that any related to
losses in the Baltic.[94] On the contrary, most are specifically located
elsewhere, the worst being the seizure of three ships coming from
Poitou, with a loss of £3,000 and forty men killed or wounded. It was
this incident which provoked the threat to impound the next Hanse
ship coming to Hull, and obviously no Yorkshire ship would risk
going to the Baltic. It is perhaps indicative that even in the mid-
1470s the York mystery of mercers, once so prominent in the English
company in Prussia, made no reference to that body in an ordinance
regulating payments to be made to the gild by masters and
apprentices at various marts. Those mentioned were Bruges,
Antwerp, Barrow and Middelburg, indicating that Yorkshire's cloth
trade was now geared to the Low Countries.[95]

The Anglo-Danish treaty of 1491 made it safer for English ships to
sail to the Baltic, and the next year the King of Denmark tried to
enlist England as an ally in his own dispute with the Hanse.[96]
Nevertheless, it is commonly asserted that English trade in the region
was now defunct, the earliest (though isolated) Sound toll register of
1497 being cited as evidence that no ships came into the Baltic that
year.[97] In fact, at the Bruges conference of 1499 the English
ambassadors raised the case of Roger Bussel of Hull, who claimed to
have been in Prussia in an English ship of 80 tuns in July 1497.[98] He
and his companions came to 'a place called Wistill' (the river
Vistula) to buy osmund and flax, where they were set upon for

---

[93] PRO, E122/98/10.   [94] *HR*, III (ii), no. 511.
[95] Sellers, *York Mercers*, p. 65.   [96] *HR*, III (iii), no. 84.
[97] N. E. Bang (ed.), *Tabeller over Skibsfart og Varetransport gennem Øresund, 1497–1660*
(Copenhagen, 1906), I, p. 2.   [98] See above, p. 247.

trading illegally. The Hanse delegates refused to entertain this charge, but their objection was based on the vagueness of the geography and the failure to name the alleged aggressors. There is nothing to disprove the claim that an English vessel was involved in an incident in Prussia in 1497. At the Bruges conference of 1521 the case was raised of another Hull vessel attacked some six miles from Danzig in 1500.[99] An even more interesting case raised on this occasion was an alleged seizure of English goods in Riga.[100] Few details were given, but the famulus of one Thomas Marten was said to have lost goods valued at 1,800 marks of Riga. The Hanse ambassadors commented that this incident was not recent, which may date it back to the 1490s, about the time of the proposed trade treaty with Riga. It was admitted that the property in question was arrested by the Grand Master of the Teutonic Order, but his action was a justifiable reprisal for the arrest in Hull of a Rostock ship in which he had merchandise of his own. Thomas Marten was in Danzig in 1517 and became involved in a legal suit which dragged on in Prussia and England from 1511 until the reign of Queen Elizabeth.[101] Scattered evidence of this sort suggests that, while English trade in the Baltic reached a very low ebb in the late fifteenth century, a precarious foothold was maintained. The corporate organisation of the merchants seems to have perished entirely. Yet there were probably a few individuals who persisted in the trade and were able to hand on experience, and possibly business contacts, from one generation to the next. This meant that when English interest in the Baltic revived in the sixteenth century it was not a totally new beginning. The later merchants did not simply inherit empty claims to privileges; they inherited knowledge of the Baltic provinces and their products, and skills in how to acquire them, a valuable legacy from the middle ages.

The build-up of trade in the sixteenth century may have come about much earlier than is generally appreciated. The second surviving Sound toll register (1503) records ten or eleven English ships in the Baltic, and the third (1528) about twenty-nine.[102] Other sources confirm the trading activities of the first two decades of the

---

[99] See above, p. 257. [100] *HR*, III (vii), no. 455.

[101] PRO, SP12/90/21. See below p. 356.

[102] *Tabeller over Skibsfart*, pp. 3–4. In the first half of the sixteenth century this source does not distinguish between ships entering and leaving the Baltic. On the assumption that most English ships going there returned safely in the same year the recorded total must be halved.

sixteenth century. Lynn merchants imported goods in a Danzig ship in 1504[103] and Lynn ships were attacked by Stralsund privateers in 1511. In August and September 1512 three Hull ships and one of Newcastle returned to Hull heavily laden with Baltic goods belonging to thirty denizen merchants.[104] When the Hull ships had sailed in April, probably bound for the Baltic, seventeen merchants had contributed to their cargoes of cloth, Scottish salt, coney skins and coverlets. Denizens imported in a Danzig ship at Hull in 1517–18, but there appear to have been no English ships coming there from the Baltic that year, nor in 1521–2.[105] At least one Hull ship made the voyage in 1525–6, but there are none which can be identified confidently in 1531–3.[106] In the early 1540s, ships of Hull, Beverley and Newcastle were employed in the trade and denizens were also importing in Danzig ships, great quantities of rye being brought in 1542.[107] The 1530s, when Danzig merchants seem to have retreated from trade with England, at least in Hull and Lynn, were probably decisive in strengthening the English stake in Baltic trade. In 1535 ships had to run the gauntlet of rival parties disputing the crown of Denmark. At Copenhagen on the outward voyage some were stopped by the Duke of Mecklenburg, a supporter of the deposed Christian II. As well as forcing them to assist him he seized much of their cloth to pay his troops, before allowing them to sail on to Danzig. When they returned in September the Sound was now under the control of Christian III, who arrested twelve or thirteen ships of London and Newcastle and detained three in his service. The merchants blamed rivals at Danzig for their second misfortune. Not only had they been restricted in what wares they might buy, they had been deliberately prevented from sailing until it was known that the Sound had changed hands and that they would be held there. While still detained in Denmark they wrote home urging the arrest of two Danzig ships making for Hull and three for London. Whatever the truth of this tale, a few days later Danzig wrote to Christian III requesting a safe-conduct for English and Dutch ships carrying the goods of Danzig merchants. The English government responded by an indiscriminate arrest of Hanseatic goods, though in the first week of November all but those belonging to Danzigers were released. The latter were detained until 2 February 1536. On 21 November Chapuys reported that some of the Danzig merchants

[103] PRO, E122/98/6.   [104] PRO, E122/64/2.
[105] PRO, E122/64/6; 202/4.   [106] PRO, E122/64/10; 202/6.
[107] PRO, E122/64/15–16.

were quite unperturbed by the arrest and felt sure that they would soon recover double the amount of both principal and interest on their losses. This meant, of course, that they believed the assets owned by Englishmen in Danzig to be greater than their own in England. English goods were still under arrest in Danzig on 25 April 1536, when the king wrote requesting their release.[108]

The troubles of 1535 and 1536 did little or nothing to stem the build-up of English trade in the Baltic. The first surviving sequence of Sound registers records 35 ships in 1536, 51 in 1537 and about 127 over the next five years. In 1543 and the following two years only one ship per year was recorded. This was presumably the result of the defensive alliance between Denmark and France, which required the closure of the Sound to enemies of France in time of war. In 1546 and 1547 seven and fourteen ships were registered, but none up to 9 March 1548, when there is a gap in the series which lasts until 1557. No amount of English cloth exported to the Baltic would justify well over 200 ships being sent there in 1536–42. The explanation is that the principal attraction of the region lay in the imports it provided, which were bulky and required a great volume of shipping. The chief commodities were grain and all manner of ships' stores, but above all cables. Twenty years later cables were still the most desirable merchandise.[109] Nearly half of all the ships (a hundred) belonged to the port of Newcastle, fifty-four belonged to London and way behind in third place was Lynn with fourteen. Newcastle ships doubtless brought grain to their home region, which was not self-sufficient in bread, and to provision northern garrisons, but many of their cargoes went to other English ports. The most likely explanation for the predominance of northern ship-owners is the fact that without a substantial export trade most vessels had to sail to the Baltic in ballast. Tyne coal admirably served this purpose, could be obtained cheaply and sold for a profit in the east. Scottish salt may have provided an alternative.

Because of his naval programme the most important single customer for Baltic imports was the king himself. In the 1530s his chief minister, Thomas Cromwell, had an active and personal interest in the region. He was frequently solicited for favours by Danzig merchants, who sent him presents, including live beavers and elks. In 1535 Richard Cavendish, one of the king's masters of

---

[108] *L & P*, 8, no. 1170; 9, nos. 246, 290–1, 323, 776, 861; 10, no. 283. *DI*, nos. 751, 867.
[109] W. Sharpe, 'The Correspondence of Thomas Sexton, Merchant of London, and his Factors in Danzig, 1550–1560' (M.A. Thesis, London University, 1952), *passim*.

ordnance, accompanied Bishop Bonner to Germany and was charged with buying up whatever naval stores he could lay his hands on. He corresponded directly with Cromwell about his success, one of his purchases being £600 of cable from a Riga merchant.[110] In 1538 William Watson was appointed royal purchasing agent in the Baltic and held this position for the rest of the reign and beyond. Official letters were regularly sent to Danzig asking the authorities to assist him to obtain naval stores for the crown. Watson's career as a Baltic merchant went back to at least 1531, since in 1543 he was in communication with a councillor of Lübeck, whom he described as having been his factor in that city for twelve years. On this occasion the councillor obliged Watson by helping him to get his own and the king's cloth off ships which he had been warned were to be attacked by the King of Sweden.[111] This incident, besides showing that the crown itself sent cloth to Prussia, proves that trade was not totally stopped during the current closure of the Sound, but continued on the Hamburg-Lübeck route.

The confirmation of the Hanse franchises by Edward VI inevitably led to a renewal of the demand for reciprocity by the growing numbers of English merchants trading with Prussia. Relations were further complicated by tension at sea – the usual accompaniment of war between England and Scotland. In the summer of 1547 English privateers seized two Stralsund ships chartered by Danzig merchants, while about the same time and in the same waters Hamburg sailors looted an English ship. The latter incident had serious repercussions, for when the Hamburg captain insolently displayed a captured English flag in Danzig it was rescued by Englishmen, who were thereupon imprisoned by the city authorities. This action alarmed the Steelyard merchants, who feared for their own privileges, and together with Lübeck urged Danzig to release the Englishmen, pay them compensation and acknowledge the principle of equal rights. Danzig very grudgingly made amends to those who had been imprisoned, but did nothing to remove the causes of more general dissatisfaction felt by English merchants. These continued to simmer until another quarrel developed in the summer of 1551. Now, 96 cloths belonging to Thomas Banaster were arrested in Danzig, as an indirect consequence of an alleged evasion of Sound duties. Smuggling, particularly of English cloth, had been a frequent subject of complaint

[110] *L & P*, 10, nos. 240, 527; 13, no. 1450; 14 (i) no. 60; (ii), no. 85.
[111] *L & P*, 18, no. 781. *DI*, no. 1161.

by the Danes in recent years. In October seventeen English merchants used the arrest of Banaster's cloth to make a general protest about their treatment in Danzig.[112] The dispute was beginning to grow to major proportions when it was overtaken by events in England. The Banaster affair may have been one catalyst, but it was probably less important than the question of cloth exports to the Low Countries, and the Merchant Adventurers were more instrumental than the Prussian traders in securing the downfall of the Hansards.

[112] *DI*, nos. 2051, 2056, 2059–61, 2064, 2067–75, 2084–6, 2367, 2370, 2375, 2378–9.

CHAPTER 6

The loss of the Hanse franchises, 1551–1611

The dispute between the Merchant Adventurers and the Hanse merchants revolved generally around exports of cloth and in particular around the role of Antwerp as a cloth mart and a source of imports. For the first few years of Edward VI's reign the Hansards successfully defended their stake in the trade. When their rivals persuaded the government to lift the restriction on the export of unfinished cloth, on the grounds that inflation had rendered it inoperable, the Hanse merchants were granted the same favour. In the summer of 1548 they were threatened with a withdrawal of this concession and the Steelyard ordered a ban on the export of all cloth to Zeeland and Brabant. Danzig protested that this action had not been sanctioned by the towns, to which the officials replied that it was designed to rouse English clothiers to support their rights.[1] The mere threat of a boycott seems to have been remarkably effective, since Hanse cloth exports in 1547–8 were the highest ever yet recorded. There was no more talk of discrimination and Hanse cloth exports continued their upward progress. In April 1550 came the first hint of the fact that Antwerp could not soak up an unlimited amount of English cloth. A group of clothiers complained that the Merchant Adventurers had abated prices, so that they were unable to dispose of their products without the loss of 20s on each piece. Summoned before the Privy Council the Adventurers decided that attack was the surest defence; foremost among their arguments was the claim that a big increase in the number of unskilled workers had resulted in overproduction and a decline in standards. They also said that since they presently held unsold stocks at Antwerp they could buy no more until these had been sold. After this the Antwerp market must have experienced a recovery, for in November 1551 the Adventurers were reported to be remarkably flushed with cash in

---

[1] *DI*, nos. 2118, 2151.

that city.[2] But at this very time their leaders were again plotting to exclude the Hansards from the cloth export trade. Their opportunity lay in the fact that the English government was currently facing a grave financial crisis and, as a partial solution, looked to Sir Thomas Gresham to refund its external debt. In the short term Gresham's activities were likely to be harmful to the Merchant Adventurers, so to buy them off the government was willing to support an attack on the Hanse.[3]

The weakest point in the Hanse defence lay in the activities of a group of merchants, chiefly though no exclusively from Cologne, who had virtually abjured their home towns to settle permanently in Antwerp. They nevertheless continued to claim the use of Hanse franchises both in Antwerp and London. Because of their close connections with other Antwerp residents these men were peculiarly tempted not only to trade with their own goods but to colour those of Dutch and Italian merchants operating from that city.[4] These 'renegades', who now contributed nothing towards the economy or charges of their home towns, were hardly less resented by loyal Hanse merchants than by Englishmen. On the other hand, it was difficult to control them and the most radical solution, which would have been to denounce them to the English government, was not an option since this would have endangered the whole organisation. This could be done, however, by the Merchant Adventurers, for the most certain way to provoke the crown into action was to convince it of the loss of revenue caused by colouring. As it turned out, the scandal of colouring was brought into the open in July 1551 by the death of Andreas Mohr, who was not one of the Antwerp exiles, but resided in the London Steelyard as factor for a Danzig firm. His papers showed that with the knowledge of his principals he had engaged in large-scale colouring of non-Hanse goods. This led firstly to the arrest of his firm's goods and then in November to a number of prosecutions in the court of the mayor of London alleging fraudulent customs practices.[5]

The Merchant Adventurers seized the opportunity presented by this exposure to mount a wholesale attack on the Hanse franchises. At the beginning of 1551 the Hansards had been routinely licensed

---

[2] *APC*, 3, pp. 19–20. G. D. Ramsay, *The City of London in International Politics at the Accession of Elizabeth Tudor* (Manchester, 1975), p. 62.

[3] Ramsay, *City of London*, pp. 51–3.   [4] *KI*, 1, nos. 605, 611–25.

[5] *KI*, 1, nos. 636, 646, *DI*, nos. 2357, 2387, K. Friedland, 'Der Plan des Dr. Heinrich Suderman zur Wiederstellung der Hanse', *Jahrbuch des Kölnischen Geschichtsverein*, 31–2 (1956–7), 193–4, 199–203.

to export cloth and to import Gascon wine until the following Christmas. During the course of the year Lübeck advised the removal of the Steelyard archives and treasury to Germany, though this seems to have been chiefly because of English domestic unrest, and no steps were taken to carry it through. When the time came for the licence to be renewed the Merchant Adventurers were ready to act. On 7 December a stop was put upon Hanse cloth exports and a few days later the Privy Council began to consider the case against them. On 29 December the Steelyard was given a copy of the charges and told to prepare a defence.[6] The case made by the Adventurers was that (1) all privileges claimed by the Steelyard were invalid in English law, since the merchants did not possess a sufficient corporation to exercise them; (2) none of their charters named particular individuals or towns so that there was no way of knowing who ought to enjoy the pretended privileges; (3) as a result the Steelyard admitted whomsoever it pleased, at a cost to the king's revenue of £17,000 a year; (4) even were the privileges valid the beneficiaries ought not to colour strangers' goods, as they allegedly did; (5) for 100 years after the grant of the pretended privileges the Hansards had been content to trade between their own ports and England, but now, despite a recognisance made in the reign of Henry VII, they meddled with the trade of the Low Countries; (6) the Hanse charters had been forfeited in the reign of Edward IV and renewed only upon condition that Englishmen should enjoy reciprocal rights, which were still denied.[7]

After the Hansards had delivered their defence a small committee headed by the Solicitor General was appointed to scrutinise it. The Privy Council discussed the matter on 9 February 1552, but deferred judgement until the 24th of that month. The decision then went against the Steelyard, the justification being precisely the case prepared by the Merchant Adventurers and described above. The franchises were suspended until such time as the merchants could produce proof that they ought to enjoy them; until then they were to trade on the same footing as all other aliens. Two ambassadors of the Wendish towns arrived in London three days before the verdict of the Privy Council was delivered and remained until July trying to get it reversed, but they gained only two concessions. These were that 2,857 cloths and 36 pieces of lead bought before the suspension might pay the old rates of duty if exported before 1 November, and

[6] *APC*, 3, pp. 86, 441, 453, *KI*, 1, nos. 610, 630, 734.
[7] PRO, SP10/14/10–11. BL, Add. MS 48019 fos. 125d–126d.

that until midsummer 1553 imports native to Hanseatic regions should be taxed only at traditional rates. The door was not closed upon further talks provided that they took place in England, and to this end the Hanse was invited to send a full-scale embassy.[8]

Immediately after its franchises were suspended the Steelyard demanded that all Hanse merchants should abstain from buying English cloth, either in England or in Antwerp. They also wanted all towns to take steps to prevent Hanse products from reaching England, whether at the hands of their own citizens, Englishmen or third parties, such as the Dutch. This boycott was confirmed, though not without vigorous debate, in a diet at Lübeck in November 1552. The crisis laid bare the conflicting interests of the member towns. Months before, and again at the diet, Cologne objected to the prohibition upon buying English cloth at Antwerp. It argued that this would simply result in Flemings and Brabanters buying more cloth and taking over the trade with upper Germany. Cologne supported the ban on exporting to England, since its merchants now had little stake in this trade. On the other hand the east-Baltic towns opposed the ban on exports to England, as did Hamburg, though Lübeck sided with Cologne on this matter.[9] Such dissension gives credence to a later English claim (February 1555) that the blockade, though maintained for nineteen months, was largely ineffective. It was alleged that during this time English merchants increased their own exports of cloth, to the profit of themselves and the crown. There had been no shortage of northern wares in London and, while the prices of a few increased, those of a greater number were substantially reduced. Furthermore, the London–Antwerp exchange rate moved from 18s to 24s and the Merchant Adventurers imported specie to the value of £80,000 sterling. By February 1555 the boycott was at an end, but the prices of most northern wares were higher than they had ever been, the exchange rate had fallen again to 21s and was likely to go lower, while the Adventurers were no longer importing specie but repatriating their assets in the form of wares.[10] This propaganda was intended to persuade the government that the country had nothing to fear from a renewal of the Hanseatic blockade, and no great reliance may be placed on the implied process of cause and effect.

---

[8] *APC*, 3, pp. 460, 475, 487–9; 4, pp. 42–3, 92–3, 98. *CPR*, 1550–3, p. 346. *DI*, nos. 2387, 2398. *KI*, 1, nos. 647–9, 678–9, 687, 690–1, 693–6, 700, 705.
[9] *DI*, nos. 2414, 2416, 2423–4, 2428. *KI*, 1, no. 644, docs. 9 (p. 351), 10 (p. 353); nos. 666–8.
[10] PRO, SP 11/5 (v). BL, Add. MS 48019, fo. 23.

The diet of November 1552 decided in principle to accept the invitation to send an embassy to London, but left the details to be settled in another diet to be held in the following May. This next assembly confirmed the decision and towards the end of June 1553 a large delegation gathered at Antwerp in readiness for the crossing to England. Their plans were disrupted by the death of the king on 6 July and uncertainty about the succession. In the event the bulk of the embassy waited at Bruges while four of their number went as an advance party to London, arriving there in time to witness the triumphant entry of Queen Mary on 3 August. According to their report they found a friend in Lord Paget, Keeper of the Privy Seal. On 27 August all the Hanse envoys were received by the queen and this was followed by talks with the Privy Council, which proceeded relatively smoothly.[11] By 24 October agreement was reached to reverse the judgement of Edward VI and on 1 November the queen confirmed the ancient charters.[12] The government took the precaution of reserving its position on several points, notably that Englishmen should enjoy reciprocity, particularly in Prussia, and that there must be some limitation of the export of unfinished cloth to the Low Countries. But for the time being the Hanse had defeated the claim that privileged imports should come only from their own regions. Most of the embassy now returned home, but three of its number remained until February 1554 negotiating about matters still in contention and supervising the reform of the Steelyard. By the middle of January a compromise had been reached about the export of unfinished cloth, and the queen again confirmed the franchises and freed the Hanse from the tunnage and poundage granted by parliament a few months before. The merchants were allowed to export unfinished cloth for a period of three years, but none was to be sold in Antwerp for the next three months.[13] The merchants of north-west Germany, particularly those of Hamburg, were increasingly exporting white cloth for finishing in their own towns and were unwilling to risk a total ban on exports just to preserve the Rhinelanders' right to sell at Antwerp. Accordingly, they demanded that the latter should honour the agreement made with England. In July 1554 at a Hanse diet Cologne claimed that pressure being put on the exiles settled in Antwerp was already leading to a fall in sales there. The diet decreed that similar steps should be taken by other

[11] *DI*, doc. 9 (pp. 846–55). *KI*, 1, nos. 841–62.
[12] BL, Add. MS 48019, fos. 117–117d. *KI*, 1, nos. 856–8.
[13] *CPR*, 1553–4, pp. 58–9. *KI*, 1, nos. 892–3, 905.

towns of the Rhineland circle. At the end of the year, however, it was necessary to renew the pressure in the face of continued complaints by the English about the revival of Hanse trade.[14] In a submission to the Privy Council the Adventurers put the total number of cloths exported at Hanse rates between 21 January and Christmas 1554 at 34,450, of which 11,200 were sold in the prohibited areas of Zeeland and Antwerp.[15] The Adventurers claimed that many of the latter were still coloured on behalf of Dutch merchants. Nor was just cloth involved in the trade revival; in December the Steelyard itself admitted that more ships from Bremen, Hamburg and Danzig had imported salt and other French goods into England than for a long time past.[16]

One of the main reasons for the success of the Hanse ambassadors in the autumn and winter of 1553–4 was the fact that Sir Thomas Gresham and the Merchant Adventurers had temporarily fallen out of favour, because of their association with the Duke of Northumberland, who had unsuccessfully tried to put Lady Jane Gray on the throne. However, Gresham's star soon began to rise again as he persuaded the new regime of the continued value of his financial expertise. On Christmas Eve the Steelyard reported that London merchants now stood high in the government's favour and it was feared that they would soon secure the downfall of the Hanse.[17] The fatal blow was struck on 26 February 1555, when the Adventurers submitted to the Privy Council an 'information to explain the confusion of their good order in the Low Countries and to reform the abuses of the Hanse'.[18] In general terms they reiterated old complaints about the unfair advantage gained by the Hansards from lower rates of custom and about the indefinite membership of the organisation, which led to defrauding of the queen's Exchequer. In particular they alleged that Hanse sales of cloth in Antwerp had upset the market and caused prices to fall; further, by maintaining permanent sales outlets in that city the Hansards discouraged buyers from visiting the Cold Mart at Barrow, where the Adventurers were then trying to reactivate their own staple. It was proposed that the Hansards be bound not to sell English goods in the Low Countries nor in any adjacent place, unless it was a member town of the Hanse. If they claimed the right of transit then they should be made to pass through the town where the Adventurers fixed their staple, so that the latter could supervise them. However, the Adventurers were now

---

[14] *KI*, 1, nos. 1046, 1057, doc. 16 (p. 378).   [15] BL, Add. MS 48019, fo. 124.
[16] *DI*, no. 2826.   [17] *Ibid.*, no. 2830.   [18] PRO, sp11/5 (v).

not concerned merely to obtain a monopoly of sales within the Low Countries; they feared for the very survival of their staple. They complained that workers were being seduced to migrate from Antwerp to Hanse towns to promote the finishing of English cloth in those places, thereby diminishing trade at the staple. It was claimed that Hamburg and Lübeck had the advantage of being nearer than Antwerp to the marts of Leipzig and Frankfurt, where much finished cloth was sold. The Adventurers' solution was that the Hansards be forbidden to export any but finished cloth.

On 19 March 1555 the Privy Council issued new regulations for the conduct of Hanse trade, which included closer scrutiny by customs officials and the providing of recognisances to prevent fraud. More seriously, quotas were to be applied for the next twelve months pending another full-scale conference between England and the Hanse. During this time Hansards were not to sell any cloth in the Spanish Netherlands, and not more than one in four of all other exports should be unfinished; not more than one quarter of all imports ought to be from non-Hanseatic regions. These measures failed to satisfy the Adventurers, who were determined to cripple Hanse trade and throughout the summer encouraged the London authorities to defy Privy Council orders to release Hanse-owned cloth which had been arrested earlier and to allow Hansards to trade in Blackwell Hall.[19]

A Hanse diet considered the new crisis at Lübeck in July 1555. As ever, a compromise between conflicting interests had to be found. Danzig was not much concerned about the question of unfinished cloth, but was adamantly opposed to the payment of higher customs duties and demanded the expulsion of any merchant who did so. It did not favour a formal ban on Hanse vessels trading from Spain and France to England, but hoped that shippers would exercise voluntary restraint. Cologne, the member most badly affected, had given very careful consideration to its position, and a memorandum drawn up by Dr Heinrich Suderman, its leading diplomat, had examined the consequences of four possible courses of action, ranging from simply accepting the new restrictions to waging open war on English trade. Not surprisingly, extreme action was ruled out; instead, the city recommended that a small delegation be sent to England, which would be cheaper and more effective than a full-scale embassy. Its chief bargaining counter was to be the threat of a boycott of all

---

[19] *APC*, 5, pp. 115–16, 161, 165. *DI*, no. 2876. *KI*, 1, docs. 19–21 (pp. 385–9).

English cloth, which the Hanse would endeavour to sustain throughout the empire, not merely in its member towns. It was hoped that the marriage of Queen Mary to Philip, a prince of the Empire and sovereign ruler of much of the Low Countries, could be exploited. In the event, the Cologne plan was adopted. The diet banned Hanse exports from France and Spain to England, and advised Cologne to reduce its cloth exports for a while, but immediate retaliation in any form was ruled out. Dr Suderman and Dr Herman Plönnies of Lübeck were appointed to go to England, but not until the autumn, when the situation might have improved. They arrived in London on 14 December.[20]

Suderman and Plönnies were formally received by the queen on 26 December, but despite their impatience the English would not get down to detailed discussions until the Christmas festivities were over. Between that time and their final audience with the queen on 19 April 1556 they had many sessions with members of the Privy Council and officials and merchants of London.[21] The latter talks were particularly acrimonious and the Hansards were blamed for many English bankruptcies during the previous four years. The fruits of the negotiations were little enough. The quota of unfinished cloth was increased from one in four to one in three, but the ban on sales in the Low Countries remained, as did the quota of one quarter for non-Hanseatic imports. Since the Londoners would not give an inch, it fell to the Privy Council to order them to ease their pressure on the Hansards. Although they were not yet readmitted to Blackwell Hall they might buy cloth from country clothiers in houses near the Steelyard, and the city was not to interfere; they were allowed to pack their own cloth, but subject to the scrutiny of the official packer, to whom they were to pay slightly increased fees. The mayor was to stop exacting a prise of imported salt and was not to fix the prices of corn, fish and other victuals imported by Hansards. Cloth presently under arrest was to be restored and any which had been sold paid for; a major legal suit then in process was to be suspended for the time being. All these concessions were for one year only and were conditional upon a full-scale embassy coming to England within that time to settle matters once and for all.

The concession that the Hansards might pass cloth through the Low Countries provided that they did not sell it there was soon negated. In June 1556 the Adventurers decided not to ship any cloth

[20] *DI*, no. 2870. *KI*, 1, docs. 24–6 (pp. 391–8).
[21] *SPF*, 1553–8, pp. 216, 220. *APC*, 5, pp. 252–7. *KI*, 1, doc. 28 (pp. 400–18).

to their staple until the following November and persuaded the government to ban alien exports in the same period. While this may have been intended to apply only to cloth going to and through the Low Countries, the customs officials ruled otherwise and the Steelyard soon reported that all trade was stopped, save that cloth already in its possession might be shipped to Hamburg, Bremen and Kampen. When trade was resumed in the autumn it was demanded that Hanse merchants exporting to the Low Countries should execute a bond not to sell cloth in Antwerp. This they refused to do and accordingly were given licence only to export some 600–700 cloths already in their possession. The Privy Council's insistence that the agreement of March 1556 should be strictly observed led to a further stoppage of trade at the end of the twelve months, on the grounds that the Hanse embassy had not arrived within the allotted time. The only concession was that the merchants might export coloured cloths already in their possession up to the number of 2,000.[22]

The arrival of Hanse delegates in May 1557 was a diplomatic fiasco. In place of the full-scale embassy which the English demanded there came only Dr Suderman and Dr Herman Focke of Lübeck. Worse still, their credentials were addressed only to King Philip of Spain and England and the outraged Privy Council refused to acknowledge them. Instead, the councillors held a series of stormy meetings with members of the Steelyard, at one of which, Lord Paget, formerly described as a friend of the Hanse, castigated as 'unfriendly, unnatural, unchristian, Turkish, tartar and barbaric' the action of Danzig in currently refusing to ship corn to England. So fraught was the climate that the secretary of the Steelyard sent forty-two of their ancient charters to Antwerp for safe keeping by the Bruges *Kontor*. When the failure of the embassy was reported to a diet convened in September 1557, it prepared a comprehensive plan for a total boycott of English cloth and the withholding of all commodities controlled by members of the Hanse. This was not to be put into effect until there had been one more attempt at a peaceful solution. The queen responded on 6 October by reiterating that the privileges of the Hanse must necessarily be limited by the laws and interests of her own country, but nevertheless she proposed that another embassy be sent to discuss the matter. This reply was

---

[22] *APC*, 5, p. 295; 6, pp. 33–4, 73. *KI*, 1, no. 1236.

regarded as unsatisfactory, so that Cologne and some other towns regarded the trade sanctions as automatically coming into effect. But as early as 20 November the former was complaining that the boycott of cloth was being disregarded, particularly by Hamburg.[23]

The merchants who remained in the London Steelyard disapproved of the boycott and urged acceptance of the invitation to send another embassy. In February 1558, alarmed by reports reaching England that the Hanse was conspiring with Denmark and France to make an offensive alliance against England and Spain, they renewed this demand. Accordingly, a five-man delegation, again led by Dr Suderman, arrived in London on 26 April. Much of their time was taken up in negotiating the release of large numbers of Hanse ships which had been, and still were being, arrested at sea and forced into English ports. Most of these were engaged in the Bay salt trade. The first concern of the English was to deny their military use to France, though they also sought to press some of them into their own service and demanded guarantees for the safety of English ships and goods allegedly arrested in Hanse ports. Apart from securing the release of most of the ships the embassy was quite fruitless, though discussions continued fitfully until the end of August. Throughout this period both the Merchant Adventurers and merchants trading to Prussia bombarded the Privy Council with evidence against the Hanse. When the envoys departed the queen wrote to the Hanse blaming the failure of their mission upon their lack of powers. During the time they were in England the export duty on cloth, which until now had remained at the level first set in 1347, was increased to 6s 8d for denizens and 14s 6d for all aliens, including Hansards. This was yet one more obstacle in the way of a settlement, particularly since Englishmen, as it appeared to Suderman, were inclined to accept the increase.[24]

By this time the Hanse merchants were finding it difficult to sustain the trade sanctions. In September 1558 Danzig complained that strangers were reaping the benefit and intimated that it wished to allow its own merchants to sell stocks of English-made cloth currently stockpiled there. When a Hanse diet met the following month it relaxed the restrictions by permitting its members to buy English wares in the Low Countries and to sell Hanse goods there for

---

[23] *KI*, 1, nos. 1396, 1438, 1469, 1474, 1483, 1488, docs. 35 (pp. 430–3), 38–9 (pp. 439–45).
[24] *APC*, 6, pp. 315, 340–2, 378–9, 387. *SPF*, 1552–8, pp. 365–86. *KI*, 1, nos. 1491, 1551, 1592, 1616. *DI*, doc. 15 (pp. 860–6).

export to England, though they were still forbidden to deal directly with Englishmen and the latter were not allowed to trade in Hanse towns. Communications passed between the towns about the desirability of sending another embassy to England and about the powers to be afforded to envoys, but these were interrupted by the death of Queen Mary in November. In a letter congratulating the new queen upon her accession, the Hanse requested the restoration of its privileges and awaited the reaction. Not until July 1559 did Elizabeth deign to reply. She thanked the Hansards for their good wishes, but complained about their treatment of her subjects. There could be no question of restoring the privileges in their entirety, but she was willing to discuss the matter if an embassy came to England.[25]

Throughout these months the Hanse maintained its prohibition upon direct trade with England, but as a goodwill gesture the queen's agent in Danzig was allowed to export a quantity of naval stores. The English, however, had not been idle. Elizabeth appealed to the King of Poland to extend his protection to her subjects and continued to explore the possibility of setting up an English staple for Baltic trade in the duchy of Holstein. In the last months of Mary's reign a cargo of cloth had been sent to Holstein in the custody of William Earl, factor of Sir William Garrard, alderman and merchant of London. Initial reaction was unfavourable, for the duke put forward several conditions which Earl thought his countrymen were unlikely to accept. However, in April 1559 Armigill Wade, a former clerk of the Privy Council, was sent as an official envoy with very precise instructions. With the help of Earl he was to investigate the suitability of the ports of Holstein for the conduct of Anglo-Baltic trade; he was to determine the extent of Hanseatic privileges in Holstein and Scandinavia and to find out if the duke would cooperate in an attempt to get them abolished; he was to enquire about the duke's religion and, if he was of Protestant persuasion, he should intimate the queen's sympathy; finally, he was to negotiate for the queen a large loan of silver, which was believed to be available in Holstein at a low rate of interest. Nothing came from this second overture to Holstein except a modest loan.[26]

In August 1559 a sparsely attended Hanseatic diet finally agreed that an embassy should be sent to England and that meanwhile another request should be made for the resumption of trade on the

---

[25] *SPF*, 1558–9, pp. 354–5. *KI*, I, nos. 1624, 1680, 1711, doc. 41 (p. 452).

[26] *SPF*, 1558–9, pp. 12–13, 42–3, 203, 217–18. Ramsay, *City of London*, pp. 225, 227–8.

basis of the ancient rates of duty. As early as 23 August the queen ordered that a licence be issued for the Steelyard to export 456 cloths already in their possession, but an official reply was not sent to the diet until 31 December. It said that no promises could be given about future customs rates, but if agreement could not be reached at the forthcoming conference, for which 1 April was proposed as the starting date, the queen would herself determine the rates according to justice and reason. In the early part of 1560 the bargaining strength of the Hanse was not inconsiderable, since England could not then afford to be too intransigent. The country was engaged in a massive armaments programme to counter the threat of French interference in Scotland. When the Regent of the Netherlands banned the export of arms to England at the end of January 1560 they had to be shipped from Hamburg. The Hanse ports were also needed for the embarkation of German mercenaries. Finally, negotiations were going on for a large loan from Count Volrad von Mansfeld, whose family controlled the chief Thuringian copper and silver mines, and he was insistent that it should be guaranteed by the Steelyard.[27] The last consideration was perhaps the least important, since there could hardly be any question of such a guarantee unless the queen capitulated entirely to the Hanse demands, which was unthinkable.

The Hanse delegates, again led by Dr Suderman, arrived in London at the end of April 1560 and were briefly received by the queen on 5 May. They were disconcerted by the coolness of their reception, particularly on the part of Secretary Cecil. After a formal session on 21 May, talks languished until well into June, for the English government was preoccupied with the crisis in Scotland. The illnesses of the Lord Treasurer, the Marquess of Winchester, and Suderman further contributed to the delay. Even then the energies of the delegates could not be devoted exclusively to the principle of the Hanseatic franchises, since they were continually urged by the Steelyard to raise immediate problems relating to Hanseatic ships which had put into English ports and fallen foul of customs officials and city authorities in London. One of the chief obstacles to the renewal of privileges was the continued opposition of the Merchant Adventurers, who were consulted by the Privy Council at every turn. The Hanse envoys were dismayed to hear a rumour that the Adventurers had offered the queen a loan of

[27] PRO, SP12/6/23. *SPF*, 1559–60, pp. 258, 455, 476; 1560–1, pp. 10, 18, 20, 189. *KI*, I, nos. 1726, 1730–1, 1775.

£40,000 if she would send them away empty-handed. At the beginning of July the Hansards made it clear that, while they might be prepared to pay higher rates of duty, they would not accept any limitation upon their freedom of trade, save for the obvious exception that they should not trade with the queen's enemies. In the middle of that month the Privy Council handed over a document entitled 'moderatio in commercio inclitae societatis Hansae', which contained a statement of the principles upon which the Hansards would be allowed to trade. It began by pointing out that any privileges should be enjoyed only by genuine members of the German Hanse and the Gildhall of Germans in London, so there must be a firm definition as to who these might be. Any privileges were applicable only to direct trade between England and the Hanse regions and in commodities native to each. The ancient customs advantage over denizens was abolished, but there might be parity with denizens in direct trade. There was to be freedom of trade in all places in England, but saving the liberties of any which could prove a right to exclude Hansards. All the foregoing was dependent on the principle of reciprocity.[28]

After considering the English 'moderatio' the envoys submitted an alternative plan which was designed to protect their trade in non-Hanseatic goods, but which, they said, would augment the queen's revenue by many thousands of pounds. If this plan was not immediately acceptable it was to be referred to an arbitrator, and the names of the Emperor and Philip of Spain were suggested. The Englishmen were not to be turned at this stage of the game and simply refused to consider the proposal, on the grounds that the queen was absent from London and the Council was too busy with other matters. The next day (31 July) the envoys under protest handed over a list of sixty-six towns which were presently members of the Hanse and of thirteen former members which were eligible for readmission. Even at a first sight of this document the English negotiators raised objections to the inclusion of the towns of Livonia. In the same session the Germans requested clarification of what precisely was meant by customs parity with denizens and sought an assurance that they would enjoy the fullest measure of free trade within the city of London. The last point was regarded as being of the utmost importance, yet it was a guarantee which the Privy

---

[28] *KI*, 1, docs. 45 (pp. 463–4), 47 (pp. 465–7), 56 (pp. 475–86).

Councillors were either unable or unwilling to provide. After a few more days of hard bargaining the English submitted their final offers (5 August) in the form of a draft treaty, which they demanded should be ratified by the Hanse within six months. The treaty proposed that the Hansards should pay the same rates of duty as denizens upon cloth and all other products exported directly to their member towns and upon native products imported from thence. No sort of cloth was to be re-exported from those places to Antwerp or anywhere else in Flanders, Brabant, Holland and Zeeland, nor any kerseys to Italy. All trade between England and non-Hanse ports was subject to alien rates of duty, save for rebates of 1d in the pound on the value of imports and 1s on exports. The relative positions were to be maintained in the event of future increases in customs rates. The only Hanseatic privilege specifically confirmed was the right to pack their own cloth. Other than this, it was merely said that the liberties should be as they were before the present treaty. This would have exposed the merchants to renewed harassment in London. As always, the position of the Hanse in England was conditional upon recognition of the principle of reciprocity.[29]

The day after being presented with the treaty the Hanse envoys produced their own much lengthier draft.[30] They agreed to pay the actual rates of duty now proposed, but the form of words used in the draft would have protected the Hansards from any future increase in either denizen or alien rates. More importantly, they proposed that the ban on the sale of cloth in the Low Countries should be a voluntary measure limited to two years, during which time the authorities of that region should themselves rule whether it was lawful for England to impose such a ban upon its rivals. They also included firm guarantees as to the freedom of trade in London and wanted the time allowed for the Hanse to confirm the treaty extended to eight months. The English dismissed this draft, insisting that the Hansards must either accept or reject their version as it stood; furthermore, they reduced the time allowed for ratification to a mere two months. Not unnaturally, the envoys protested that the last requirement was an impossibility and requested that they be allowed until 1 July 1561 without prejudice to the offer. The latter date was finally conceded and, after a few more meetings with the Steelyard and English officials to arrange a *modus vivendi* until July,

---

[29] *Ibid.*, docs. 48–9 (pp. 467–8), 51 (pp. 469–70).   [30] *Ibid.*, doc. 52 (pp. 470–3).

the envoys left London on 19 August. As a result of last-minute negotiations it was agreed that Hanseatic trade should continue on the basis of the draft English treaty, but cloth exports were allowed only under licence, in an attempt to ensure that the restrictions were observed.

Failing a full diet of the Hanse the attitude of its members to the English terms had to be determined in provincial diets and by written communications passing between the chief towns. On 15 May 1561 a letter was sent to Elizabeth saying that the treaty could not be ratified. The queen's reply, sent on 7 July, indicated that even so trade might continue on the terms she had dictated. Despite a renewed clamour from her own subjects, Elizabeth could not afford to adopt a more severe line at this time, since she was still dependent upon Hanse ports for the supply of munitions. They were continually pressing for assurances that she would not send weapons to Muscovy for use in its war against Livonia and would have needed little provocation to cut off the supply entirely. The Hanse found it difficult to accept the loss of its ancient privileges and entertained the vain hope that force might succeed where diplomacy had failed. Because of England's isolation in the early 1560s it was thought that another power might be joined in a common cause against her. One candidate was France, since Elizabeth was not reconciled to the loss of Calais and to achieve her ends was inclined to give aid and comfort to the French Huguenots. When a Hanse diet was convened in the summer of 1562 consideration was given to abandoning the London Steelyard in favour of a *Kontor* at Rouen, and at the same time banning English merchants from Hanseatic regions. Heinrich Suderman, the acknowledged expert on Anglo-Hanseatic relations, consistently favoured an understanding with the Low Countries. The strength of his argument lay in the fact that England's cloth trade was still almost entirely dependent on Antwerp, yet its future in that place was far from assured. Contemporary attitudes towards the conduct of the trade meant that if Antwerp was closed to the English merchants then they would have to find another staple; the only alternative was one of the German ports.[31]

England's relations with the government of the Low Countries began to deteriorate soon after Elizabeth's accession. Among the causes were her refusal to marry Philip of Spain, her acceptance of Protestant refugees and a belief that she was plotting with

[31] *Ibid.*, nos. 1970, 1984, 2009, docs. 64 (pp. 500–2), 67 (pp. 517–18), 70 (p. 258). *SPF*, 1564–5, pp. 543–4.

malcontented local nobles. This did not itself affect relations between the Merchant Adventurers and the Lords of Antwerp (the governing body of the city), for the latter frequently chafed at control from Brussels. There was some loss of local sympathy in 1562–3 when English privateers, licensed to attack French ships, inflicted serious losses on neutral trade. But when the blow came it was struck by the Brussels government, which in November 1563 banned the import of English wool and cloth into any port in the Countries until the following February. This was represented as a quarantine measure to prevent the introduction of the plague then raging in London. The real reason was the belief that pressure applied at this time, when England was still threatened by France, would force the queen to be more accommodating to the interests of Spain and its Netherlands dependency.[32]

When the Merchant Adventurers found themselves excluded from the Netherlands they prevailed upon the government to ban all exports of cloth, so that their rivals might not enjoy an advantage. No exception was made in favour of those who exported to places outside the Netherlands, so this move hit the north Germans as well as Cologners and others who traded in Antwerp or merely used Netherlands ports in transit. On 17 March 1564 Hamburg city council wrote to Elizabeth complaining about the damage to their economy and requesting an exemption in favour of their citizens. They also proposed that the Adventurers should transfer their staple to Hamburg, where they would be accorded equal trading rights with burghers. Richard Ehrenberg, the authority on Anglo-Hamburg relations in this period, expressed astonishment at the offer, which was to be taken up three years later. He held that it disregarded the basic Hanseatic tenet that aliens should not trade in member towns on equal terms with burghers. However, this view disregards the fact that since 1437 the Hanse as a whole, with the notable exception of Prussia, had in principle accepted that Englishmen should enjoy reciprocal rights. Admittedly, the Hanse's good faith was seldom put to the test, since until the mid-sixteenth century Englishmen had little direct interest in any Hanse towns except those of the eastern Baltic. In reply to Hamburg's offer Elizabeth said that it was up to the Adventurers to determine for themselves where they fixed the staple, since this was not a matter of public policy. The city was encouraged by this answer, but the die

---

[32] For a full discussion of this episode, Ramsay, *City of London*, pp. 179–210.

had already been cast. The Adventurers had decided to set up a staple elsewhere, and this was certainly not done without the closest consultation with the government. In January 1564 the Privy Council had drawn up a series of questions to be answered by the Adventurers, which amongst others asked how they might respond to a prolonged exclusion from the Low Countries. It emerged that the only places considered to be practical alternatives to Antwerp for a cloth staple were Hamburg and the port of Emden in East Friesland. When the Brussels government extended the ban on English wool and cloth until Easter 1564, negotiations were begun with the ruler of East Friesland about the setting up of a staple. These proceeded rapidly and smoothly, with the result that a cloth fleet of forty to fifty ships sailed to Emden in May 1564. To ensure the success of the venture the government on 23 March proclaimed a ban on all imports from the Netherlands, the intention being that all wares normally bought at Antwerp would be admitted to England only if they first passed through Emden.[33]

Although Emden was not a Hanse town Hamburg merchants began to buy from the Adventurers at the new staple and the number of cloths finished in Hamburg quickly doubled. This development, like the earlier invitation to the Adventurers to come to Hamburg, did nothing to endear that city to fellow members of the Hanse. Heinrich Suderman, even before he received confirmation of the invitation, had warned of the dangers which would flow from a separate agreement between England and Hamburg. This would prejudice the bargaining power of the Hanse, and additionally any town which received the staple must incur the enmity of the Netherlands. In May the merchants remaining in the Steelyard complained about Hamburg's attitude, which they saw as undermining their efforts to get Elizabeth to remove the ban on their own trade. Shortly before, they had a limited success in gaining permission to export the residue (about 800) of the 5,000 unfinished cloths specified in the last licence issued to them before the ban on exports, provided that they did not sell these east of Emden. The interpretation of the safeguard gave rise to a dispute between the Adventurers and Cologne merchants, with each trying to persuade

[33] PRO, SP12/15/67; 33/26. *SPF*, 1564–5, pp. 58, 105, 158, 316. R. Ehrenburg, *Hamburg und England im Zeitalter der Königin Elisabeth* (Jena, 1896), pp. 76, 79, 310–12. For a full discussion of the first English cloth staple at Emden, B. Hagedorn, *Ostfrieslands Handel und Schiffahrt im 16. Jahrhundert* (Berlin, 1910), I, pp. 170–202. Ramsay, *City of London*, pp. 252–83; G. D. Ramsay (ed.), *The Politics of a Tudor Merchant Adventurer: A Letter to the Earls of East Friesland* (Manchester, 1979).

the ruler of Emden that its version was correct. The former claimed that the Hanse cloth should not be shipped to Emden, which meant that the Cologne men would have to pass it through Hamburg. The latter asserted that there was no impediment to their using Emden, provided that they did not send cloth into the Netherlands, only to Germany. The Englishmen's purpose was to delay the arrival of the Steelyard cloth so that it could not compete with the stocks they held in Emden. To the same end they sought to delay the packing of Hanse cloth before export. On 24 June, ten days after the official opening of the new mart, Thomas Aldersey, deputy governor of the company, complained to Cecil from Emden that 'certain Easterlings' there were trying to persuade potential customers to hold back by promising that within six weeks they would be able to sell English cloth more cheaply than current prices. This charge is confirmed by one of Heinrich Suderman's letters, dated sixteen days earlier, which tells of his own efforts to prevent not only Hamburgers but his fellow Cologners and others from buying from Englishmen in Emden. The Adventurers' concern was not simply about Hansards selling cloth in Emden, for they were rapidly becoming aware that they would themselves have to find a market beyond that port. The need arose from the fact that the Brussels government had forbidden the import of cloth from the new staple into the Netherlands and also banned all exports to Emden, so denying Englishmen cargoes for the return leg of their enterprise. In the absence of buyers at Emden some Adventurers decided to take their stock to the great autumn mart at Frankfurt on Main, but since much of it was white cloth they needed to have it finished and dyed on the way. Cologne was an obvious choice for the work and on 18 July Suderman wrote that 800–900 English-owned cloths were imminently expected there.[34]

Suderman's animosity towards England did not stop at attempting to blight the prospects of its staple at Emden. At the beginning of August he attended a diet of the Hanse towns of the Rhineland third and reminded them that they had suffered more than any other section of the Hanse from the loss of privileges in England. He urged that a firm alliance with the Netherlands must lead to their restoration. Shortly afterwards a rumour reached England that this provincial diet had agreed to a six-year ban on the import of English cloth unless the privileges were restored and would recommend this to an impending diet of the whole Hanse. Another rumour was that

[34] PRO, SP12/34/5. *SPF*, 1564–5, pp. 125, 138, 164. *KI*, 1. nos. 2323, 2329, 2334, 2346, 2355, 2364, 2385.

the Cologne authorities were hostile to the activities of Englishmen at the Frankfurt fair and had imposed a tax of one thaler (about 5s sterling) on all English-owned cloth finished in their city. The rumours came at an inopportune time for the London Steelyard, which had just succeeded in negotiating that each year for the next four years its members might export a total of 5,000 unfinished cloths. They were dissatisfied with the quota, but it was better than nothing and they did not want it jeopardised straight away. At the behest of the Privy Council the Steelyard wrote to Cologne seeking assurances that Englishmen would not be taxed on cloth brought to the city, and demanding that a Hanse delegation should come to England to discuss the perennial complaint that Hanse merchants should not enjoy privileges which were denied to Englishmen in their parts. Cologne replied immediately that the rumour resulted from a misunderstanding, for although the question of a tax had been considered it had not been imposed and there was no intention of doing so.[35]

At the Hanse diet in September 1564 there was much advice against taking hasty measures against England. The Steelyard wrote that an alliance with the Netherlands would lead to its own undoing, while the city of Cologne opposed this before an embassy went to England to seek a peaceful solution to differences. The diet decided against an embassy, but drafted a strongly worded letter to the queen complaining about continued harassment of Steelyard merchants by the city of London. It also drew up instructions for Heinrich Suderman to negotiate with the Netherlands for an alliance against England. Suderman pursued this task with enthusiasm but he was too late, for the English government had already arranged to hold peace talks with the Netherlanders. The queen was now willing to settle on terms which were acceptable to Brussels in the previous spring, and the latter had no need for Hanse assistance. The Hanse was thus reduced to the role of a suppliant begging the regent to raise its grievances, but without mentioning the name of Suderman who was now regarded with deep suspicion in England.[36]

At the beginning of 1565 the Merchant Adventurers gave up their Emden enterprise and the main axis of trade was restored to Antwerp, even though formal peace talks had yet to begin. A conference was initiated that summer but never brought to a

---

[35] *APC*, 7, p. 147. *SPF*, 1564–5, pp. 191, 197. *KI*, 1, nos. 2402, 2404, 2418, doc. 72 (p. 532). PRO, sp12/34/57. [36] *KI*, 1, nos. 2421–3, 2433, doc. 74 (p. 540).

conclusion, and the return to Antwerp was short-lived. As the religious and civil tumult spread throughout the Netherlands in 1565 and 1566 all foreign merchants increasingly felt themselves threatened and began to consider alternative bases for their business. In September 1566 Sir Thomas Gresham recommended that the Adventurers should seek a new staple, so that they would not become caught up in the war. Shortly afterwards, George Gilpin, secretary of the company, made a brief journey to Hamburg to spy out the land, and in January 1567 the alderman of the Steelyard informed Heinrich Suderman that the Adventurers had decided to move their staple to that city. There can be no doubt that this step was taken in closest consultation with the government. The move may already have been decided in principle, but it was not until April, following greater pressure upon Protestants in the Low Countries, that the council of the Adventurers in Antwerp gave formal powers to a three-man delegation to negotiate the setting up of a staple in Hamburg. This returned to Antwerp, its mission successful, on 29 July.[37]

While the English envoys were in Hamburg, a Hanse diet met in Lübeck. Cologne proposed that they should recognise the impossibility of recovering their lost privileges at present and should temporise, while not abandoning hope of success in the future. This was more or less the policy adopted, though it is noteworthy that from this time the Hanse sought to involve the authority of the Empire more than in the past. This may have been in recognition of the fact that English merchants were beginning to venture into the interior of Germany and were becoming susceptible to pressure in quarters where hitherto they had been relatively immune. The diet itself took no action about Hamburg's dealings with the Merchant Adventurers, but on 9 June Heinrich Suderman, in his role as Hanse syndic, made a notarial protest in the presence of members of the city council of Lübeck. He also sent George Laffarts, secretary of the Antwerp *Kontor*, to Hamburg, where he repeated the protest before the city fathers. Lübeck supported this step and, affecting the part of a friendly neighbour, advised Hamburg to act cautiously. Hamburg councillors reacted vigorously to the interference, asserting that an agreement with the Adventurers would benefit all the Hanse, but that in any event theirs was a free city which had the right to adopt any policy which suited its inhabitants. Regarding the latter point,

---

[37] Ehrenburg, *Hamburg*, p. 82. *KI*, 1, no. 2986.

on 28 June Morris Zimmerman, alderman of the London Steelyard, wrote to Suderman that Hamburg city council did not have the support of that community for its present actions. This reflects the opposition of the Hamburg *Englandfahrer*, who on 5 June petitioned against the reception of the Adventurers. Ehrenberg believes that the town as a whole was behind the council, for in the mid-1560s the civic coffers were virtually empty and the arrival of the staple was seen as part of a more prosperous future.[38]

Despite all protests, on 19 July a formal agreement of no fewer than fifty-six points was signed between Hamburg and the Merchant Adventurers, which was to regulate English trade in the city for the next ten years.[39] Ehrenberg regarded the terms as exceptionally favourable to the Englishmen, a fact which he ascribed to the weak bargaining power of the city. The English claimed to possess even greater privileges in Antwerp and Emden, but the Hamburg council were unaware of how precarious their position was in Antwerp and how bad trade had been in Emden. Foremost in the agreement was the recognition by the city of the authority of the Merchant Adventurers Company, thus enabling its officials to discipline its members. A court was to be established for this purpose, though the city had jurisdiction in criminal matters. Civil cases between Adventurers and burghers or other outsiders were to be heard by the city, unless the latter elected to accept the verdict of the English court; the city was to provide adequate buildings for these purposes. Additionally, if the Adventurers gave three weeks' warning of the arrival of a cloth fleet the council would ensure that they were provided with good warehouses at a fair rent. Other assistance included the use of a crane, free of charge. The company could introduce up to six alien warehousemen, but if more were required they must be engaged locally. It had strictly to observe local staple regulations, which meant that all loading and unloading had to be done in the city and nowhere else on the Elbe, and there were restrictions on the trade in certain goods, such as grain and munitions. Otherwise freedom of trade was limited only by certain measures to protect local interests. The Adventurers might act as their own brokers and could buy and sell with outsiders as well as with burghers. They were forbidden to retail cloth in the city, except between themselves. Imported kerseys could be dyed locally in any fashion for their own use, but any other cloth finished in Hamburg

---

[38] *KI*, I, nos. 3097–8, 3122, 3124–5, 3129, 3136–7, docs. 89–90 (pp. 589–93). Ehrenburg, *Hamburg*, pp. 85–6.   [39] Ehrenburg, *Hamburg*, pp. 312–26.

on behalf of the Adventurers must be done in a fashion which fitted it for sale in Frankfurt, Leipzig or upper Germany. Cloth so prepared must not be sold by them to non-burghers within the city, but taken to its ultimate destination. Undressed cloths, or all those finished in England, could be disposed of without such restrictions. At the start of the negotiations the authorities had hoped to persuade the Adventurers to pay an import duty of 3s on each cloth, compared with 1s paid by burghers. This was refused, on the grounds that it was higher than the duty levied in Antwerp. In the final outcome it was agreed that the Adventurers should pay the same as natives on all imports and exports.

Despite the advantageous terms negotiated with Hamburg the Adventurers saw them primarily as an insurance measure and were inclined to persist with their Antwerp trade for as long as possible. As late as 28 February 1568 governor Marsh wrote to Hamburg that it was intended to send only a small part of their cloth to the city that year. This was immediately followed by a deterioration in the security of Englishmen in Antwerp, and in April it was reported that twelve shiploads of cloth would be going to Hamburg. In the event, that summer the Adventurers sent only four ships of their own and took space in one Hamburg-owned ship. On 29 December 1568, following Elizabeth's seizure of the Duke of Alva's treasure ships, all Englishmen who remained in Antwerp were placed under house arrest and there could be no question of sending any more cloth to the city. On 19 January 1569 the Adventurers informed the Privy Council that they had a large stock ready for export, which must go to either Hamburg or Emden. They asked for measures such as had been implemented when the staple was last removed from Antwerp, namely a total ban on exports to the Netherlands and a ban on the import by aliens of any goods, save from the place which the Adventurers should designate as their staple. As late as 1 March they complained that a strict ban had not yet been proclaimed, merely a warning to denizens to forbear, which left aliens trading with impunity.[40]

Hamburg was chosen by the Adventurers in preference to Emden, and on 20 February the French ambassador reported that a fleet was on the point of leaving London. The sailing was delayed until late April, but was swollen from the fifteen ships mentioned in the ambassador's first dispatch to twenty-eight, including three chartered

---

[40] PRO, SP12/49/9, 12, 14, 30, 56. Ehrenburg, *Hamburg*, p. 102.

by the Steelyard and two by Italian merchants. It was protected by seven warships supplied by the queen to thwart the Duke of Alva, who was reported to have alerted forty-five vessels in Zeeland to watch out for the Englishmen. In the event, Alva was unwilling to mount the attack without a direct order from King Philip and the entire cargo, worth up to a half-a-million crowns, was brought safely to Hamburg by 27 May. In September 1569 a second fleet of twenty-five to thirty merchantmen and two warships went to Hamburg, with 30,000–40,000 cloths of better quality than the previous consignment, and estimated to be worth at least £200,000. In spring 1570 there was a third convoy of fifty ships and five escorts. There is no evidence of another fleet in 1570, but one was sent early in 1571. The practical as well as the moral support of the queen for these ventures was assured on a number of counts. Apart from the obvious fact that trade routes had to be kept open so that customs receipts did not suffer, the government arranged to borrow some of the receipts of cloth sales in Hamburg. The money was used to underwrite a Protestant alliance being organised in an attempt to counter the military successes of the Duke of Alva in the Low Countries. Elizabeth received £40,000 from the proceeds of the first voyage in 1569, but the fact that much cloth was 'sold' to recipients of the subsidies suggests that many of them may have received payment in kind.[41]

The willingness of individual members of the Merchant Adventurers company to continue support for the Hamburg venture obviously depended on two factors – the warmth of the reception which they or their agents received in the city and the degree of commercial success. On the first score the observance of their religious practice was the most important consideration. Ehrenberg admits that the clauses dealing with freedom of worship were the least satisfactory part of the Anglo-Hamburg treaty. He justified this from the city's standpoint by the need to protect its established Lutheran Church from more radical forms of Protestantism. Worship became a major issue as early as March 1570 when Sir Richard Clough, leader of the Englishmen in the city, died and the local clergy tried to prevent his countrymen from burying him with their own rites. From that time until the end of their sojourn in the city English correspondence is full of bitter complaints about religious intolerance. More than once it was said that the Adventurers should

[41] Ehrenburg, *Hamburg*, pp. 105–13.

move to Emden, where they would be free to observe their own faith, though it was conceded that for trade purposes this place was less well situated than Hamburg.[42]

It is more difficult to judge the commercial success of the enterprise. In July 1571 an Adventurer claimed that wool and cloth sold at Hamburg for 10–15 per cent less than the usual Antwerp prices, while some goods bought for return to England cost 30 per cent more. Ehrenburg gives figures from the Hamburg archives which shed some light on the volume of trade. Appendix 4a shows that the amount of English cloth finished in the city in the twelve months following the shipment of 1568 increased by about one-third, but in the year after the first consignment of 1569 it more than doubled. This early peak was succeeded by a two- or three-year decline, but then there was a steady recovery during the remainder of the English sojourn. The remarkably swift response to the increase in cloth imports does not necessarily mean that there had been a vast unused finishing capacity in Hamburg before this, though there may have been some. The increase was due in large part to an influx of cloth workers from the Low Countries, attracted by the prospect of employment and the hope of religious freedom. Ehrenberg estimated that during the first four years or so the Adventurers contributed an average of at least 18,000 cloths to the total taken up by local industry and also sold averages of around 34,000 cloths and 21,000 kerseys to strangers. He mistakenly believed that the Steelyard export licence was increased from 5,000 to 15,000 per annum in 1568; it was increased to 8,000 in June 1570. But he also made the point that, after first increasing, the cloth trade of the Hamburg *Englandfahrer* dwindled, since finishers could buy more cheaply from the Adventurers.[43]

While the expansion of the finishing industry in Hamburg made a welcome contribution to English exports it could not take up all the cloth which had formerly been sold in Antwerp. The Adventurers had therefore to explore more distant markets, for which Hamburg was simply the continental port of entry. Some of those who shipped in the first fleet of 1569 intended to take their cloth to Italy and some may have continued to do so throughout the period of the Hamburg staple.[44] In 1576–7 non-Hanse aliens, which means overwhelmingly Italians, sent 17,017 kerseys and a few hundred other cloths to

---

[42] *Ibid.*, p. 115.
[43] *SPD, Addenda*, 1566–79, p. 356. Ehrenburg, *Hamburg*, pp. 112, 118, 327–8. PRO, SP12/71/25.   [44] *SPF*, 1569–71, p. 80.

Hamburg,[45] while Italians and four or five Englishmen had cloth ready to pass the same way early in 1579. In the long run, of course, the routing of cloth overland through such a northerly port was not a viable proposition and, once the sea-passage to the Mediterranean became safe, trade was transferred to it. But other Englishmen besides those bound for Italy ventured beyond Hamburg. We have already seen that during the period at Emden some Adventurers took their own cloth to Frankfurt fair. Some continued to do so after the return to Antwerp and the need was even greater after the settlement at Hamburg. However, some went much further, for the Bavarian city of Nüremburg, which was developing a cloth finishing industry of its own, opened its gates to them. The Nüremburgers had formerly bought cloth at Antwerp and were prepared to seek it at Hamburg, but they also offered concessions to Englishmen who settled in their city. This opportunity was soon disavowed by the Adventurers Company. It was official policy not to sell cloth outside the designated mart, for it was believed to be more profitable to make the foreigner come for it than take it to him. In the words of John Wheeler, a later secretary of the company, 'A commodity sought for at the Mart Towns is more esteemed by the seeker thereof there, than if it were brought home and offered to him to sell at his own doors, and the merchant's proverb is "That there is twenty in the hundred difference between Will you buy? and Will you sell?".'[46] Despite the company's disapproval some Adventurers settled at Nüremburg and may have been joined by interlopers. Theirs seems to have been a precarious business, for in 1579 they complained that their purchases in Nüremburg were many times the value of the cloth they sold there. This may lend some credence to Wheeler's defence of the company's policy.

The amount of unfinished cloth sent forward from Hamburg seems to have peaked about 1571 or 1572 and then declined considerably. Unfortunately the records do not distinguish between exports still in the possession of the Adventurers and those bought in the city by strangers.[47] Several factors contributed to the decline of inland trade. First, there was a widespread failure of harvests in 1571, which actually led to requests to Elizabeth to permit English

---

[45] PRO, SP12/119/47, printed in Ehrenburg, *Hamburg*, pp. 330–1, but incorrectly dated as 1577–8. Other copies are PRO, SP12/127/88 and BL, Add. MS 48009, fos. 1079–85. See below p. 359.   [46] J. Wheeler, *A Treatise of Commerce* (London, 1601), p. 51.
[47] See appendix 4b.

corn to be exported to Hamburg and Emden. The dearth resulted in severe hunger, if not famine, in Germany and the Low Countries in 1572. More important in the longer term was the diversion by the Adventurers of some of their trade back to Emden and Antwerp. English interlopers had continued to bring cloth to Emden after the withdrawal of the staple in 1565 and in the early 1570s there was a marked increase in trade there. This was because there was still a considerable demand for English cloth in the Netherlands despite an official ban on its import. In June 1571, when the Dutch sea beggars blockaded the river Ems, there were thirteen English vessels in the port. During 1571 over seventy came there, including two or three sent officially by the Adventurers Company. During the next two years the company sent another five ships.[48] Unfortunately, the interlopers had paid local customs duties, so the Counts of East Friesland and the town council now demanded that the Adventurers did the same. This led to a protracted dispute, since the Englishmen insisted that they should still enjoy the privileges negotiated in 1564. It also encouraged the return to Antwerp, which became possible with the gradual improvement in relations between England and Spain from early in 1572; the following year trade with the Netherlands was officially reinstated. Some Adventurers now returned to Antwerp, but there was little prospect of restoring lost glories. All the sea approaches to the city were dominated by the sea beggars, who did not observe the rights of neutrals and acted as a general deterrent to trade. The return to Antwerp was limited and short-lived, for in November 1576 the Adventurers again left the city after it was plundered by mutinous Spanish troops.

The latest collapse of the Antwerp mart meant that the Adventurers must again depend more heavily upon Hamburg. Unfortunately, that city was coming under increasing pressure not to renew the company's privileges, which were soon due to expire. This pressure must be traced back to 1572, when on 1 May Heinrich Suderman wrote to the London Steelyard requesting it to send a delegation to a full Hanse diet, the first for five years, which was soon to assemble at Lübeck. In his reply Morris Zimmerman, the alderman, said that he believed that the queen herself was willing to restore the Hanse privileges, but that she was opposed by certain of the Privy Council, urged on as always by the city of London. A

---

[48] Hagedorn, *Ostfrieslands Handel*, 1, pp. 200–2.

memorandum drawn up by the Steelyard for consideration by the diet focussed attention on restrictions upon its trade in London.[49] Coming at that time, such complaints must be received cautiously. The city had certainly not given up its formal opposition to Hanse claims to privileges, but during much of the time when the Adventurers had a staple in Hamburg there were few prosecutions. This relative complacency resulted no doubt from the counsel of London cloth exporters, as well as pressure from the government. The memorandum also complained about recent acts of parliament, particularly the statute of 1567 which required each cloth exporter to take one fully dressed piece for every nine unfinished pieces. This made no allowance for the fact that while there was a limited overseas market for cloth dressed in England by no means every merchant had access to it. Objection was also made to the renewal in 1571 of fifteenth-century statutes requiring certain aliens, including Hansards, to import bowstaves; for most of them that trade was now obsolete. Finally, the Steelyard complained about Hamburg's reception of the Merchant Adventurers. It claimed that even the treaty of Utrecht guaranteed Englishmen only such rights as they enjoyed prior to 1474, but Hamburg had gone beyond this and granted them privileges which they had never enjoyed before.

The address of the Steelyard, supported by Heinrich Suderman, ensured that Hamburg's actions came under scrutiny in the diet – this, despite the fact that at a preliminary meeting of Wendish towns in February 1572 Hamburg, by threatening to boycott the diet, had extracted from her neighbours a promise that they would not criticise her on this account. In the July diet the Hamburg representative defended his town by pointing out that its reception of the Adventurers was in no way responsible for the loss of Hanseatic privileges. On the contrary, it had enabled the Steelyard to obtain an increase in its quota of unfinished cloth, while Hamburg had been able to intercede with the English government about piracies committed recently against other Hanse towns. Furthermore, Hamburg challenged the Steelyard's interpretation of the treaty of Utrecht; its intention was not simply to confirm rights enjoyed by Englishmen before 1474, but to make them as free in Hanse towns as Hansards were in England. Ironically, this was the very proposition which Englishmen had been advancing since the

---

[49] *KI*, 2, no. 104, docs. 3 (p. 341), 5 (pp. 348–52).

fourteenth century. In the face of this spirited defence the diet did not attempt to impose sanctions on Hamburg, though it did lecture the city on the folly of its ways. It claimed that if Hamburg had not provided the Adventurers with a refuge, their exclusion from the Netherlands and a strategic dependence on Baltic trade would already have forced the English government to restore the privileges.[50]

Before dispersing, the diet wrote separate letters to Queen Elizabeth and Lord Burghley requesting confirmation of ancient privileges and exemption from recent legislation. In reply Burghley said that any confirmation must expressly include all the points of the draft treaty of 1560, which the Hanse had so far refused to accept. In regard to particular complaints, the Privy Council prevaricated about cloth exports and salt imports, but said that it would be satisfied if the Hanse complied with the spirit of the legislation about bowstaves, rather than obeyed the letter of the law. Despite this negative response the renewal of contact between the diet and the English government seems to have encouraged new initiatives. In January 1573 the Earl of Leicester notified the Steelyard that if it made the queen an interest-free loan of £40,000 she would confirm the privileges in full. The few merchants who remained there were very much in favour of this and discussions went on for several months. There was, of course, no way in which such a loan could be raised without the support of the towns, and the opposition of Cologne and Lübeck eventually killed the idea. The prospect of a German loan was revived towards the end of 1575, when one Roland Fox offered the queen his services to raise £100,000 in the Rhineland. This led to direct negotiations between the government and the city of Cologne, which ended abortively in August 1576. But the English were reluctant to take no for an answer and as late as February 1577 Walsingham was still pressing the Steelyard on this matter. Given the mood of the times it is somewhat surprising that there appears to have been little contact between the English government and a Hanseatic delegation which was in London between September and December 1574. This was made up of Heinrich Suderman and two representatives each of Cologne, Lübeck and Hamburg. It originated in a resolution in the diet of 1572 to investigate the finances of the London Steelyard, but was not

---

[50] *Ibid.*, 2, docs. 12–13 (pp. 364–9).

put in hand until now. Presumably, the delegation's activities were largely restricted to the diet's original intention, though it had a few talks with English officials about various matters, such as the tax on salt.[51]

Towards the end of 1575 there was an increase in hostility towards the activities of Steelyard merchants in London, possibly prompted by the coming assembly of parliament. As well as involving the queen's loan, which has been discussed above, it may have been intended as a warning of what would happen if the English privileges in Hamburg were not renewed. In April 1576 Morris Zimmerman wrote to Heinrich Suderman saying that English merchants were making threats about what they would do if they were excluded from that city. He also said that, if turned out, they would try to gain entry to Stade or Bremen, preferably the former. If the harassment was intended as a warning to Hamburg it was unwise and counter-productive. In 1572 and 1575 the city had defied its allies but in the diet of August 1576 it could not ignore arguments that it would be intolerable to renew its agreement with England while Hansards were being oppressed in London. It therefore gave an undertaking not to do so without consulting its Wendish neighbours. On 19 July 1577, the tenth anniversary of the Anglo-Hamburg treaty, the council formally proclaimed that it had now expired. Under its terms Englishmen had a full year to remain peaceably in the city, and pains were taken to point out that during this time the treaty might be renegotiated. The cordial note of the proclamation so alarmed the Steelyard that it wrote to Suderman warning him of the possibility of secret dealings between Hamburg and England, and advising that the former be reminded of the promise given to the diet the previous year. The Adventurers were hopeful of a renewal, encouraged perhaps by the opinion of their own lawyers that there was no justification for Hamburg's denunciation of the treaty.[52]

The English government itself took the initiative in seeking the renewal of the treaty. The queen's letter, dated 8 October 1577, was taken to Hamburg by Dr Palley, who was to negotiate with Christopher Hoddeson, who had been in the city since 23 September. Hoddeson had been sent over in charge of £20,000 sterling, mostly

---

[51] *Ibid.*, 2, nos. 203, 207, 272, 278, 282, 297, 302, 311, 323, 504–6, 511, 563, docs. 18–19 (pp. 399–400), 32–6 (pp. 411–17), 40–1 (pp. 428–30), 52 (pp. 460–1), 56–7 (pp. 468–70). *SPF*, 1572–4, p. 199.

[52] *KI*, 2, nos. 802, 1179, docs. 64 (p. 478), 75 (pp. 492–3). *SPF*, 1577–8, p. 426.

in the form of silver and gold bullion. The queen seems to have had no immediate use for the money in that place, but wanted to establish a contingency fund on the continent. Before he left England Hoddeson had proposed that it be lent to the Merchant Adventurers at 6 per cent interest and two months' call, or if the government did not favour this then it might be deposited in one of the chief cities of north-west Germany. In the event the money became an embarrassment, since no city would take it even at 5 per cent, while the Adventurers wanted no more than £15,000 Flemish and a deal was complicated by the problem of exchange rates. A memorandum drawn up in England for Lord Burghley therefore advised that the bulk of the fund be repatriated, leaving £5,000 in the hands of Hoddeson to finance his mission.[53]

Much to his disgust Hoddeson found himself chosen by the Adventurers as their deputy governor and treasurer in Hamburg, and because he could not disclose the true reason for his presence he was unable to refuse the post. He and Palley presented the queen's request to the city council on 5 January 1578 and received an answer ten days later. The council said that because of its promise to the diet it could not make an immediate decision. It merely undertook to decide the matter before the expiry of·the year's grace on 19 July. This displeased the English, both because of the consultation with other towns and because nothing would be settled by February, which was the month when the Adventurers usually sent a fleet to Hamburg. Hoddeson suspected that the delay was deliberately designed to secure one or other of two ends; either the Adventurers would hold back their fleet, leaving the Steelyard merchants to corner the market, or they would ship cloth, patronising Hamburg to the bitter end, and then finding themselves burdened with tolls after July. He therefore recommended that neither Adventurers nor any other merchants should be allowed to export cloth to Hamburg until the treaty was renewed; pressure should also be put on the Steelyard to intercede with the Hanse.[54]

Despite Hamburg's protestation that it must consult its neighbours it was in no hurry to do so. On 14 January 1578 Zimmerman wrote to Suderman that he knew nothing of what was going on, since both Hamburg and the English were very secretive. Elizabeth again wrote to Hamburg on 28 February demanding a renewal of

---

[53] *KI*, 2, doc. 70 (p. 487). *SPF*, 1577–8, pp. 426–40.   [54] *SPF*, 1577–8, pp. 458–60.

privileges without delay or diminution. Negotiations were still continuing and by 16 March it had been agreed in principle that the Steelyard quota of unfinished cloth should be increased by 3,000 or 4,000, but the queen would not sign the necessary warrant until Hamburg had renewed its treaty with the Adventurers. Hamburg did not reply to the queen's letter and the matter hung fire until the assembly of a Wendish diet in June, but the city remained under heavy pressure from all sections of the Hanse. The representatives at the diet were probably misled by an unjustifiably confident report by George Liseman, secretary of the Steelyard. He said that English merchants were now so hard pressed that they had virtually nowhere to sell their cloth but the Empire. It was therefore a very favourable time to demand the restoration of their ancient privileges, or at least the greater part of them, for without this the redress of particular grievances was useless. Four days later (9 June) the Hamburg representative announced that the city would expel the Adventurers if its allies insisted, which they did. The same day the diet wrote to the queen that her subjects did not need special privileges in Hamburg, for if she would only confirm the treaty of Utrecht they could trade freely in all Hanse towns. On 14 June Hamburg council itself wrote to Elizabeth, still not categorically refusing to renew the treaty, but making that step conditional upon greater freedom for Hanseatic merchants in England. Finally, on 20 June in Hamburg the council formally announced to the Adventurers that their privileges would be absolutely terminated on 28 November next. The following day it turned down a plea to extend the time limit until 12 March 1579, but stated that between November and March the Adventurers might dispose of any goods remaining to them upon the same conditions as other aliens.[55]

When news of Hamburg's final decision reached London the Adventurers went immediately to the Privy Council and in turn Steelyard officials were summoned to provide an explanation. They were advised that the Adventurers were demanding not merely the renewal of the Hamburg agreement, but also full implementation of their ancient claim to reciprocity in all Hanse territories, as expressed in clause four of the treaty of Utrecht; if the claim was not met the Hansards would be deprived of such privileges as they continued to enjoy in England. Because of fear of reprisals there was no question of an immediate clamp down on Hanse trade, but the government

[55] *KI*, 2, nos. 1221, docs. 74 (pp. 491–2), 77 (p. 494), 85 (p. 505), 81 (pp. 498–9), 87–8 (pp. 509–10). *SPF*, 1578–9, p. 22. BL, Lansdowne 25/74.

was urged not to allow any increase in their cloth exports beyond the recent level, in order to prevent the accumulation of a stockpile which would allow them to defy the Adventurers, at least for a little while. In August 1578 a warrant was issued for the export of 2,000 cloths, but a warning was given that no more would be released until the matter of the Englishmen in Hamburg was settled. Hanseatic letters of this period were not optimistic of a favourable outcome and indicate that even the Earl of Leicester, who among the queen's intimates was the most well disposed towards them, held out hopes of nothing better than a settlement based on the 1560 compromise. On 15 October the queen wrote formally to the Hanse saying that its privileges in England would be ended unless those of the Adventurers were restored in Hamburg. This was interpreted by Steelyard officials as meaning that their situation was about to become worse than at any time since 1557–8. Despite their gloom, which prompted them to consider exporting their ceremonial silver to a safer place, they engaged in serious and protracted talks with members of the government; hopes of a settlement waxed and waned. At the beginning of November 1578 Morris Zimmerman reported a speech of Leicester, in which he portrayed the queen as Hercules and again said that there could be no question of restoring to the Hanse the privileges of the treaty of Utrecht, but at most confirming the draft treaty of 1560. A week later Zimmerman wrote that talks with Leicester and Secretary Walsingham were going well and, were it not for the constant agitation of the Merchant Adventurers, might soon be brought to a satisfactory conclusion. On 6 December, however, he claimed that Walsingham was the chief mouthpiece in the Council of the Adventurers. Rumours that Leicester might be willing to concede the 1560 compromise, even if Hamburg did not renew its charter to the Adventurers, spurred the latter to more direct action. By 2 December they had persuaded the city of London to exclude Steelyard merchants from Blackwell Hall and to suspend all other privileges, thus reducing them to the status of aliens at the very time when it was seeking to re-introduce hosting laws and other obsolete customs. The government was not prepared to tolerate such blatant interference and city officials were summoned to the Privy Council to account for their behaviour. On 9 December the Privy Council published a decree, allowing the Steelyard merchants until 25 March 1579 to demonstrate that Englishmen enjoyed the same privileges in Hamburg and other Hanse towns as they themselves claimed in London and elsewhere in England;

failing this they would be treated like all other aliens. Since the burden of proof lay upon the Hansards they were in a difficult position. However, at the end of that month they succeeded with great difficulty in getting the London edict suspended on the grounds that it prejudiced the queen's decree of 9 December.[56]

During this period the Merchant Adventurers constantly complained about their treatment in Hamburg, particularly about attempts to dispose of real estate which they had acquired there. Even so, the government would not press the Hanse too hard. In December 1578 Zimmerman reported that the queen expected a delegation and she would welcome this, even though she was not prepared to issue an invitation herself. In January the Steelyard merchants were promised a licence for a further 3,000 cloths. Nevertheless, not until 17 February 1579 did Lübeck draft a reply to the queen's letter of the previous October and this did not reach its destination until 20 March, just five days before the expiry of the ultimatum of 9 December. It merely said that the English demands would be discussed in a diet which was due to meet on 25 July.[57]

Once the 25 March deadline had passed the Adventurers pressed for the immediate implementation of the December decree, but the Privy Council delayed until 7 April, when it announced that the sanctions would be suspended until after the meeting of the diet. If that body did not give satisfaction the decree would then be enforced. Pressure upon the Germans was increased by the decision that merchants might continue to trade upon payment of the rates of duty charged since 1560, but must also give bonds for the payment of full alien rates, which would be forfeit if the diet decided against the Englishmen. Additionally, the mayor of London was authorised to begin proceedings against Hanse merchants who traded with non-citizens, provided that no final decision was taken in any case without the permission of the Privy Council. In response to the Adventurers' plea for a total ban on trade with all ports between Emden and the river Skawe, the council's response was decidedly lukewarm. During the late winter and spring exports had been halted while Burghley collected information about the general level

---

[56] *SPF*, 1578–9, pp. 112–14. *APC*, 10, pp. 300–2, 419. *KI*, 2, nos. 1333, 1341, 1346, 1356, 1360, 1364, 1371, docs. 89–92 (pp. 511–17), 94 (pp. 518–19), 97 (p. 522), 99–100 (pp. 526–9), 102 (pp. 532–3). PRO, sp12/127/15.
[57] *KI*, 2, nos. 1378, 1398, doc. 103 (pp. 533–5). *SPF*, 1578–9, pp. 382, 494. *Calendar of Salisbury MSS*, 2, p. 232.

of trade with Hamburg over the last two years and about goods which denizen and alien merchants now had ready to ship there. This done, the Privy Council decided that denizens who were not free of the Merchant Adventurers or the new Spanish Company might export cloth and any other non-prohibited goods currently in their possession to whatsoever port they chose, including Hamburg. When present stocks were spent they must obey an injunction to avoid all ports between Emden and the Skawe. Alien merchants other than Netherlanders (primarily Italians) were permitted to ship current stocks to Hamburg, provided that they did not sell in that city but passed on to upper Germany or Italy. Afterwards, they too were to observe the injunction. Some four or five Englishmen who sought permission to send a small quantity of kerseys in their company were allowed to do so. Any Netherlanders who were accustomed to ship cloth via Hamburg were allowed to continue without limit of time, but only in the usual quantities and without colouring for other aliens or Englishmen. Finally, Hamburg merchants were also allowed to ship their usual quantities, for sale only in their own city.[58]

During the run up to the Hanseatic diet the advice of Steelyard officials, as well as that of Heinrich Suderman, was to take a firm stand, either by banning trade with England and trying to exclude cloth from the Empire or, alternatively, burdening denizen-owned cloth with import duties equal to the higher export rates which now faced Hanse merchants. The fact that there were now only four merchants resident at the Steelyard seems to have decided them to throw caution to the wind. They prepared a number of detailed memoranda for consideration by the diet.[59] These claimed that in recent years Hanse trade had been completely undermined, not only because Englishmen could sell cloth in Germany more cheaply than the Steelyard merchants, but also because the former could now get return goods, such as linen, on more favourable terms. It was alleged that even English shipping costs now matched those of the Hanse and this posed a threat to the latter's fleet. The situation was not thought to be irreversible, since England's economy depended upon cloth exports, for which Germany and eastern Europe were the principle markets; nor could England survive without imports from

---

[58] PRO, sp12/130/33. *SPF*, 1578–9, pp. 468–9, 481–2, 496. *KI*, 2, doc. 106 (pp. 539–41). *Calendar of Salisbury MSS*, 2, pp. 232–3, 238.
[59] *KI*, 2, docs. 107–14 (pp. 540–53).

Hanse regions. To keep Englishmen in their place it was necessary not only to confirm their exclusion from Hamburg, but also to deny them access to any other German mart. The latter point had reference not only to the danger that the Englishmen might obtain a refuge in another Elbe port, such as Stade, as an alternative to Hamburg, but also to the more imminent possibility that they might obtain a staple for their Baltic trade in the Prussian port of Elbing.

The critical Hanse diet began on 22 June 1579 and continued until late August, but the refusal to accept the latest English demands had been taken and a formal address to the queen had been drafted by 8 July. It was decided that Danzig and Cologne should provide envoys to go to England with Heinrich Suderman, the Hanse syndic. In the event Suderman did not make the journey, so the main burden of the negotiations fell upon George Liseman, secretary of the Steelyard. The queen's reply to the Hanse letter, drawn up on 8 September, intimated that despite its intransigence she would not yet enforce the decision of the previous April, so that there might be time for reconsideration. On 13 September the Hanse envoys met the Privy Council to receive answers to three questions which they had submitted in advance. The alleged purpose of the meeting was to ensure that the envoys fully understood the English position and did not misrepresent it to the diet. But the answers given to them were far from unambiguous. In reply to the query as to whether Hanse merchants should enjoy customs equality with Englishmen, it was said that they must pay the rates recently levied on them; in answer to the request for cloth-export licences, it was said that they would have a sufficiency of licences, provided that they gave security to observe any current regulations concerning sales; the answer to a question about freedom of trade within England was that it remained as in former times. When the envoys demanded that their merchants should be released from any securities given in consequence of the April decree this was refused, and finally they were told that all the English concessions were dependent upon the restoration of the former privileges in Hamburg.[60]

In November 1579 George Liseman went again to Germany in an attempt to persuade the towns to adopt retaliatory measures against English trade. Since the government would not issue export licences

---

[60] *Ibid.*, docs. 115 (pp. 573–8), 121–2 (pp. 597–9). *APC*, 11, p. 262.

unless the merchants gave security to pay alien duties, the Steelyard wanted a similar step to be taken in Hanse towns. It also advocated a blockade of Narva and a ban on Englishmen's trade in Danzig, Elbing and Königsberg. Failing a full diet of the Hanse Liseman managed to arrange a conference between the Hamburg city council and representatives of Lübeck and Bremen. This began on 22 December but found difficulty in reaching agreement. Hamburg wanted to proceed cautiously, while Liseman urged immediate retaliation; Hamburg was willing to send another embassy to England, but Lübeck was against this. Finally, on 30 December the conference decided that if the English government continued to exact security for payment of alien customs then a similar security, amounting to $7\frac{3}{4}$ per cent of the value of their goods, should be taken from English merchants in Hanse towns. For the moment this decision was not to be implemented, but it was hinted at in a letter to Elizabeth dated 29 December, which reached its destination in mid-February.[61]

Meanwhile, the Steelyard had reopened talks with the Privy Council and was reconsidering its official policy of refusing to give security for the payment of alien customs. This was because some merchants, particularly those of Cologne, wanted to comply in order to obtain export licences, but were refusing to pay scot to the *Kontor* if they eventually had to pay alien rates. In February 1580 Lübeck complained to Cologne that because of this the English had gained the impression that the city and its third were not wholeheartedly with the Hanse. One factor which weakened Zimmerman's opposition to bonds was an initial optimism that they would not be forfeit, since he believed that ultimately the government would decline to treat the Hansards as aliens. As late as 24 January 1580 he was relying on verbal assurances that no decision had yet been taken. He was profoundly shocked to be told that day that the matter had been decided against the Hanse. Even as late as 6 February the Privy Council declined to commit this to writing. On 21 February Zimmerman was told that the Hamburg letter of 29 December made no difference to the decision, but only a fortnight later was he given written notification of this for transmission to the Hanse. He believed that the procrastination was designed to allow the Merchant Adventurers time to re-establish a staple at Emden

[61] *KI*, 2, nos. 1466, 1660, 1671–2, 1696, 1700, docs. 126 (pp. 610–16), 129 (pp. 618–620). Ehrenburg, *Hamburg*, p. 154.

and the Eastland merchants theirs at Elbing. Only when these parties felt assured of their ends did the government let the final blow fall upon the Steelyard. Inevitably, Zimmerman smelt corruption; on 10 January he had reported that the Adventurers had given rich new year's gifts to the Privy Council and that his side ought to do the same.[62]

Even though the government seemed to have made up its mind to treat the Hansards as aliens, the decision was at first only partly implemented. On 19 March 1580 the Steelyard secretary went before a public notary in London and swore that a Cologne merchant had been prevented from exporting cloth unless he paid the full alien duty in ready money. Three days later word was sent to Lübeck that bonds were no longer acceptable for cloth presented for export, but Thomas Smith, farmer of the London import duties, had promised that he would not yet levy alien rates on imports. It was urged that the time had now come to retaliate. In fact, preliminary steps were already being taken. On 13 March Lübeck, having received news of the Privy Council's verbal decision of 21 February, wrote to Cologne urging it to take security from English-owned goods. On 24 March the latter city instructed hosts to certify the authorities about all Englishmen and their goods, though money was not yet demanded. Only in June did the chief western towns, including Hamburg, begin to levy money at the rate of $7\frac{3}{4}$ per cent on English-owned goods, which would be refunded if and when Hanse merchants were repaid in England. The Steelyard had wanted a rate of 20 per cent. When the Privy Council heard of the charge in September it immediately ordered that an additional tax of $7\frac{3}{4}$ per cent be imposed upon all Hanse imports and exports. Although not unexpected, this move nevertheless led to second thoughts in some of the Hanse towns, particularly when coupled with protests within Germany against their own action. One complaint came from the Augsburg firm which handled the entire production of the Hungarian copper mines, selling much of it to Englishmen at Hamburg. The firm solicited the Emperor to write to Hamburg asking it to review the discriminatory tax. More effective was the direct action of English merchants who began to avoid the town in favour of smaller ports on the Elbe. As if to emphasise the choice open to Hamburg Elizabeth wrote a friendly letter and the Merchant Adventurers sent an envoy requesting renewal of their

---

[62] *KI*, 2, nos. 1702, 1707, 1713–17, 1719, 1730–1, 1734, docs. 132 (p. 623), 136 (p. 627). *APC*, 11, p. 406.

privileges. Interested townsfolk pressed the city fathers to do this. Hamburg's dilemma was apparent when in November 1580 its representative walked out of a conference held at Lüneberg to prepare a case for submission by the Hanse to a forthcoming imperial diet. Those who remained decided that in every Hanse town all persons handling merchandise, even that only in transit, must swear that no Englishmen had any financial interest in it. Failure to do so would result in the imposition of a $7\frac{3}{4}$ per cent tax, even if this had already been charged in another town. Moreover this was no longer to be treated merely as security, but as a non-refundable levy to finance the campaign against England.[63]

Unfortunately for the Hanse the days had long passed when it could unilaterally attempt to determine the fate of English merchants and English manufactures in central and eastern Europe. Commercially, it had to take account of the interests of powerful cities in southern Germany which had prospered in the sixteenth century; constitutionally, it relied upon the cooperation of the imperial authorities in Germany, and of the King of Poland for help to control the Prussian towns. The first priority was to seek an imperial ban on the Merchant Adventurers' staple in Emden. After their expulsion from Hamburg the Adventurers had removed their court to Antwerp, where it remained until 1582, when it was transferred to Middelburg. But as early as January 1580 Morris Zimmerman claimed that only one third of the membership traded at Antwerp. The remainder resorted chiefly to Emden, where their numbers built up rapidly after August 1579, when company representatives gained provisional assent of the two counts of East Friesland to the restoration of their former privileges. Only one thing disappointed them – the levying of taxes on their trade between Emden and inland towns. This stemmed from the fact that the first Adventurers to return, like the interlopers who were there before them, used Emden merely as a port of entry and exit for the continent. This was unproductive from the counts' point of view. Comital tolls were not levied on trade to and from England and if Englishmen did not halt at Emden there was less incentive for interior merchants to come to the town. The latter would have paid tolls as they came and went, so in their absence Englishmen were required to make up the deficit from their trade into Germany.[64]

---

[63] PRO, SP12/136/67. *APC*, 12, p. 206. *KI*, 2, nos. 1754, 1757, docs. 139 (p. 632), 143–4 (pp. 639–42). *SPF*, 1579–80, pp. 475; Addenda, 1553–83, p. 559. Ehrenburg, *Hamburg*, pp. 155–8.   [64] *KI*, 2, no. 1713. *SPF*, 1579–80, p. 147; Jan.–June 1583, p. 528.

Hagedorn contends that the English privileges were renewed despite the initial hostility of Edzard, the elder and more powerful of the two counts.[65] In fact, this hostility, suggested by a letter he sent to Queen Elizabeth in December 1579, was more apparent than real.[66] He began by complaining about the ingratitude displayed by the Adventurers in their untimely withdrawal from his town in 1565, and no doubt his resentment on this score was real enough. But the remainder of the letter reflected the official policy of the Merchant Adventurers, who may themselves have prompted Edzard to write in this vein. He complained that Italians and other aliens were still free to export cloth to Hamburg and other ports in the Low Countries, and also imported from these places. Furthermore, both interlopers, that is Englishmen not free of the Merchant Adventurers Company, and stragglers, freemen who disregarded the injunction to confine their business to the official mart, bought and sold at Hamburg and elsewhere in Germany. Edzard's claim that such activities were as harmful to the company as to himself were echoed by governor Christopher Hoddesdon, in a letter sent to Burghley in March 1580 from Emden, whither he had gone to formalise the new agreement with the counts.[67] Hoddesdon complained that he had bargained with a Brunswick merchant for £2,000 of saltpetre to be delivered at Emden, but the latter broke the contract because of the great demand for gunpowder by Englishmen still at Hamburg. Prices were soaring from 'no other cause than the greediness of our own merchants, as the thing itself will more effectually declare, if this disordered running to Hamburg do not stay itself, or be shortly stayed by your means'. In the same letter Hoddesdon reported that Edzard's animosity towards England stemmed chiefly from resentment of the fact that his younger brother was in receipt of a pension from the queen, while he had nothing. Later correspondence shows that what he really wanted was a token of Elizabeth's esteem and that a grant of the garter might win him over just as effectively.[68] Despite Edzard's misgivings that England was still trying to recover privileges in Hamburg, he agreed that the company might remain at Emden for six years.

As early as January 1580 Lübeck drew up a memorandum which was to form the basis of the Hanse case against the Merchant Adventurers for the remainder of the sixteenth century. It alleged that the company was a monopoly, injurious to the Empire, and as

[65] Hagedorn, *Ostfrieslands Handel*, 2, p. 30.   [66] *SPF*, 1579–80, pp. 102–4.
[67] *Ibid.*, pp. 188–90.   [68] *Ibid.*, pp. 197–200, 213–14, 270.

such should be outlawed on the basis of an imperial law of 1548. As a first step it called for the expulsion of the Adventurers from Emden. Repeatedly over the next few years most of the constitutional components of the Empire expressed sympathy with the Hanse. But without the active support of the Emperor Rudolf, which was not forthcoming, nothing could be done to harm its rivals. The Emperor first wrote to the Counts of East Friesland calling upon them to expel the Adventurers in June 1580, but they refuted the charges against the Englishmen and allowed them to remain. Following further complaints the Emperor again ordered the counts not to harbour the Adventurers and made representations to the queen. But in February 1581 he announced that he was powerless to impose fiscal sanctions on English trade or to ban the import of cloth; such steps could be taken only by an imperial diet, after receipt of conclusive proof that the Adventurers operated a monopoly. In March he decreed that the penal tax of $7\frac{3}{4}$ per cent must cease. Since the Hanse was still lobbying for support it had no choice but to obey. Many towns were secretly glad of a face-saving excuse to lift the tax, which was tending to destroy their own trade as south-German merchants diverted traffic from traditional routes to avoid places like Lüneberg which imposed it. Some towns had already followed Hamburg's example and abolished it. All this was reported gleefully by Hoddesdon, who concluded that the tax had done little harm to English trade.[69]

In July 1581 the remnants of the Steelyard community, feeling themselves to be utterly abandoned by the Hanse towns, approached the Privy Council and suggested that the privileged status which they had enjoyed until March 1580 should be reinstated in exchange for the return of the Merchant Adventurers to Hamburg on the terms prevailing until 1578. They also asked that the new tax of $7\frac{3}{4}$ per cent should be ended, since it was no longer being levied in Germany. Under questioning they admitted that they had no authority from the Hanse to make the first offer and that they had only hearsay knowledge of the suspension of the tax. In October, therefore, the Privy Council pronounced that they could take no action on either matter, pending some formal statement by a Hanse diet which was shortly to meet in Lübeck. On 4 November the diet revoked the $7\frac{3}{4}$ per cent tax, but its statement about the Hamburg residency was regarded as so unsatisfactory that the Privy Council, under pressure from both the Adventurers and the Eastland

[69] *SPF*, 1579–80, pp. 364–7; Jan. 1581–Apr. 1582, pp. 196–8; Jan–June 1583, pp. 586–7. *KI*, 2, nos. 1710, 1781, 1796, 1799–1800, 1853, 1862.

Company, declined for the moment to remove its own tax. Finally, at the end of January 1582 the Council agreed to suspend the tax for four months, to allow time for the Hanse to clarify their attitude towards English merchants. Writs sent to customs collectors ordered them not to collect the tax until further notice; there is no evidence that it was reimposed, despite the fact that no reply came within the allotted time.[70]

Notwithstanding the Steelyard's conviction that it had been abandoned, the Hanse submitted its case against the Adventurers to the imperial diet which met at Augsburg in the summer of 1582. The outcome was disappointing, despite the fact that all chambers approved a decree which outlawed the Merchant Adventurers from the Empire, on the grounds that they constituted a monopoly. When the diet dispersed the Emperor refused to publish the decree, contenting himself with more representations to Queen Elizabeth and the Counts of East Friesland. Contemporaries believed, and most German historians have accepted, that the frustration of the diet's decision was due to bribery of the imperial Chancellor. On the other hand, J. R. Marcus believes that Emperor Rudolf was simply unwilling to provoke a clash between himself and the queen.[71] The English success, whether due to bribery or sound argument, owed much to the energies of George Gilpin, secretary of the Merchant Adventurers, who had been sent to the diet to present their case. Fortunately, he managed to avoid the fate of Daniel Rogers, an ambassador dispatched to the Emperor in 1580, who had been captured and imprisoned by the Spaniards.[72]

Throughout 1583 the Emperor ignored complaints from princes and provincial estates all over Germany that he had not published the imperial ban on the Adventurers. Finally, in June 1584 following an appeal from the Electors, he felt compelled to justify his position and formally stated that the time was inopportune, since a ban would harm the Empire as a whole. He urged that the Hanse should accept an invitation given by Elizabeth more than a year before to send a delegation to England to discuss their differences. This move was timed to coincide with a diet of the Wendish towns at Lübeck.

[70] *APC*, 13, pp. 226–7, 317–18, 323. PRO, SP12/149/59; 150/32–4; 152/16–17. *KI*, 2, docs. 154 (pp. 684–8), 162 (pp. 700–1), 164 (pp. 708–12).

[71] J. R. Marcus, *Die handelspolitischen Beziehungen zwischen England und Deutschland in den Jahren 1576–1585* (Berlin, 1925), p. 61.

[72] *SPF*, Jan. 1581–Apr. 1581, pp. 490–1, 596–7, 635; Jan.–June 1583, pp. 305–10, 621–41.

When it was decided to convene a diet of the whole Hanse in September, Hamburg announced its support for the proposed embassy, since there appeared to be no way that England could be forced into submission. Lübeck was hostile, but agreed that Hamburg should privately arrange for Steelyard merchants to have exploratory talks with the Privy Council. These duly took place and the merchants again proposed that their franchises should be restored in return for a revival of the English residence at Hamburg. They wanted the queen to send an embassy to the coming diet, with full powers to negotiate this. The Privy Council replied that once the Adventurers were reinstated at Hamburg then the Hanse privileges would be restored, to the extent that they had been enjoyed during the present reign. But the queen's representative would not go to the Hanse; it was incumbent upon them to send a mission to England. The Steelyard was prepared to support this, as was Hamburg, but the formal proposition was opposed by Heinrich Suderman in a typically voluminous historical memorandum which he submitted to the diet when it belatedly met in November 1584. The official reason for the refusal to negotiate in England was that the Emperor and the Kings of Poland and Spain were all interested parties, but none of them would be willing to send an ambassador there. Utrecht, Antwerp or Bruges were put forward as alternative venues. Nevertheless, the diet did agree that George Liseman and Dr John Schulte should go to England for further exploratory talks. They were to report back to the towns of Lübeck, Hamburg, Bremen and Lüneberg, which together were empowered to act executively on this matter.[73]

Liseman and Schulte were in London from June to November 1585, but to no avail. The mission was handicapped by Liseman's distrust of Schulte, for he believed that the latter was concerned only to secure the return of the Adventurers to Hamburg, his own city, and was prepared to sacrifice the wider interests of the Hanse to this end. But personal discord was not the main reason for the failure of the talks; this stemmed from the fact that the envoys were not empowered to meet the minimum English demand, which was a firm guarantee of the restoration of the Hamburg residency. As a result of the talks of the previous autumn it had been assumed that ambassadors would be authorised to negotiate on this matter, and

[73] *SPF*, July 1583–July 1584, pp. 513–14, 517; Aug. 1584–Aug. 1585, p. 140. *KI*, 2, nos. 2199, 2201, 2208, 2215–16, docs. 182–5 (pp. 762–74).

there was great disappointment that this was not the case. Burghley was not at all reassured by Schulte's private promise that the residence would be restored as soon as England reinstated the Hanse privileges. The chief obstacle to a settlement was that neither side was prepared to make the first move, though the position was complicated by the patently untrue claims of each that the other already enjoyed freedom of trade. It cannot be said that the Englishmen were not serious in their will to settle, since the Privy Council took the precaution of obtaining the queen's signature to a document promising to reduce Hanse customs duties to the level prevailing before December 1578. This may in itself have been no mean achievement given the scène which took place when the envoys had their first audience with the queen on 5 July. She was angry because letters brought with them from the Emperor were written in German, which she could not read, and she mocked Schulte throughout a formal speech which he made in Latin, a language in which she was fluent.[74]

Soon after their return to Germany Liseman wrote to Heinrich Suderman warning of the duplicity of Schulte and Hamburg, saying that they were still conspiring to secure the return of the English residency. A letter sent by Schulte on 6 March 1586 to Burghley and Walsingham proves that this suspicion was wholly justified. He admitted that since the breakdown of the recent negotiations he regarded it as his duty to look after the interests of his own town, which required the return of the Merchant Adventurers. One of his last actions in England was covertly to arrange with Sir John Saltonstall, governor of the company, for the dispatch of a representative to Hamburg to discuss the matter with the city. This envoy, John Roberts, was now about to return to England bearing Schulte's letter, outlining proposals for the residency and a formal invitation from the senate of Hamburg to the queen to send an ambassador empowered to make a treaty. Schulte's own letter shows that he was very apprehensive about the reception which might be given to these overtures. He feared that the English would resent the absence of detail. Much remained to be settled in future talks in Hamburg and this conflicted with the principle of negotiating only in England. In so far as they went the proposals were not as advantageous to the Adventurers as the privileges enjoyed during the earlier sojourn in the city. Schulte anticipated rejection, but

[74] *SPF*, Aug. 1584–Aug. 1585, pp. 659, 666, 669–70, 673, 677, 679–80, 687–8, 695–8; Sept. 1585–May 1586, pp. 12–13, 17–20, 71–4, 138–9, 145. *KI*, 2, docs. 197–224 (pp. 809–73).

urged that, even if the Adventurers would not commit themselves to ten years, they should try 'for a year or two' to see whether they could trade in the city on these terms 'without loss'. He strongly dissociated himself and his city from letters sent to the queen by the other three towns which had been empowered by the Hanse diet to act executively:

The tenor of these letters was not confirmed by us, nor were they written by our consent or at our request. So that I leave your lordships to judge how far the men of Hamburg should be bound by them. I think myself that you ought not to be deterred by them from your plan, for affairs are no longer in that condition that we think it necessary to require the consent of other states.

All things considered, it is not surprising that Schulte requested 'these letters to be kept carefully, lest they come into the hands of those who are not favourable to this business and have it in their power to harm me'. He said that his opponents boasted that by bribery they could obtain information from any English official.[75]

As Schulte feared, Hamburg's proposals were ill-received by the Privy Council and, at first, by the Merchant Adventurers. This, rather than an imperial mandate to Hamburg forbidding it to negotiate further with England, was the obstacle to progress throughout the summer of 1586. But Hamburg was still anxious to woo back the Adventurers and in August renewed its invitation in more seductive terms. It was emphasised that what was needed from England was simply a promise of partial restitution of the Hanse privileges, and though this had to be sincere it did not need to be the most 'solemn kind' of state guarantee. Moreover, a member of the Merchant Adventurers Company could serve as envoy, rather than a fully accredited state ambassador. The pledge was also renewed that Hamburg would not be dictated to by the rest of the Hanse. This softening of tone coincided with increasing difficulties in the only markets officially open to the Merchant Adventurers and led the latter to ask their government to permit the reopening of negotiations. The agreement between the Adventurers and the rulers of Emden had expired early in 1586 and was reluctantly renewed for one year. The staple brought little benefit to the counts and their subjects, who were also unhappy about England's attitude towards their own trade with the neighbouring Spanish-occupied provinces of the north-eastern Netherlands. The Dutch rebels

[75] *Ibid.*, doc. 222 (pp. 853–5). *SPF*, Sept. 1585–May 1586, pp. 420–5, 431.

mounted a strong blockade of the river Ems to prevent supplies reaching the Spaniards, and the Earl of Leicester did nothing to restrain them when he assumed command of operations in the Low Countries. Indeed, Leicester, convinced that Emden actively favoured Spain, tried to persuade the Merchant Adventurers to abandon that town and direct all their cloth to Holland and Zeeland. This they would not do, since the occupation of Nijmegen by the Spaniards in 1585 barred the way between those provinces and Germany. Moreover, they feared that too close a proximity to Leicester would make them an easy target for forced loans.[76]

With the Spanish market now closed to English cloth the Privy Council foresaw a trade recession if the Adventurers left Emden, and countermanded Leicester's request to the company. Nevertheless, by the autumn of 1586 the merchants were holding back from purchases in England and this led the clothiers to complain to the Privy Council. The outcome was that at Christmas the Adventurers agreed that, despite unsold stocks, the company would borrow money at its corporate charge to buy up cloth lying unsold at Blackwell Hall at the end of each week, provided that clothiers did not bring more than the usual amounts nor attempt to increase prices. Failing this, members of the Staple company would be allowed to buy any cloth unsold after noon on Fridays and export it to any place overseas, notwithstanding the Adventurers' monopoly. If the intervention of the staplers did not take up all the slack then unenfranchised Englishmen would be allowed to participate, and even aliens. For a time the Adventurers honoured the agreement, but in the spring they complained of overstocking at Emden and Middelburg and the government was compelled to throw open the trade to all and sundry. On 16 May 1587 the alderman of the Steelyard was informed by Walsingham that as an act of special grace his members might buy cloth at Blackwell Hall and export it at denizen rates, though it was emphasised that this was in anticipation of Englishmen obtaining freedom of trade in Hamburg and other Hanse towns. As well as providing relief for the clothiers the gesture was intended to smooth the path for the Adventurers, who had finally been authorised to send a delegation to Hamburg to resume negotiations about the residency.[77]

The English party, led by governor Richard Saltonstall and Dr Giles Fletcher, reached Hamburg on 3 June 1587 with six ships

---

[76] *Ibid.*, pp. 385, 479–81, 502; June 1586–June 1588, pp. 68–76, 102–3.
[77] *APC*, 14, pp. 273–5. *KI*, 2, doc. 235 (pp. 893–4).

laden with cloth. The first matter to be determined was the toll to be levied on the present shipment. The Englishmen charged the senate with duplicity, in first having agreed to a rate and then the very next day increasing it, on the grounds that they could not otherwise obtain the support of the townsmen. Subsequent negotiations about the future of the residency were equally bitter and were finally broken off by the Englishmen on 22 August, when it became clear that the senate was unwilling to grant more than a temporary agreement for the Adventurers to trade in Hamburg until Easter 1588. The many letters sent home and surviving memoranda share the blame widely for the failure of the talks. First, the Englishmen castigated the alderman of the Steelyard who had written to Hamburg pointing out that the current crisis in the cloth industry weakened their bargaining power. The Steelyard also complained about recent new imposts on trade, particularly a patent which gave Sir Walter Raleigh a charge on overlengths of exported cloth. English Staplers and interlopers were also accused of undermining their fellow countrymen by advertising the current suspension of the Adventurers' monopoly. One of the reasons why the Hamburg senate's offer was rejected was that it would have allowed all Englishmen to trade in the city. But most malign influence was attributed to Dr Westondorp of Groningen, who had come to Hamburg as an envoy of the Duke of Parma, governor of the Spanish Netherlands, and continuously inflamed the senate against England. The Englishmen dismissed the claim that before granting a permanent residence the city would have to consult Spain, the German princes and other Hanse towns, since its invitation to negotiate had explicitly said that no consideration would be given to the wishes of third parties. But now a territorial dispute with Denmark disinclined Hamburg to alienate its allies.[78]

At an early stage in the dispute about tolls the English commissioners sent three Adventurers to Stade, a small town on the western side of the Elbe estuary, a few miles downstream from Hamburg. This place had been considered as a possible staple during several earlier crises. The town authorities offered much lower tolls than Hamburg, both on the present shipment and future consignments, but demanded that the English should break off all negotiations with Hamburg. At first the latter were not prepared to do this, but on 22 August, immediately after receiving the senate's

[78] *Ibid.*, doc. 238 (p. 899), *SPF*, June 1586–June 1588, pp. 313–15, 320–1, 348–9, 352, 365–6, 393, 397–405, 408, 429, 456–60.

latest offer, they decamped to Stade, without even lodging a formal notification that the talks were at an end. The senate then repented of its earlier stubbornness and sent messengers to Stade, entreating the Englishmen to return and reopen negotiations. There was no longer any talk of obtaining the consent of the Hanse or any other party, and the Adventurers were offered terms which were claimed to be substantially the same as those of 1567. One glaring omission was a firm guarantee of freedom of worship. Because of the opposition of the city churches the senate was unable to embody this principle in a formal treaty, though it offered to provide a secret guarantee. Religion seems to have presented no problems at Stade. Unimpressed by Hamburg's renewed offers, at the end of September the Adventurers signed an agreement to establish a staple at Stade for a term of ten years.

Having failed to prevent the accord between the Adventurers and Stade the Hamburg senate now worked to destroy it. Pressure upon Stade to expel the Adventurers was exerted via the town's overlord, the cathedral chapter of the archdiocese of Bremen. A more direct threat was the stationing of warships at the mouth of the Elbe in an effort to exact a toll known as tun and beacon money. Isolated English vessels were made to take their cargoes to Hamburg, but no attempt was made against large fleets. For a time there was hope of persuading the English government to force the Adventurers to cancel their agreement and accept Hamburg's terms. In response the Adventurers named three conditions for going to Hamburg, two of which were virtually unattainable. These were privileges as favourable as they now enjoyed in Stade, the agreement of Stade itself to surrender the staple and the endorsement of a Hamburg residency by the Hanse. The fact that it was now the Englishmen who were making the last demand suggests that they had given up any serious consideration of returning to Hamburg. In May 1588 the Privy Council decided in favour of the Adventurers, writing to Hamburg that it had but itself to blame for losing the staple, which could only be recovered when the three conditions were satisfied. At the same time the privileged cloth exports enjoyed by Steelyard merchants for the past year were terminated. They were informed that they might no longer export at denizen rates, except for any cloths already in their possession and provided that these were taken to Stade and sold there. Hamburg was still not ready to concede defeat. Between July and September 1588 its secretary, Sebastian a Bergen, tried vainly to persuade the Privy Council to reverse its decision. One sticking point was the continued failure to allow freedom of worship. Equally important was the question of trade between the Hanse and Spain. Not only were Hamburg's merchants deeply involved but Hamburg ships were now the main carriers of trade originating in other Hanse towns. A prerequisite of the return of the residency was the suppression of the trade in grain and munitions, and acceptance of an English right of search. The Privy Council was particularly concerned about large stores of iron ordnance, which were believed to be going from England itself to Hamburg and thence to Spain.[79]

In the summer of 1588 the Archbishop and Chapter of Bremen tried to settle the dispute between Hamburg and Stade, suggesting various forms of compromise. But with the failure of mediation the church sided with Stade and, when the Emperor ordered the latter to expel the Englishmen in January 1589, it requested that the publication of the decree be suspended until a meeting of the imperial estates. In June William Milward, an envoy of the queen who had arrived in Germany the previous April, reported that after consulting the Electors the Emperor had agreed to this. A new appeal to the Emperor from a Hanse diet in September 1591 met with no response. With the support of its overlord and inactivity on the part of the Emperor, Stade simply ignored pleas, warnings and threats about its English guests which poured in from many quarters, including Lübeck, Denmark, the King of Spain and the Duke of Parma. For several years the Merchant Adventurers were in little danger of losing their new base of operation. Their main worries related to English interlopers who continued to trade at Hamburg, and in providing protection for their own cloth convoys. The latter was a serious problem, since there was a constant fear that Hanse ships with letters of marque might attack the fleets. In 1591, when the queen was offered £200 to provide escorts or 'wafters', she contemptuously refused it as too little. Yet the company was compelled to provide escorts, which were inspected by royal navy controllers and if they were deemed insufficient the fleet was not allowed to sail.[80]

---

[79] *Ibid.*, pp. 611–12, 646–7; July–Dec. 1588, pp. 1, 226–8, 360; Jan.–July 1589, p. 240. *APC*, pp. 77–87, 229, 238. *KI*, 2, nos. 2496, 2501, 2503, 2516, 2543–4, doc. 253 (p. 922).
[80] *Ibid.*, nos. 2608–9. *SPF*, June 1586–June 1588, p. 645; Jan.–July 1589, pp. 51–2, 197–8, 241–2, 280, 331. *APC*, 21, pp. 58–9.

The Hanse diet which met between June and August 1591 made vague noises about the English staples at Stade and Elbing, but they were rather low down in an order of priorities. Some towns saw little point in expelling the Adventurers from Stade merely to see them return to Hamburg. At first Lübeck had warned Stade against harbouring the Englishmen, but a little later William Milward reported that Lübeck preferred this arrangement to a staple at Hamburg, which was already considered too rich and proud a neighbour. For others in the late 1580s and early 1590s the 'English question' meant the payment of compensation for losses incurred in their trade with Spain. As early as November 1585 England had given formal notice that she would intercept any ships believed to be carrying corn or munitions to Spain. The chief effect of this warning was to divert Hanse voyages to Spain around Scotland and Ireland. Following the defeat of the Armada the issue became more important than ever, since the English believed that Baltic ships and ship-building material would go to re-equip the Spanish navy, and grain was still accounted a strategic good. On 18 May 1589 the Privy Council issued orders to Sir John Norris and Sir Francis Drake, currently leading an expedition to Portugal, to stop the Baltic corn fleet then making for Iberia. Early in June sixty Hanse merchantmen sailed into the arms of the Englishmen at Cascaes in Portugal and were promptly dispatched to England. Shortly afterwards the Earl of Cumberland seized another eleven Hanse ships. From late July and for many months to come the Privy Council sent out a plethora of orders and counter-orders about these spoils. At first it was decided that all goods classed as contraband should be confiscated, but other wares and the ships themselves were to be released. On hearing rumours that the Hanse was to summon a special diet to concert a plan for revenge the Council ordered that all but the smallest ships should be detained until after that event. Most of the ships were released gradually during the course of 1590, and the diet, which eventually met in 1591, was then given a stern warning not to interfere. In November 1589 and February 1590 Steelyard officials were again warned of the consequences of trading with Spain and in January 1592 the Privy Council published a more exact definition of goods which were accounted contraband. England continued to intercept Hanse ships to search for such wares, but there were no more mass seizures until the end of 1596. The object now was not to deny material to Spain, but to obtain corn to prevent famine in

England and to victual troops in Ireland. This policy persisted throughout 1597 and 1598 and was directed against Dutch as well as Hanse ships, for Amsterdam had become the great entrepôt for the Baltic grain trade and the good burghers had no qualms about supplying their Spanish enemy.[81]

The complaint about the staple at Stade was revived by the Hanse when the imperial diet met in 1594. Elizabeth's envoy, Christopher Parkin, persuaded the representatives not to vote for a ban upon Englishmen, but they called upon the Emperor to intercede with the queen for the restoration of Hanse privileges in England. This he did not do until July 1595, but the request was denied. In November 1596 the Hanse renewed its application to the Emperor, which this time met with a very different response. In March 1597 the Imperial Council advised the expulsion of the Adventurers and a mandate to this effect was drafted in August. It alleged that the Company of Merchant Adventurers constituted a monopoly, which harmed the Empire by raising the price of cloth. All subjects were forbidden to deal with members of the company, who were allowed three months from the date of publication of the edict in any town to remove themselves and their property. Proclamations began to be made from the end of September, and in Stade itself on 28 October 1597. The Englishmen attempted to have the edict recalled, and dispatched envoys to friendly German princes and to the Emperor. At first they were optimistic of success and consequently retaliation against German merchants still operating in England proceeded at a leisurely pace. In January 1598 a formal prohibition was made against the latter, except for any subjects of the King of Poland who could demonstrate that they were no longer associated with the Hanse nor privy to the imperial action. The Lord Mayor of London was instructed to take possession of the Steelyard, but execution of the order was repeatedly postponed until July, when the few merchants who remained there were given several days grace to remove their possessions.[82]

When it became clear that an early removal of the imperial ban was not to be expected a split developed in the ranks of the Merchant

Adventurers. Many continued to trade at Stade and publicly declared themselves to be interlopers, hoping thereby to escape the consequences of the ban on the grounds that they were not part of a monopoly. They were encouraged in this by the Stade authorities and abetted by the Lord Mayor of London, Sir Richard Saltonstall, who, although a former governor of the company, issued them with certificates which identified them as interlopers. Officially, the company abjured Stade and, declining invitations from Groningen and Emden, declared that its only staple was to be held at Middelburg, where the court had been since 1582. It prevailed upon the government to ban exports to the rivers Elbe and Ems and to require bonds from all exporters, save those in the Eastland and Mediterranean trades, to deliver cloth only to Middelburg. The order was soon amended, not only to make it clear that France and Muscovy lay outside the company's monopoly, but also to allow merchants to take 'reasonable quantities' of cloths, bays and kerseys to Amsterdam and other places in Holland and Zeeland, as they were said to be accustomed to do. The opposition drew up memorials pointing out the alleged disadvantages of Middelburg compared with the Elbe ports. Merchants were said to be deterred from coming out of Germany to the former town, both because of fear of neighbouring Spanish garrisons and a long land journey burdened by tolls. Additionally, big English ships which had voyaged to the Elbe could not negotiate the Zeeland shallows, which left exports to small vessels which returned home in ballast. It was not only dissident members of the company and traditional interlopers who opposed attempts to funnel trade through Middelburg. There were also complaints from clothiers and the Masters of Trinity House, on the grounds that such regulations restricted the vent of cloth and impinged upon the freedom of navigation. In November 1598 the Privy Council, while denying any intention of limiting the traditional privileges of the Adventurers' company, declared that it had no wish to interfere with the legitimate rights of other parties. It therefore withdrew its recent proclamation that bonds should be given to export only to Middelburg. This was an implicit recognition of the fact that interlopers would continue to trade on the Elbe. The move did not immediately reconcile the company with its dissident members, but in the event it was the former which had to compromise to prevent mass defection to the ranks of out-and-out interlopers. From the autumn of 1598

Englishmen again traded at Stade, Hamburg and Bremen without hindrance from local authorities. Lübeck continued to insist that the imperial ban was directed at all English-owned cloth, but the other towns and south-German merchants maintained that interlopers were not part of a monopoly and therefore did not come under the ban. Those who did not simply ignore the edict easily obtained certificates of exemption from the Emperor himself. Thus in July 1599 dissident Adventurers claimed that during the previous twelve months they had sent eighteen ships to Stade, with an average of 2,000 cloths apiece. This situation so threatened the fabric of the company that it had to retreat from its insistence upon a sole staple at Middelburg. At first it sanctioned alternative trade only at Emden, where many members dealt from the autumn of 1598 to the spring of 1601. However, while trade at Stade was virtually toll free, Emden tolls on cloth and goods bought for return to England were double the rates which had been charged there in the 1580s. This made merchants receptive to a formal invitation to return to Stade, which was given by the town council in February 1601 and quickly accepted by the company and the crown. Thereafter, exports to Emden gradually declined and in the next year none at all went there. As early as June 1601 the company was officially loading six ships for Stade, and in order that the market should not be spoiled the Privy Council ordered the stay of three interloper ships which were about to sail there. At the same time instructions were given to punish merchants who had taken cloth to Hamburg in defiance of a recent proclamation that Emden and Stade were to be the only ports open for trade with Germany.[83]

Although the Merchant Adventurers Company was directly involved in the return to Stade and Emden it was necessary to give the impression that it was not operating a monopoly. This it did by not holding a court in either place and by various other subterfuges, such as exposing cloth for sale every day instead of only on appointed days. The kernel of the monopoly – regulation of supply – remained, but outward conformity to superficial imperial requirements ensured that Englishmen were unmolested at Stade. In 1607, in return for a renewed assurance that no monopoly existed nor was intended, the company even persuaded the Emperor to allow it to reopen its residency and make regulations for the conduct of its members. This

[83] *Ibid.*, pp. 199–203. *APC*, 29, pp. 24–5, 112, 299, 302–3; 31, pp. 440, 451. PRO, SP12/175/93; 265–71.

provoked the Hanse into pressing once more for the enforcement of the imperial ban. Paradoxically, this reflex and futile response reopened the question of where the staple should be located and resulted ultimately in its return to Hamburg, with privileges basically the same as those given in 1567. Stade bid desperately to retain it, but offers were received from Hamburg, Bremen and Emden, as well as from the King of Denmark on behalf of the town of Krempe. The prize finally went to Hamburg, with the Adventurers returning there for the last time in 1611.[84] In 1688 the company's charter was revoked by act of parliament and it lost its legal monopoly, but the membership reorganised as the Hamburg Company and continued to trade in the city until expelled by Napoleon in 1809.

The merchants who throughout this book have been described as Hanseatics gave up active trade in England long before the Adventurers disappeared from Germany, but by a strange quirk their descendants retained a tenuous link with the past for almost half a century longer than the latter group. Since the Hanseatics appear on the pages of history long before the Merchant Adventurers there is a measure of poetic justice about this. The last chance for the Hanseatics to re-establish themselves in England came after the return of the Adventurers to Stade in 1601. In the autumn of 1602 an embassy, headed nominally by Ralph, Lord Eure, went to Germany for talks with representatives of the King of Denmark. It also made contact with Ehrenfried von Minckwitz, an imperial agent who was examining claims that the Adventurers had given up their monopolistic practices. In March 1603 there was a conference in Bremen between the English envoys, Minckwitz and representatives of the Hanse towns. Talks went on for several weeks but were ended by the death of Queen Elizabeth. They were officially resumed in July 1604, when the last full-scale Hanseatic embassy ever to visit England presented its credentials to James I. The Hanse offered to give up its opposition to an English staple in Germany in return for a favoured status for its members in England. It no longer demanded the restoration of the medieval franchises, which had given it an advantage over Englishmen. Nevertheless, the equality of status which it requested was rather more extensive than Elizabeth had been prepared to allow between 1560 and 1578. During that

---

[84] Ehrenburg, *Hamburg*, pp. 210, 227.

period Hanseatics had paid denizen rates of duty only on goods originating in, or exported to, such places as Englishmen recognised as legitimate 'Hanseatic regions'. Now it was demanded that this definition should embrace all European imports except those from France, Spain and Italy. This would have allowed Hanseatics to pay denizen rates on the produce of southern Germany and central Europe. Such goods made up a large part of the stock in trade of the Merchant Adventurers, so the proposal was not acceptable to this group. Equally unacceptable were other demands, such as full freedom of trade in England, including access to Blackwell Hall, and a guaranteed export quota of 30,000 cloths.[85] The Hanse delegation departed empty-handed at the end of September 1604, but in 1606 the few merchants remaining in London received a consolation prize – the return of the Steelyard, which had been in the hands of the crown since 1598. Six merchants had quarters there in 1610, when it was temporarily sealed up by the Lord Mayor of London because of threats alleged to have been made against Englishmen in Hamburg and Lübeck. Five were still resident in 1620, but in 1632 they were reported to be long gone. The medieval buildings were destroyed during the great fire of London, but the complex was rebuilt and until 1853 the title remained vested in the towns of Lübeck, Hamburg and Bremen as trustees of the now defunct Hanse. The property was then sold and shortly afterwards the site disappeared under Cannon Street railway station, ironically at the very time when German historians were beginning to be conscious of the lost glories of the medieval Hanse.[86]

Analysis of the political relations between the Hanseatic merchants and the last three Tudor monarchs has shown that the medieval franchises were not destroyed with a single blow, but whittled away gradually. The fiscal advantage over denizens came to an end at the beginning of Elizabeth's reign and in 1579 the merchants were reduced to the status of aliens. Freedom of trade, which above all implied the right to export cloth without restraint, was lost earlier. It survived for no more than twelve months after the departure of the embassy which sought to make good the damage done in the reign of Edward VI. Hanse cloth exports were resumed on 24 January

---

[85] For a full discussion see R. Grassby, 'Die letzten Verhandlungen zwischen England und der Hanse, 1603–4', *HG*, 76 (1958), 73–120.
[86] P. Norman, 'Notes on the Later History of the Steelyard in London', *Archaelogia*, 61 (1909), 389–426.

1554 and by the following Michaelmas had reached 27,903.[87] The Merchant Adventurers, who had access to the customs records, put the total dispatched between that January and Christmas at 35,450,[88] which more or less agrees with the figure of 36,000 from January to November used by Heinrich Suderman for certain calculations he made about Hanse trade at that time.[89] This year was not only the last in which there was virtually free trade in cloth, but also the last in which the Hanse merchants were able to export anything like the volume which they had grown accustomed to handling in recent years. As a result of the January agreement the Hanse were allowed to ship an unlimited amount of unfinished cloths up to the value of £6 each for a period of three years, subject only to an informal understanding that for the first three months they should not sell any cloth in Antwerp.[90] The prices above which it was illegal to export unfinished broadcloth were last altered by statute in 1542, when they were raised to £4 for white cloths and £3 for coloureds. Inflation soon made these figures unrealistic, but as an alternative to further statutory action the ceiling was raised by use of the monarch's dispensing power. The distinction between white and coloured cloths was abandoned, but £6 (in the case of short-cloths) became and remained the conventional figure.

The Merchant Adventurers alleged that 11,200 cloths out of the total given above were consigned to Antwerp and Arnemuiden. They did not actually claim that any had been sent during the forbidden period and they could not legitimately complain about sales at Antwerp later in the year, despite the fact that many exports were clearly timed to catch the Bammas mart. Instead they sought to show arithmetically that the Hansards must have coloured cloth for other aliens, thereby depriving the crown of the higher rate of duty which it should have received from the latter. The 'proofs' consisted of the 'facts' that most Hanse cloth exporters did not import anything in their own names, the total value of their cloth exports exceeded imports by £154,366 3s 4d (actually £150,348 13s 4d) and during the recent Hanse trade boycott many Dutch merchants had exported cloth, but few did so now. Therefore Hansards must be colouring cloth for Netherlanders. The argument that because Hanse merchants did not import wares they could have no cash of their own to buy cloth is so absurd that it is difficult to see whom it was meant to persuade. Members of the Privy Council, for whom the memorial

---

[87] PRO, E122/87/4.   [88] BL, Add. MS 48019, fo. 124.
[89] Friedland, 'Heinrich Suderman', p. 231.   [90] *CPR*, 1553–4, p. 58.

was drawn up, must have known that a large part of the cloth trade was financed with bills of exchange. The only merit of this document is that it confirms that the Hanse still had a very large import deficit. This probably approached, though it did not reach, the figure given by the Adventurers, who made no allowance for non-cloth exports and, more importantly, used official values of imported goods, which were less than true values. Whether or not the Hanse merchants observed the letter of the agreement with the Privy Council it was less than wise of them to have sold almost one third of their entire export for the year in the Low Countries. They were well aware of the resentment this caused among Englishmen and also that it was the official policy of the Hanse to disengage from this market. Much of the cloth sold in Antwerp belonged to men who had established a domicile in that city. Six of these (three originating from Cologne, one from Danzig, one from Nijmegen and one unlocated) have been identified as exporting a total of 4,648 cloths (17 per cent) between January and Michaelmas.[91] Other merchants were probably less guilty, but not necessarily blameless; merchants did not send cloth only to their own towns. Apart from the above-mentioned proportion, the January–Michaelmas trade was handled by merchants of Cologne (20 per cent), Hamburg (20 per cent), Danzig (17 per cent), Bremen (7 per cent) and unidentified (20 per cent).

The stagnation of Hanse exports which resulted from the renewed attack of the Merchant Adventurers in 1555 became a complete stoppage after the increase in duty in 1558. In August 1559 Queen Elizabeth wrote to the Marquess of Winchester authorising the export of 456 cloths which had lain in the merchants' hands unshipped for a long time, because they could not pay the new duty without the consent of the 'head and governors of their company the other side of the sea'.[92] They were required, however, to provide security to pay by the end of the following January, whatever level of custom should have been determined upon. Despite the fact that no agreement was reached they were then allowed to continue shipping on payment of only the old rate of 1s plus bonds for the residue. Between Michaelmas 1559 and 15 September 1560 over 6,000 cloths were shipped in this way; only on the latter date did immediate payment of a full 6s 8d duty begin.[93] In September 1560 strict conditions were laid down for future trade. The merchants were forbidden to sell any cloth exported at the denizen rate of duty

[91] Friedland, 'Hamburger Englandfahrer', appendix.   [92] PRO, SP 12/6/23.
[93] PRO, 356/28.

in Brabant, Flanders, Holland or Zeeland, even if it had first been dispatched to a Hanse town; nor were they to sell kerseys in Italy. There was no limit to the total amount of cloth they might export to their own ports, but the quota of undressed cloths was fixed at 5,000, worth up to £6 each. No guarantee was given of a perpetual quota. On 10 October 1560 Winchester wrote to Cecil passing on the thanks of the Steelyard for the licence for undressed cloth, but pointing out that they presently had some 2,000 such cloths worth more than £6, which they wished to get away before winter, while the promise of export at denizen rates held good. In February 1561 the queen informed Winchester that despite the complaints of the Merchant Adventurers the Steelyard might export 600 undressed cloths, provided they gave security not to sell them in the Low Countries. This appears to have been additional to the initial quota for 5,000 and the Steelyard may have obtained yet more licences, since they exported around 12,000 undressed cloths in 1560–1. The generous treatment of the Hanse merchants at this time was possibly due in large measure to the advocacy of the Marquess of Winchester. In April, he wrote to Cecil recommending them in very glowing terms; 'the alderman and merchants of the stillyard be verie honest and conformable, and do good service daily to the quene and the realme in bringing in of corne and other comodities and therefore I wish the continuance of the quenes majesties favour toward them – they be the best and most conformable straunge merchants that contynue in the realme'. For several years at least Winchester continued to protect the Hansards from interference by the Merchant Adventurers.[94]

At this time the Merchant Adventurers were still benefiting from the liberal cloth policy inherited from the reign of Mary. Then they were allowed to export unlimited numbers of white short-cloths up to the price of £6 each. Quotas were set for long-cloths above the value of £6, but they were sufficiently high not to cause problems. There is no evidence that merchants had to pay directly for licences and one may assume that freedom of export was allowed in return for the general financial help given by the company to the crown. In April 1559 the Adventurers received a patent to export during the queen's pleasure an unlimited number of short-cloths up to £6 each and 6,000 long-cloths above that price. In August 1560 they received

[94] *CPR*, 1558–60, p. 420. PRO, sp12/14/6; 16/15, 58.

a licence for a further 8,000 long-cloths.[95] Despite the Merchant Adventurers' own freedom of trade the renaissance of Hanse cloth exports after Michaelmas 1560 provoked them into a renewal of the witch-hunt against their rivals. Figures produced by the Adventurers give the total Hanse export between Michaelmas 1560 and Christmas 1561 as 20,926 short-cloths, of which almost 63 per cent was white broadcloth, 37 per cent coloured and dressed broadcloth and the negligible balance kerseys and dozens.[96] The Adventurers alleged that between 6 February and 1 November 1561 Hanse merchants had shipped to Antwerp a total of 1,617 cloths. This was not itself illegal, though from the earlier of those dates security had to be provided against breaking bulk in the city. As evidence that a misdemeanour had been committed the Adventurers gave the names of five Hanse merchants who had paid Antwerp import duty on a total of 607 cloths, 117 kerseys and 30 cottons. But none of these five was recorded as owning any part of the 1,617 cloths legally entered in the queen's export rolls, so they would not have provided bonds which could now be declared forfeit. The Adventurers therefore suggested that the value of the 607 cloths and other pieces should be forfeited on the grounds that they had not been exported in the names of the true owners, as English law required. They further maintained that in the space of a year certain burgesses of Antwerp, whose names were also missing from the queen's rolls, had imported 2,621 cloths, 6,721 kerseys, 3,216 cottons and 2,231 dozens; therefore, like numbers must have been coloured for them by Hanse merchants. The injustice of this claim should have been apparent from the Adventurers' own memorandum, which gave the total non-broadcloth exports of the Hanse to all ports, including their own, as a mere 148 kerseys, 447 dozens and 82 pieces of checked cottons. It was therefore impossible for them to have exported or re-exported large numbers of such cloths to Antwerp.

In 1561–2 Secretary Cecil probably exercised much greater control over the issue of licences to the Hansards. On 21 January 1562 Winchester wrote to him, passing on the thanks of the Steelyard for a recent licence for 400 cloths worth less than £6 each and requesting a new licence for 6,000 cloths, which would satisfy their needs only until Easter. For the whole year they required a licence for 10,000 to 12,000 cloths and Winchester suggested the

---

[95] *CPR*, 1558–60, pp. 110–11, 491.   [96] PRO, sp12/20/43.

immediate issue of a warrant for 12,000. In fact it is highly probable that no new warrant was issued before July at the earliest, though the total Hanse export of all kinds of cloth amounted to just over 10,000 in the fiscal year 1561–2. The delay was associated with an entirely new plan which was being hammered out to regulate the export of unfinished cloth. When published this was found to have sacrificed even the interest of the Merchant Adventurers to the private profit of the queen's favourite, Robert, Lord Dudley. In July 1562 Dudley received a series of patents which empowered him to sell a virtually unlimited number of licences to export unfinished cloth for the next six years. It was already agreed in principle that a free licence for 30,000 cloths should be reserved for the Merchant Adventurers, but this was not enrolled before January 1563. The licence was valid for only a year and restricted to cloths worth £6 or less. In November 1563 negotiations were under way for a renewal on the same terms, but just then all exports were banned because of the dispute with Brussels. In July 1564 the Adventurers were given a free licence at the queen's pleasure, that is until recall, of 25,000 cloths per annum up to £6 and a further 5,000 above that price. This quota, which was allowed throughout the reign of Elizabeth and beyond, did not suffice for their needs and they had therefore to buy additional licences from Dudley and a succession of courtiers and government officials who acquired grants similar to his.[97]

Like the Merchant Adventurers the merchants of the Steelyard now received a free licence to export undressed cloth, but in their case limited to 5,000. The first operational date is not known, but by May 1563 the merchants were petitioning for an additional licence. A draft of a warrant directed to the Lord Treasurer authorised them to export 5,000 a year, subject to the proviso that all exported since 1 October last should count as part of this year's quota. In the event, the warrant, given under the queen's signet, was not issued until 7 July. It permitted the export of 5,000 cloths in the twelve months beginning 3 July just past, but any in excess of 5,000 exported since 3 July 1562 (the commencement of Dudley's monopoly) were to count as part of this year's quota, so that the total in two years should not exceed 10,000.[98] Unlike the free licence of the Adventurers that of the Steelyard was not issued in perpetuity and, though it was renewed each year, the difference between the two caused practical problems. In July 1566 Adam Wachendorf wrote to Suderman

[97] *CPR*, 1560–3, pp. 244–5, 621; 1563–6, p. 180. PRO, SP12/21/24; 31/9, 11, 14.
[98] PRO, SP12/28/21–2; 29/20.

saying that he was having great difficulty in getting hold of the royal warrant because of the queen's constant travelling.[99] A more serious difficulty arose after parliament passed a bill promoted by the cloth-workers' company the following year. This required exporters to take one dressed cloth for every nine undressed. An exception was allowed in the case of undressed cloth exported on existing licences, which meant that of the Merchant Adventurers Company and probably Dudley's licence, though the latter was near its ter-mination. Cloth exported on the Steelyard licence was not recognised as exempt, despite the fact that the only difference between it and the Adventurers' licence was that the former had to be warranted afresh each year. Some Hanse merchants exported finished cloth and the total was quite considerable, but not all wished to do so, so it was necessary to petition to be relieved of the requirement. A draft exists of a letter showing that it was intended to allow this request, but it is not known whether the intention was executed.[100]

In June 1570 the Hanse free licence for unfinished cloth was increased to 8,000 and thereafter was renewed each year at this figure until the Adventurers were expelled from Hamburg in 1578. Both before and after 1570 total exports generally exceeded the permitted quota. The difference between the two figures included dressed cloths and certain types of unfinished cloth which could legally be exported without a licence. Nevertheless, the question arises as to whether the merchants were able to supplement their collective licence by purchasing additional licences. The answer is that they were unable to do so before 1568, since the Merchant Adventurers bought Dudley's grant from him, perhaps with the very purpose of ensuring that he did not sell licences to Hansards. After 1568 the licensing system became more complex and it is difficult to get a clear picture of how the Merchant Adventurers, let alone the Steelyard, acquired licences in excess of their free quota. In 1570 a grant to Sir Henry Neville pioneered a new type of licence, which as a result of a loophole presented a marvellous opportunity to milk the queen's Exchequer. This was greedily emulated by Cecil and Walsingham, but since the full potential of the grants was only realised if they were passed on to other aliens it is unlikely that any of these licences were bought either by denizens or Hansards. In April 1577 Walsingham received a new grant of 30,000 cloths, much less damaging to the crown, since the queen was to receive full

---

[99] *KI*, 1, no. 2640. [100] PRO, SP12/48, 71; 77/67.

customs. This time it was a practical proposition to sell licences to Hansards, and Walsingham probably did so in the first year of operation. Early in 1578, however, the Steelyard pressed for an increase in their free licence as part of a deal to secure the extension of the Adventurers' residence in Hamburg. In March Thomas Wilson, the queen's private secretary, wrote to Burghley that she was 'content' that the Steelyard should have 3,000 to 4,000 above their usual number and 'Mr Secretary (Walsingham) hath willingly yielded – preferring public before his own private commoditie.'[101] A warrant for an additional 3,000 was actually drawn up, but not released because the Adventurers were expelled from Hamburg. The latter development not only prevented the Steelyard from obtaining an increase in its licence but virtually destroyed its existing trade. Separate figures for Hanse cloth exports are not available after 1578, but it is clear that the totals of those taxed at alien rates allow room for the inclusion of few Hanse cloths, or none at all.[102]

In 1564 the Exchequer introduced a new type of customs record – the port book. It was not long before the petty customer of London exports (who dealt with the cloth trade in that port) began to disregard the careful instructions issued for keeping the books, and the second surviving example (1571) is deeply flawed.[103] On the other hand, the first (Easter–Michaelmas 1565) was kept meticulously and allows a detailed breakdown to be made of Hanse cloth exports in that period – the last time this can be done.[104] Exports totalled 7,620 (out of 10,156 for the whole year 1564–5), customed in the names of twenty-seven merchants. Thirteen were Hamburgers, but they shipped only 22·4 per cent of the total, compared with 47·3 per cent credited to four Lübeckers; four Cologners had 17·2 per cent, three Danzigers 12·2 per cent, while the remainder (less than 1 per cent) belonged to one merchant from Osnabrück, one from Suell and one whose town was not given. The origins of the merchants provides little guidance to the destinations of the cloth. Almost one fifth of the total went in seven English ships, said to be going to Danzig. Little more than one sixth of these cargoes was in the names of Danzig merchants, the rest being in the names of Lübeckers. Danzig was almost certainly receiving more cloth than this, since both the Danzig and Lübeck merchants also shipped an even greater amount of cloth to Hamburg and Amsterdam. Either of these groups may have sold that cloth in north-west Germany, but

---

[101] *CPR*, 1569–72, pp. 6, 407; 1572–5, p. 281; 1577–8, p. 345. BL, Lansdowne 25/74.
[102] See appendix 3.   [103] PRO, E190/5/1.   [104] PRO, E190/2/1.

it is just as likely to have gone overland to a west-Baltic port for transhipment to the east. In 1565 Denmark severely curtailed traffic through the Sound because of war with Sweden, and Hanseatic voyages, not merely to England but to all western ports, were almost at a standstill. To complicate matters still further the amount of cloth intended for sale in Hamburg cannot be deduced from that shipped there directly, either by the city's own merchants or by all the Hansards. Some cloth simply passed through the city, but on the other hand it also received some via Amsterdam, and to a lesser extent Flushing and perhaps Antwerp. This resulted from a relative scarcity of ships passing between Hamburg and London, while Amsterdam–London sailings (and vice-versa) were second only to those between Antwerp and London. Since there was heavy traffic between Hamburg and Amsterdam it was a simple matter to trade via the Dutch port.

Danzig, Hamburg and Amsterdam between them received 80 per cent of Hanse cloth exported in this period and redistributed it in north-west Germany, Denmark, north-east Germany and Poland. These regions did not constitute a homogeneous market and there was a varying demand for different types of cloth. Overall the 1565 exports consisted of Suffolks and Gloucesters (37 per cent of each), Wiltshires (19 per cent) and the remainder made up chiefly of Hampshire kerseys and Devonshire dozens, with a mere handful of other broadcloths – Coxalls, Berkshires, Worcesters and Kents. Only Suffolks and Gloucesters went direct to Danzig, in a proportion of 4:1, while Danzig merchants shipping via other ports handled only these cloths, with a bias of more than 3:1 in favour of Suffolks. Lübeckers shipping elsewhere than to Danzig handled Suffolks, Gloucesters, Wiltshires and Hampshire kerseys in proportions of 40:40:12:8. Hamburgers took Gloucesters 52 per cent, Wiltshires 33 per cent, Suffolks 8 per cent and the balance in a mixture of other regions.

In this second half of 1564–5 only 18 per cent of Hanse cloth exports were sent to Antwerp and it is likely that few, if any, were sold in the city. This was not solely the result of the English government's control over exports. In the late 1550s the Hanse had terminated the privileges of the merchants who had until then defied its orders to relinquish their citizen rights in Antwerp. Now, as many as eight northerners and the Osnabrück merchant sent small consignments of cloth to Antwerp, but 88 per cent of that going there belonged to four merchants of Cologne and was probably destined for their home city. This may also have been true of the small amount of cloth which the latter sent to Hamburg and Flushing. Apart from a few Devon dozens and a token amount of Berkshire broadcloth the Cologners bought only Gloucesters and Wiltshires, in about equal amounts. In the light of all that has been written about the system of licences it may come as some surprise that only 23 per cent of all Hanse cloth exported in this period required licences. These were carefully recorded in the port book. Most of the rest were described as either 'worked' or 'coarse', the latter presumably indicating unfinished cloths which were not sufficiently valuable to need a licence. Wiltshire cloths were the most difficult to export without a licence and 74 per cent were supplied with them. In contrast only 21 per cent of Gloucesters and none of the Suffolks (both twice as numerous as Wiltshires) had licences. Since Wiltshires were relatively more important to the Cologners than to their colleagues they required a disproportionate share of the licences, taking 42 per cent of them even though they handled only 17 per cent of all the cloth. Subsequently, the growth of the Hamburg finishing industry created a greater demand for licences and no doubt they were distributed differently.

The decline of Antwerp in the scheme of Hanse trade with England is confirmed by the London import port book of 1567–8, the last year of normal trade in the now doomed commercial capital of the Low Countries.[105] Total imports at Hanse rates were valued at £10,136 plus 1,381½ awms of Rhine wine, of which £1,177 of the goods (11·6 per cent) and 10½ awms of wine were aboard ships coming from Antwerp. (Additionally there were two cargoes of French wine owned by Hanse merchants.) One Cologne merchant imported steel from Antwerp worth £576, another madder and onion seed worth £55, while the rest was owned by ten Hamburg, Lübeck and Danzig merchants, the bulk of whose imports came more directly from north Germany and the Baltic. All were 'genuine' Hanseatic goods, but one should not attach too much significance to the duty changes of 1560 in thus restricting trade. English complaints about Hanse competition in the import of 'neutral' goods from Antwerp before that date had been greatly exaggerated. Moreover, as early as 1552 Cologne was complacent about the prospect of a ban on the export of Hanse goods to England, since its citizens even then had little to lose. In 1567–8 the

---

[105] PRO, E190/4/2. Calendared in B. Dietz (ed.), *The Port and Trade of Elizabethan London* (London Rec. Soc., 8, 1972).

situation was no better. Apart from the Antwerp trade and a single consignment from Amsterdam, Cologne's exports to England all went via Dordrecht, but consisted only of 1,344 awms of wine and £537 of merchandise, principally bowstaves, Cologne hemp and steel. These were handled by the above-mentioned two merchants plus three others. Given the decay of traditional exports to England, such as Cologne thread, steel and weapons, wine offered the best prospects to those who still wanted to bring in goods to finance purchases of cloth. In 1575 it was reported that the German vintage promised to be the best since 1540 and merchants were urged to increase their imports, more particularly since French wine was now subject to heavy taxes.[106] Unfortunately, although the overall import of wine increased during the reign of Elizabeth, English palates did not much appreciate Rhine wine and it did not make much impact upon the market.

Some part of the decline in the share of Cologne merchants in England's trade in the mid-sixteenth century and later can be blamed on domestic factors. Nevertheless, they could with some justice complain that they suffered more than other Hansards from the cloth-licence system and the customs changes of 1560. As we have seen, the Baltic cloth trade did not depend upon licences, while Hanse trade in this region continued to enjoy customs parity with that of denizens. This did not prevent Englishmen from engrossing much of the trade, even before their rivals lost parity in 1578. As early as 1565 the ships leaving London for Danzig carried almost as much denizen cloth as Hanseatic (1,352 against 1,561). In 1567–8 denizen Eastland merchants imported into London alone £8,156 of merchandise from Danzig and Königsberg, another £729 of Baltic goods from thence or Amsterdam, and £2,018 from Narva. Another group of Englishmen, beginning to explore the possibilities of Hamburg as an alternative to Antwerp, imported goods to the value of £659. Few of the latter were Eastland goods and included some decidedly non-Hanseatic wares, such as spices. In contrast Hanseatic merchants imported only £730 of merchandise from Danzig and Königsberg and a total of £7,691 from Hamburg, Amsterdam and three other Dutch ports fed by Hamburg. The latter total included some Baltic goods, but commodities from northern Germany, such as linens, were predominant. As far as Eastland proper was concerned Englishmen had left their rivals out of sight.

---

[106] *KI*, 2, no. 678.

For reasons which are not altogether clear, 1568 became something of a landmark in denizen trade with the Baltic. When the idea of an incorporated Eastland company began to be discussed in 1578, certain parties proposed (unsuccessfully) that membership should be restricted to those who had traded there in 1568 or earlier. It may simply be that ten years seemed an appropriate qualifying period. On the other hand, in 1568 events in Prussia had caused English merchants to cling together for security and it is possible that an informal organisation, predecessor of the Eastland company, dates from that time. The affair had its origins in a legal dispute going back to 1511, suspended in 1536 when Thomas Martens returned from Danzig to England. In 1562 his son, William, revived the claim and in 1568 was able to obtain the legal distraint of Danzig property in England. Inevitably, this led to retaliation and on 26 July, eight Newcastle ships were under arrest at Danzig. A value of £8,100 was set upon six, including the goods in them chartered by Newcastle merchants, while two chartered by merchants of Lynn and London were worth £810, plus goods of undetermined value. By 9 September at least sixteen ships were under arrest. The Privy Council requested advice from Dr Daniel Lewes, which was delivered on 25 September. He observed that the London merchants involved were somewhat protected by the fact that their losses consisted of goods bought on credit, to be paid for later by English wares. Unfortunately, the Newcastle men had expended ready money on returns, allegedly over £8,000. The only way to help the latter was for the Privy Council to intervene and order the release of Danzig's ships and goods in England. This would be unfair to Martens, who had a good case, so Lewes suggested that if the Council did proceed in this manner it should order the English merchants to reimburse his legal costs to the present date, which would be no great burden to them.[107]

The buoyancy of trade in the 1560s demonstrates that the rediscovery of the Baltic by English shippers and merchants in the reign of Henry VIII was an achievement not subsequently destroyed by occasional periods of war in that region and renewed disputes with the Hanse. There is a hiatus in the Sound registers from 1548 to 1556, but in 1557 fifty-seven English ships were recorded as entering the Baltic and fifty-six coming westwards (table 19). In the

---

[107] PRO, SP12/47/2, 26, 46, 63, 81; 90/21.

latter year ships were delayed for many weeks at Danzig in retaliation for restrictions on Hanse exports, and by the autumn the Germans had ordered a boycott on trade with England. In 1558 no English ships passed through the Sound. Prussian support for the boycott soon waned and, although there are no Sound records for 1559, correspondence proves that a few English ships returned to Danzig.[108] In 1560 nine ships were recorded in the Sound, all visiting Danzig. In December of that year a group of English merchants obtained a royal licence to trade with the east country in foreign bottoms without incurring alien customs as prescribed by the navigation act of 1559.[109] Their suit alleged that they had always used strangers' ships, since English owners disliked the long, tedious voyage to the Baltic. Another reason put forward was that Eastland wares were 'very pestringe and grosse' and must be carried in 'great hulkes', of which England had but few. In fact, wares which supplied the main returns from Eastland had in the national interest been specifically exempted from the provisions of the navigation act. It may be supposed, therefore, that the 1560 licence was given so that for the present the merchants might export cloth in foreign ships without paying alien rates on it.

Elizabeth's first settlement of the Hanse problem led to an immediate increase in the number of English ships going to the Baltic. The average of movements recorded in the Sound between 1562 and 1569 was fifty-six eastwards and fifty-four westwards, but the respective figures are sixty-five and sixty-two without the years 1564–5. In these two years Denmark was restricting traffic because of its war with Sweden, and the average was then only thirty ships a year. From 1574 to 1603 the overall average of English ships recorded is ninety-four, though this comes down to seventy-six with the omission of the highly exceptional years 1578, 79, 86, 87, 95, 97 and 98. The latter resulted chiefly from unusually high grain imports. In these three decades there were no years, save that of the Spanish Armada, when the number fell way below the average. From 1562 the number of English ships visiting the Baltic each year was more than sufficient to carry the entire volume of denizen exports to that region and from 1565, at least, most undoubtedly went this way, even though the act discriminating against the use of foreign bottoms lapsed in January 1567. In 1565 English ships

---

[108] Sharpe, 'Thomas Sexton', pp. 110–11.   [109] *CPR*, 1560–3, pp. 8–9.

Table 19. *English ships recorded in the Sound tables, 1497–1603*

Year	Both ways	Year	Eastward	Westward	Year	Eastward	Westward
1497	0	1557	57	56	1583	83	81
1503	21	1558	0	0	1584	89	91
1528	57	1560	9	9	1585	63	66
1536	69	1562	51	52	1586	197	196
1537	102	1563	71	73	1587	254	259
1538	50	1564	33	33	1588	41	41
1539	25	1565	29	24	1589	78	79
1540	65	1566	87	77	1590	64	63
1541	42	1567	51	53	1591	70	72
1542	71	1568	53	45	1592	63	61
1543	1	1569	76	72	1593	82	82
1544	1	1574	72	74	1594	86	91
1545	1	1575	81	79	1595	124	123
1546	13	1576	97	102	1596	72	73
1547	28	1577	83	80	1597	149	150
1548ᵃ	0	1578	152	154	1598	111	110
		1579	105	103	1599	78	74
		1580	56	57	1600	85	77
		1581	74	73	1601	93	100
		1582	96	93	1602	68	70
					1603	67	64

ᵃ To 9 March only.

carried the entire stock of Hanse cloth sent directly to Danzig and though this probably resulted from war conditions the situation was not necessarily unique. The Sound registers show some other years in which alien vessels declared no English cloth, as well as many in which the amount was negligible.[110] A very different pattern of ship-chartering existed in the import trade. English merchants engaged foreign ships for a considerable part of their returns, to say nothing of the imports of aliens. In 1567–8 thirty ships were recorded in the port book as coming to London from Danzig, while the true number may have been as high as thirty-three. Fifteen of these vessels were English, five Danzig, two Hamburg, two Antwerp and six/nine Dutch. Two Königsberg ships came from that port. Only English ships (six) came from Narva. A similar dependence on foreign ships throughout the reign of Elizabeth is suggested by the Sound registers.[111] In the absence of many surviving English port books the registers also provide the only evidence about fluctuations in the volume and values of imports and exports through the Sound over long periods. The published tables have come in for considerable criticism, but Zins has made a valiant attempt to utilise them quantitatively and there is no need to repeat his performance.

English merchants regularly complained about attempts by the King of Denmark to increase arbitrarily the customs levied in the Sound, but they made comparatively little use of the alternative route to the Baltic (Hamburg/Lübeck). This is understandable, for the other way was not free from tolls, handling charges were higher and shipping less freely available. The removal of the Merchant Adventurers' staple to Hamburg led to an increase in the amount of traffic between there and England and encouraged some diversion of the Baltic trade. There is no indication of the volume, except in 1576–7 which may have been very untypical, since it more or less coincides with a drastic slump in the amount of English cloth recorded in the Sound (calendar year 1577).[112] The information is contained in a brief prepared by the Merchant Adventurers after they had been expelled from Hamburg and were trying to persuade the government to prohibit all trade with that port.[113] *Inter alia* it gives the exports of non-Adventurers from London to Hamburg. These consisted of woollen cloths equivalent to around 3,400 short-

---

[110] H. Zins, *England and the Baltic in the Elizabethan Era* (Manchester, 1972), table 7.3 (p. 169).
[111] *Ibid.*, tables 6.5, 6.6 (pp. 146–7).   [112] *Ibid.*, table 7.3 (p. 169).
[113] PRO, SP12/119/47; 127/88. BL, Add. MS fos. 1079–85.

cloths, other textiles, including bays, cottons and worsteds, and some non-textiles. For the moment it suited the purposes of the Adventurers to ignore the fact that some of these goods may have been sold in Hamburg by interlopers, and they alleged that all of the woollens and most of the other goods were simply in transit to Eastland. They urged that there was no reason for such traffic to continue and that the English navy would benefit if all goods went through the Sound. They also claimed that it was a falsehood for Eastland merchants to pretend that by coming to Hamburg they avoided the attention of the King of Denmark, since they passed through his dominions on leaving the city. The Eastland merchants were not ready to abandon Hamburg simply because the Adventurers had been driven out. In April 1580, shortly after their incorporation, they petitioned the Privy Council that the port was necessary to a trade which they had built up with Spain and the Levant. Rather vaguely they claimed that they bought 'wax and other commodities in Lübeck, Lüneburg and places thereabouts', which they exported through Hamburg. Despite the opposition of the Adventurers the Council agreed that, if the Eastlanders gave a bond of £4,000 not to bring anything to England, they might send up to four ships a year from Hamburg to Spain or the Levant.[114]

The 1580 agreement allowed the Eastland Company to continue to ship cloth from England to Hamburg, provided that none was unpacked or sold there. However, it is unlikely that much use was now made of this route to the Baltic. Since the withdrawal of Englishmen's privileges the toll levied upon them passing cloth through Hamburg had allegedly been increased fivefold. Moreover, since the end of 1577 they had become *personae non gratae* in Lübeck. This was the result of injudicious attempts to export from thence to Narva, possibly to avoid the attention of the English Russia Company. John Chapell of London paid £1,200 for copper at Hamburg, only to have it confiscated when he came to ship it at Lübeck.[115] Narva had fallen to the Muscovites in 1558 and despite the protests of Hanseatic and Scandinavian powers Englishmen began to visit the port, probably in 1563 when the first ship was recorded as returning from there. Trade peaked in 1566 when no fewer than forty-two out of seventy-seven English ships sailing westward through the Sound came from Narva. In these years the

---

[114] *APC*, 11, pp. 439–41. [115] *SPF*, 1578–9, pp. 494–5. PRO, SP12/149/4–5.

trade was in the hands of private merchants but was opposed by the Russia Company, which in the mid-1550s had instituted a trade with Muscovy via the North Cape, the White Sea and Archangel. The Russia Company regarded the new Narva trade as a breach of its monopoly. At the end of 1566 the company, having failed to stamp it out, obtained a parliamentary decision that Narva was included in its monopoly.[116] After that the trade declined, even though the company sent ships there and interlopers were not entirely frightened away. In 1574 thirteen English ships came from Narva, but none during the next three years. The attempt to revive the trade in 1577 failed. Four ships came from there in 1578, but in succeeding years a number which had made the voyage were seized by Swedes as they returned. In 1581 Russia lost the town and for the remainder of the sixteenth century only one English vessel is recorded as coming from Narva.

The frustrated attempt to revive trade with Narva coincided with a more significant change in the pattern of English activity in the Baltic. Until now interest was concentrated on Danzig, as it had been during the middle ages. In 1577 this city revolted against its Polish suzerain and trade came to a virtual standstill. Only six English ships were recorded as coming from there, compared with ninety-five in the previous year. The immediate gainer was Königsberg, from which sixty departures were recorded that year, whereas formerly there had been hardly any. Königsberg managed to retain some of this business, but in the long run the chief beneficiary of the turn of events was Elbing, which earlier had even less appeal to Englishmen than Königsberg. Elbing made its first overtures in 1578, but after the incorporation of England's Baltic Merchants as the Eastland Company in August 1579 negotiations began in earnest for the establishment in the town of a staple for cloth.[117] Prospects for the staple were for some time in doubt. As well as the vigorous opposition of Danzig and the Hanse, and the lukewarmness of many Englishmen, the company feared that a staple could not succeed as long as aliens were free to export cloth to wherever they wished in the Baltic.[118] In fact the abolition of Hanseatic customs parity with Englishmen had already eliminated the opposition. The cloth staple was successfully established, but

[116] T. S. Willan, *The Early History of the Russia Company* (Manchester, 1956), pp. 67–77.
[117] The early history of the Eastland Company is found most conveniently in Zins, *England and the Baltic*, pp. 54–133.   [118] PRO, SP12/146/51.

Elbing did not gain a complete monopoly of returns to England. Its location and port facilities were not of the best and some merchants preferred to buy Polish goods elsewhere. From 1582 Elbing was recorded as the departure point for most home-coming English ships, but each year a fair sprinkling left Danzig and Königsberg. If it were possible to take account of the repatriation of English-owned goods in foreign vessels then the continuing role of the alternative ports would be seen to be greater. Danzig remained the outlet for Polish grain and in years of dearth in western Europe it was the destination of the additional English ships which sped to the Baltic. However, it was Elbing which provided Englishmen with the privileges which they had sought, and been denied, for a century and a half. They enjoyed these until the town was ruined by Swedish invasions during the Thirty Years War. From Elbing the Englishmen no doubt contemplated with satisfaction the discomfiture of their old Hanse rivals, but there still remained the Dutch. That is another story, however.[119]

[119] For Eastland trade in the seventeenth century see R. W. K. Hinton, *The Eastland Trade and the Common Weal in the Seventeenth Century* (Cambridge 1959). J. K. Fedorowicz, *England's Baltic Trade in the Early Seventeenth Century* (Cambridge, 1980). B. E. Supple, *Commercial Crisis and Change in England, 1600–1642* (Cambridge, 1964).

Conclusion

The last Hanse diet, at which only nine towns were represented, was held in 1669. In reality the organisation had ceased to function long before that. Some small sense of purpose survived into the second decade of the seventeenth century, but the events of the Thirty Years War, above all the domination of northern Europe (including much of Germany) by Sweden, finally proved that the Hanse had no place in the modern world. What needs to be explained, however, is not why it finally succumbed now but why it had lasted so long. The Hanse was essentially an institution of the middle ages and its demise was heralded when the Muscovites closed the Novgorod *Kontor* in 1494. This *Kontor* was reopened in 1514, but it was never the same again. Novgorod had lost much of its importance by 1494, so to that extent its closure was more of a symbol than a critical blow. Nevertheless, it is generally accepted that the decline of the Hanse dates from the late fifteenth century. One possible cause which has been identified is the reorganisation and expansion of trade routes which began about that time. On the one hand, the geographical discoveries resulted ultimately in a world-wide trade centred on the Atlantic ports. On the other hand, aggressive firms of merchants based in south-German cities such as Augsburg, Nüremberg and Ulm began to divert trade in their direction. The first development is sometimes alleged to have turned the Baltic into a backwater and thereby weakened the Hanse. There is little or no foundation for this conclusion, since for the most part the new commerce was not competitive with the traditional trade of the Hanse. One of the earliest results of the discoveries was to turn Antwerp into the entrepôt of the Portuguese spice trade. This was detrimental to the Italian spice trade which came via the Levant, but did no harm to the Hanse. The only obvious development which may have been detrimental to Hanse interests was the opening up of the

Newfoundland cod fishery. This provided an alternative to Lübeck's Bergen trade and Hamburg's more recent stake in the Iceland fishery. Overall, the expansion which resulted from the discoveries did nothing to diminish the real size of Baltic trade, even though it meant that the latter was now a proportionally smaller part of total European trade. In the late sixteenth and early seventeenth centuries the trade of some Hanse sea-ports was larger than in the heyday of the organisation. The second development mentioned above is a different proposition. The south-German cities prospered from their intermediate position between north-west Europe and Italy and to that extent they did no harm to the Hanse. But they also provided alternative (land) access to and from central and eastern Europe and therefore detracted from Hanseatic sea-borne trade. For a time the Fuggers even posed a serious threat to Hanse firms in the Baltic itself.

South-German merchants were not the first outsiders to threaten Hanse trade and the seeds of decline were in place long before the end of the fifteenth century. They were scattered at the very time that the Hanse of merchants was giving way to the Hanse of towns. What is meant by decline is not simply a reduction of trade but the weakening of the Hanse as an institution. But before reviewing the decline let us recall the strength and uniqueness of the Hanse. The economic development of the Baltic region in the twelfth and thirteenth centuries is fundamentally important. At that time German merchants enjoyed a near monopoly of the trade between north-eastern and western Europe and that fact has often been seen as a sufficient explanation for the further development of their association. The theory is that because of their usefulness they were welcomed by their hosts, who recognised their fellowship and gave them valuable privileges which underpinned the Hanse. There must have been rather more to it than that. At the same time as the Germans provided a link between the Baltic and the west, Italians were performing a similar function between the west and the Mediterranean. But the latter developed in a very different manner from the former. Far from organising themselves into a single commercial entity, Italians did not even favour such unions for individual city stakes. Nor did they acquire commercial privileges as the Hanse did. It may be that the precocity of Italian business techniques hindered collective action beyond a certain point. At an early date merchants learnt how to pool their resources to finance societies or companies which traded throughout Europe. Drawing strength from their own size the companies may have eschewed close cooperation even with fellow citizens lest this led to the disclosure of secrets. But even if this explains why the Italians did not progress in a certain way it does not account for the German success. Unfortunately, barring nebulous and unprovable assertions such as 'national characteristics' no succinct explanation can be provided here.

By the middle of the fourteenth century the generosity widely extended to Hanse merchants in earlier times was disappearing. There were a number of reasons for this. In some quarters a growing sense of national identity cannot entirely be ruled out, but on the whole sentiments were more practically based. Princes reliant upon taxes were reluctant to allow Hansards to pay less than others, as were their subjects, of course. Some western communities were no longer satisfied to rely upon the Hanse as intermediaries with the Baltic, but had merchants of their own anxious to assume the role. Naturally, the latter expected to be allowed favours similar to those enjoyed by Hanse merchants in their countries. If these were refused they tended to side with internal interests agitating for the cancellation of Hanse privileges. In these circumstances the Hanse of merchants gave way to the Hanse of towns. It may be that autonomous merchant communities based abroad were regarded as inadequate even to defend the privileges enjoyed in their host countries. It is more obvious that they could not take it upon themselves to promise reciprocal rights in Hanse towns. The latter was entirely within the remit of the towns themselves, so it was inevitable that these should become more directly involved in the organisation. The new version of the Hanse was essentially defensive. It was unable to eliminate competition in trade, but it may have contained it within smaller limits than would otherwise have been the case. It also succeeded in preserving Hanse privileges abroad. Nevertheless, there was an internal contradiction within the Hanse, which was already a source of weakness. Now as before, the organisation existed solely to protect the commercial interests of its members. But they did not all share the same interests. Indeed, the interests of some actually conflicted with those of others. The three main power blocs of Cologne and the Rhine towns, Lübeck and the north-western maritime towns, and the Prussian towns frequently had a divergence of interests, particularly when it came to relations with outside agents. One of the functions of the diet was to try to smooth over such difficulties, but it was not always successful. In the end conflict of interest played a large part in the break-up of the Hanse.

Throughout its history, trade with England was of great importance to the Hanse. Trade was not conducted in a vacuum. A political dialogue, now in a low key, now in a higher, ensured that the wheels of commerce remained in motion, sometimes smoothly, sometimes erratically. At first negotiations were widely spread out, and between times merchants went routinely about their business. Later the dialogue was almost continuous and it was advisable for men to keep themselves informed about the current state of play, so that if necessary they could conclude their business quickly and depart without loss. Of course, some were so deeply committed that a quick withdrawal was impossible. These provided the backbone of Hanse trade in England and ensured that it survived many hard blows. Previous chapters have tried to describe and explain in some detail both the trade itself and the political dialogue. Now, in a résumé of the most important points an attempt will be made to show how the Hanse experience in England was typical (or untypical) of its general history.

Imperial, German-speaking merchants were visiting England long before the beginnings of the Hanse. They enjoyed limited privileges and may even have been loosely organised, but it cannot be shown that they left any legacy to their successors. They came from two slightly separated regions. The staple trade of those from the valley of the Meuse was the import of metal goods, which were manufactured in their home district. This region, part of the 'middle kingdom' which emerged from the ruins of Charlemagne's Empire, was peripheral to the later German Empire and its towns never became members of the Hanse. Dinant was an anomaly, since in England, but only there, its merchants were allowed to avail themselves of Hanse privileges. Further east another centre of activity was the ancient city of Cologne. This also supplied high-class metal goods to England, but made from steel rather than copper, brass and laton, which were the specialities of the Meuse towns. These metals and artefacts formed part of the stock of Hanse merchants for as long as they continued to trade with England. The Rhine merchants also imported wine. It is unlikely that Rhenish wine ever enjoyed a major share of the English market, since early on it had to compete with a home-grown product and wine from

Normandy. Later, all these vintages gave way to a flood of Gascon wine, but a trickle continued to come to England from the Rhine valley.

By the second half of the twelfth century Cologne merchants visiting England were well organised and beginning to acquire the privileges which later were regarded as an important part of the inheritance of the Hanse. Their headquarters, the London Gildhall, developed into the Steelyard, one of the four great medieval *Kontore*. The Cologne organisation, however, even with the addition of other Westphalian towns was not the German Hanse, and it is doubtful that left to its own devices it would have acquired such a large stake in English trade as the wider community eventually did. Reinforcements came in the early thirteenth century from towns on the North Sea and Baltic coasts. Notwithstanding the view that an inter-town organisation of these merchants operating in the Baltic was the core of the Hanse, it is difficult to see exactly how that body fits into the English scene in the first half of the thirteenth century. A group, which is never defined more closely than 'merchants of Gotland', possessed valuable privileges before the 1220s. But citizens of the key towns of Lübeck and Hamburg do not seem to have shared these, at least not automatically. The latter were still obtaining their first privileges and looking for English recognition of their hanses at a considerably later date. It is possible that individual Lübeck and Hamburg merchants who also traded with Gotland were able to lay claim to the earlier privileges, while their fellow citizens generally could not. This would explain the need for Lübeck and Hamburg to press their suits independently, though it draws attention to the limited membership of the Gotland community. The latter point need not be stressed too strongly, since it is generally accepted that the fully developed Hanse did not come from a single organisation or event. It resulted from an amalgamation of interests which had formerly been separate.

Events in England in the early years of Edward I's reign were of major importance in the history of the Hanse, though what was happening in Flanders at roughly the same time was equally significant. These countries were the real melting-pot of Hanseatic interests, and developments here carry more weight than those at Bergen or Novgorod. The geographical position of England and Flanders accounts for this; the northern and eastern outposts did not attract merchants from so many different towns and regions as the former. In England, Cologne and the northern merchants seem to have realised that it was better to unite to defend or extend their trade rather than continue their separate ways, competing not only with Englishmen and other aliens but even between themselves. Obviously, similar political considerations prevailed in other countries visited by Hanse merchants. England is somewhat different in that the political marriage of interests does not seem to have led to as great a pressure for the concentration of trade as there was elsewhere. Concentrations of trade in overseas countries were greatest at Bergen and Novgorod, but the northern merchants also wanted to make Bruges into a staple for Baltic goods coming to the Low Countries and for cloth exported from that region. They were only partly successful in this, not least because a number of Dutch towns were themselves members of the Hanse. Additionally, from the early fifteenth century Antwerp attracted Cologne merchants; the draw of the Brabant city was resisted by other groups, but in the following century it replaced Bruges as the seat of the *Kontor*. In England the London *Kontor* was clearly the leader of the Hanse community before the end of the thirteenth century, but its authority to tax the provincial *Kontore* was disputed for a very long time to come. Trade at Boston was greater than that at London until the late fourteenth century and only thereafter did the latter gradually acquire a virtual monopoly of trade. Even in the sixteenth century it was possible for there to be a substantial, albeit temporary, revival of trade at Hull. Trade at the provincial ports had a distinctly regional bias – Lübeck at Boston, Prussians at Hull, Bremen at Lynn, Hamburg at Yarmouth, Cologne at Ipswich. London trade tended to be more mixed, though dominated by Rhinelanders except in its last years. There is no evidence of any deliberate attempt to discourage trade in the provinces. The decline there was the result partly of commercial forces and partly of accidents of one sort or another. Dishonesty was at the bottom of the Hamburg men's withdrawal from Yarmouth, but their being found out may be classed as accidental. The decline of the Boston *Kontor* was more complex. The bitterness of the quarrel between Lübeck and England was obviously of importance, but it was not necessarily the decisive factor. Some weight must be allowed to the decline of the Bergen staple, which was the mainstay of the Boston trade. Consideration should also be given to Boston's own decline in the fifteenth century, though care must be taken not to confuse cause and effect.

The German merchants in England had organised themselves into a single community by the 1280s. More importantly, their organisation was then formally recognised by the government of the host nation and became the focus for commercial privileges. The significance and the timing of this cannot be overstressed. A century later English merchants trying to establish themselves in Prussia sought recognition of their fellowship from the government of that country. This was long refused and the denial caused the English a great deal of trouble. Had the Germans in England not acted when they did, they might not have done so at all and the omission could have been fatal. Edward I was ready to assist all alien merchants (at a price) and in 1303 issued the *Carta Mercatoria*. This may have lulled the merchants into a false sense of security, and the Hansards even neglected to renew their own charters when Edward II confirmed the *Carta Mercatoria*. Had aliens generally basked in such royal favour two or three decades before, then the pressure upon the Germans to sink their regional differences might have been less. Fortunately, the Hansards belatedly secured the confirmation of their individual charters, so they were protected when the lords ordainer cancelled the *Carta Mercatoria* in 1311. In succeeding years they were even able to obtain an extension of their privileges, for the king himself was not hostile to them, and anyway they paid him handsomely. Again the Hanse had a good sense of timing, for by the 1320s the tide was moving against them. The accession of Edward III put an end to the critical inspection of their franchises which was taking place at that time and they obtained a renewal of their charters. Never again did they neglect to do this at the beginning of each reign, though sometimes they were forced to wait several years for a formal confirmation. Each act of renewal added another layer of authority and while parliament was ready to tear up the charters unless Englishmen gained something in return the crown was more circumspect. Parliament began to interest itself in the matter of alien trade in the reign of Edward III. Its earliest statutes favoured aliens, reinforcing rights enjoyed previously only by virtue of the king's prerogative. But from the 1370s almost every intervention of the commons was hostile. By now the rights promised to alien merchants in the *Carta Mercatoria* were totally disregarded and there is no doubt that without their own charters the Hansards would have been no better off than the others.

Despite recognition of the Hanse community in England before the end of the thirteenth century it seems to have been many decades before the crown looked beyond this group. Indeed, if one depended solely on English sources there would be no evidence until after the middle of the fourteenth century that the *Englandfahrer* were part of a larger organisation. The community enjoyed a great degree of autonomy and may have exaggerated this to their hosts. The English were concerned lest the franchises be enjoyed by too many Germans, so it would not be sensible to let them know just how big or integrated the Hanse actually was. As late as the 1350s, during the Curtys affair, the London Gildhall categorically denied that its members had any connection with the Bruges *Kontor*. It is difficult to accept this statement at its face value and the English may only have feigned to believe it as a way out of a dilemma. In the 1370s the crown and the Hanse diet came face to face, apparently for the first time. The diet seems to have brought itself to the attention of the king; though no doubt it had been presented with letters which he had earlier sent separately to a number of towns. After this the English realised that there was little point in entering into serious negotiations unless these were sanctioned by the diet. Agreements which concerned the Hanse as a whole were discussed and ratified in a diet, but could only be enforced in individual towns after further ratification by their councils. England neither knew nor cared whether every single town ratified treaties, since the vast majority had no direct contact with England or Englishmen. Obviously, this indifference did not extend to all. In 1447 the Hanse franchises were suspended on the grounds that Prussia had not yet ratified and implemented the treaty made ten years earlier. Common sense might suggest that all that was necessary in such a situation was for England unilaterally to deny privileges to the merchants of any town or region which wilfully disregarded a treaty. In 1449 English envoys offered to restore the franchises, subject to the exclusion of Prussians until they ratified the 1437 treaty. Lübeck argued against this on the grounds that the Hanse's constitution did not allow privileges belonging to the organisation as a whole to be denied to any individual members. Nevertheless, England imposed its own solution in the 1450s and perhaps in later times. At the end of the fifteenth century Riga claimed that its merchants were excluded from the franchises because it had never ratified the treaty of Utrecht (1474). This may be true, though it seems just as likely that they found themselves in that situation by simple neglect of active trade. Other members of the Hanse argued that ratification of the treaty even at this late date should be enough to solve Riga's problem.

What was earlier described as an internal contradiction within the Hanse – the conflict of interests between members – is particularly relevant to its relationship with England. Not all clashes of interest were permanent, but there were certain well-established tendencies. For example, Prussia was frequently ready to support organised boycotts of English-made cloth, indeed it was often in the forefront of such proposals. On the other hand it was reluctant to observe prohibitions on the export of goods to England, except when this happened to suit its own immediate interest. After the early fifteenth century Prussia almost alone was the target of English ambitions in the Baltic. It bitterly resented the 'sell-out' of 1437 and the pressure from other towns, even as late as 1474, for it to accept that treaty. No doubt the others were motivated by self-interest, but they cannot have been uninfluenced by the fact that Prussia itself had a poor record of Hanse solidarity – resulting partly from what appears to have been a trait of headstrongness. Prussia's isolated dispute with England in the 1380s was the result of a precipitate response to an act of piracy. During the more general crisis in the early fifteenth century Prussia undertook not to make a separate peace, but then went back on its word. This led to a prolonged coolness which had hardly disappeared before the renewed troubles of the 1430s. Again the Grand Master first promised to respect collective decisions of the Hanse, but then gave binding orders to his envoy and ruled that he alone could speak for Prussia. In 1451 Prussian delegates to the Anglo-Hanse conference at Utrecht were supplied with secret instructions authorising them to make a separate peace if there was no general settlement. On the other hand, in 1453 Danzig (soon to break away from the Teutonic Order) vetoed a letter addressed to Henry VI in which the Grand Master dissociated his subjects from the rest of the Hanse.

Of all the towns those of the Rhineland were least willing to quarrel with England. They escaped lightly from the activities of privateers and had no objections to English trade in the Baltic. Their main concern was the retention of the franchises, but they opposed trade boycotts because of the damage these did to their own business. In the 1390s Dortmund recommended the payment of compensation for English losses at the hands of the *Vitalienbruder*. Thereafter, Cologne was the chief advocate of the policy of appeasement, and if its advice was not heeded it was always ready to consider independent action. The city was involved in the first attempts to reach a settlement in the 1430s, but was not represented in the embassy of 1436 which finally worked out a treaty. It actually sent a delegation of its own to England, which was believed to be undermining the position of the Hanse. Its merchants disregarded the diet's ban on the export of cloth (though they were not alone in this) and, if the efforts of the official Hanse envoys had not been successful, it is possible that the events of 1468–74 would have been anticipated. Cologne cannot be absolved from sharing the blame for this later crisis with Denmark and England. Its merchants immediately dissociated themselves from the innocent victims of English anger and their action was endorsed by their home city. This must have encouraged the government to persist in its immoderate action, in defiance of counsel from other quarters which urged restraint. Nor is there any evidence that Cologne ever attempted to mediate between England and the rest of the Hanse during the struggle which followed. Cologne merchants were lucky perhaps to be readmitted to the Hanse community in England in 1478. Ironically, in the sixteenth century they were the prime cause of disharmony between England and the Hanse, since they were the most active rivals of the Merchant Adventurers in Antwerp.

The main concerns of the maritime towns of north-western Germany were the preservation of the franchises and the safety of their shipping against any form of interference by England. Their business was more diversified than that of Cologne and the Prussian towns and more representative of the Hanse as a whole. After the early fifteenth century they were not in themselves of great interest to the English until the collapse of Antwerp. The Merchant Adventurers then looked around for an alternative cloth staple. Their attempts to woo Hamburg and Stade were divisive of the Hanse, but by then it was already so decayed that the additional strain may have made little difference. The last point which needs to be made about the divisions within the Hanse takes the form of a question. Was the conflict of interests which stands out in a study of Anglo-Hanse relations merely a symptom of the general weakness of the organisation or was it a cause, indeed a deep-seated cause, of that weakness? No certain answer can be given. Conflict of interests also existed in other areas of Hanse trade, though they may have been less serious than here. Cologne's recklessness in defending its trade with England must have been one of the severest blows to the Hanse, since it was struck at a time when there was still some vitality in the organisation. The relative importance of the other stresses caused by the English connection is less easy to assess.

It is something of a paradox that the treaty of 1437 which has been discussed above as a cause of division within the Hanse was described in an earlier chapter as a considerable achievement. The merchants gained several useful concessions, above all freedom from tunnage and poundage which they had been claiming for the previous ninety years. Admittedly, Englishmen gained a tax concession in return, but only the Prussians were concerned about that and they could never be forced to implement it. After some shilly-shallying about lack of reciprocity the English government stoically accepted immunity from tunnage and poundage as part of the traditional franchises. It was allowed without a murmur when all the other privileges were restored in the treaty of Utrecht. Had England emerged victorious from the tussle of 1468–74 the whole panoply of Hanse privileges would have disappeared without trace, the first such clean sweep in Europe. England did not win, but neither did it lose; it compromised with the Hanse because the war had become an embarrassment. There is nothing surprising about the restoration of the franchises as part of the compromise. They were medieval, but they were not yet a relic of medievalism, since England's trade was still medieval. Moreover, there was no major commercial opposition to the Hanseatics at that particular time. English trade in the Baltic was for the moment defunct, and although the Merchant Adventurers had earlier expressed concern about Hanse activities in the Low Countries their opposition was not yet intense. On the other hand, it is surprising that the franchises remained almost intact until the middle of the sixteenth century. There was some whittling away of the edges in the reign of Henry VII – for example, the ban on the export of unfinished cloth and the imposition of poundage on lead, but not much else. In 1521 Thomas More bluntly told Hanse envoys that the king could drive their merchants from his country any day that he chose. Cardinal Wolsey had both the power and the will. In all probability it was only the making of an alliance with the Emperor which saved the Hansards in 1522. By the time the alliance was terminated in 1525 Wolsey seems to have lost interest in the matter. Even so, the franchises were undoubtedly now an anachronism. England's trade was burgeoning and hardly stood in need of the Hansards, so why allow them to pay lower customs duties than Englishmen and undercut the Merchant Adventurers in Antwerp? The revival of English activity in the Baltic complicated the situation and the decision in 1538 to give other alien merchants customs parity with denizens may have obfuscated the position of the Hansards. But when the tax concession to aliens was ended in 1545 the Hanseatic anomaly must have become glaringly obvious, particularly since their cloth exports soared to levels higher than ever before. Anxieties about the future of the Antwerp market led to the mid-century crisis, involving the suspension by Edward VI of the franchises and a lengthy, self-imposed Hanse boycott of trade with England. The government of Mary saw fit to restore the franchises in their entirety, partly because the Merchant Adventurers were temporarily in disfavour and partly, no doubt, because a quarrel with the Hanse was an unnecessary complication on top of other problems. The respite was brief. Before long severe restrictions were placed on Hanse trade, though its fiscal advantage was retained almost until the very end of the reign. The latter was then partially demolished when there was a general increase in cloth duties and Hansards were made liable to pay the full alien rate. A permanent solution was not worked out until Elizabeth was firmly established on the throne. This left the Hanse considerably better off than they would have been but for the premature death of Edward VI. At that time they were treated simply as aliens and were likely to remain that way. Now they enjoyed customs parity with Englishmen in trade with their own regions (including cloth exports). In trade between England and third parties they paid higher duties than natives, but enjoyed a slight advantage over other aliens. This compromise lasted until 1578, when it was destroyed by an act of short-sighted folly on the part of the Hanse. At this date the remnants of the Hanse privileges were not seriously disputed by any group of English merchants. Competition against the Merchant Adventurers had largely been eliminated by tight quotas on the export of unfinished cloth. English merchants were well-entrenched in the Baltic and no longer needed the threat of abolition of Hanse privileges to maintain themselves there. As far as England was concerned, the privileges were now merely a bargaining pawn in the dispute about the staple at Hamburg. Rational diplomacy by the Hanse would have saved the privileges and even provided them with an increase in the cloth quota. Instead they threw everything away in a vain attempt to keep the Merchant Adventurers out of the continent. This was a battle they could not win, but the stand cost them the privileges and this resulted inevitably in the loss of their remaining trade with England.

The final battleground fought over by Englishmen and Hansards was a new one, but over the centuries scenes of conflict had shifted many times. The one venue in which there was a continuous engagement was England itself. Here the issue was whether Hansards should be subject to the conditions which Englishmen sought to impose upon all visiting alien merchants – length of stay, hosting regulations, terms upon which goods might be bought or sold, the specification of natives with whom trade was actually permitted, personal taxation – as well as the taxation of trade itself and the prohibition of certain imports and exports. As we have seen, the Hansards acquired charters which theoretically gave them immunity against parliamentary statutes, which in the course of time reinforced the prescriptive claims of English towns and cities. These did not prevent a guerrilla battle on this front from start to finish. One signal English success was the exclusion of Hansards, together with other aliens, from the wool trade. This was achieved not so much by discriminatory taxation (though that may have helped), but by the creation of a staple, not in England itself but still on English territory. The first foreign field of conflict may have been Norway, though inability to maintain grain exports may already have been causing an English withdrawal from that country when the Hanseatics began to dominate its economy in the late thirteenth century. The Hanse's stranglehold on Norway's overseas trade embraced that with England, and Englishmen seem to have made only fitful attempts to recover this in the fourteenth and fifteenth centuries. Among the factors which bore upon this lack of resolution was the establishment of the Iceland fishery, which itself became a minor area of Anglo-Hanse conflict towards the end of the fifteenth century.

Until shortly after the middle of the fourteenth century trade between England and the Baltic remained largely or entirely in the hands of Hanse merchants. Then Englishmen rapidly established a business which exceeded that of their rivals. The initial attraction may have been the Skania fairs which served as a distribution centre for western cloth and where return cargoes of herrings could be bought with a minimum of trouble. Englishmen were drawn also to the Hanse towns of the west Baltic, but soon the lure of the east was stronger. Danzig, at the mouth of the river Vistula, was the gateway to much of central and eastern Europe. The English even had ambitions to extend their trade to Livonia, but made little or no headway there. The greater attraction of the eastern over the western region lay in the fact that besides providing a good market for cloth it gave more direct access to goods (other than herrings) which supplied return cargoes. Also, the natives of the eastern towns, despite a large investment in shipping, seem to have been less dedicated to overseas trade than those of the west. This allowed Englishmen (and other aliens) to establish themselves in the import and export trade. Native tolerance of the strangers did not extend to conceding them a stake in Prussia's internal trade nor the use of the country as a base for a wider penetration of eastern Europe. On the other hand Englishmen claimed these rights as a corollary of the privileges enjoyed by the Hanse in England. This gave rise to disputes between hosts and visitors throughout the period of English trade in Prussia. The English acquired legal rights by the treaties of 1388 and 1409, but these could not always be exercised, particularly in Danzig. The treaty of 1437 confirmed existing rights and even appeared to provide immunity from taxation, but it was never ratified by Prussia. After that the conditions in which Englishmen traded in Prussia were less favourable than in the best of earlier times.

English trade with the Baltic peaked in the late fourteenth or early fifteenth century and declined thereafter. By the 1460s it was at a very low ebb. To that extent it is a mistake to say that the Anglo-Hanse war of 1468–74 destroyed the trade. What it did was to ensure that Englishmen did not make another concerted effort to recover the lost ground after the expedition of 1468 was frustrated by the Danes. It is also incorrect to say that in the treaty of Utrecht the English abandoned their claim to reciprocal rights and that this accounts for their absence from the Baltic in the late fifteenth century. As far as legal-political relations with the Hanse are concerned, it was no more difficult, but no easier, to trade with Prussia or other Hanse towns after 1474 than before 1468. It is true that English trade with the Baltic remained at a very low level, but the constraining factor was the hostility of Denmark. It may be presumed that Hanse merchants now gained the edge over their rivals in this region. The size of the traffic cannot be established but it was probably smaller than it had been in earlier times. English merchants did not disappear totally from the Baltic and a few stalwarts provided the basis for a recovery, which began soon after 1500 and can be remarked strongly by the 1530s. Thereafter, there were occasionally short periods in which trade was temporarily suspended, but no real setbacks. The foundation of the Eastland Company finally put Englishmen in possession of the privileged position to which their predecessors had aspired in vain – ironically at the very time that the Hanseatics lost the last vestiges of their privileges in England.

As English interest in the Baltic waned in the late fifteenth century tension began to grow between the Merchant Adventurers and the Hanseatics in the Low Countries. But, contrary to what has often been stated, there was little or no direct connection between these two developments. The origins of the Merchant Adventurers and the staple trade in the provinces of Zeeland and Brabant date back to the early fifteenth century. About the same time Cologne merchants began to realise the potential of this region for their trade in general and their English trade in particular. There is evidence of rivalry between the two groups by the 1460s, but it became intense only towards the end of the century and later, with the great increase in cloth exports to the Low Countries. The Elizabethan settlement left the Englishmen in command of the Antwerp market, but the fruits of victory soon withered on the vine, as Antwerp lost its role as an international mart and cloth-finishing centre. This meant that the Merchant Adventurers had to turn their attentions elsewhere. Some, appreciating the importance of south Germany and central Europe as a market for cloth and a source of imports, wanted to open up direct trade with the interior. But official company policy adhered to the traditional concept of a staple mart, and its leaders directed their energies to finding an alternative to Antwerp. Emden and Middelburg were tried, but did not really fit the bill. The Adventurers turned therefore to the estuary of the Elbe, the gateway to much of Germany and middle Europe. Thus it was that the very heartland of the German Hanse became the final battleground of the two rivals. The Adventurers gained a foothold in Hamburg and held it until long after the demise of the Hanse.

Gildhall certificates

At the beginning of Henry IV's reign the Hanseatics were advised that their privileges should be enjoyed only by those merchants and shippers who bore sealed letters of identification from their native towns. To what extent, if any, this rule was enforced is not known, although compliance ought to have been a relatively simple matter. During negotiations early in Edward IV's reign the king's lawyers ruled that only members of the London Gildhall were entitled to use the franchises. This was probably a device to restrict the number of provincial merchants who escaped payment of tunnage and poundage. Everyone claiming immunity now had to be certified by Gildhall officials as a member of that organisation. The check continued until at least the reign of Henry VIII, and there are many surviving certificates from throughout the period. They were sent up to the Exchequer by the customs collector with his particulars of account to establish the claim for allowances. Anomalies in the dates of some of the earliest certificates raise doubts about the integrity of those operating the system. The first is addressed to the customs collectors of Hull from the alderman and merchants of the Gildhall, and was allegedly sealed by them on 9 July 1463.[1] The certificate names seventeen men but gives no details of their trade, and was returned to the Exchequer with the relevant particulars of account and a separate, undated schedule of another nineteen names, this time with the value of each man's goods. Between them, certificate and schedule name all but three of the Hanse captains, sailors and merchants importing in three Danzig ships which came to Hull on 22 and 24 August 1463. The first explanation which springs to mind is that on 9 July the Gildhall sent to Hull the names of those known to be importing there in the near future. When the ships arrived, the customs officials would have found not only goods belonging to these

---

[1] Childs, *Hull Customs Accounts*, p. 64.

men, but merchandise of another twenty-two who also claimed Hanse privileges. Many of the latter, having only small amounts, may have been sailors. Since their claim to concessionary rates could not immediately be allowed their names were scheduled. (Why three out of twenty-two names were omitted, unless by oversight, is not apparent.) Unfortunately, this explanation cannot be entirely correct, since all but one name in both certificate and schedule are listed in precisely the same order as they appear in the customs particular. The single exception establishes conclusively that the certificate, as well as the schedule, was copied from customs documents. The second name in the customs particular must have been accidentally overlooked when a draft of the certificate was being prepared and therefore stands not in second, but in final, place in the existing certificate. This suggests that the certificate was deliberately antedated, moreover with a date that is demonstrably false. The next Hull certificate lists all who imported and exported there in May and June 1465, again in the same order as they appear in the customs particular, but this time it is dated 19 February 1466.[2] There is a similar dating problem relating to the earliest certificate for Lynn, attached to the particular covering the period 19 November 1464 to 19 November 1465.[3] On 22 November 1465 the Gildhall certified twenty-four men, and on the following day wrote another certificate with two more names, which must have been accidentally omitted from the first. The twenty-six names are a complete record of all Hanse merchants importing and exporting at Lynn, between 27 February and 8 October 1465. No one was left uncertified and again all the names occur in the same chronological order as in the customs particular, proving that the certificate was copied from the particular. Since the year of account ended only on 19 November there is no way in which the necessary information would have been available for certificates to be written in the London Gildhall three and four days later. Theoretically, it is possible that a representative of the Gildhall examined daybooks of the customs immediately after the end of the period of account and wrote the certificates at Lynn. Given the example of Hull, it is more likely that these are ante-dated certificates, though on this occasion the discrepancy is not quite as glaringly obvious. What lay behind this is a mystery as yet unsolved.

In one respect the new system of certification could be of benefit

---

[2] *Ibid.*, p. 95. [3] PRO, E122/97/4.

to the London Steelyard. If enforced it would have provided them with a record of all who claimed Hanse privileges, even the 'tramps' who infrequently brought cargoes of salt and wine to provincial ports, where there was not regular Hanse trade. This would have enabled them to collect scot from such casual traders, had they been minded to do so. On the other hand there were certain aspects of the system which they found irksome. In November 1465 Steelyard officials wrote to Lübeck pointing out that they were not familiar with many of the names being submitted to them.[4] They suggested that, whenever many merchants from a town sent goods in one vessel, they should not enter all their names separately on the manifest, but allocate ownership between a limited number. This was dangerous advice and if accepted could have made merchants liable to prosecution on the charge of colouring, since English law required that all goods imported and exported should be customed in the name of the real owner.

[4] *HR*, II (v), no. 376.

Hanse trade figures in the late fifteenth century

During the 1460s the customs officials of several ports occasionally totalled the value of Hanseatic goods (including cloth) which would have paid poundage subsidy, but for the merchants' immunity. Unfortunately, only those of Hull did so with any regularity so a statistical series cannot be established.[1] On the other hand, even a random figure sometimes provides valuable evidence. Thus between 28 August 1467 and 30 September 1468 the total value of Hanse goods (which did not include any cloth) recorded at Sandwich was £2,585. This proves that the Steelyard merchants were still using the port for their import business. Later, by the terms of the treaty of Utrecht the Hanse merchants were allowed to retain their petty customs payments until the financial indemnity awarded to them had been settled. This resulted in a distinction being made in every port between the Hanse and alien share of the petty custom. Unfortunately, once the indemnity had been paid off there was no pressing reason to keep a separate account of Hanse payments and the practice gradually died out. While it lasted it is possible to gain a reasonably accurate picture of total Hanse trade. The following tables record the figures for ports where there was a regular business. Details are not supplied for ports where trade was small and sporadic, but such trade was included in the estimate supplied in an earlier chapter.[2]

[1] For the Hull figures see Childs, *Hull Customs Accounts*, table 3, p. 230.
[2] See above, p. 272.

	London Merchandise (£)	London Wax (cwt)	Cloths	Cologne cloths
Mich. 1474–5 June 1475[a]	not known	not known	385	
5 June 1475–Mich. 1475[a]	4,288	294	1,238	1,472 (12 months)
Mich. 1475–Mich. 1476[a]	7,908	1,159	5,281	2,999[b]
Mich. 1476–20 Nov. 1477[a]	7,488	1,161	5,375	2,930
20 Nov. 1477–9 July 1478[a]	6,539	821	3,002	2,261
9 July 1478–Mich. 1479[c]	16,209	1,354	11,449	
Mich. 1479–Mich. 1480	16,701	1,628	10,068	
Mich. 1480–Mich. 1481	22,281	2,839	14,079	
Mich. 1481–Mich. 1482	22,534	3,561	13,386	
Mich. 1482–24 July 1483	16,246	1,739	7,490	
24 July 1483–Mich. 1484	20,601	892	13,074	
Mich. 1484–17 Sept. 1485	22,320	1,843	13,756	
17 Sept. 1485–10 Dec. 1486	23,911	1,994	14,139	
10 Dec. 1486–16 July 1487	6,632	527	3,210	
16 July 1487–Mich. 1488	not known	3,492	13,188	
Mich. 1488–Mich. 1489	30,160	2,784	13,724	

[a] First three columns exclude Cologne.
[b] Includes merchants of Veere, but their average 1476–9 was only 75 p.a.
[c] Now includes Cologne.

Mich.–Mich.[a]	Hull		Boston		Lynn		
	Merchandise (£)	Cloths	Merchandise (£)	Cloths	Merchandise (£)	Cloths	Wax (cwt)
1474–5	1,115[b]	444	1[f]	31	146[k]	270	9
1475–6	1,183[c]	438	436	283	528[k]	307	37
1476–7	1,532	435	0	0	177[k]	84	1
1477–8	397	208	681	548	477[k]	129	17
1478–9	1,670	232	377	195	237[k]	187	20
1479–80	1,610	791	415	265	410[k]	183	47
1480–1	2,484	915	417	242	294[l]	184	44
1481–2	3,907	690	816	62	895	181	50
1482–3	2,037	387	546	214	318	79	0
1483–4	1,903	334	211	152	424	89	14
1484–5	2,158[d]	29	458	283	661[m]	145	0
1485–6	1,693[e]	337	0	0	256[n]	46	0
1486–7	2,509	68[f]	0	0	501[o]	192	0
1487–8	319	116	263	67	1,032	280	50
1488–9	not known	43[g]	395	32	2,006	777	81
1489–90	c. 1,184	105	1,177	31	461	32	0
1490–1	0	0	0	0	not known	30	54
1491–2	not known	148	1,512	146[f]	1,226	338	25
1492–3	3,037	619	0	0	not known	480	45
1493–4	3,247	444[h]	0	0	308	17	0

[a] Except where otherwise indicated.
[d] To 22 Aug.
[g] 19 cwt wax also.
[j] 74 cwt wax also.
[m] To 22 Aug.

[b] 22 Aug.–8 Aug.
[e] From 22 Aug.
[h] 45 cwt wax also.
[k] 13 Nov.–13 Nov.
[n] From 17 Sept.

[c] From 8 Aug.
[f] 135 cwt wax also.
[i] From 2 Nov.
[l] 13 Nov.–Mich.
[o] From 26 Oct.

	Sandwich		Ipswich			
Mich.–Mich.[a]	Merchandise (£)			Merchandise (£)	Wax (cwt)	Cloths
1474–5[b]	204[h]	Mich. 1474–8 Nov. 1475		1,470	56	349
1475–6[b]	313[h]	8 Nov. 1475–8 Nov. 1476		496	37	851
1476–7[c]	764[i]	8 Nov. 1476–8 Nov. 1477		301	19	30
1477–8	379[j]	8 Nov, 1477–8 Oct. 1478		55	0	158
1478–9	89[h]	8 Oct. 1478–14 Oct. 1479		255	28	155
1479–80	1,639	14 Oct. 1479–14 Oct. 1480		251	0	194
1480–1	1,512	14 Oct. 1480–Mich. 1481		1,147	7	146
1481–2	840	Mich. 1481–Mich. 1482		317	7	228
1482–3[d]	1,993[k]	Mich. 1482–24 July 1483		336	1	35
1483–4	1,914	24 July 1483–Mich. 1484		0	0	0
1484–5[e]	1,739	Mich. 1484–22 Aug. 1485		643	17	273
1485–6[f]	2,243	22 Aug. 1485–Mich. 1486		347	0	7
1486–7	not known	Mich. 1486–Mich. 1487		1,129	19	348
1487–8	2,648	Mich. 1487–26 Dec. 1487		502	16	187
1488–9[g]	83					

[a] Except where otherwise indicated.
[d] To 25 July.
[g] To 13 June.
[j] Plus £58 Cologne.

[b] 17 Nov.–17 Nov.
[e] To 22 August.
[h] Excluding Cologne.
[k] 8 cloths also.

[c] 17 Nov.–Mich.
[f] From 16 September.
[i] Plus £60 Cologne.

Elizabethan cloth exports

During the last two years of Henry VIII's reign enrolment of the customs accounts became very erratic and was given up entirely during the next two reigns. The practice recommenced with effect from Michaelmas 1559 and continued until 1604, when it was abandoned for ever. Despite the fact that Hanse cloth exports were now taxed at denizen rates they continued to be recorded separately until 1579, when they began to pay alien rates. Thereafter it is not possible to distinguish Hanse exports from those of other aliens, but the marked fall in the combined figures of the two groups suggests that there was very little Hanse export. During the brief interlude in 1586–7 when Hansards were again allowed to export at denizen rates, their trade is not distinguished from that of natives. By the 1560s Hanse and other alien cloth exports were virtually confined to London; for the trade of this port see the accompanying table.[1]

Figures given in the enrolled accounts form the official record of all cloths (converted to notional short-cloths) which paid custom to the crown. They provide the only possibility of establishing trends in trade, but must nevertheless be used with extreme caution. The figures do not include the duty-free wrapper allowance, which was one cloth in every ten at London and all provincial ports except Hull and Newcastle, where it was two in ten. In order to calculate true exports, many figures in customs accounts have to be adjusted upwards. Unfortunately, it is not known when the wrapper allowance was introduced, though there is some evidence for it in the early sixteenth century. If the allowance came in suddenly and uniformly then there would have been an artificial drop of 10 per cent in recorded exports, which really requires an upward adjustment. Hanse and other alien exports are not affected by this

[1] At Hull Hansards exported 94 cloths in 1559–60, 15 in 1561–2 and 106 in 1562–3. A few were also exported in other years until 1566, but are not distinguished from those of denizens.

problem in the 1550s and earlier, since neither group then received a wrapper allowance. Indeed, it is likely that the allowance was originally given to denizens to reduce their fiscal disadvantage *vis à vis* Hansards. The latter gained the allowance in 1560 when it was determined that they should pay the same custom as denizens. Other aliens never received a wrapper allowance, but were given a smaller rebate in their cash payment; in their case this requires no adjustment of the recorded cloth figures.

Another problem which arises when comparing Elizabethan cloth exports with those of earlier periods (and also different years within this reign) concerns the size of the short-cloth. The customs definition of a short-cloth was altered several times in the second half of the sixteenth century, but most drastically in 1584, when Sir Walter Raleigh was granted a lease of overlengths. The inclusion or exclusion of overlengths after that date makes a difference of more than 10 per cent in recorded exports. Finally, it must be noted that the figures for the years 1569–72 should be regarded sceptically. In this period some of the customs officers were heavily 'massaging' their port books, partly – though allegedly not entirely – for criminal purposes. The figures given here show the official attempt to set the record straight.

	Denizen	Hanse	London cloth exports Alien		Denizen	Alien
1559–60	89,864	8,381	11,444	1582–3	95,452	3,566
1560–1	59,556	16,425	5,866	1583–4	89,370	4,645
1561–2	55,735	10,133	8,714	1584–5	94,760[a]	5,539[a]
1562–3	32,161	12,115	7,955	1585–6	95,858[a]	7,064[a]
1563–4	41,603	9,038	5,838	1586–7	90,390[a]	6,211[a]
1564–5	106,076	10,156	17,824	1587–8	79,601[a]	6,270[a]
1565–6	59,654	12,278	10,249	1588–9	103,945[a]	5,134[a]
1566–7	56,504	8,211	4,424	1589–90	94,277[a]	4,628[a]
1567–8	71,814	14,906	6,877	1590–1	84,481[a]	3,939[a]
1568–9	72,561	12,204	11,683	1591–2	106,101	3,656
1569–70	60,569	22,907	7,728	1592–3	82,746	2,478
1570–1	67,951	4,962	5,336	1593–4	No details in acct.	
1571–2	49,447	8,443	5,695	1594–5	111,506	3,475
1572–3	73,351	5,779	536	1595–6	No acct. found	
1573–4	71,573	11,583	8,900	1596–7	56,159	2,606
1574–5	74,696	14,667	9,890	1597–8	105,267	6,284
1575–6	85,348	16,499	6,505	1598–9	81,568	6,281
1576–7	74,873	13,536	6,455	1599–1600	106,362	4,599
1577–8	78,512	12,677	9,628	1600–1	100,380	4,195
1578–9	83,735	3,723	9,965	1601–2	113,512	5,072
1579–80	92,137		7,718	1602–3	acct. corrupt	2,465
1580–1	91,436		5,225	1603–4	113,785	5
1581–2	92,228		4,974			

[a] Figs. *exclude* overlengths from 25 March 1584 to Easter 1591. Thereafter overlengths are *included*.
Source: PRO, E356/28–9.

English cloth dyed in Hamburg, 1535–1612

	Stals[a]		Stals
1536, ante 18 May	614	1 Sept. 1564–30 June 1565	8,014
18 May 1536–12 Apr. 1537	811	1 Aug. 1565–30 Aug. 1566	8,296
1537–8[b]	1,252	30 Aug. 1566–30 Aug. 1567⎫	3,795
1538–9	1,352	28 Jan. 1567–30 July 1568 ⎭	2,166
1539–40	2,123	30 Aug. 1567–30 Aug. 1568	6,125
1540–1	2,512	30 Aug. 1568–30 Aug. 1569	8,185
1541–2	2,648	30 Aug. 1569–30 Sept. 1570	18,987
1542–3	2,983	25 Sept. 1570–29 Sept. 1571	14,114
1543–4	2,865	29 Sept. 1571–29 Sept. 1573	21,098
1544–5	4,220	5 June 1573–31 Dec. 1574	24,777
1545–6	3,289	1575–6[c]	26,648
1546–7	3,274	1577–8	29,354
1547–8	3,397	1579–80	19,462
1548–9	4,590	1581–2	25,410
1549–50	5,485	1583–4	24,116
1550–1	5,620	1585–6	29,510
1551–2	5,719	1587–8	39,261
1552–3	3,099	1589–90	29,380
1553–4	4,182	1591–2	27,191
1554–5	6,208	1593–4	22,215
1555–6	3,123	1595–6	25,334
1556–7	4,371	1597–8	18,949
1557–8	4,069	1599–1600	23,702
1558–9	1,249	1601–2	24,731
1559–60	5,071	1603–4	23,786
1560–1	4,759	1605–6	29,362
1561–2	4,085	1607–8	31,885
1562–3	4,204	1609–10	25,666
1 June 1563–30 July 1564	3,381	1611–12	25,022

[a] The *stal* was a local unit, larger than a short-cloth.
[b] From 1537 to 1563, twelve months, May to May.
[c] Hereafter, periods of two calendar years.

English cloth forwarded from Hamburg without local handiwork 1568–1605

(I) Tolls collected by the city (in Hamburg pounds)			
1568–9[a]	320	1590–1	31
1569–70	8,696	1591–2	16
1570–1	12,473	1592–3	26
1571–2	11,147	1593–4	22
1572–3	7,492	1594–5	13
1573–4	8,320	1595–6	1
1574–5	5,067	1596–7	8
1575–6	3,430	1597–8	12
1576–7	5,590	1598–9	267
1577–8	6,224	1599–1600	479
1578–9	3,753	1600–1	210
1579[b]	402	1601–2	101
1587–8[c]	795	1602–3	9
1588–9	51	1603–4	5
1589–90	20	1604–5	7

[a] From 6 Aug. 1568–22 Feb. 1569. Thereafter finance year 22 Feb.–22 Feb.
[b] Until November 1579.
[c] From November 1587.

(II) Varieties of cloth forwarded					
	Broadcloths	Kerseys	Dozens	Cottons	Frieses	Bays
1568–9	1,295	35	0	0	0	0
1569–70	28,798	19,686	224	0	0	817
1570–1	39,195	26,599	481	110	293	398
1571–2	35,715	19,319	577	31	680	492
1572–3	24,654	13,860	2,166	0	355	218

Bibliography

ORIGINAL AUTHORITIES: UNPUBLISHED
PUBLIC RECORD OFFICE

Parliamentary and Council Proceedings, C49. Exchequer Accounts Various, E101. Customs Accounts, E122. King's Remembrancer's Memoranda Rolls, E159. Port Books, E190. Enrolled Accounts of Custom and Subsidy, E356. Enrolled Miscellaneous Accounts, E358. Enrolled Foreign Accounts, E364. Lord Treasurer's Remembrancer's Memoranda Rolls, E368. Pipe Rolls, E372. Ancient Correspondence, SC1. State papers, SP

BRITISH LIBRARY

Additional Manuscripts. Lansdowne Papers. Cotton Manuscripts

ORIGINAL AUTHORITIES: PUBLISHED

Acts of the Privy Council of England, New Series, *1542–1631* (London, 1890–1964)

Beverley Town Documents, ed. A. F. Leach (Selden Soc., 14, London, 1900)

Calendar of Chancery Warrants, 1244–1326 (London, 1927)

Calendar of Charter Rolls, 1226–1516 (London, 1903–27)

Calendar of Close Rolls, 1272–1509 (London, 1892–1963)

Calendar of Early Mayors' Court Rolls, ed. A. H. Thomas (Cambridge, 1924)

Calendar of Fine Rolls, 1272–1509 (London, 1911–62)

Calendar of Liberate Rolls, 1226–72 (London, 1916–24)

Calendar of Patent Rolls, 1232–1509, 1547–82 (London, 1906–1986)

Calendar of Plea and Memoranda Rolls of the City of London, 1323–1482, ed. A. H. Thomas and P. E. Jones (Cambridge, 1926–61)

Calendar of Salisbury Manuscripts (Historical MS Commission, 9, London, 1888)

Calendar of Signet Letters of Henry IV and Henry V, ed. J. L. Kirby (London, 1978)

Calendar of State Papers, Domestic, 1547–1610 (London, 1856–69)

Calendar of State Papers, Foreign, 1547–1589 (London, 1861–1950)

Close Rolls, 1227–72 (London, 1902–38)

Curia Regis Rolls, 12 (London, 1957)

The Customs Accounts of Hull, 1453–1490, ed. W. Childs (Yorks. Arch. Soc., 144, 1986)

Danziger Inventar, 1531–9, ed. P. Simson (Inventare Hansische Archive des 16. Jahrhunderts, 3, Munich and Leipzig, 1913)

The Early English Customs System, ed. N. S. B. Gras (Cambridge, Mass., 1926)

England's Export Trade, 1275–1546, ed. E. M. Carus-Wilson and O. Coleman (Oxford, 1963)

The Eyre of London, 1321, ed. H. M. Cam (Selden Soc., 85–6, London, 1968–9)

Foedera, Conventiones, Literae, et cuiuscunque generis Acta Publica inter Reges Angliae, ed. T. Rymer and R. Sanderson (3rd edn, The Hague, 1739–45)

Hanseakten aus England, 1275 bis 1412, ed. K. Kunze (Halle, 1891)

Hansisches Urkundenbuch, ed. K. Höhlbaum and others (Halle and Leipzig, 1876–1939)

Journals of the House of Lords (London, 1846)

Kölner Inventar, ed. K. Höhlbaum (Inventare Hansische Archive des 16. Jahrhunderts, 1–2, Leipzig, 1896–1903)

The Laws of the Kings of England from Edmund to Henry I, ed. A. J. Robertson (Cambridge, 1925)

Letter Books of the City of London, ed. R. R. Sharpe (London, 1899–1911)

Letters and Papers, Foreign and Domestic, of Henry VIII, 1509–47 (London, 1864–1932)

The Libelle of Englyshe Polycye, ed. G. Warner (Oxford, 1926)

List and Analysis of State Papers, Foreign, 1584–94 (London, 1964–89)

Literae Cantuarienses, ed. J. B. Sheppard (London, 1887–9)

The London Eyre of 1244, ed. H. M. Chew and M. Weinbaum (London Rec. Soc., 6, 1970)

'A London Municipal Collection of the Reign of John', ed. M. Bateson, *EHR*, 17 (1902), 495–502

Munimenta Gildhallae Londoniensis, ed. H. T. Riley (London, 1859–62)

Patent Rolls, 1216–32 (London, 1901–3)

Placitorum in Domo Capitulari Westmonasteriensi Asservatorum Abbreviatio (London, 1811)

The Politics of a Tudor Merchant Adventurer: A Letter to the Earls of East Friesland, ed. G. D. Ramsay (Manchester 1979)

The Port and Trade of Elizabethan London, ed. B. Dietz (London Rec. Soc., 8, 1972)

Proceedings and Ordinances of the Privy Council, ed. N. H. Nicholas (London, 1834–7)

Die Recesse und Andere Akten der Hansetage, Series I, 1256–1430, ed. K. Koppmann (Leipzig, 1870–97); II, 1431–76, ed. G. von der Ropp

(Leipzig, 1876–92); III, 1476–1530, ed. D. Schäfer and F. Techen (Leipzig and Munich, 1881–1913)

Records of the Borough of Leicester, ed. M. Bateson, I (London, 1899)

Rotuli Hundredorum (London, 1812–18)

Rotuli Litterarum Patentium, 1201–16 (London, 1835)

Rotuli Parliamentorum (London, 1785–1832)

Rotulorum Originalium in Curia Scaccarii Abbreviatio (London, 1805–10)

Royal and Historical Letters during the Reign of Henry the Fourth, ed. F. C. Hingeston, I (London, 1860), 2 (London, 1965)

State Papers during the Reign of King Henry VIII (London, 1830–52)

Statutes of the Realm (London, 1810–28)

Tabeller over Skibsfart og Varetransport gennem Øresund, 1497–1660, ed. N. E. Bang (Copenhagen, 1906)

A Treatise of Commerce, by J. Wheeler (London, 1601)

Tudor Royal Proclamations, ed. P. L. Hughes and J. F. Larkin (Newhaven and London, 1964)

Urkundliche Geschichte des Hansischen Stahlhofes zu London, ed. J. M. Lappenberg (Hamburg, 1851)

Walsingham, T., *Historia Anglicana*, ed. H. T. Riley (London, 1863)

William Ashbourne's Book, ed. D. M. Owen (Norfolk Rec. Soc., 48, 1981)

The York Mercers and Merchant Adventurers, 1356–1917, ed. M. Sellers (Surtees Soc., 129, 1917)

SECONDARY WORKS

Alexander, G. M. V., 'The Life and Career of Edmund Bonner, Bishop of London, until his Deprivation in 1549' (Ph.D. thesis, London, 1960)

Bartlett, J. N., 'Some Aspects of the Economy of York in the Later Middle Ages, 1300–1550' (Ph.D. thesis, London, 1958)

Bjork, D. J., 'The Peace of Stralsund, 1370', *Speculum*, 7 (1932), 447–76

Bolton, J. L., 'Alien Merchants in England in the Reign of Henry VI, 1422–61' (B.Litt. thesis, Oxford, 1971)

The Medieval English Economy, 1150–1500 (London, 1980)

von Brandt, A., 'Die Hanse als mittelalterliche Wirtschafts-organisation – Entstehen, Daseinsformen, Aufgaben', in A. von Brandt and others, *Die Deutsche Hanse als Mittler zwischen Ost und West* (Wissenschaftliche Abhandlungen der Arbeitsgemeinschaft für Forschung des Landes Nordrhein-Westfalen, 27, Cologne and Opladen, 1963, pp. 9–38

Bridbury, A. R., *Medieval English Clothmaking: An Economic Survey* (London, 1982)

Britnell, R. H., *Growth and Decline in Colchester, 1300–1525* (Cambridge, 1986)

Brooke, C., and Keir, G., *London, 800–1216* (London, 1975)

Burgon, J. W., *The Life and Times of Sir Thomas Gresham* (London, 1839)

Carsten, F. L., *The Origins of Prussia* (Oxford, 1954)

Carus-Wilson, E. M., *Medieval Merchant Venturers* (2nd edn, London, 1967)

Chrimes, S. B., *Henry VII* (London, 1972)

Christensen, A. E., 'Scandinavia and the Advance of the Hanseatics', *Scandinavian Economic History Review*, 5 (1957), 89–117

Christiansen, E., *The Northern Crusades* (London, 1980)

Dollinger, P., *The German Hansa* (London, 1964)

Ehrenburg, R., *Hamburg und England im Zeitalter der Königin Elisabeth* (Jena, 1896)

Ellmers, D., 'Die Entstehung der Hanse', *HG*, 103 (1985), 2–40

Engel, K., 'Die Organisation der deutsch-hansischen Kaufleute in England im 14 und 15 Jahrhundert bis Utrechter Frieden von 1474', *HG*, 19 (1913), 445–517; 20 (1914), 173–225

Fedorowicz, J. K., *England's Baltic Trade in the Early Seventeenth Century* (Cambridge, 1980)

Fisher, F. J., 'Commercial Trends and Policy in Sixteenth Century England', *EcHR*, 10 (1940), 95–117

Ford, C. J., 'Piracy or Policy: The Crisis in the Channel, 1400–1403', *Trans. Roy. Hist. Soc.*, Series 5, 29 (1979), 63–77

Friedland, K., 'Der Plan des Dr. Heinrich Suderman zur Wiederstellung der Hanse', *Jahrbuch des Kölnischen Geschichsverein*, 31–2 (1956–7), 184–242

'Hamburger Englandfahrer, 1512–57', *Zeitschrift des Vereins für Hamburgische Geschichte*, 46 (1960), 1–42

Gould, J. D., *The Great Debasement* (Oxford, 1970)

Grassby, R., 'Die letzten Verhandlungen zwischen England und der Hanse, 1603–4', *HG*, 76 (1958), 73–120

Gross, C., *The Gild Merchant* (London, 1890)

Hagedorn, B., *Ostfrieslands Handel und Schiffahrt im 16. Jahrhundert* (Berlin, 1910)

Ostfrieslands Handel und Schiffahrt vom Ausgang des 16. Jahrhunderts bis zum Westfälischen Frieden, 1580–1648 (Berlin, 1912)

Harding, V. A., 'Some Documentary Sources for the Import and Distribution of Foreign Textiles in Later Medieval England', *Textile History*, 18 (1987), 205–18

Hatcher, J., *English Tin Production and Trade before 1550* (Oxford, 1973)

Hinton, R. W. K., *The Eastland Trade and the Common Weal in the Seventeenth Century* (Cambridge, 1959)

Holmes, G., *The Good Parliament* (Oxford, 1975)

Jenks, S., 'Die Ordnung für die englische Handelskolonie in Danzig (23 Mai 1405)', in *Danzig in acht Jahrhunderten*, ed. B. Jähnig and P. Letkemann (Münster, Westph., 1985), pp. 102–20

'Das Schreiberbuch des John Thorp und der hansische Handel in London, 1457–9', *HG*, 101 (1983), 67–113

England, die Hanse und Preussen: Handel und Diplomatie, 1377–1461 (Habilitationsschrift, Free University of Berlin, 1985)

'War die Hanse kreditfeindlich?', *Vierteljahrschrift für Sozial- und Wirtschaftsgeschichte*, 69 (1982), 305–38

Kendall, P. M., *Warwick the Kingmaker* (London, 1957)

Kingsford, C. L., *Prejudice and Promise in Fifteenth Century England* (Oxford, 1925)

Kumlien, K., 'Hansischer Handel und Hansekaufleute in Skandinavien', in A. von Brandt and others, *Die Deutsche Hanse als Mittler zwischen Ost und West*, pp. 78–101

Kurzinna, W., 'Der Name Stalhof', *HG*, 18 (1912), 429–61

Lauffer, W., 'Danzigs Schiff und Wahrenverkehr am Ende des XV Jahrhunderts', *Zeitschrift des Westpreussischen Geschichtsverein*, 33 (1894), 1–44

Lloyd, T. H., *Alien Merchants in England in the High Middle Ages* (Brighton, 1983)

    The English Wool Trade in the Middle Ages (Cambridge, 1977)

    'Overseas Trade and the English Money Supply in the Fourteenth Century', in N. J. Mayhew (ed.), *Edwardian Monetary Affairs* (British Arch. Soc. Reports, 36, Oxford, 1977), pp. 96–124

Lönig, G. A., 'Deutsche und Gotländer in England im 13 Jahrhundert', *HG*, 67–8 (1942–3), 65–93

Loomis, L. R., *The Council of Constance* (London, 1962)

Marcus, J. R., *Die handelspolitischen Beziehungen zwischen England und Deutschland in den Jahren 1576–85* (Berlin, 1925)

Martin, J., *Treasure of the Land of Darkness* (Cambridge, 1986)

Miller, E., 'The Economic Policies of Governments: France and England', in M. M. Postan, E. E. Rich and E. Miller (eds.), *Economic Organisation and Policies in the Middle Ages* (Cambridge Economic History of Europe, 3, Cambridge, 1963), p. 291

    'Medieval York', in P. M. Tillot (ed.), *The City of York* (The Victoria History of the Counties of England, London, 1961), pp. 25–116

Munro, J. H. A., *Wool, Cloth and Gold: The Struggle for Bullion in Anglo-Burgundian Trade, 1340–1478* (Toronto, 1973)

Nicholas, D., 'The English Trade at Bruges in the Last Years of Edward III', *Journal of Medieval History*, 5 (1979), 23–61

Norman, P., 'Notes on the Later History of the Steelyard in London', *Archaeologia*, 61 (1909), 389–426

Parker, V., *The Making of Kings Lynn* (London, 1971)

Pauli, R., 'Die Stahlhofskaufleute und Luthers Schriften', *HG*, (1871), 153–62

Peters, I.-M., *Hansekaufleute als Gläubiger der englische Krone, 1294–1350* (Cologne and Vienna, 1978)

Petri, F., 'Die Stellung der Südersee- und IJsselstädte im Flandrisch-Hansischen Raum', *HG*, 79 (1961), 34–57

Pistono, S. P., 'Henry IV and the English Privateers', *EHR*, 99 (1975), 322–30

Postan, M. M., 'The Economic and Political Relations of England and the German Hanse from 1400 to 1475', in E. Power and M. M. Postan, *Studies in English Trade in the Fifteenth Century* (London, 1933), pp. 91–153

Power, E., and Postan, M. M., *Studies in English Trade in the Fifteenth Century* (London, 1933)

Ramsay, G. D., *The City of London in International Politics at the Accession of Elizabeth Tudor* (Manchester, 1975)

The Queen's Merchants and the Revolt of the Netherlands (Manchester, 1986)

Ramsey, P., 'Overseas Trade in the Reign of Henry VII: The Evidence of the Customs Accounts', *EcHR*, Series 2, 6 (1953), 173–82

Richmond, C. F., 'Royal Administration and the Keeping of the Seas, 1422–85' (D.Phil. thesis, Oxford, 1963)

Ross, C., *Edward IV* (London, 1974)

Ruddock, A., *Italian Merchants and Shipping in Southampton, 1270–1600* (Southampton, 1951)

Scarisbrook, J. J., *Henry VIII* (London, 1968)

Schanz, G., *Englische Handelspolitik gegen Ende des Mittelalters* (Leipzig, 1881)

Schulz, F., *Die Hanse und England von Eduards III. bis auf Heinrichs VIII. Zeit* (Berlin, 1911)

Sharpe, W., 'The Correspondence of Thomas Sexton, Merchant of London, and his Factors in Danzig, 1550–1560' (M.A. thesis, London University, 1952)

Stein, W., 'Die Hanse und England beim Ausgang des hundertjährigen Krieges', *HG*, 26 (1921), 27–126

Die Hanse und England. Ein hansisch-englischer Seekrieg im 15. Jahrhundert (Hansische Pfingstblätter, 1, Leipzig, 1905)

'Die Hansebruderschaft der Kölner Englandfahrer und ihr Statut vom Jahre 1324', *HG* (1908), 197–240

Stone, L., 'State Control in Sixteenth Century England', *EcHR*, 17 (1947), 103–20

Supple, B. E., *Commercial Crisis and Change in England, 1600–1642* (Cambridge, 1964)

Thielemanns, M. R., *Bourgogne et Angleterre: Relations Politiques et Economiques entre les Pays-Bas Bourguignons et L'Angleterre* (Brussels, 1966)

Veale, E. M., *The English Fur Trade in the Later Middle Ages* (Oxford, 1966)

Weinbaum, M., 'Stalhof und Deutsche Gildhalle zu London', *HG*, (1929), 45–65

Wernham, R. B., *Before the Armada* (Oxford, 1966)

Willan, T. S., *The Early History of the Russia Company* (Manchester, 1956)

Wylie, J. M., *History of England under Henry the Fourth* (London, 1884–98)

Zins, H., *England and the Baltic in the Elizabethan Era* (Manchester, 1972)

Index

Admiral's court, 112, 143, 155
Agincourt, battle of, 139, 159
Albany, Duke of, 235
Albert of Hohenzollern, Grand Master, 10
Alien trade regulations, 30, 55–6, 58, 69, 101, 109–10, 236–7, 269–70; see also *Carta Mercatoria*
Almain, merchants of, 25, 27, 35, 75
Alva, Duke of, 313–14
Amsterdam, 116, 352–3, 355
Anglo-Hanse conferences: (1375), 51–4; (1379), 59–60; (1394), 71; (1406), 117; (1407), 118–20, 126; (1434), 142–4; (1435), 144–5; (1436–7), 145–50; (1449), 180, 182; (1451), 186–8; (1462–3), 197–8; (1465), 199–200; (1469), 205; (1473–4), 209–17; (1491), 242–5; (1497), 246; (1499), 246–50; (1520), 254–6; (1521), 256–8; (1552), 294; (1553–4), 296–7; (1555–6), 299; (1557), 300; (1560), 303–6; (1603–4), 345–6
Anglo-Hanse treaties: (1437), 150–6, 174, 176, 180, 212, 214–15, 217; (1474), 209–17, 236, 239, 248–9, 251; (1560), 305
Anglo-Prussian conferences: (1386), 64; (1388), 65–6; (1389), 67–8; (1391), 67; (1403), 114–15; (1404), 115; (1405), 117; (1407), 120; (1408–9), 120–2; (1419), 129; (1429), 136; (1447), 178–9
Anglo-Prussian treaties: (1388), 65–7, 72, 77, 123; (1409), 121–5, 151, 153
Antwerp, 14, 146, 165, 242–5, 264, 292–3, 295–6, 306–7, 311–12, 315, 317, 346, 354, 368
Arnemuiden, 346
Arras, congress of, 146
Askham, William, 122
Attendorn, 36

Attendorn, Ralph de, 23
Augsburg, 328, 332, 363

Banaster, Thomas, 290–1
Barenbroek, Hans, 234
Bartholomew of Hull (ship), 129
Bay fleet, 133–4, 175, 180–2, 189, 193
Bayonne, 82
Beaufort, Cardinal, 133
Bebys, John, 65, 67
Bek, Sir John, 170
Belle, John, 251
Belt, The, 190
Bergen, 5, 49, 53, 82–4, 88, 94, 137, 179, 228, 275, 367
Bergen op Zoom, 165
Bergenfahrer, 85, 137–8, 148, 161, 165, 225, 227
Berwick, 122
Beverley, 1, 88–9, 288
Billingsgate tolls, 17
Birmingham, Henry, 185–6
Blackwell Hall, 298–9, 323, 336, 345
Bonner, Edmund, Bishop of London, 262, 290
Bordeaux, 82, 85, 176, 238
Borowe, Thomas, 144
Boston, 17, 20, 26, 35–6, 39–40, 43, 51–2, 62, 75, 82–7, 134, 137–8, 161, 166, 219, 225, 227, 232–4, 275, 277
Botill, Robert, Prior of the Order of St John, 186
Bows, 49, 318
Brampton, William, 117–18
Brandenburg, 8
Brandon, John, 111
Braunsberg, 66, 87
Brekerfeld, Arnold, 282
Bremen, 14, 16–17, 91, 112, 138, 191, 242, 300, 320, 347
Brill, 91

396

Printed in the United States
By Bookmasters